UNCONVENTIONAL
FLYING OBJECTS
a scientific analysis

*"Paul Hill has done a masterful job ferreting out the
basic science and technology behind the elusive UFO
characteristics **and demonstrating they are just advanced
and exotic extensions of our own technologies.** Perhaps
this book will help bring solid consideration for making
all that is known about extraterrestrial craft publicly
available."*

—*Edgar Mitchell, Sc.D.,*
Apollo 14 Astronaut

PAUL R. HILL
UNCONVENTIONAL FLYING OBJECTS

a
scientific
analysis

HAMPTON ROADS
PUBLISHING COMPANY, INC.

for the evolving human spirit

Publisher's note: To preserve the authenticity of
the manuscript, we have used the author's original
sketches and drawings whenever possible.
All other drawings are computer-generated.
Thanks to Robert M. Wood, Ph.D., for his invaluable
assistance in bringing this book to fruition.

Cover design by Jonathan and Matthew Friedman

For more information write:

Hampton Roads Publishing Company, Inc.
1125 Stoney Ridge Road
Charlottesville, VA 22902

434-296-2772
fax: 434-296-5096
e-mail: hrpc@hrpub.com
www.hrpub.com

If you are unable to order this book from your local
bookseller, you may order directly from the publisher.
Call 1-800-766-8009.

ISBN 1-57174-027-9

10 9 8 7 6 5

Printed on acid-free paper in the United States

Contents

FOREWORD

Nearly 30 years ago I met Paul Hill in his office at NASA—Langley. For different reasons, we had both begun examining the evidence of unidentified flying objects, trying to understand how they would operate if the current sightings were indeed factual reports. This research was in addition to our normal aerospace jobs. After Paul retired from NASA in 1970, I continued to work at McDonnell Douglas, retiring in 1993, and am now focusing my attention on the very important UFO phenomenon. During this 30-year period, I have closely followed the developments in this field, talking with some of its most prominent researchers. I would say that Paul Hill's analysis of the key issue of how UFOs operate was far ahead of its time in both its science and his scientific attitude.

In *Unconventional Flying Objects*, Paul Hill peripherally mentions his role at NASA, noting an attitude of tolerance for his interest in the UFO phenomenon, but he is careful not to mislead his reader into believing, even by inference, that NASA had an interest in UFOs. He was able to establish himself as an informal "clearing house" for UFO information passing through this government agency. As a result, he was exposed to a wide variety of direct reports, which provided him with ample data to begin his analysis.

Paul Hill worked on this book for many years, completing it in 1975. Although the book relies on sighting reports from the 1950s through the mid-1970s, the material is far from outdated; rather, many of these cases have become classics in the field of UFO reporting, only amplified by sightings in the years to follow. These early reports reveal excellent clues about the underlying science and technology of UFOs. Reports since this period would add very few new dimensions to Hill's documentation. His material even includes early reports of humanoid occupants and communication with them—predating more recent abduction claims—and comments on other current inquiries such as the value and limitations of hypnotic regression.

Hill's approach was 20 years ahead of its time. He never became trapped in the endless speculation about the reality of UFOs; he accepted the reports at face value and let his analysis of the observed phenomenon speak for itself. And his methodology was impeccable. He took the reported observations and then directly evaluated alternative hypotheses, exploring all relevant avenues of inquiry. His comprehensive breakdowns include size, color, halos, clouds, wakes, jitter, heat, maneuvers, performance, sound, solidity, landing, weight, nests and rings, propulsion, propulsive forces, force fields, radiation, merging systems, occupants, collecting, interference, weaponry, and artifacts.

Hill's attitude about the sacrosanct laws of physics is strictly deductive: the laws should be changed to reflect the data instead of vice versa. This unbiased approach gives a new understanding of classic UFO cases, leading to more comprehensive understanding of them, such as the now-famous 1952 RB-47 case over the Gulf of Mexico. More generally, Hill's scientific interpretations of the sightings are especially coherent. For example, his own 1962 sighting reveals two objects rotating around each other 200-feet apart with a period of one second yields 123g, a classic calculation. Hill uses his detailed knowledge of dynamics to perform many calculations relating observed motion and the forces that might cause them. The book also includes cases with "before its time" calculations of how the objects could travel both subsonically and supersonically and make no noise. And the arguments supporting a gravity field are excellent, and are extremely cogent, consistent with a 1994 paper by Haisch and Puthoff showing that the control of gravity and inertia are now technically feasible.

Although written in technically precise language, the book can easily be understood by laymen with non-technical backgrounds, because Hill sticks to the central principles of flight, dynamics, and electricity, using them to embrace the remarkable set of anomalous reports he has compiled from many sources. The information unfolds like a mystery story unraveling its plot. The case histories are clearly written and easy to follow, and have the advantage of getting to the main point without wasting time on irrelevant details. Calculations are simple, understandable, and checkable throughout—one of the necessary conditions for good technical work, often missing in UFO literature. Sketches are simple and focus on the point in question, as if Hill were drawing them on the blackboard in his office for the visiting reader.

The author's Introduction is extremely helpful in guiding the reader through this interesting volume. Paul Hill's *Unconventional Flying Objects: a Scientific Analysis* is an excellent reference guide for the researcher, a wake-up call for the skeptic, a model for the case investigator, a review of fundamental principles for the engineer or scientist, and a great mystery story for all trying to understand how the UFOs can really work. Hill's conclusion is that UFOs "obey, not defy, the laws of physics," lending credibility to sighting reports.

Robert M. Wood,
Ph.D. in Physics, Cornell University 1953
Aeronautical Engineer, 1953-1961, and
Research and Development Manager,
1961-1993: McDonnell Douglas
Corporation, Huntington Beach, CA

Introduction

The sighting of what has been taken to be unconventional vehicle-like objects in our skies has created great interest, surprise, and, for some, a welcome diversion to the daily routine. Others react with incredulity, even open hostility. Opinions have been sharply divided, and, as is so often the case when facts are in short supply, emotions have ruled. All must realize the tremendous potential sociological, technological, and historical impact that contact with beings from another world would create if such were established. Through the decades of the 1950s and 1960s, the believers were in the minority but, as if to make up for their lack of numbers, were very outspoken and argumentative. There was no lack of opposition after the U.S. Air Force threw down the gauntlet.

Both the believers and the nonbelievers have insisted on proof without avail, until it is now widely accepted that the proof concept does not apply, since not one of the objects has been captured and therefore none can be subjected to laboratory tests in the scientific tradition. On the other hand, proof of nonexistence is even more remote. About the best that the challengers have come up with is that the phenomena as reported seem to defy the laws of physics as we understand them. They say that for this reason the reports cannot be believed. A major intent of this book is to show that UFOs obey, not defy, the laws of physics.

One reason for the tide of opinion now running in favor of the believers, if the Gallup Poll's 51-percent figure can be so interpreted, is probably the well-known Condon Study and its recommendations which resulted in the retirement of the U.S. Air Force from their limited investigations of unconventional objects. Project Blue Book was closed. What looked at the time like a case-closed verdict of guilty against unconventional object sightings and all they might signify, in retrospect looks more like the demise of their main opposition by public institution.

Also, partly because of the outspoken opposition to the existence of unconventional objects in our skies by U.S. government institutions and sponsored studies, a scientific protest of sorts developed. Important and distinguished men of science such as Dr. James E. McDonald, atmospheric physicist; Dr. J. Allen Hynek, astronomer and for years Project Blue Book consultant; Prof. James A. Harder of the University of California, Director of Research for the Aerial Phenomena Research Organization; and others stepped forward to demand more impartial studies in order to determine what the sightings really meant. At last the UFO witness, long the butt of ridicule from all sides, had some of the heavy guns of science on his side for a change.

A common opinion among such scientists, as set forth by Dr. Hynek in *The UFO Experience*, is that a computerized study of UFO reports is required to sort fact from fiction and to establish a bona fide pattern of observations. They feel that such a study will establish to a higher degree of probability the objective existence, or nonexistence, of what the witnesses say they have observed. One of the outstanding UFO students to take the computer study approach is Dr. David Saunders, co-author of *UFOs? Yes! Where the Condon Committee Went Wrong*. He made a good start on such a study while an investigator on Condon's study project, but he was destined not to finish it owing to his separation from the project.

Fortunately, work on cataloging UFO phenomena into categories and patterns was started long ago by collectors and analysts of unconventional object reports. Notable among these are the numerous works by Coral and Jim Lorenzen, Jacques and Janine Vallee, Frank Edwards, and the National Investigating Committee for Aerial Phenomena (NICAP) under the direction of Maj. Donald Keyhoe.

Naturally, different data catalogs emphasize different features. Sporadically over a period of 25 years and during a final two-year period of concentrated effort and analysis, I have evolved my own brief catalog of UFO phenomena, summarized and substantiated in these pages. The items of this summary list of phenomena, comprising the highly repeating and therefore most believable aspects of the unconventional objects, will be called the UFO pattern. The UFO pattern, together with the more detailed information used in its compilation, forms the basis of this inquiry into possible scientific explanations. A review at this point of the bewildering array of data which constitutes the pattern should allow all readers to start on a more common footing. With regard to configurations, bear in mind that only highly repeating shapes are given.

The UFO Pattern: A Condensed Statement of Repeated Observations

CONFIGURATIONS, the highly repeating shapes.

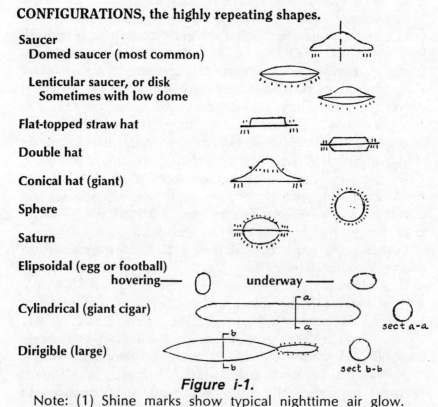

Saucer
   Domed saucer (most common)

   Lenticular saucer, or disk
     Sometimes with low dome

Flat-topped straw hat

Double hat

Conical hat (giant)

Sphere

Saturn

Elipsoidal (egg or football)
        hovering ——   **underway** ——

Cylindrical (giant cigar)

Dirigible (large)

Figure i-1.

Note: (1) Shine marks show typical nighttime air glow.
(2) Dash-dot vertical centerline is saucer axis of symmetry.
(3) Giant cigars have plumes also.

SIZE

The size range is tremendous, varying from something like 8 inches for a lenticular "foo-fighter" of World War II to well upwards of a thousand feet in length for the giant cylindrical shapes. Dirigible configurations range in the hundreds of feet, possibly larger. Saucers, spheres, and ellipsoidal configurations ordinarily range in the 1- to 30-meter size, and Saturn-like vehicles, so named because of their central rim, are frequently in the 5- to 15-meter range. Sufficient estimates of conical-hat saucers have not been made to suggest a range in size, but one was reliably estimated to be of the order of 200 meters in diameter. Obviously statistical studies are needed to further define the range of UFO sizes.

COLOR

In daylight, unconventional objects range from a brightly polished silver color to a dull aluminum appearance. Flat-bottomed saucers are often darker underneath in a central circular area or in an annular ring near the rim.

At night, there are two variations:

(a) The unconventional objects carry running lights in many patterns. Sometimes they blink, making the object look like a Christmas tree or a theater marquee.
(b) They are solidly lighted in red, orange, amber, yellow, blue or blue-violet, and brilliant white, singly or in combinations. The solid colors resemble neon lighting.

HALOS

The nighttime neon-like, solid-color luminescence emanates from an envelope of air around the objects like a halo, rather than from the vehicle directly. This halo tends to obscure the vehicle, making the edges indistinct, as we will explore further.

Around saucers and Saturns, the halo is most concentrated near the rim, more extensive below than above. (See shine marks on sketches.)

A unique cone of illuminating air is sometimes present below a saucer, giving it an ice-cream-cone appearance.

CLOUDS

The big cylindrical objects are sometimes surrounded with a white cloud, giving rise to the name "great cloud cigar." This phenomenon is less frequent with other configurations.

WAKES

Dirigible and cylindrical objects carry plume-like wakes when accelerating rapidly or moving at high speeds, grey to straw-colored in daylight, flame-colored at night. They can move slowly (100 mph) without generating the plume.

JITTER

Unconventional objects at times seem to vibrate heavily. If the object is also moving slowly, the movement seems jerky or jittery. It is difficult to know whether the jitter is an actual motion or an optical effect. For this reason, the phenomenon is listed with other appearance factors.

HEAT

No one complains that being near an unconventional object is like being near a hot stove. Heat radiations (infrared, etc.) from their surfaces or from the surrounding halos and wakes is missing except for mild sensations of warmth. This observation carries the strong implication that the surfaces, halos, and wakes are not very hot (i.e., nothing is at a red heat).

MANEUVERS

Hovering. Hovering at any altitude is common. UFOs also hover very close to the ground for substantial periods, sometimes giving the distinct impression that they are doing so instead of landing. (In other words, hovering seems to serve the same purpose as landing.)

Falling leaf or UFO-rock. This maneuver is similar to the motion of a coin falling in water. It most often occurs just before the UFO begins to hover.

Silver-dollar wobble. To duplicate this motion, give a coin a slow spin on a flat surface. This motion occurs at the end of a rapid descent as the UFO initiates hovering.

Acute-angle turn. This is another dazzling but common maneuver. The UFO decelerates rapidly to a stop at the point of the turn and accelerates rapidly in the new direction. (It requires acute observation to note the stop.) The right-angle turn (90 degrees) is a special case of the acute-angle turn.

Sudden reversal of direction. This maneuver surprises the witness because it isn't in the repertoire of Earth vehicles. It is actually an extreme acute-angle turn (180 degrees).

Bank-and-turn. The motions are in every way comparable to the motions of conventional aircraft—a familiar one at last!

Straight-away speed run. This maneuver also can be similar to the corresponding maneuver of conventional craft, but can be different in that it is just as apt to be vertical as horizontal or any angle in between.

Tilt to maneuver. While not actually a maneuver, this observation, which I have confirmed, is important. UFOs tilt to perform all maneuvers. For example, they sit level to hover, tilt forward to move forward, tilt backward to stop, bank to turn, etc.

PERFORMANCE

Speed. Speeds to about 9,000 miles per hour have been measured by radar at 60,000 feet altitude at Goose Bay, Labrador; by radar near 18,000 feet altitude over the Gulf of Mexico; and eyeballed between landmarks at about this speed and 3,500 feet altitude over Hampton Roads, Virginia.

Acceleration. The literature on unconventional objects is filled with adjectives of superlative degree to describe accelerations, but there are no numbers. Here my sightings and calculations can help; they place minimum values of observed accelerations at the order of 100 times Earth-surface gravity on two occasions, once for spheres and once for a big dirigible. (This is an order of magnitude more than Earth vehicles of comparable size, but far less than some small tube-launched or gun-launched missiles.)

Some reported sudden disappearances are quite likely cases of extreme acceleration, which may be beyond the comprehension of the testifying witness and even the case investigator. The major report pattern is either that they disappear with "lightning speed" or "incredible swiftness" or that they move off slowly.

Altitude. A half-dozen sightings of unconventional objects by orbiting astronauts place operating altitudes at near 200 nautical miles. This figure would seem to qualify these objects as space-worthy, non-atmospheric phenomena, possibly spacecraft.

SOUND

Hum, buzz, or whine. These are the characteristic sounds of the UFO at close quarters. The sound rises in both pitch and intensity seconds before and during take-off from hovering or landed condition. Sometimes moving UFOs make a slight swish-of-air sound. At other times, the observer is greeted with absolute silence.

Unconventional objects seldom create a roar or boom, even when moving at supersonic speed.

SOLIDITY

Unconventional objects have solid surfaces. This characteristic is attested to by those who have touched them, rapped on them, and listened to the thud or the whine of ricocheting bullets from rifle and point-blank pistol fire.

LANDING

The main pattern is that UFOs let down retractable landing gear before landing. The gear leaves well-defined prints in the contacted surfaces.

WEIGHT

Landing gear imprints are defined well enough to make weight estimates possible. The weight estimates indicate that modest-sized unconventional objects weigh tons.

NESTS AND RINGS

Saucers landing without use of gear in reeds or soft terrain leave "saucer nests."

Low-hovering saucers sometimes swirl down "grass rings."

Hovering saucers at times form chemically and physically altered annular rings in the earth itself. These are called "saucer rings."

Hovering saucers at times leave evidence of charred roots or wilted plants.

PROPULSION

Unconventional objects have "no visible means of support." They have no externally visible engines, power plant, or other visible means of locomotion or propulsion. As one witness put it, "So whatever made it go, I don't know," Pattern-wise, jet propulsion is absent (see Section XII).

PROPULSIVE FORCES

Assuming unconventional objects don't neutralize their nertial mass, the accelerations displayed place the propulsive forces at high values, too high to be accounted for by any aerodynamic principle.

FORCE FIELDS

Analysis of direct physical evidence shows that unconventional objects employ force fields. Invisible forces bend down or even break tree branches; bump or slow automobiles, sometimes spinning them out of control or even tipping them over; and stop people by force and even knock them down, among other observations.

RADIATION

Unconventional objects are highly radioactive (see Section IV).

MERGING SYSTEMS

Spheres and saucers have on numerous occasions been seen to separate from the large cylinders and dirigibles and re-merge with them. The small objects move with the large object as a swarm, or dart away at high speed in different directions, some swiftly returning.

OCCUPANTS

Occupants have been seen to disembark from and to re-board unconventional objects. On occasion, one or two occupants are seen. On other occasions, several occupants seem to work as a team or crew.

COLLECTING

Unconventional objects and their occupants engage in collecting things such as plants, minerals, and water, both manually and by automated processes such as suction hoses.

INTERFERENCE

Unconventional objects interrupt all electric circuitry, burn out batteries, and stop gasoline engines, but they don't affect diesel engines.

WEAPONRY

Unconventional objects employ heat beams, paralyzing beams, and force beams as tools and weapons, generally applied in moderation.

ARTIFACTS

Artifacts are hard to obtain, and even more difficult to prove bona fide. The most outstanding artifact is a fine white filament, left in the wake of unconventional vehicles, known as angel hair. It may be gathered by witnesses but disappears by sublimation, a direct change from the solid to the gaseous state of matter.

OVER AND UNDER WATER

Unconventional objects have been observed submerging into and emerging from bodies of water, as well as floating on the surface, often enough to form a pattern.

HABITS

UFOs at times appear in much greater numbers than usual. The resulting increase in the rate of UFO sightings and reports is called a *flap*. A flap may be confined to a single continent or may be worldwide. Flaps occur on a cyclic basis with two years being one of the periods.

UFOs appear to have preferred observational habits. Among preferred snooping sites are defense installations, hydroelectric installations, dams, and lakes. They also give preference to lone individuals or small groups and to isolated cars. They are sometimes attracted by blinking light signals.

UFOs are most often observed at dusk or early evening. They are frequently seen traveling or maneuvering over water, just off shore. They sometimes return to a given area within minutes or hours or return the following day, as though they had not concluded their observations.

Individuals may be taken aboard for examination. In

some cases, the person remembers the experience; in others, recall appears possible under hypnosis.

This UFO pattern—represented by this brief outline—contains the essentials of existing UFO data. This pattern in its entirety is all we have on which to base an understanding of the unconventional objects.

Having briefly reviewed the pattern, one can see what all the fuss has been about. If all this is true, the old dead universe many astronomers believed in is gone; the new live universe they now accept is verified, with exobiology assuming major importance; new viewpoints are given to old mythologies; religions are affected; ideas about space-travel difficulties are shattered; interest in exploration beyond the solar system is heightened; all natural sciences are given tremendous impetus; emotional involvements will be heightened; dogma of all types will be shattered. With the entire twentieth century being a period of scientific revolution, the establishment of unconventional objects as fact would add much to the revolutions, perhaps a quantum jump as some have suggested.

Be all that as it may, the process of acceptance takes time. Anyone who has read Dr. Thomas S. Kuhn's fascinating book, *The Structure of Scientific Revolutions*, must know that the acceptance of the UFO has to be the gradual process that it is turning out to be because it is man's nature, and scientific history, that old ideas are discarded only after new ideas are firmly established. It often takes new generations to squarely face new facts. Dr. Kuhn says:

> No part of the aim of normal science is to call forth new sorts of phenomena; indeed those that will not fit the box are often not seen at all. Nor do scientists normally aim to invent new theories, and they are often intolerant of those invented by others. Instead, normal-scientific research is directed to the articulation of those phenomena and theories that the paradigm already supplies (p. 24).

> Let us assume that crises are a necessary precondition for the emergence of new theories and ask how scientists respond to their existence. Part of the answer, as obvious as it is important,

can first be discovered by noting what scientists never do when confronted by severe and even prolonged anomalies. Though they may begin to lose faith and then to consider alternatives, they never renounce the paradigm that led them to the crisis. They do not, that is, treat anomalies as counter instances, though in the vocabulary of philosophy of science that is what they are (p. 77).

New facts and theories have to form a neat, logical package before they can be accepted, and justifiably so; otherwise technological chaos would reign. Therein lies the problem. Some degree of technological sense has to be made of the unconventional object, even to make "seeing believing." Otherwise, we are still apt to be in mythology, or dealing with the occult. If there be any doubt about this, look how members of occult groups have grabbed the ball and are sprinting with it. They have now been joined by a few parapsychologists who do little better. A prominent parapsychologist, in attempting to link the mind with UFOs, has suggested they are projected here by vast mental powers.

Objective

I seek the answers to unconventional objects in the physical sciences. Indeed, the main questions posed by the UFOs can best be formulated and asked in terms of the engineering sciences. As an example, I support the questioning viewpoint of Dr. Bruce Rogers, expressed in his article in the December 1973 *UFO Investigator*, entitled "UFOs: Their Performance Characteristics." After giving various speed and acceleration performance examples, including the case of the 9000-mph UFO in Goose Bay, Labrador, he duly asks why they don't burn up when moving at such speeds in the earth's atmosphere, and how the occupants can stand the high accelerations. Continuing the engineering science view, he questions how the vast power needed to drive them can be packaged in the limited space available, pointing out that an atomic power plant would never fit. Dr. Rogers concludes, "There is much that is mystifying about UFOs, and woefully little information about them. But, there is one thing about which there can be no doubt. Whoever builds and operates these vehicles possess a technology incredibly advanced beyond anything known on our planet."

UFOs are indeed a technological challenge, and serious work to explain them in terms of the physical sciences is long overdue. Professor James Harder is one of the prominent scientists who have repeatedly expressed this view for a number of years. In the *APRO Bulletin* for March/April 1973, he said:

> Who among UFO investigators has not wished for a clear, closeup, detailed photograph of a UFO? And what would it prove? Surely it would help settle the question, still on some agendas, of whether UFOs actually exist . . . however, is it not time to go beyond that issue to a host of scientific problems and questions that are raised once one has accepted the fact of UFO existence? It seems to me that we should be well into a second phase of UFO investigations in which the object is not so much to prove the existence of UFOs as to try and understand more about them.

The main objective of the analyses in this book is to present what can be explained of the UFO pattern in terms of today's scientific principles. If much of the pattern can be so explained, those crying "defying the laws of physics" will be discredited, making the UFO more understandable and therefore more acceptable. For the reasons stated by Dr. Kuhn, a lot of scientific sense has to be made of the UFO enigma to make UFOs acceptable. In simple terms, pieces of the jigsaw puzzle have to be fitted into place to the point where the casual observer can see the picture forming. Then the clever bystander, always present, can suggest a piece here and there to aid the progress as well as to correct misfits, for teamwork is essential in the end. But a start must be made.

Early Beginnings

I made my beginning analysis of unconventional object maneuvers in the 1950s. This work was no doubt stimulated by my sighting of unconventional objects on July 16, 1952. My sighting was made at the peak of the flap for that year, tightly sandwiched between the July 14 Pan American Airways sighting in my own neighborhood and the great Washington D.C. flap on July 19, 1952. My sighting was investigated by Project Blue Book, classified as unknown, and given first public mention by Major Edward Ruppelt on pages 157-58 in his *Report on Unidentified Flying Objects.*

My background of flight experiments with rocket-supported platforms was pertinent to the understanding of the control of unconventional objects, that is, to the understanding of how they maneuver. It enabled me to correlate their tilt-to-control maneuvers fifteen years before that idea came to a member of the Condon Project. In his book, Dr. David Saunders says, ". . . information might be gleaned from a careful analysis of the relation (if any) between attitude changes (tilting) of a single UFO and changes in its direction, or speed of flight. Questions along these lines were a part of my UFO reporting questionnaire that the project never got around to using" (p. 232).

While I did not invent the idea of flying platforms, I built the first ones capable of flight testing and capable of testing flight maneuvers. They were of the type which tilt-to-control, the thrust remaining coincident with the axis of symmetry. I did not realize until after I had experienced the superb controllability of my device that unconventional objects might be controlled on the same principles. If this thought was correct, I had a nearly perfect piece of equipment for simulating their maneuvers. Another encouraging aspect was that saucer UFOs even looked like a flying platform.

I was soon doing the pendulum-rock and falling leaf, the sudden reversals, banking-to-turn, and the silver-dollar wobble, surely the first UFO maneuver flight simulations. I did them as much because they came naturally and I enjoyed doing them, as for any other reason. Although some data about some of them, such as the falling leaf and sudden reversals, was common even then, data about others, such as the bank-to-turn, was in short supply and the experiments were almost ahead of the data. But as the data rolled in through the 1950s, the correctness of the UFO maneuver simulations became more and more evident. By the time I saw the Tremonton, Utah, movies of maneuvering disks (see Section XI) in slow and stop motion, in which I could make out the circular planforms and the edge-on fadeouts as well as the elliptic in-between on banking turns, I was totally convinced that the analysis of UFO maneuvers as presented in Section XI is the correct one.

I was prevented from making any pronouncements about this application of my work by official National Advisory Committee for Aeronautics (NACA) policy. That policy was that flying saucers are nonexistent. The NACA Director, Dr. Hugh L. Dryden, made a public pronouncement to that effect at about that time, and I had been instructed by my superior in official channels that my name could not be used in connection with my sighting or in any way that would implicate the NACA with these objects. NACA research officials were all scientists with management training in which the necessity for unambiguous policy had been emphasized. Clearly, I was destined to remain as unidentified as the flying objects. When the name of the organization was changed from NACA to NASA, the National Aeronautics and Space Administration, the same officials remained in charge, and one could notice no change in policy. The only difference was that individuals were going into space; when astronauts sighted unknowns in space, a grounded official couldn't rationally contradict them. But they could shut them off the air (*APRO Bulletin*, February 1976).

Rationale and Disciplines in the Analyses

The rationale used in the analyses is primarily simple logic, and the usual fitting of evidence to theory in what has come to be accepted as the "scientific method." Perhaps the previous paragraphs regarding the fitting of flight maneuver data to a control theory is a fair example, although we are not usually so fortunate as to have laboratory simulations.

In some cases, a process of elimination is used, a process suggested by that fictional detective, Sherlock Holmes, whose admonition was to first eliminate the impossible, for it is in the remaining possibilities, however improbable, that the answers are to be found. Since "impossible" is a dangerous word to associate with unconventional objects, the concepts eliminated are those which do not fit the data, or the UFO pattern. Section V presents an example. All the known particles of modern physics, together with their antiparticles (with the possible exception of the four neutrinos) are eliminated as propulsion possibilities in the following sense. A beam of high speed particles shot out from the UFO cannot be a realistic basis for their propulsion because such beams would have gross effects, such as gross heating or lasting radioactivity, not evident in the UFO pattern.

On the other hand, it is well known that any process of elimination, however well based, is circumstantial evidence of the weakest character with respect to the positive identification of a single result. Fortunately, while I was eliminating all known forms of propulsion possibilities except acceleration fields, I uncovered a substantial body of direct evidence that UFOs use and direct acceleration fields in the proper direction for propulsion. This is nearly the same as saying they direct force fields; this trait is so listed in the UFO pattern outline and supported by the data of Section VI. The next consideration is whether the field is electric, magnetic, gravitational in nature, or something else.

But the unconventional object can be explained by no one phenomenon such as magnetic-field propulsion or gravitational propulsion; nor can it be explained by any one technology. A multi-disciplinary approach is a minimum requirement. In considering the correctness of a group of theories resulting from a broad approach, one needs a yardstick which will enable the viewer to stand back and take the measure of the picture forming as the pieces of the jigsaw puzzle are fitted together. A good yardstick was found in *UFOs and Diamagnetism*. According to the author, Eugene Burt, a leading physicist wrote the following statement in criticism of Burt's theory:

I see little point in a debate on a particular, essentially ad hoc hypothesis. What counts in the structure of scientific concepts and theories is not the workability of an hypothesis concerning a particular phenomenon but the entire network or matrix of ideas including this particular phenomenon and everything else with which it is connected. The test of correctness it not a single line of logic but the internal consistency of the whole network— one must be able to traverse the network in any direction and have things hang together without contradictions (p. 117).

This masterful statement applies to UFO theory as well as to all branches of organized knowledge. I am trying to conform to it.

What's a Good Name?

While an appropriate name for unconventional objects is beyond the scope of this book, I thought I should point out that *UFO* is not a reasonable name or acronym, and explain what I mean when I use it.

One to two hundred years ago, science was called natural philosophy, and scientists were known as natural philosophers, or naturalists. When a field naturalist made a discovery, he first identified the find as something new or a variant of organized knowledge. He then classified it, and gave it a descriptive name. Now when we discover an unconventional object, we identify it as "unidentified" and name it the same! On the first page of *The Report on Unidentified Flying Objects*, we find whom to thank for this contradiction. Major Edward Ruppelt says, "UFO is the official term that I created to replace the words flying saucers."

One suspects that a field naturalist would have done considerably better, as naming was their specialty. Ruppelt scored a complete miss on two out of three words: *unidentified* and *flying*. It is assumed that anyone with a good dictionary can see why unidentified is a misnomer. As to flying, the atmosphere has no more than nuisance value to the unconventional craft, which, unlike aircraft, use the atmosphere neither for support nor for locomotion. Unconventional objects, or craft, don't fly. They are vectored along trajectories.

Even the word *object* is almost totally undescriptive, except that it correctly indicates something solid, and not a mere plasma, light, mirage, or other form of natural phenomena.

Borrowing the adjective *unconventional* from Coral Lorenzen's usage, I use *unconventional object* until a more descriptive name appears or is accepted. Since UFO is shorter and so well known, this acronym is used with the understanding that the U stands for unconventional. UO would be more accurate, but I do not propose it, preferring to leave naming to people with the proper talent.

The term *saucer* is used to refer to a craft that moves through the atmosphere without an obvious means of support or propulsion, a form of unconventional object as we have described it. A saucer is characteristically shaped like two saucers placed lip-to-lip and may have a rounded dome or cupola on top. Alternatively, it may be shaped like a straw hat or a single inverted saucer or bowl. Saucers are characteristically surrounded by an ionized atmosphere, or plasma, that gives them nighttime illumination in red, orange, yellow, green, blue, or white, and often gives them a mist-shrouded appearance. They are silent except for a hum or buzz noticeable to near observers.

The acronym UFO is a wider generic term than *saucer*. It refers also to unconventional objects of other shapes as well: spherical, Saturn-shaped, egg-shaped (ellipsoidal), dirigible-shaped, and cigar-shaped. Specifically, UFOs are vehicles capable of operation both in space and in the earth's atmosphere.

At no time does the term UFO refer to a UFO report or to a misidentified object or natural phenomenon.

Data Sources

There is now a lot of good UFO data, thanks to the private organizations whose people have encouraged UFO reporting and have investigated, filed, and cataloged the data, published it in bulletin and book form, and are continuing to do so. In writing this analysis, I have placed major reliance on these sources; I could have done nothing without them. The bulletins to which I refer are the *APRO Bulletin*, published by the Aerial Phenomena Research Organization of Tucson, Arizona, and the *UFO Investigator*, published by the National Investigations Committee on Aerial Phenomena of Kensington, Maryland.

Many complaints have been noted about the lack of hard UFO data. It has been the nature of UFO data to be primarily in anecdotal form. Still, some measurements and many good estimates have been made of the UFO phenomena which have been parametrically classified. While there is admittedly a shortage of hard data, I do not subscribe to the complaints. It is my experience that exploratory research is usually done with a modicum of good data, and UFO research simply fits the rule. I believe that the problem is less with the data than the data readers. As Professor of Philosophy Emerson Shideler said, we need "to be readier to accept phenomena as reported" (*APRO Bulletin*, November/December 1971). That *is* the data. On occasion I knowingly use data that some have rejected as false, but those who have rejected it are usually those who reject all data not explainable as natural phenomena. The first step in this analysis is to accept the data that fits a consistent pattern.

There are hard data shortages in the measurement of gravitational and magnetic fields near UFOs and in the measurement of electromagnetic wave characteristics from the lower gamma wave frequency through x-ray, ultraviolet, visible, and even radio frequencies. Insofar as the understanding of UFOs is concerned, more high acceleration data would definitely help. However, there is already enough speed data to show that in our atmosphere UFOs have speeds that cannot be matched by aircraft or rockets.

Organization of the Analysis

The analysis is broken into sections, each covering a general topic. To some degree the order of the topics is determined by which questions can be most firmly answered. UFO theories or explanations can be considered either as possible or plausible explanations, or as real explanations. I have ordered the topics as I have so that the first dozen or so sections should entertain theory with a high probability of being the real explanation. (I never was one who lacked the courage of my convictions.) The remaining sections, beginning with supersonic aerodynamics, present what should be at least good possibilities. This unusual ordering presumably has the psychological advantage of seeking areas of agreement between author and reader early in the book. Section XVIII, on interstellar travel time, however, is straight, bona fide science, and can hardly be wrong unless the entire twentieth-century physics is wrong. It therefore does not necessarily follow that explanations offered in the second half are less real. Groundwork and technical considerations come into the ordering also.

Section I is a simple presentation with the aim of making the reader realize that the UFO is a solid, down-to-earth object or machine, not some nebulous natural phenomenon.

Section II treats UFO speed and acceleration performance because performance has been such a point of public concern. I have never seen UFO acceleration data. Accelerations are invariably described by adjectives, mainly superlatives bordering on or including the infinite. While these descriptions are sensational, they are bad science. I therefore take the liberty of boring the reader with two formulas useful in the calculation of acceleration, and illustrate the procedure to obtain what may be the first acceleration data. At least the data is new, for it is taken from my own sightings, which happen to suit.

With some preliminaries out of the way, Section III begins to hammer out an explanation of the most commonly observed UFO phenomenon, their glowing halo. A hundred years ago this illuminating ion sheath around a UFO would have been the same total mystery to science that it is today to the casual observer. But with today's quantum-mechanical principles, the explanation is a piece of cake. The A and B of quantum mechanics is explained, if not the C to Z, as it pertains to molecular ionization.

Section IV substantiates Section III by showing radio-activity in the x-ray range to be the obvious cause of the ion sheath.

Section V eliminates high speed ejected particles as a possible means of UFO propulsion.

From there, the analysis progresses toward the field explanation of UFO propulsion in an order that is self-explanatory.

Section I
Physical Properties and Effects

A. Introductory Statement

Physical evidence exists that UFOs are real, solid, massive, machine-like vehicles, as evidenced, for example, by their retractable landing gear and the deep impressions made by the landing gear in various solid-earth surfaces.

Sighting records show, however, that they often do not land, but on close approach to the earth hover a few feet above its surface. If they stay any length of time, the plant roots and soil humus below the UFO are apt to be scorched and chemically altered, as may be tree branches and trunks on the side facing the UFO. Light-weight green plants, such as grass, are more apt to be only wilted or unaffected.

People are not immune. They sometimes receive ultra-violet eye and skin burns resembling sunburn. Very close observers have received burns ranging from flesh burns to injuries with all the symptoms of radiation poisoning.

B. Evidence of Weight and Massiveness

EXAMPLE I-B1.

In *Flying Saucers Over Spain*, UFO student Antonio Rebera gives an interesting account of the landing of a saucer on February 6, 1966, at Aluche, Spain, a suburb of Madrid with new apartment buildings interspersed with open spaces. The saucer landed in an open space, perhaps larger than a city block. From the street bordering the clear area, witness Jose Louis Jordan watched a luminous, fiery disk approach, hover momentarily, and land at about 8:00 P.M. During its approach, it lowered a tripod landing gear which it sat down on. The saucer was shaped like two big rimmed pie pans placed rim-to-rim and was estimated to be 10 to 12 meters in diameter. In a few minutes it rose, the landing gear disappearing as it did so. Sr. Jordan was overcome by the experience. Instinctively he tried to locate other witnesses, but he was too late. The vehicle had gone, but it had left impressive evidence of its visit. Pressed into the hard Spanish soil were three neat footprints of the landing gear, arranged in an equilateral triangle of 6 meters (19.7 feet), imprint to imprint. The prints were rectangular with rounded corners and each had a raised X-mark of half-round cross section on the bottom. The dimensions were given in centimeters.

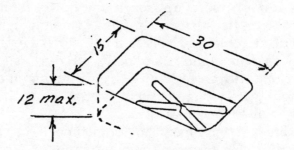

Figure I-1.

The prints were therefore about 6 by 12 inches in plan and nearly 5 inches deep, although one was shallower. The raised X-print looked something like the traction markings on a tire tread. Hundreds of Madrillenos came to witness the UFO tracks. They had clearly been made by a heavy or massive vehicle in a vertical landing, as the prints were clear-cut.

EXAMPLE I-B2

Near Gault, Ontario, on July, 30, 1957, 15-year-old Ted Stevens stood and watched a round, silver-colored object hover for 40 minutes before it landed in a corn-stubble field about 300 yards distant, according *UFO, The Whole Story,* by Coral and Jim Lorenzen. A burned circle and two impressions in the ground remained as evidence of the landing. Investigators of the incident were hard put to explain the impressions as the ground was nearly rock-hard, and the prints were pressed into the ground, not dug. The consensus of all who studied the evidence was that something very heavy had rested there.

EXAMPLE I-B3

On a late afternoon (5:50 P.M.) of April 1964, police patrolman Lonnie Zamora of Socorro, New Mexico, drove his patrol car off the highway and followed a desert trail to investigate a roar and flash of blue flame near a dynamite shack. This story is detailed in *Flying Saucers: The Startling Evidence of the Invasion From Outer Space*, by Coral Lorenzen (pp. 218-21).

As Zamora approached the area where the shack was located, he caught a glimpse of a white vehicle standing on end (which he first took to be a car) with two small individuals standing by it dressed in what looked like white mechanics' uniforms. One of the figures appeared to turn and look toward him. Zamora called fellow officer Sergeant Chavez for assistance. He then drove up and across the next mesa, where he stopped and got out. Taking three steps toward the gully ahead, he could again see the vehicle, which was not a car but a cylindrical object standing on end. Suddenly there was a roar from the object as it kicked up dust. Zamora threw himself to the ground and, looking up, saw the vehicle rising on a very shallow, slanted trajectory. He got up and started to run, but hit the car, knocking off his glasses. The roar ceased, giving way to a high-pitched whine as the object cleared the dynamite shack by only about 20 feet.

Sergeant Chavez soon arrived, and the two went down to the gully to inspect the area. A mesquite bush at the center of the landing site was still burning. There were four 8x12-inch wedge-shaped depressions, 3 to 4 inches deep. The ground was very uneven, and the arrangement of the marks "indicated self-leveling gear."

Jacques Vallee, a scientific conservative, also investigated this landing. In *Challenge to Science*, he says, "The investigation also revealed that the craft was not built by amateurs; it had landed on uneven terrain, firmly set on four legs of unequal length in such a way as to put the center of gravity in the best position" (p. 35).

EXAMPLE I-B4

According to *Flying Saucers: Serious Business* (pp. 58-59) and other sources, Marius Dewilde, who lived about a mile from Quaroble, France, went to bed at 10:15 P.M. on September 10, 1954. A few minutes later he got up and went to see why his dog was howling. Outside, his dog came crawling up to him, and he switched on his flashlight to look around. He could make out, some distance from the house, a large dark object on the railroad. Only 20 feet away, in the beam of his light, he saw two humanoid figures about 3½ feet tall and wearing shiny helmets similar to those worn by divers. Associating the figures with the object on the tracks, Dewilde ran to interpose himself between the figures and the tracks. At that time a bright beam from the object stopped him. He told police, "I could only stand there as if paralyzed. I could not move my arms or legs. I could not yell. I was helpless when that light was on me."

He saw an opening appear in the dark object, and shortly thereafter it left by rising straight up.

The incident was investigated by the French Air Force and Department of Territorial Security. Where Dewilde said the object rested, five deep indentations were pressed into the wooden crossties. Experts who examined the indentations and the crosstie material estimated the weight of the object to be 30 tons. Dewilde described the object as approximately football-shaped, roughly 6 meters long by 3 meters high.

In all of these instances, the objects were clearly very heavy to have left such impressive prints. In the last case, we have what should be a reliable minimum weight estimate of 30 tons because the crumbling strength of various woods is well known.

For the three centuries since Newton's time it has been known that each pound of weight is due to the acceleration of gravity acting on each unit of mass. Thus we must conclude that UFOs are both heavy and massive, at least when landed. While this is a simple concept, it is too important to pass over lightly. When this concept is taken at face value, it can be immediately deduced that each of the UFOs which made the prints, being heavy and massive, required a lot of thrust to lift off and even more to accelerate. The strong implication is that their invisible power plants and thrust generators are powerful ones.

Since we are fortunate enough to have estimated dimensions from the Quaroble case, let us check on the mass density to get a comparison with Earthcraft. If we make the logical assumption that the UFO shape was ellipsoidal with the 6 meters being the axial length l and 3 meters the cross-diameter d, the volume is given by

$$V = \left(\frac{4}{3}\right)\pi\left(\frac{1}{2}\right)\left(\frac{d}{2}\right)^2$$

$$= 9\pi \quad = 28.27 \text{ cubic meters}$$

Assuming short tons, of 2000 lb./ton, 30 tons converts to 27,200 kilograms of mass. To get mass density, we divide mass by volume and get 965 kilograms per cubic meter. Since water has a mass density of 1000 kg per cubic meter, the Quaroble UFO was about 96 percent as dense as water, very close to the density of a submarine. It is several times more dense than a jet aircraft.

This density, if representative, could explain the observed underwater operation and the apparent multiphibious nature of the UFO. It's particularly important that we take note that an object of this density, equipped with a retractable landing gear, is a very substantial "flying" machine made to land on land and having properties consistent with operation from water surfaces or even underwater.

In some cases, saucer UFOs land in swampy areas by simply making a belly landing. Such a landing distributes the load and leaves a shallow, saucer-like depression, sometimes with swirled-down reeds or grass, that is called a saucer-nest. *Flying Saucers: Here and Now* presents a photo of such a nest (Edwards 32-35).

According to the July/August 1974 *APRO Bulletin*, APRO has adopted as one of its goals the analysis of ground traces left by UFOs to determine their weight. The technique will involve the taking of core samples and penetrometer readings at the site, together with laboratory analysis in Tucson. The soil bearing strength will be carefully measured and the UFO weight computed from this data and the dimensions of the impressions. This realistic program should furnish needed data.

The landed data shows that UFOs are massive while landed. In Section VII we shall encounter impressive evidence that UFOs use high thrust while in flight, which is highly inconsistent with the assumption made by some UFO investigators that UFOs reduce mass to zero. With no mass they would not need and could not use high thrust. In Section II, where we will address performance, we shall see that observed accelerations are high, but not so high as to require an escalation of hypothesis to zero mass, or even to mass control for their explanation. In other words, all can be explained by ordinary mass densities and excellent thrusting capability. In this view, UFOs are very good machines, without miracles.

For those interested in the theory on which some have based their mass-control ideas, let me add that it is an interpretation of Einstein's general theory of relativity, and other "metric" theories of gravitation. Einstein related the property of local inertial mass to the mass of the universe, as Mach did before him and others since. The property of local inertial mass depends on the action of all the mass and gravity of the universe. The interpreters reason logically that if there were a perfect gravity shield surrounding local matter its inertial mass would be zero.

Physicists have hunted for a gravity shield for over half a century and have determined in the laboratory to high precision that no matter forms a gravity shield to the slightest measurable degree. Astronomers have been in agreement with this result because they know that during a solar eclipse, if the interposition of the mass of the moon between the sun and the earth had any shielding effect, the earth's orbit would be perturbed. It is not.

The acceptance of twentieth-century science at face value is at experimental odds with basing mass control on the shielding possibility. I sometimes wonder about the possibility of an alternate idea. Possibly inertial mass could be reduced, if not by shielding, by the superposition of a negative gravity field of antigravitons on the normal gravity field of gravitons to cancel the effect of the two fields, one against the other. I do not, however, seriously propose this, particularly for the UFO scout ships such as saucers, spheres, ellipsoids, etc., for which available data provides strong evidence of massiveness.

For the big dirigible and cigar UFOs, which are presumably the interstellar starships, I know of no landing data or other strong direct evidence of great massiveness and the possibility remains open that these large vehicles may have an artificially reduced mass. This possible distinction between the scouts and the starships was suggested to me by Dr. James Harder. He also suggested a theoretical means for the reduction of the mass of interstellar vehicles based on the quark theory of matter. This theory is discussed in Section XIX.

C. Evidence of Solidity and Hardness

We have just provided evidence of solidity, for who ever heard of a massive object, weighing in the range of several tons, that didn't have solid surfaces? Also, it is certain that the landing gear of the UFOs in the examples cited were of harder material than the earth or crossties on which they rested. The principle that "the indenter is harder than the indent" underlies hardness testing, although it is not usually the direct basis for the laboratory testing of material hardness. The direct basis is simply the depth of the dent made by a small hard object under a prescribed loading.

Other evidence of solidity and hardness is given by the sound of bullets striking UFOs. UFOs have been shot at hundreds of times. On many occasions, the bullets have been heard to impact. On other occasions, the distinctive whine of ricochets has been heard. For brevity, only one example is given here. Another example is given in Section VII.

EXAMPLE I-C1

On May 13, 1967, at 1:45 A.M., Michael Campeadore was driving nearing St. George, Utah, when he heard a loud humming sound (Lorenzen, *UFOs Over the Americas*, 46). It was so unusual that he put on his brakes and jumped out of his car. It was then that he noticed a huge object, about 40 to 50 feet in diameter, hovering 25 to 35 feet above his car. Thoroughly frightened, he loaded an ammunition clip into his 0.25 caliber pistol and squeezed off point-blank shots. He heard the bullets hit and ricochet as if they had struck metal.

The ricochet of bullets in this and similar cases indicate that the UFO shell is composed of a hard material, or at least presents a hard surface, for if it did not the bullets would penetrate rather than glance off in a ricochet.

EXAMPLE I-C2

Two eleven-year-old San Diego, California, boys sneaked up on a UFO in a darkened vacant lot and rapped on it with a flashlight. They too performed a useful experiment, demonstrating solidity. Their case was one of those seriously studied by *The National Enquirer* UFO panel in their "best evidence short of conclusive proof" contest (*UFO Investigator*, February 1974). When struck with the flashlight, the UFO flared up red, began to whine, and took off—as, meanwhile, so did the boys.

D. Conclusion

We have examined, briefly, the available types of data pertaining primarily to the structural properties of the UFO. This data includes the properties of weight, mass, solidity, hardness, and density. The UFO properties in each case are not unlike the corresponding properties of Earth vehicles. The lone point on mass density placed that particular vehicle more or less in the range of a loaded rocket system, or a submarine, and heavier than a jet aircraft.

These down-to-earth physical properties—that is, the similarity of the physical properties of unconventional machines to those of Earth machines—tend to confirm that the investigation and study of the UFO by means of the physical sciences is the correct approach. The variable-geometry property of their retractable and adjustable landing gear also confirms that, structurally, here are ordinary machines as we know them. On the one hand, as machines, they seem to very much belong to our universe. On the other hand, they are unexplainable in terms of natural phenomena such as ball lightning, air plasmas, and the like, even though they show all the characteristics of being surrounded with a plasma. The latter point will be discussed in great detail in Section III.

In the following section, we briefly discuss the unconventional machine's fabulous performance.

Section II
Performance

A. Performance as an Aid to Identification

Anything, to be surely classed as a UFO, must meet one of two criteria. Either it has to be seen from a sufficiently short distance to be certain that its configuration is not that of any conventional craft, or its speed, acceleration, or maneuver performance has to be such that no airplane, helicopter, missile, or balloon could possibly account for it. For example, if something goes faster than an airplane, and the same craft slows to a hovering condition, it is a UFO. Even if it goes only 500 mph and also hovers, it is probably a UFO because helicopters can't go 500 mph. These statements say that range-of-speed capability is more important in the identification of an unconventional object than high speed itself. These criteria tend to eliminate from serious consideration as UFOs meteors as well as objects which are only seen moving slowly at high altitude, especially balloons. It need not eliminate unidentified (usually non-orbiting) objects seen in space by astronomical telescopes, of which there have been a fair number of sightings. These have to be natural objects or spacecraft. Several of the half-dozen or more unidentifieds sighted in space by U.S. astronauts pass the performance criteria; maneuvering in space, or going in a westward orbit as was the green object seen by Gordon Cooper near Perth, Australia, is evidence of superior performance sufficient enough to identify them as unconventional (space) craft, or UFOs.

The best and surest way to determine aircraft and UFO speeds is with radar. This is usually military-base or airport radar, unless the craft is being observed at a missile range, in which case there should be special radars coupled to path-plotting chart boards, giving a permanent record. Radars are instruments made to measure how position in space varies with time. From this data, speed is readily obtained, and if the data is recorded, the acceleration performance can be computed.

The radar is a reliable instrument. Radar is sufficiently reliable to entrust to it and its operators the lives of the public traveling by commercial airline and the lives of all military plane crews and passengers as well.

Theadolites, which provide position in space by optical triangulation, give satisfactory data, but besides being relatively rare instruments, they require 3 crews of 2 each for their operation and are therefore usually in a non-ready status.

Speed and acceleration are the performance parameters discussed in this section. Maneuver performance is discussed in Section XI, following the laying of more groundwork.

B. Speed

Nearly everyone knows that speed is the trademark of the UFO.

The only question is, have their speeds actually been measured, and so definitely known? The answer is emphatically yes. Two of the best sources of speed data are Maj. Edward J. Ruppelt's *Report on Unidentified Flying Objects* and Maj. Donald E. Keyhoe's *Flying Saucers From Outer Space* because they present the early speed data measured by Air Force radar before such data was classified by JANAP (Joint Army, Navy, Air Force Publication) 146 and AFR (Air Force Regulation prohibiting data release) 200-2.

EXAMPLE II-B1

Only one example of speed will be given, one involving multiple radar measurement with visual confirmation. This report is old but still valid. It was released to Keyhoe by the Air Force's UFO public relations officer, Al Chop, before JANAP 146 was issued (Keyhoe, 161-65). The bomber heading was not given.

Just before dawn on December 6, 1952, on a bright

moonlit night, a B-29 bomber was cruising at 18,000 feet over the Gulf of Mexico, 100 miles south of the Louisiana coast. Approaching the end of a night practice flight to Florida, radar operator Lt. Coleman was watching the main radarscope looking for the coastline. At 5:25 A.M., a fast-moving target appeared on the scope, approaching from ahead, or 12 o'clock. Coleman was amazed because it moved 13 nautical miles between sweeps of the radar. Grabbing his stopwatch, he timed it and computed the speed at 5,240 mph. He reported this to Captain Harter, who replied, "That's impossible. Recalibrate your set."

As Coleman recalibrated his set, 4 other blips came on the screen at 12 o'clock, approaching the B-29. Coleman reported that the radar was in order. The 4 unknowns appeared not only on Coleman's scope, but also on the captain's scope and on the navigator's scope. As one of the 4 objects came by, Master Sergeant Bailey, assisting Coleman, sprang to the right waist blister and peered out. To his astonishment, he saw a blue-lit object streak by, far enough to the side that he could follow its annular motion.

By this time, a second group of blips appeared on all three scopes, also coming in from 12 o'clock, but their courses missed the bomber by miles. This group also traveled at over 5,000 mph. At 5:31, all seemed clear.

For a minute the tense airmen relaxed. Then a third group appeared, also coming in from 12 o'clock. Lt. Coleman used the stopwatch while Sgt. Bailey computed the speed to be over 5,000 mph. This time the navigator beat Bailey to the waist blister and watched two of the machines streak by, mere blurs of blue-white light at that speed.

Capt. Harter studied his scope. Forty miles behind, a group of 5 cut across his path and, turning, headed straight for the bomber. But they slowed and fell in behind, pacing the bomber for about 10 seconds while the captain held his breath.

This group then turned aside and picked up speed again. All watched their scopes while the 5 targets approached a huge machine that made a half-inch spot on the scope. Amazed, they watched the 5 smaller blips merge with the large one. The big machine swiftly accelerated. Coleman called Capt. Harter.

"We clocked it," said Coleman. "You won't believe this. It was making over 9,000 mph."

"I believe it, all right," replied Harter. "That's just what I figured."

Here we have not only accurate, instrumented speed data, but an elegant mother-ship story from the Air Force's own people and equipment.

No part of the radar data indicates that the sightings could be explained by meteors or meteoroids. Specifically, the following points are inconsistent with meteoroid travel.

1. Five thousand mph is too slow for meteoroids.

2. Several course changes were made.

3. The objects were observed coming head-on and following.

4. Two instances of acceleration (speed increases) were noted.

5. Meteors don't rendezvous.

The objects could not have been conventional craft, for the following reasons:

1. Conventional craft don't cruise at 5,000 mph in level flight at 18,000 feet altitude. If they did, they would burn up.

2. U.S. rocket planes of that time period used only boost-glide trajectories, heading westward toward Edwards Air Base, Muroc, California, far to the west and over land.

3. Conventional craft don't make a blue streak. In this case, the blue light tends to confirm the sighting of unconventional objects, as this is their characteristic color at high-power operation (further explanation in Section III).

C. Acceleration

DATA

In the early 1950s, I studied the UFO pattern and noticed their propensity for visiting defense installations, flight over water, evening visits, and return appearances. Within a 20-mile radius of the Langley Research Center in Hampton, Virginia, where I was employed, were located over a dozen defense installations, and we were almost surrounded by water. On July 16, 1952, after the Pan American pilots made headlines in the local paper by reporting disks passing below their airliner near Hampton, I thought, "This is the night. They may be back."

Accordingly, expecting conformance to the pattern, at 5 minutes to 8 P.M., just at twilight, a companion and I arrived at the Hampton Roads waterfront, parked, and started to watch the skies for UFOs. At 8:00, I said to my companion, "I'd give a thousand dollars for a good look at a UFO." No sooner were the words spoken than here they came, up over the southern horizon, slightly east of a collision course with the observers. We kept an eye on them as they approached, getting out of the car to do so. They came in side by side at about 500 mph, at what was learned later by triangulation to be 15,000 to 18,000 feet altitude. From all angles they looked like amber traffic lights a couple of blocks away, which would make them spheres about 13 to 20 feet in diameter.

They slowed into a left turn to pass directly over our heads toward the west. They practically came to a stop as they approached. It was then that they started their strange jitter, a surprising phenomenon. First one leaped a little way ahead of the other as fast as or faster than the eye could follow—you couldn't be sure. Then the other seemed to jump ahead. They kept up these odd mincing steps for a few seconds as they passed overhead, while we craned our necks. Then, after passing zenith, they made an astounding maneuver. Maintaining their spacing of about 200 feet, they revolved in a horizontal circle, about a common center, at a rate of at least once per second. After a few revolutions, and without a pause, they switched their revolutions into a vertical plane, keeping up the same amazing rate. Awe-stricken, I reached my hand out to the car for support saying, "Nothing can do that. Those are really saucers."

That was halfway into a 3-minute sighting. Up to that point I had just been a fascinated spectator. Now they had convinced me. At that moment, I realized that here were visitors from another world. There is a lot of truth in the old saying, "It's different when it happens to you." It was within my line of business to know that no Earthcraft could remotely approach those maneuvers.

Within seconds of the circling maneuver, an identical sphere came in from the Atlantic Ocean on an ascending course over lower Chesapeake Bay and joined the others, falling in below. For a few seconds they seemed to float along, then began accelerating slowly toward the south as a fourth amber sphere came in from the James River to build the group up to a formation of four as they headed south. I thought, "A-ha, the circling maneuver was a rendezvous signal."

The sphere that came in from the Atlantic had evidently cruised northward, just offshore. This was learned in a visit to Norfolk, Virginia, looking for additional data. One of the Norfolk papers carried an article about it. A Virginia Beach bus driver was going north along the coast when a lone passenger had come forward a few minutes before 8:00 P.M. and tapped him on the shoulder, calling his attention to a strange, orange or amber fiery-looking sphere out over the water. The driver was sufficiently impressed to stop the bus, and together they watched the fiery sphere cruising northward parallel to shore, just above the water's surface. This was obviously the first object that answered the rendezvous signal. My instant impression was that these vehicles were surveying the East Coast. If they had good resolving power, perhaps I was in their survey.

It was subsequently learned that a ferryboat load of passengers, docked at Old Point and waiting to make the overnight trip to Washington, had witnessed the entire event, among them the President of the Newport News Shipbuilding and Dry Dock Corporation. The next morning the Newport News *Daily Press* carried a two-inch banner headline, FLYING SAUCERS OVER HAMPTON ROADS. The detailed report had been made to the *Press* by an Air Force captain, a fighter pilot. Our observations agreed even to the estimated 500 mph speed. However, one thing puzzled me. The *Press* article said that aircraft spotters who had been on duty reported nothing. Determined to check this out, I got a list of spotters on duty the night in question and visited them individually in their homes. They all said they saw the UFOs and knew that they were not aircraft. The head spotter said that he had been instructed by the Richmond Filter Center, operated by the Air Force, to report aircraft, and no nonsense, and so had said nothing. However, they gave me the data needed for triangulation to obtain altitude.

Reporting the incident to my NACA boss next morning was a mistake. "What had you been drinking?" were his first, and almost his last, words. Knowing my duty was to report to Air Force Intelligence, I went to the local ATIC Office. The desk officer and his secretary listened to my story, then he reported to his chief. I caught the gist of their conversation:

"Are you sure he saw the saucers?" asked the chief.

"Yes, I know he saw them. Do you want to interview him?"

"No, you go ahead."

I signed a statement written by the secretary. The intelligence officer complained that I should have run to a phone and called Tactical Air Command Headquarters so that they could have tried an intercept. With a few Yes Sir's, I left. At the time, I already had a growing aversion to the Air Force's attempted intercepts, but why discuss policy at the bottom of the totem pole?

ACCELERATION DEFINITIONS AND IMPORTANCE

Acceleration is the change in velocity per second. While many can estimate speed just by watching, few if any can so estimate acceleration. It has to be computed, an easy task in certain simple cases which we shall review.

For extremely high-performance vehicles such as rockets and UFOs, the most convenient unit of acceleration is Earth (surface) gravity. Thus, acceleration is given in multiples of Earth gravity, commonly called g's, or just g. At 10 g, for example, the acceleration is 10 times that of a freely falling body near the Earth's surface. This usage avoids the confusing basic units such as meters per second per second.

Because of the shortage of acceleration data, and because of the importance of such data to UFO locomotion theory, I present the two most common methods of estimation in the hope that this information will result in new data. The first method applies to turning trajectories, the second to straight-line trajectories.

ACCELERATION IN A TURNING TRAJECTORY

For our purposes we can think of any portion of a curved path, or trajectory, as a segment of a circle having a radius, r, normal to the path. Any object moving along this portion of the curved path has an acceleration, a, also normal to the path and pointed along r toward the center of curvature. The formula to compete this acceleration requires the following four symbols. The use of British or metric units of measure makes no difference in the result.

Symbols	British	Metric
r, radius of curvature of path	feet	meters
V, velocity of object	ft/sec	m/sec
g, Earth gravity	32.2 ft/sec^2	9.8 m/sec^2
a, acceleration of object	multiples of Earth g or g's	

Then for any curved trajectory, the magnitude of the turning acceleration is computed by the square of velocity divided by radius times gravity:

$$a = \frac{v^2}{rg} \qquad (2\text{-}1)$$

Using this formula, we can compute the approximate acceleration of the circling spheres estimated to have a turning radius of 100 feet. Since they circled steadily about once per second, their velocity was:

$$V = \frac{\text{circumference of circle}}{\text{time per revolution}} = \frac{2\pi r}{t}$$

$$= \frac{(2)(3.14)(100)}{(1)} = 628 \, \frac{ft}{sec}$$

and their acceleration was approximately:

$$a = \frac{V^2}{rg} = \frac{(628)(628)}{(100)(32.2)} = 122 \, g$$

Considering probable errors, this figure should be rounded off to the order of 100 g.

ACCELERATION IN A STRAIGHT-LINE TRAJECTORY

The computation of the acceleration in a straight line from a standing start (hovering) requires the introduction of one new symbol, s, the distance traveled in the time t. Assuming that the acceleration is constant, acceleration is computed by:

$$a = \frac{2s}{gt^2} \qquad \text{in g units, or g's} \qquad (2\text{-}2)$$

Also, with constant acceleration from a standing start, the velocity reached in the time t is given by:

$$V = \frac{2s}{t} \qquad \text{consistent units} \qquad (2\text{-}3)$$

We can approximate the acceleration and speed of the big dirigible-type UFO that I observed (detailed in Section XII) going a measured 5 miles in about 4 seconds, assuming its acceleration to be constant, and that it started from rest instead of the estimated initial speed of 100 mph:

$$a = \frac{2s}{gt^2} = \frac{(2)(5)(5,280)}{(32.2)(4)(4)} = 102 \, g \qquad \text{approximately}$$

The velocity reached was:

$$V = \frac{2s}{t} = \frac{(2)(5)(5,280)}{4} = 13,200 \text{ ft/sec}$$
$$= 9,000 \text{ mph}$$

This speed just happens to equal the speed measured by B-29 radar in the earlier example.

To take initial velocity V_1 into account in the computation of acceleration requires the use of the following formula:

$$a = \frac{2(s - V_1 t)}{gt^2} \quad g's \qquad (2\text{-}4)$$

For the initial speed of 100 mph, we substitute for V_1 its equivalent of 147 ft/sec, and the other numbers as before. The equation gives the acceleration of the big dirigible at just 100 g.

CONCLUSION

Such acceleration performance is an order of magnitude beyond the capability (10 g) of Earth-type aircraft, and is well beyond large missile performance. However, the small World War II tube-launched antitank Bazooka missile had a linear acceleration of several hundred g, and the acceleration of cannon-launched missiles runs into the thousands of g's. For example, the U.S. Army's cannon-launched guided projectile (CLGP) has to withstand cannon-launch environments of over 7,000 g and is designed to withstand 9,000 g (*Aviation Week & S.T.*, October 13, 1975). This vehicle has wings and tail, and maneuvers as needed to strike tank targets up to 8 kilometers distant. Critical to its functioning was the development and packaging of its gyroscope, delicate optics, and electronics to withstand the g forces.

The building of small missiles containing computers, guidance, instrumentation, and telemeters to withstand 100 g loadings has been within the state-of-the-art for over two decades. Remarks to the effect that observed UFO accelerations would crush all known materials are very poorly founded.

D. Optical Effects of High Acceleration

"In nature . . . discontinuities do not take place."
—Dr. Joseph G. Coffin,
mathematical physicist
(*Vector Analysis*, 96)

In general, I disagree with the occasional description of some UFO maneuvers as instantaneous. *Sudden* is the proper word. I hold with the scientific community that all physical occurrences require a finite time. The quote by Dr. Coffin, above, makes the same point. This is not quibbling over a small difference in time. It is a basically important point of physics. Thus, while we are wearing our science caps we will be wary of the chap who says that a UFO left instantly when the phrase "so quickly I didn't see it go" would serve as well and not smudge up our science caps.

Generally speaking, I have faith in the UFO witness, particularly when the sighting is from close up. What follows is not a criticism of the witness, but some comments on the limitations of his observations due to the visual-mental reaction time required. Everyone who has watched a magician perform should realize that such limitations exist.

The validity of this viewpoint in explaining the apparent disappearance of even large objects will be illustrated by an incident that occurred at the Wallops Island (research vehicle) test range. We were doing a research model flight test for one of the military services, utilizing one of our high acceleration vehicle systems to drive the research model to the required supersonic speed. This particular branch of the services had their own missile test range and experienced cameramen. Although it was against our usual regulations, their management prevailed on us to allow them to utilize their own movie tracking crew in addition to ours to assure good camera coverage. The model launch was in the 15 to 20 g range, increasing as the rocket weight decreased. During countdown, which comes over loudspeakers, all cameras were ready and running, all eyes on the vehicle. On the count of zero, the visiting cameramen did not see the vehicle leave! They reacted rapidly and panned up the smoke trail as rapidly as they could, but their cameras never caught a glimpse of the model-rocket system. Their previous experience in tracking lower acceleration vehicles had left them totally unprepared to follow a really high performance vehicle. Our highly selected and highly trained camera crew got their usual fine movies only because they knew from experience how to lead the action, and the incredible panning rates required.

On the highest performance vehicles it is common for visitors with a professional interest in the flight to not see the vehicle launch, even though they know when and where it is going. If they glance up the smoke trail quickly enough, they are apt to get a glimpse of it as it disappears from sight. We are speaking of vehicles with a minimum length of 20 feet.

"What happened?" is a not untypical reaction and question.

"Good flight," the usual answer.

"I didn't see a thing; it was too fast. How could you tell it was a good flight?"

"I was in the radar chart room. If you step into the chart room you can watch the radar read-out automatically plot the vehicle trajectory."

Anyone who has watched aerial objects moving away in daylight knows how easy it is to lose sight of the object, and how troublesome to get one's eyes back on it. When UFOs are said to disappear, the witness may be right, but I believe the impression is explained by a combination of visual acuity and witness reaction time. Of course, at night all such reports are without merit. The UFO has to but blink out all its lights to give the impression it disappeared, even though it has not moved.

The instant disappearance reports are one of the reasons that many in the scientific community have brushed UFOs aside for "defying the laws of physics." The right angle turn and sudden reversal of direction are two others. The latter, easily explained, will be discussed in the section on saucer maneuvers. We will address the right angle turn now.

At the Langley Research Center, I became a sort of clearing house for local UFO sightings. We had good reports because they were made by scientist- and engineer-types who had volunteered for aircraft spotting duty. An instrument scientist from the Instrument Research Division related to me his sighting of a UFO making a right angle turn. While on night spotter duty, he saw what looked like a meteor descending vertically at extreme speed from high altitude. Before reaching the ground, however, it came abruptly to a stop, and without hesitation accelerated horizontally to a high velocity. It was then that he realized it couldn't be a meteor. It had followed a very rapid square-cornered trajectory which is sometimes part of the UFO pattern. This UFO was going fast near the corner, but decelerated rapidly to a stop at the corner. Then, without noticeable hesitation, it accelerated rapidly in a horizontal direction. Thus it actually came to a stop at the corner, however briefly. This is the point that technically untrained observers would very likely have missed. No laws of physics have been violated or even threatened. (Note that this maneuver would be perfect for the avoidance of radar surveillance.)

It is my conclusion, to borrow a phrase used frequently by Dr. T. Allen Hynek, that no UFO maneuver requires an escalation of hypothesis beyond well-controlled high acceleration for its explanation. In other words, high thrust-to-weight ratio and thrust-vector control explain them. These are ordinary engineering concepts of this century, and will be treated in detail in Section XI. Fortunately, the usual UFO disappearance report is that it took off at tremendous speed and disappeared in seconds, a description which should strain no one's sensibilities as it is in strict conformance with this century's science.

Section III
Illumination

"UFOs are largely confined to a silver color in the daytime and a kaleidoscope of colors at night."
—Coral and Jim Lorenzen

A. General Statement and Summary of Coverage

UFO illumination is a difficult subject because of the large variety and detail of the nighttime colors displayed and the detailed quantum physics involved. There are two main types of UFO lighting: (1) the ordinary running lights and spotlight beams, and (2) the sheath of illumination surrounding the UFO. The ordinary UFO spotlight beams are obviously used to light terrain and objects at night. However, some luminous beams may be weapons, having as a purpose the projection of heat, the disruption of electric and electronic equipment, and even the temporary paralysis of individuals. The running lights are at least as complicated as those of cars, boats, and aircraft, and perhaps as superficial, and no more will be said about them. However, in this section the sheath of illumination surrounding a UFO at night will be pursued in as much detail as possible, as it doubtless has some basic connection with UFO operation—not a cause, but an effect.

There is really no secret as to what this illuminated and illuminating sheath of atmosphere around the UFO is. It is a sheath of ionized and excited air molecules often called a plasma. It has all the many characteristics of ionized and excited air molecules, and has no characteristics not attributable to ionized and excited air molecules with expected contaminants; thus the illumination is tied to an air plasma. I am not suggesting anything original, as it has been suggested by many that such is the case. Indeed, any physicist who has made a study of UFOs must know they are characteristically surrounded by an air plasma. The terms *ionized* and *excited* will be explained shortly.

The phenomenon of ionized and excited atmospheric molecules around a UFO also ties together a number of related mysteries about the UFO. It accounts for the general nighttime appearance of the UFO: the many observed colors, the fiery, neon-like look, the self-illuminating character, the fuzzy, indefinite or even indiscernible outline, yet an appearance of solidity behind the light. It also accounts for the general lack of heat radiation despite the fact that they sometimes look fiery or even like a flaming ball of fire, and even the ultraviolet burns sometimes received by close viewers of UFOs with a blue plasma. In the daytime the same plasma is present, but usually invisible. Morning and evening, it is partly visible. Giant cigars and dirigibles are exceptions, for they can lay down a plasma wake or cloud visible in the daytime. The ion sheath also accounts for some daytime UFO characteristics such as a shimmering haze, nebulosity of the atmosphere or even smoke-like effects sometimes observed when high contaminant concentrations and chemical actions may be presumed to be present.

While there remain many unknown details about the quantum mechanics and spectral behavior of the plasma sheath, there is really only one important secret and that is the exact nature of its cause. Several possibilities enter the arena, and these will be reviewed later, when we narrow the cause down to a power-plant-connected, ionizing, wave-type radiation from the UFO.

Finally, since we will find that the UFO is radioactive, radiating intense radiations of x-ray frequencies, the most likely single candidate for the ionizing radiations of importance are those in the x-ray bracket. Particulate radiation, other than the electrons supplied by the atmosphere in the ionization process, we will see, are almost ruled out.

Among the minor unsolved mysteries of the plasma sheath is the following question: bearing in mind that two or more spectral colors combine to form a color which may be a surprise to all but the color experts, is the observer really seeing the color he thinks he is seeing? This subject is not treated in detail, but a suggestion is made for resolving the problem experimentally.

B. Sample Data on Colors and Illumination

EXAMPLE III-B1

Near Ponta Poran, in southern Brazil, on December 21, 1957, a party of Brazilians were driving a jeep along a country road about 6:30 P.M. on a cloudy evening (Lorenzen, *UFO: The Whole Story*, 148-50). Two near-spherical UFOs were seen following a horizontal course, but they oscillated from side to side with a wobbling motion. One of them stopped, then dived at the Jeep while the other one circled overhead. While they maneuvered, their illumination was intense, coming mainly from a bright silvery glow surrounding the lower hemisphere, which gave the vehicles an aspect of brilliance although their outlines seemed obscured by this very illumination. The vehicles appeared to be twins. Each one intermittently sent a brilliant beam of light at the Jeep, which, however, had no effect on the motor, and the driver kept going the best he could. When he hesitated, one would shine a beam of light on the road ahead and the other would hover over the illuminated spot as if to land. When it finally did land, the illumination intensity died down and the outline became clear. It was an oblate, or flattened spheroid about 15 feet in diameter and was surrounded by a flat ring at the equator which seemed to rotate.

The upper hemisphere, or hemispheroid, was a fiery red, as was the ring, and, again, the bottom was lighted by a silvery glow. There were no other features, such as doors or windows, visible. There also was no heat, odor, or perceptible noise. The vehicles were excellent examples of the classic Saturn-type UFO.

EXAMPLE III-B2

On the night of February 18, 1968, at Vashon Island, Washington, three young men drove to a gravel pit near which a saucer had been seen earlier (Lorenzen, *UFO: The Whole Story*, 163). It was still there but had moved directly over a pond within the pit. One of the young men, Joseph Frabush, described the object as lens-shaped, made of shiny metal, and about 30 feet in diameter. The lighting was a blue-white glow. Frabush had difficulty describing the light, but insisted that the vehicle was lighted by a reflected light rather than light generated by the vehicle (surface) itself, even though there were no lighting sources in the area.

Of course the source was the atmosphere, and the light *was* reflected by the shiny surface. An unusual part of this story relates to a strange bit of residual physical evidence. When the UFO left, the pond was found frozen over, although air temperatures had been above freezing for days.

EXAMPLE III-B3

Near Madrid, Spain, eyewitness Antonio Pardo and his family saw a UFO in the daylight, just as the sun was setting (Ribera and Farriols, 86). Photographs were taken, and the shape was clearly that of two pie pans lip-to-lip, the configuration we have categorized as a double-hat saucer.

In a letter to writer Antonio Ribera, which I have translated, witness Antonio Pardo said, "The color was orange . . . All the witnesses could appreciate a uniform brilliance all around the periphery, as if it were a neon lamp. We are sure that if it had been seen at night we would have seen it with its own light. Even in daylight the luminous contrast was evident."

EXAMPLE III-B4

In another observation documented, three fighter bombers took off from the deck of a carrier off the coast of Korea on an early morning flight to bomb a truck convoy in the Yalu River valley (Lorenzen, *Flying Saucers*, 30). As the sun came up they were flying northward over the valley at 10,000 feet. The lead pilot was startled to see two large shadows moving at high speed along the ground, coming from the northwest. He looked up and saw that two huge UFOs were causing the shadows. His radar showed that they were moving at a relative velocity of 1,000 to 1,200 mph when they suddenly stopped, assuming the velocity of the planes at a distance of a mile and a half. They seemed to begin a jittering or fibrillating motion. The pilot's reaction was to shoot. He readied his guns and gun cameras, but the radar went haywire. The screen bloomed, becoming very bright, and he realized the radar had been jammed. He called the carrier, but each frequency that he tried was successively jammed by a buzzing a moment after he turned it on. All the while, the objects were jittering out ahead, maintaining the speed of the planes.

The pilot used reference points on the windshield and the previously determined range to determine their size. They were between 600 and 700 feet in diameter! They were shaped like conical hats with oblong ports in the crown, through which copper-green lights shone. The objects had a shiny, silvery appearance with a reddish glow surrounding them. Above the ports was a shimmering red ring, encircling the top portion. The bottom was black except near the periphery, which glowed red. The black part never jittered.

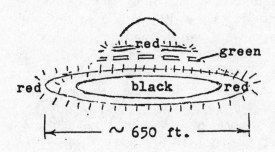

Figure III-1.

The objects then began maneuvering around the flight squadron, circling above and below. At this time all six men in the three planes experienced a feeling of warmth in the airplanes and a high-frequency vibration.

After the flight, they found that all the gun camera film had been exposed or fogged, and that the luminous paint used on the instrument dials had become extremely bright; the paint had been rejuvenated.

In this account, we have not only the red glowing atmospheric illumination, which was strong enough to be seen in the morning daylight, but a very strong suggestion of the reason for it. A radiation from the UFO energetic enough to activate luminous paint and to penetrate camera cases could excite nearby atmospheric molecules to radiate colors, as will be discussed.

EXAMPLE III-B5

On the night of April 20, 1969, near Browntown, Wisconsin, Mr. and Mrs. Robert Phillips witnessed a spectacular light phenomenon (*APRO Bulletin*, May-June 1969, p. 8). They stopped their car to observe. As the light approached, it looked like a luminous yellow-orange cone, point down. However, when it hovered near their car they could see that it was actually shaped like a kettle drum, with a diffuse, axisymmetric cone of light below. As this UFO started to move slowly, parallel with the road, the Phillips paced it with their car. As the UFO moved along, its color changed to an orange-red, then to a bright red. Meanwhile, as it moved, the intensity of the glowing cone diminished to the point where its actual shape was well-defined.

Since the Phillips at first mistook the luminosity for the shape of the UFO, I wonder how many others fall into the same trap but never see the real shape well-defined. Similar circumstances could easily account for the nighttime reports of ice-cream-cone UFOs, for example. We shall return to the conical light phenomenon later, for it tells us that UFOs are capable of focusing their powerful ionizing radiations, in this case into an axisymmetric cone.

EXAMPLE III-B6

We shall finally consider a case in which a UFO lit up with the blue-white appearance of an electric arc. This sighting occurred at 7:00 P.M., November 2, 1971, on a farm near Delphos, Kansas (*APRO Bulletins*, November-December 1971 and March-April 1972). Sixteen-year-old Ronald Johnson was tending his sheep when he heard a rumbling noise and went to investigate. As he approached the back side of the barn, he saw a saucer-type UFO hovering what he thought to be one foot above ground level. The UFO then lit up like an electric arc, having the blue-white appearance of an electric welding arc. This "arc flash," as it was described, began at the bottom and almost instantly enveloped the entire object. He stood and watched the lighted object for about 4 minutes before it took off. As it did so, the rumbling sound changed to a high pitch. Meanwhile, Ronald underwent a partial and temporary loss of vision, and afterward he suffered from the symptoms of a mild ultraviolet eyeburn.

Ronald called his parents, who came out in time to see the brightly lit UFO disappearing in the distance. Examination of the spot where the saucer had hovered showed an annular ring, known as a "saucer ring," in which the ground had been chemically altered, obviously by radiations from the saucer. Ronald was quoted as saying that the UFO also displayed orange and red colors, but no details were given on that aspect.

This case is only one of many in which blue-lit UFOs have caused skin or eye burns resembling electric arc burns, according to the doctors of patients who required treatment. This fact doesn't mean that the ionized atmosphere is an electric arc, although it radiates like one. Rather, it means that ionized atmospheric nitrogen radiates very strongly in the ultraviolet frequencies, whatever the cause of the ionization.

C. Ionization and Quantum Light Processes

At low altitudes, atmospheric gas molecules such as nitrogen and oxygen consist of two atoms each, like dumbbells, held together by a sharing of their outer electrons. The electrons of such molecules, unless disturbed by a collision with an energetic particle or photon, remain in their lowest energy state, called the ground state. Above the various electron ground-state energy levels are numerous energy-level vacancies. When a sufficiently energetic wave (photon) or particle generated by the UFO collides with a molecular electron in the surrounding atmosphere, the electron is impelled past all energy-level vacancies and outside the molecule. The electron becomes a free entity, rattling around between molecules. The molecule that lost the electron is said to be ionized; it is a positive ion. If the freed electron attaches to a neutral molecule, a negative ion is formed. If a free electron enters a positive ion, it usually enters one of the normally vacant energy levels and gives off a light quanta (photon) having an energy equal to that given up by the electron. Thus a relatively fast electron would give off a relatively energetic photon, say in the ultraviolet, or blue range.

This electron, occupying what is normally an energy-level vacancy, is in an unstable state. It can't remain because it is attracted toward lower states by the central positive charges. The molecule containing the unstable electron is said to be excited. The electron may cascade down through successively lower energy levels until it arrives at the unfilled ground state, successively giving off light quanta with energies just equal to each change of energy level by the electron. These emissions from the excited molecule depend strongly on the atomic structure and energy-level vacancies of the particular element involved, but are modified by molecular spin. In excited atoms, the energy transitions are distinct, as is the atomic spectral lines. In excited molecules, on the contrary, the temperature-dependent energy of the rotating "dumbbells" is enough to make the spectra appear to be a continuum, having peaks at high energy concentrations and valleys in the frequency regions in between, where fewer photons are emitted.

Finally, the energy the electron imparts to each photon determines its wavelength and color. Air molecules can radiate in a kaleidoscope of colors, any color of the spectrum.

The following equation, in slightly different form, was first used by Einstein in 1905 to explain the photoelectric effect. It is basic to all light phenomena.

Let E = energy of light photon in electron volts, eV. One eV is the energy delivered to an electron which moves through a 1-volt drop in electric potential.

λ = wavelength of light photon in Angstroms, Å. One Angstrom = 10^{-10} meters.

Then λ equals 12,400 divided by E, or

$$\lambda = \frac{12,400}{E} \qquad (3\text{-}1)$$

This equation gives us the following color chart connecting photon energy, wavelength, and color. > means greater than; < means less than.

Color Chart

Photon Energy, eV	Resulting λ, Å	Corresponding Color
> 3.26	< 3800	ultraviolet
3.26 - 2.58	3800 - 4800	blue
2.58 - 2.21	4800 - 5600	green
2.21 - 2.10	5600 - 5900	yellow
2.07 - 2.00	6000 - 6200	orange
1.97 - 1.65	6300 - 7500	red
< 1.65	> 7500	infrared

The following notes should be made concerning this chart:

1. All UFO colors stem from energetic, ionizing radiation or radiations, generated by the UFO, which ionize the air.

2. Of all the visible colors, red and orange correspond to the least energy, according to this chart. They are also the two most common colors associated with UFO low-power operation, such as hovering or low-power maneuvers. The electrons have been given the ionization energy, but not much more, and cascade down in small energy drops corresponding to red or orange. This is statistically probable, as there are more small drops available than big ones.

3. According to the color chart, blue requires a relatively high activation energy. Blue, white, and blue-white are the common colors at high-power operation. The blue of the high-power maneuver or high-speed operation corresponds to the strong radiation peaks of nitrogen which will be discussed next. A blend of all the colors tends to white; but with the blues predominating, the blend gives a blue-white, as in an electric arc.

D. Physical Data

Figures III-2 and III-3 show the relative spectral radiance of nitrogen and air, over a very large range of wavelength, when excited by a 10 keV electron beam. The visible spectrum runs from about 3800 to 7500 angstroms, and the colors that can be activated by the ionization are spotted on the figures. It should be perfectly clear that air can radiate in any or all colors. The bulk of the emissions seem to come from the N_2 1st negative, Gayden green, and N_2 1st positive spectral series of nitrogen, and the individual color peaks are very clear of Figure III-2. Still, as we can judge by comparing it to Figure III-3, atmospheric oxygen adds radiance in the green, yellow, orange, and particularly red. Excited in this gross manner that excites all emissions at once, it appears to the eye as blue-white. More sophisticated equipment could excite a single color. In fact, the peak for the usually-used nitrogen laser line at 3371 Angstroms is clearly visible in both figures. This is not a hint that UFOs use lasers to control the colors, but UFOs do radiate invisible wave energy with ionizing capability, and there is no reason to think that this radiation does not have distinctive frequency components and energy levels. The UFO colors constitute evidence that they do.

OPTICAL INFARED CHARACTERISTICS

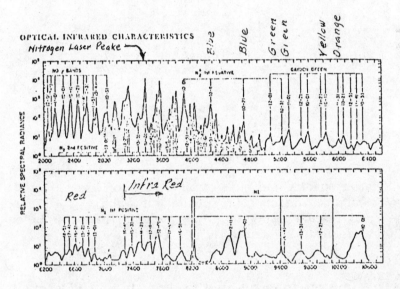

WAVE LENGTH IN ANGSTROMS

Figure III-2.

Relative spectral radiance of nitrogen at 22 Torr (closely approximating one millimeter of mercury) excited by 10 keV electrons. The effective spectral slit width was 18Å and the total scanning time approximately 90 minutes. Below 3200Å the relative intensity is less certain.

* One Torr approximates one millimeter of mercury.

OPTICAL INFARED CHARACTERISTICS

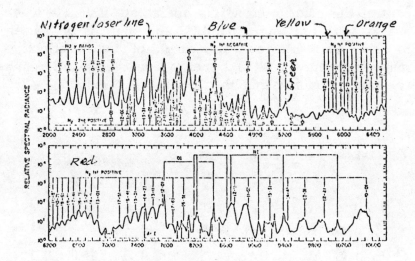

WAVE LENGTH IN ANGSTROMS

Figure III-3.

Relative spectral radiance of air at 22 Torr excited by 10 keV electrons. The effective spectral slit width was 18Å and the total scanning time approximately 90 minutes. Below 3200Å the relative intensity is less certain.

The implications of all this are clear. UFOs excite different spectral peaks and colors, or different color combinations, as we saw in the Ponta Poran incident (Example III-B1), depending on the type of UFO and its operating condition. In particular, the illumination comes directly from the air and not from the vehicle surface, as the witnesses in several of the preceding examples so well pointed out.

E. Brightness

The ionization energy has two components, energy level and amount. So far we have discussed the colors in terms of energy level only, in units of electron volts per event and per photon generated. We have said nothing about either the amount of activation energy per unit area, per second (power per unit area) that the UFO emits in the form of ionizing radiation or the resulting number of photons generated in the ion relaxation process. If events are occurring well below ion-saturation levels, the number of ions created per unit volume per second and the equivalent number relaxing and giving off photons should be proportional to the activation power per unit area. Hence the light intensity, which is proportional to the number of photons passing a given area per second, is also proportional to the ion-activational power the UFO emits.

When a hovering UFO starts to maneuver, it necessarily increases thrust (lift) and power. In such a circumstance, the UFO is generally observed to brighten rather than change color, as the witnesses observed in Example III-B1. This brightness would be the result of an increase in the activation power that the UFO puts out, exactly as just explained, while the energy levels of individual events stay fixed. This concept is simply standard quantum mechanics, which explains the changes in brightness as well as the color of the air surrounding a UFO at night.

The brightness change together with the UFO power change clearly show that the UFO radiation causing the brightness is an integral part of the power system. On the other hand, the observed atmospheric colors are a by-product of the power plant radiation quite dependent on the properties of the atmosphere. The colors would probably be quite different on any other planet, and would be characteristic of that planet's atmosphere.

F. The Fuzzy or Invisible UFO Outline

The quantum mechanical explanation for the indistinct or invisible outline of the UFO at night is particularly straightforward. In excited molecules, the downward drop of the electron through various energy levels is a reversible process. When two molecules each have an electron in an unstable upper energy level u, that drop to a lower level l, they each give off a photon with an energy equal to the difference in the energy levels u and l. If the photon from the first molecule properly encounters the second, it puts the electron right back from level l to level u, the reverse of the relaxation process. This is why the spectroscopist says that the absorption spectrum of a gas is equal to its emission spectrum. Any wavelength which a gas emits it can, and does, absorb. Since the excited air emits in the visible wavelengths, it absorbs in the same wavelengths, and there is a critical distance of a few feet of plasma that will absorb the passing light. In other words, beyond a few feet of thickness a plasma is essentially opaque to light of its own emission frequencies.

At night, when the witness must see the UFO by its own light, it follows that if the plasma is fully developed (saturated with ions) the plasma can completely obscure the UFO, for the critical distance is small. In the more general case where the UFO is operating at a lower radiation, the witness can see the UFO surface directly ahead, looking normal to the surface through the least amount of plasma. The light reflected from that surface reaches his eye. But when he looks for the outline, he must look obliquely through a greater thickness of plasma. The light from the edge will be partly or all absorbed, making the edge indistinct or invisible. This is why the witness says, "I'm sure the object was solid, but I couldn't see its shape." If the UFO radiation dies down as the witness watches, the entire UFO becomes visible because the actual plasma thickness becomes less than critical.

The opaqueness of various plasmas to passing radiation has many counterparts in modern technology. The principle is used in the furnace design of steam turbine-electric power plants which are designed to heat the boiler tubes by gas radiation. The designer makes the plasma thickness "seen" by the boiler tubes a little greater than the critical plasma thickness, so a maximum of radiated energy reaches the tubes. A greater thickness would do no good, as the radiation can pass no further. Another example can be seen in vehicles re-entering the earth's atmosphere from orbit or from a lunar trip. While the plasma sheath is at a maximum, there is a complete radio communications blackout, for even the radio frequencies can't pass through the critical plasma thickness. That some are hot and some are cold makes no difference. The degree of ionization and excitation is what counts.

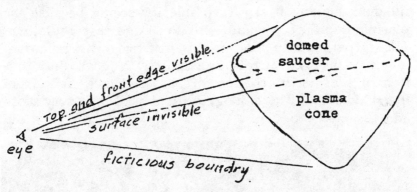

Figure III-4. Effect of plasma thickness on visibility.

The absorption characteristics of the plasma can also partly account for a daytime hazy or smoky appearance of the atmosphere around the UFO. When the surrounding illumination is brighter than the plasma, the plasma absorption may be greater than its emission, making it look darker, or hazy, as in Ray Hawks' sighting in Section IX (Lorenzen, *UFO, The Whole Story*, 224). If it looks very dark or smoky, the UFO primary radiation is probably inducing chemical reactions of the atmospheric impurities, perhaps, for example, smog. Atmospheric impurities could be very important in the interpretation of UFO data because, as is well known, impurities in a gas can make ionization linger.

Figure III-5 is a photo of a pertinent experiment. The Langley Research Center of NASA has developed a technique for ionizing the air in a supersonic wind tunnel in order to photograph a test model by ion light. It is a simple way to study the air flow and shockwave system. The photo is that of a small model under test. The N_2 1st negative blue peaks of nitrogen are activated by shooting a stream of electrons crosswise and up-stream of the model. These are the same ions which give the UFO its blue color at high power. The light color (blue in the original photo) around the model is a zone of compressed, ionized air created by the surrounding supersonic shock envelope under study. It is by this light that we see the model. while this photo is almost full-size, making it size favorable for seeing because the plasma depths are small, still the edges are indistinct. This is particularly true, in this instance, with regard to the windshield, which is obscured by a local concentration of plasma which doesn't pass reflected light from the windshield. The analogy with the UFO is very close and essentially obvious.

Figure III-5. Graphic illustration of indistinct outline.

Supersonic wind-tunnel model under test, photographed by N_2^+ ion-plasma light.

G. A Word of Caution on Color

At present, we don't know for certain, when we see a given UFO color such as yellow or green, whether we are looking at a single color of narrow frequency band, or at two or more colors spread over a wide range of frequencies, giving the same effect on the eye. The theory of colors due to mixed light frequencies is complicated and is beyond the scope of this book. However, photographing UFOs with tri-color cameras would seem to be a good way to get a reading on the real spectral colors being emitted. These cameras take 3 pictures in 3 colors by the use of filters—an old but effective method, invented by Grassmann in 1853. Astronomers are now using tri-color photography to determine the real colors radiated by emission nebulas (Miller 39). Emission spectral lines are identified. Spectrographic grating attachments for ordinary cameras have been tried, and apparently failed due to insufficient light intensity from the UFO (Saunders and Harkins). Spectrometers, used to get spectral energy distributions, are very elaborate for field use.

The following section, on radiation data and analyses, is also pertinent to pinpointing the exact radiation cause of atmospheric ionization.

Section IV
How Hot Is UFO Radiation?

A. The Radiation Questions

From ionization, heating, and vibration data, we have gotten some pretty definite indications that UFOs are radiating energy. The following questions are now being asked. Of what energy level is the radiation? What is its intensity? From the observed data what can be judged regarding its basic type? That is, is the UFO radiating high energy waves, or high energy, ionizing particles? Do these facts, whatever they are, give us useful information about the propulsion system? Can we answer these questions now, or must we await field investigations with expensive scientific equipment combined with lots of good luck?

The answers to these questions can be roughly given now; more refined answers will require more data. An important connection between these answers and the power plant system will be discussed in Section V.

B. David and Goliath, and Other Radiation Data

EXAMPLE IV-B1

In spite of several proposals and a few plans, the scientific world at large has produced essentially no measured, documented, and published UFO data. By contrast, David took his trusty Geiger counter and, without thought of budget money for field investigations or elaborate data gathering programs, went looking for Goliath. The event was the UFO reported in the vicinity of Lexington, Alabama, beginning December 27, 1972. David was APRO Field Investigator Bill Rogers. His agile efforts were reported in the *APRO Bulletin* for January-February 1973.

On January 30, at 6:30 P.M., Bill Rogers arrived in Lexington. Actually, he had an excellent field plan. He and two companions in one car and three other individuals in three other cars went in different directions and kept in touch by radio. Rogers had received three alert calls by 9:00 P.M.., but each time he had been too late to witness anything. Heading back on highway 101, Rogers decided to visit the new garbage dump, which had been the location of a UFO in prior reports. At about a mile from the dump, he spotted a yellowish-orange-to-white light moving slowly, just above tree-top level and about a mile to his right. He got out of the car with his companions, and they studied the object with binoculars. After about a minute, the object moved up about 40 feet, and they could see that it had a shape between a sphere and an egg (ellipsoidal). It then descended as if going to land. The trio piled into the car and headed toward the UFO while Rogers checked his Geiger counter. They could see it as they rounded a sharp curve where the dump starts; they stopped the car in a skid, but by the time they all jumped out the object had descended behind a hill. The glow was still visible, however. A second later it came up, and the Geiger counter showed a reading of 400 volts and 250 milliroentgens. Then it went back down behind the hill and the counter reading returned to normal. This sequence was repeated several times with the same readings being obtained each time it rose. Rogers pointed a flashlight beam at the object. The object fluttered a little and descended again. The fifth time the object went down, its glow went out as if a light had been turned off. The men attempted to reach the spot by car, but they could not. They therefore called it a night.

EXAMPLE IV-B2

The *APRO Bulletin* of July-August 1969 reported that near Bogota, Colombia, on the July 4, 1969, a farm family witnessed a UFO shaped like an egg standing on end (ellipsoidal). Mauricio Gnecco, age 13, sent signals in imitation Morse code with his flashlight, whereupon the UFO approached the house and hovered between two tall trees located 150 feet from the farmhouse. There it remained about 5 seconds. It was 4-6 feet tall, yellow-orange in color, with an arc of light around it. It made no sound as it hovered before 11 witnesses. The UFO then flew over a nearby hill and was obscured from view. Mr. Arcesio Bermudez, who was the only one unafraid, took the flashlight from Mauricio and ran after the UFO. He later said that he approached to within about 20 feet of the UFO, which was landed on its two legs. He called to the other male adult, Louis Carbajal, "Louis, come here. Look at this Martian." He claimed he saw a person inside. Mauricio and Andres Franco, also 13, watched the UFO from the top of a nearby hill. They said that it blinked on and off. Finally it left, rising high in the sky and disappearing toward Bogota.

Within two days Arcesio Bermudez was taken very ill. His temperature dropped to 95 degrees F. Within a few days he had black vomits (from prior internal bleeding), and diarrhea with blood flow. He died in Bogota on July 12, at 11:45 P.M., just 8 days after his prolonged close encounter with the UFO. At 10:00 A.M. on July 12, he had been attended by Dr. Louis Borda, and at 7:30 P.M. by Dr. Cesar Esmeral. They ascribed death to gastroenteritis which has various causes, among them severe radiation poisoning. The Colombia Institute of Nuclear Affairs said that Bermudez's illness was characterized by symptoms similar to those caused by a lethal dose of gamma rays.

None of the other witnesses, all of whom were much less exposed, were affected.

EXAMPLE IV-B3

According the Lorenzens (*UFO, The Whole Story*, 291), a radiation case occurred in the courtyard of a hospital at Mendoza, Argentina, in August 1967. One of the nurses watched as a saucer, described as having a mush-

room shape, came in for a landing nearby in the courtyard. (From other stories, I have concluded that a short,
thick stem below a saucer is an adjustable-length landing
gear.) The saucer glowed such a brilliant red that she
had to cover her eyes with her hand, and a buzzing
noise accompanied the landing. A few minutes elapsed
before she ventured to look again; when she did, she
saw the saucer flashing red and blue lights and flying
away. A medical examination of the 46-year-old woman
was made. Although she was in good condition, a scientist of the Argentine Atomic Energy Commission said
she had been exposed to radiation. The radiation from
the saucer also had apparently been strong enough to
affect the ground, for there was a burned-looking grey
spot at the place where she indicated the saucer had sat
down.

EXAMPLE IV-B4

The Lorenzens also report that Steve Michalak, age 52,
an amateur prospector from Winnipeg, Manitoba, had a
close encounter with a landed saucer with serious results
to his health (*UFOs Over the Americas* 38-41). On May
20, 1967, Michalak was on one of his prospecting trips
near Falcon Lake. He was taking rock samples when, at
12:15 P.M., he noticed two red glowing objects moving at
high speed and very low altitude. One of the objects sat
down nearby, while the other hovered, then left.
Michalak was concealed by brush, so he sat and
sketched the machine while he watched it. On the
ground it looked like stainless steel, but it was radiating
heat in rainbow colors. In 20-30 minutes a door opened
and he could hear a high-pitched sound like a motor
running. He thought he heard voices, and tried commu-
nicating in English, Russian, Italian, Polish, and German,
but to no avail. The door merely closed, and the motor
sound could no longer be heard.

He reached out his gloved hand and touched the
machine, with the result that his rubberized glove melted
enough to slip off. The machine then began to turn
counterclockwise and took off, as Michalak felt a hot air

blast or other force pushing him to his left. He was left with his clothes on fire, minor burns on his face, and second- and third-degree burns on his chest in a perfect checkerboard pattern. Michalak was hospitalized, and the case was published in the *APRO Bulletin*.

Dr. Horace C. Dudley is APRO's advisor in radiation physics. He was Chief of the Radioisotope Laboratory, United States Naval Hospital, St. Albans, New York, from 1952 through 1962. Portions of his opinion on the case follow: "Mrs. Michalak's description of her husband's nausea and vomiting followed by diarrhea and loss of weight and the drop in the lymphocyte count is a classical picture of severe whole body radiation with x-rays or gamma rays. I would guess that Mr. Michalak received on the order of 100-200 roentgens. It is very fortunate that this dose of radiation lasted only a very short time or he would certainly have received a lethal dose."

EXAMPLE IV-B5

The son of the sheriff of Price County, Wisconsin, had received a new set of bow and arrows. According to the Lorenzens (*UFO, The Whole Story*, 226), he and another boy went out to try the bow and arrows at 4:30 P.M. on November 3, 1960. In the area of a gravel pit, they heard a high-pitched humming sound and felt the air become warm. Looking around for the noise source, they saw an aluminum-colored object on a hill where they had just been. The boys ran toward it to get a better look, but it rose into the sky and disappeared. The boys felt the ground where the object had sat down and found it quite warm.

Drawings made by the boys showed a domed saucer, and questioning by an APRO investigator revealed its diameter to be 20-25 feet. A check of the vicinity with a Geiger counter showed no abnormal radioactivity.

EXAMPLE IV-B6

Ruppelt reported a well-documented case in which scoutmaster named Desvgers encountered a big saucer hovering over a palmetto thicket (Ruppelt 176-86). When Desvgers noticed the object over his head, he struck at it with his machete, and for his trouble received in his face a ball of flame which also singed his arms, burned his nostrils, burned holes in his cap, and rendered him unconscious.

Ruppelt considered this an important incident and investigated personally. He sent samples of the soil below where Desvgers said the saucer hovered to be tested by the Air Force Materials Laboratory at Wright Patterson. He also sent the machete. The only evidential findings of the entire investigation besides the burns, attested to by an examining doctor, were the following:

- The Materials Laboratory found the roots of the grass to be charred, but not the above-ground foliage. The soil had to be heated to 300 degrees F. to duplicate the charring. (How could Desvgers have done this without burning the grass?)
- Regarding the machete, "No knife was ever tested for so many things . . . They found nothing, just a plain unmagnetized, unradioactive, unheated, common, everyday knife."
- Ruppelt said, "We checked the area with a Geiger counter, not expecting to find anything. We didn't."

C. Radiation Analysis

WAVE OR PARTICLE? OF WHAT MINIMUM ENERGY?

According to modern physics, the energy radiating from a UFO has to be carried by energetic waves or energetic particles. For reinforcement, I quote from *Elementary Modern Physics* (Weidner and Sells 23): "Waves and particles play such an important role in physics because they represent the only two modes of energy transport. We can transport energy from one point in space to a second point only by sending a particle from the first to the second site, or by sending a wave from the first to the second site."

We don't have a measurement for Rogers' distance from the UFO when he took the readings (Example IV-B1), but recalling that he saw the UFO from about a mile away, then drove a little closer, let us assume for the purpose of discussion that he got to within a kilometer (0.62 mile). Charged particles have a limited range in the atmosphere because they collide frequently with atomic electrons and finally give up all their energy. Neutral particles could hardly be the energy carriers because they cannot activate (ionize the gas in) an ordinary counter. The following table gives the range of typical charged particles in sea-level atmosphere (Weidner and Sells 321).

Kinetic Energy, Millions of eV	RANGE IN AIR, METERS		
	Alpha Particle	Proton	Electron
1	0.005	0.023	3.14
5	1.035	0.34	20.0
10	1.107	1.17	41.0

At an energy of 10 million eV, computation shows, the electron is moving at 99.88 percent of light speed. Actually, for UFO radiation this table extends to too high an energy level in the last row, and even in the second, as we shall see. But even if 10 million volt electrons were radiated, they would be absorbed by the atmosphere in 41 meters, and wouldn't work the counter at 1,000 meters, or even at 100 meters.

Photons (waves), on the other hand, do not have what could be called a range limit in air. They have absorption coefficients, and attenuation, meaning that a certain percentage of the photons are scattered or absorbed in a given distance, then in the next equal distance the same percentage is scattered or absorbed, and so on, in an exponential-type decay. Theoretically, some get to the target. Those that do get to the target on an unwavering straight line arrive with all their initial energy, and can therefore actuate the counter and give a reading. From the Geiger counter reading and the other data, we tentatively conclude that the ellipsoidal UFO radiated potent wave-type, ionizing radiation into the surrounding atmosphere.

In *Elementary Modern Physics* (Weidner and Sells 324), the following statement is made in a discussion about gas-filled counters, of which the Geiger counter is the most common type: "Recall that the energy required to produce one ion pair in a gas is typically 25 to 40 eV." In other words, it takes a minimum of about 25 eV to ionize a gas in the ordinary conditions of a counter. But 25 eV just happens to approximate the energy level that divides the ultraviolet and the x-ray wave lengths on the electromagnetic spectrum. The indication, therefore, is that *the UFO-radiated waves have an energy level in the x-ray range*, or even higher, although we have not yet discussed the upper energy-level limit. In general, the Geiger counter cannot give the wave energy, for it is not a wave analyzer, but it gives radiation exposure dose rate. However, it seems worth mentioning at this point that the examples in which radiation sickness was substantiated by the statements of radiation experts also substantiates that both the ellipsoidal and saucer UFOs radiate in the x-ray energy range or possibly higher, in the range of gamma rays.

RADIATION EXPOSURE: DOSE AND DOSE RATE

To understand what the Geiger counter reading means, we must define the unit of its measurement, the *roentgen*. The roentgen is a measure of x-ray or gamma ray exposure dose. One roentgen is the exposure to 86 ergs of x-ray or gamma ray energy. A Geiger counter reading of 250 milliroentgen means the exposure dose at that place is 250 milliroentgen in an hour's time, or a quarter roentgen per hour. The Radiation Health and Safety Act passed by the U.S. Congress in 1968 set the safe exposure limit at 0.5 milliroentgens, or 0.0005 roentgen per hour, to determine safe standards for manufactured products. The UFO radiation of 250 milliroentgen measured repeatedly by Bill Rogers was 500 times the legal safe limit where he was standing. That reading clearly establishes that UFO as radioactive. The exposure dose rate would be even higher close to the UFO, and it's worthwhile to discuss that point further at this juncture.

We have already decided that the counter was probably worked by x-ray or gamma ray photons, because the distance was probably beyond the range of charged particles. The attenuation of photons can be thought of as the consequence of two factors—an inverse square geometrical factor and the attenuation (scattering and absorption) of the atmosphere. I do not have complete data for scattering in the three-dimensional case and will therefore leave the accurate computation of distance effects to the radiation experts. However, an extremely crude and overly conservative (it underestimates the radiation) approximation can be made by considering the inverse square effect only. For example, if the counter were 1,000 meters from the UFO when the quarter roentgen reading was taken, then, by the inverse square, the exposure dose at 6 meters would be 7,000 roentgen per hour. In the Bogota example cited, 6 meters is about the distance Bermudez said he stood from the ellipsoidal UFO. If he had stood for 10 minutes at this exposure rate, his exposure dose would have been over 1,100 roentgen. This would be lethal, as full-body exposure to 800 roentgen is considered lethal, and half that, or 400 roentgen, is lethal about 50 percent of the time. Bermudez was just too close. At 200 feet instead of 20 feet he would have been exposed to less than one percent as much radiation, and would have been relatively safe.

Given Rogers' actual distance from the UFO at the time of measurement and some detail on the counter used, radiation experts can calculate the radiation intensity as it varied with distance from the UFO, taking everything into consideration. Their figures will doubtless come out larger than those given here.

UPPER LIMIT OF RADIATION ENERGY

In examples IV-B5 and IV-B6, there was no indication of residual radioactivity after the UFOs had left, according to the Geiger counter readings taken. These two accounts are typical in showing no residual radioactivity of the ground or anything else in the vicinity. There have been cases in which residual radioactivity was present, but such cases are extremely rare, and outside the norm. For UFOs to leave the ground radioactive they would have to emit radiation capable of initiating nuclear reactions in the soil and rocks, forming unstable isotopes which would continue to emit secondary radiations. The initiation of nuclear reactions could be caused by the emission of gamma rays with an energy of about three million electron volts or higher. Therefore UFOs do not radiate photons with an energy greater than three million electron volts. This energy level is into the lower gamma ray spectrum, but, on a logarithmic scale, is not far above the top of the x-ray band.

THE MOST PROBABLE PHOTON FREQUENCY RANGE

There is a very general phenomenon of nature known as *resonance* which usually means that some recipient of vibratory energy responds well to a particular vibrational frequency and, conversely, if agitated will have a vibrational output of that frequency. The organ pipe is tuned to its note and the radio receiver to the incoming electromagnetic wave frequency. Size is important to resonant frequency. Going down in size, the frequency gets higher. On the molecular level, rotating (dumbbell) molecules of oxygen and nitrogen gas are in tune with infrared frequencies. Individual electrons in the outer shell are more in tune with visible and ultraviolet light frequencies. Oxygen and nitrogen both have two inner electrons, the K-shell electrons, that have vibrational frequencies corresponding to x-rays. They are very apt to become involved in x-ray reactions provided the passing x-rays are of the appropriate frequencies. In keeping with their small shell dimension, the frequency should be high, of the order of 10^{17}

(100,000,000,000,000,000) to 10^{18} cycles per second. X-rays run from about 10^{16} to 10^{20} cycles per second.

To see that the most probable interaction frequency range is somewhat limited, consider the practice of taking x-ray photographs with high frequency or hard x-rays. Such rays readily penetrate organic matter composed mainly of hydrogen, carbon, nitrogen, and oxygen, but penetrate calcium-rich bone with difficulty, being stopped by ejecting K-shell electrons from the calcium atoms. Thus the hard x-rays are more resonant with the K electrons of the heavier atom and pass by the very N and O atoms we are interested in, and the H atoms as well, which phenomenon may have some interest from the viewpoint of moisture in the atmosphere. This truth is verified by a glance at the developed x-ray film.

On the high-frequency side of resonance, there is a gradual fading of reaction probability, but on the low side there is a sharper cut off corresponding to the energy required to eject a K electron. This energy corresponds to a frequency of about 1.2×10^{17} cycles per second for nitrogen and more like 1.6×10^{17} cycles per second for oxygen. (The K x-ray spectral lines for nitrogen and oxygen, caused by an electron dropping from the outer shell to the K shell, should have frequencies of about ¾ of the approximate ionization frequencies given here.)

Of course, the x-rays have more than ample energy to eject outer-shell electrons, but they are not well tuned to do so. The greater probability is that the ultraviolet radiations get involved when an outer-shell electron drops down to fill a K-shell vacancy, leaving another vacancy which, when filled, causes the emission of ultraviolet or visible light. The ultraviolet light is then propagated from molecule to molecule, as is the visible light. The ultraviolet light can cause repeated ionizations.

One can tell from this description that I do not think ultraviolet waves emanating from the UFO could be a primary cause of ionization, by ejecting outer-shell electrons. How could they be when even a piece of paper or a window pane stops ultraviolet light? The highest-probability route is K-shell electron ejection by soft-to-medium x-rays, and the subsequent relaxation process which emits a K x-ray photon, an ultraviolet photon, and perhaps several visible photons. Since most of the initial x-ray photon energy is used up in ejecting the K electron, there is a low-energy electron product from the reaction. In attaching to a molecule, it could give off a color, possibly even red. A less probable route is the ejection of outer-shell electrons by the x-rays. This would liberate high-energy electrons which would ionize any molecules they struck.

I have no faith in the probability of microwaves influencing the ionization process as has been suggested (McCampbell). The air ionization experiments by microwave energy done in the laboratory under low-pressure conditions such as 0.01 millimeters of pressure are not valid at sea-level pressures. At sea-level, the molecules are so closely spaced that they can't resonate at microwave frequencies. Even if they could, with the millions of microwave receivers in existence the UFO would be emitting such a quantity of microwaves that it would be one of the easiest objects in the world to track, not one of the hardest.

CONCLUSION AND COMMENT

From the analysis in this section, I conclude that UFOs radiate between 25 electron volts, which is the bottom of the x-ray band, and 3 million electron volts, which is into the lower end of the gamma ray spectrum. This radiation readily accounts for the radiation sickness reported in various cases, because the radiation data taken by Bill Rogers indicates not only that the radiation is a type to cause trouble, but that it has adequate intensity to be very serious.

It is furthermore noted that x-rays or mild gamma rays are quite adequate to cause the ion-sheath so universally seen surrounding the UFO. Conversely, the existence of the ionized air around the UFO lends weight to the concept of high-intensity x-ray type radiations from the UFO. X-rays would also penetrate a few inches of soil, giving up their energy to plant-root depths. Soil being a thermal insulator, the heat would escape slowly and the temperature would build up with time below a low-hovering UFO. Most ground heating data is from saucer-type UFOs, and these are the ones known to focus their ionizing radiations downward with considerable accuracy, because of the observed saucer ion cones and saucer ring data.

By way of review, we further note that the visible colors come from the ionized atmosphere surrounding the UFO, not from the UFO, except by reflection from the UFO surface, as noted by Frabush (Example III-B2). The same is true for the intense ultraviolet that gives the skin burns when the telltale strong blue of strong nitrogen ionization is present.

Putting this information altogether, we can see the beginning of a UFO theory matrix which hangs together when criss-crossed from several directions, as indicated in the introduction.

Section V
Energetic Particle Ejection as a Propulsion Possibility

A. A 34-Particle Universe

Any scientific examination of the UFO puzzle must answer this question: Are UFOs propelled by the ejection of any of the elementary particles of matter? Since some types of elementary particles can pass through the atmosphere at high velocities without being noticed, a sufficient number of them could impart a high thrust to the UFO and still comply with the well-known UFO characteristic—no visible means of support. Therefore, the question must be taken seriously. Offhand, it looks like they could be, but the real question is, are they?

This question is related to the question of jet propulsion, in that mass is being ejected in both cases, but in jet propulsion streams of gas—either atoms or molecules—are ejected, not elementary particles. Elementary particles, such as electrons, protons, neutrons, and pions are the building blocks of atoms.

Astronomers have determined by spectroscopy that the known universe is composed of the same elements and particles as the solar system, and, insofar as can be determined, they follow the same rules of chemistry and quantum mechanics everywhere. Physicists therefore consider particles to have a universal nature. To be systematic and thorough, we refer to Table V-1, A 34-Particle Universe. This table and all particle physics used in this section can be found in *Elementary Modern Physics* (Weidner and Sells). The 34-particle universe concept was developed in 1953 by M. Gell-Mann, and has since been successfully used to predict nuclear reactions. It includes all the known (discovered) particles except the "resonance particles" that have decomposition times of about 10^{-31} seconds (ie, the reciprocal of 10 followed by 31 zeros) and would not make it through the UFO skin, if that were the route followed, before decomposing into a shower of particles as given in the table. We are therefore being quite complete in examining the 34 particles. We shall include also, however, the compound particles found in cosmic rays and used in nuclear reaction research, the deuteron or heavy hydrogen atomic nucleus and the alpha particle or helium nucleus. These both carry a positive charge.

Note that in the particle columns the antiparticles (particles of antimatter) get equal billing with the particle and must be counted to come out to 34.

Table V-1
A 34-Particle Universe

Name	Particle	Anti-Particle	Elec.. Charge	Rest Mass	Rest Energy MeV	Mean Life, Sec	Principal Decay Mode
Baryon Family							
Hyperons:							
omega	Ω^-	Ω^+	-1	3272	1672	1.1×10^{-10}	$\Xi + \pi^-$
xi	Ξ^-	Ξ^+	-1	2586	1321	1.7×10^{-10}	$\Lambda^{o+}\ \pi^-$
	Ξ^0	$\overline{\Xi}^0$	0	2573	1315	$2.9 \times 10\text{-}10$	$\Lambda^{o+}\ \pi^o$
sigma	Σ^-	$\overline{\Sigma}^+$	-1	2343	1197	$1.7 \times 10\text{-}10$	$n + \pi^-$
	Σ^0	$\overline{\Sigma}^0$	0	2334	1192	10^{-14}	$\Lambda^o + \delta$
	Σ^+	$\overline{\Sigma}^-$	+1	2327	1190	$8.1 \times 10\text{-}11$	$p + \pi^o$
lambda	Λ^0	$\overline{\Lambda}^0$	0	2183	1115	$2.5 \times 10\text{-}10$	$p + \pi^-$
Nucleons:							
neutron	n^0	$\overline{n}^0$	0	1839	939.5	1.0×10^3	$p + e + \overline{v}_e$
proton	p^+	p^-	+1	1836	938.3	∞	
Meson Family							
kaon	K^0	$\overline{K}^0$	0	974	498	$8.7 \times 10\text{-}11$	$\pi^+ + \pi^-$
						5.3×10^{-9}	$\pi^+ + e^- + \overline{v}_e$
	K^+	K^-	+1	966	494	1.2×10^{-10}	$\mu^+ + v_\mu$
pion	π^+	π^-	+1	273	140	$2.6 \times 10\text{-}8$	$\mu^+ + v_\mu$
	π^-	π^+	-1	273	140	$2.6 \times 10\text{-}8$	$\mu^- + \overline{v}_\mu$
	π^0	π^0(self)	0	264	135	1.8×10^{-16}	$\gamma + \gamma$
Lepton Family							
muon	μ^-	μ^+	-1	207	106	$2.2 \times 10\text{-}6$	$e + \overline{v}_e + v_\mu$
electron	e^-	e^+	-1	1	.51	∞	
μ neutrino	v_μ	$\overline{v}_\mu$	0	0	0	∞	
e neutrino	v_e	$\overline{v}_e$	0	0	0	∞	
Photon	γ^0	γ^0(self)	0	0	0	∞	

B. The Charged Particles

As a superscript to each particle symbol in Table V-1, there is either a plus sign (+), a minus sign (-), or a zero (0), indicating the particle carries a unit positive charge, a unit negative charge, or no charge. We first consider the charged particles, carrying a plus or a minus.

To obtain high thrust with particle ejection with a reasonable number of particles requires that each one be energetic, so that it will carry as much momentum as possible. The thrust is simply equal to the momentum of each particle (mass times velocity) times the number of particles ejected per second.

The following reasons rule out the use of charged, energetic particles for UFO propulsion:

(1) My experience with the effect of high-energy charged particles penetrating metal and plastic simulations of space structures is limited to electron stream bombardment, the accelerating electric potential (a variable) being several million eV supplied by a van de Graff electrostatic generator. The electron beam cut the structures to shreds in a few hours. The electron is the lightest of the charged particles; heavier particles such as protons, deutrons, or alpha particles would have the same result in less time. The point is, with no particle apertures in general evidence, how would charged particles get through the shell without cutting their way?

(2) Consider the UFO in Example I-B2, whose weight was estimated as 30 tons, or 27,216 kg. Assume the UFO accelerates protons to 1 GeV, one billion electron volts. This gives them a velocity of 0.875 c, where c is the velocity of light, or 2.623×10^8 meters/sec. At this speed the relativistic mass of each proton is 18.8176×10^{-31} kg, which is more than double its rest mass of 9.10908×10^{-31} kg. The number of particles per second required to support the UFO in hovering flight is:

$$\text{no/sec} = \frac{\text{UFO weight in Newtons}}{(\text{mass of proton})(\text{velocity of proton})}$$

$$= \frac{(27{,}216 \text{ kg})(9.8 \text{ Newtons per kg})}{(18.817 \times 10^{-31} \text{ kg})(2.623 \times 10^{8} \text{ m/sec})}$$

$$= 5.403 \times 10^{26} \text{ protons/sec}$$

Each proton carries a charge of 1.6×10^{-19} coulombs. The beam current is:

$$\text{Beam current} = (5.403 \times 10^{26})(1.60 \times 10^{-19})$$

$$= 86 \text{ million amperes}$$

There is no way for an electrically isolated UFO to neutralize this fantastic current. Bolts of lightning would have to continually pass between the UFO and the ground, and of course this is not observed. Considering that an electric welding machine can be plugged into a 110-volt circuit and not blow a 30-ampere fuse, can you imagine the brightness of a charged particle beam of 86 million amperes? It's out of the question.

(3) Charged particles would have a big air drag, and would create high downward and outward air currents at ground level, just as a heavy helicopter does. No such winds are in evidence.

(4) If accelerated to over three million electron volts, a charged particle beam would leave the ground radio-active. This is not observed.

(5) The beam energy can get out of hand. We will see in subsection D (Photons), what can happen. A beam of charged antiparticles would increase the hazard of high-beam energy by adding possible annihilation reactions.

C. The Neutral Particles

Atomic nuclei are shielded from charged particles both by the surrounding electrons and by their own electric charge. Neither of these defenses is valid against the neutral particles, which are therefore prone to strike the nucleus and initiate nuclear reactions. Neutral particles also have a greater penetration capability than charged particles of equal weight and velocity and would therefore penetrate further into the ground.

MESONS

In the meson family, the kaon (K^0) and pion (π^0) are both emissaries of the strong nuclear force. On high-energy impacts with the nuclei of various elements of the earth, excited nuclei and radioactive decay would surely occur in various reactions and on a big scale. The residual radioactivity would give a strong Geiger counter reading, but this is not observed. The antiparticle of K^0 would surely have a similar effect. The ground below a hovering UFO would probably also absorb enough kinetic and radioactive energy in depth to remain warm for days. Neither effect is noted.

THE BARYON FAMILY

The xi zero, sigma zero, and lambda zero hyperons are all products of high-energy particle collisions in high-energy particle experiments. They have much more rest energy than the ordinary atomic components such as neutrons, protons, and pions into which they decay with high-energy releases. If a hovering UFO used a high-energy stream of these particles, the ground would be both radioactive and heated in depth. A beam of high-energy neutrons would have the same effect, as is well known. The comments that were made about the mesons apply here as well.

LEPTONS, THE LIGHT PARTICLES

The electron was eliminated in the discussion of charged particles.

In this family the four neutrinos will remain candidates for the propulsion system until a later section, as they would have none of the misfit features listed in this section. For example, they would not cause radioactivity, ionization, or excessive heating because their absorption is so small. They should thus go unnoticed, there being no direct way to observe their use. There are, however, ways to notice that they are *not* being used, as we shall discover.

D. Photons

Although photons have the aspects of electromagnetic waves, they may also be considered as particles, as in Table V-1. I hope this discussion of photon rocketry for near-earth application will enliven what I fear is otherwise a dull technical section.

A photon rocket is one which gets its thrust from an intense beam of photons. There is no restriction on wavelength. A photon rocket is really unsuitable for near-earth operation at near-earth speeds, because of the excessive energy in the photon beam. The beam-energy problem is two-pronged; the UFO would have to generate it, and it also has to be dissipated.

The basic difference between a chemical rocket and a photon rocket lies in the difference between the chemical rocket's jet velocity and the photon beam's light velocity. A chemical rocket has a jet velocity on the order of $3x10^3$ (3,000) meters per second, while the photon-beam velocity is $3x10^8$ meters per second, or 100,000 times faster. This results in very high mass economy for the photon rocket, but gives very bad energy economy at near-earth speeds. For a valid comparison of the two, we consider the chemical rocket to be an ideal one, with all its chemical energy converted to jet kinetic energy, which is nearly the case for space rockets. Then we consider a chemical and a photon rocket of equal thrust, and therefore equal momentum per second in the jet and photon beam. Then the ratio of the relativistic energy in the photon beam $(E=mc^2)$ to the kinetic energy in the rocket jet $(\frac{1}{2} mv^2)$ is just twice the ratio of light speed to chemical-jet speed. Using the velocity ratio of 100,000, the energy ratio is therefore 200,000.

To put these statements into understandable form, consider the UFO in Section I which had an estimated weight of 60,000 pounds. The energy of its beam would be roughly 2,000 times greater than the jet energy of a Saturn class rocket with a thrust of 6 million pounds. Those big rockets require many tons of water per second on the concrete jet deflectors to keep the deflectors from eroding away by scouring and vaporizing. The photon beam energy of this saucer (if it were propelled in such a ridiculous manner) would have enough energy to vaporize 118 thousand tons of water per second! (You read it right.) Furthermore, such a vehicle hovering over water would just about do it, too, for a photon rocket beam can correctly be thought of as pure energy in wave form ready to be delivered upon contact with matter. If such a UFO hovered over water, vast clouds of condensed vapor would obscure everything. When the UFO hovered low over land, this beam would vaporize the ground so fast the UFO would have no place to land. Never mind the takeoff. From what?

Of course, this is William Markowitz's, argument turned around. He said the heat would disintegrate the UFO; therefore they don't exist. A very clever argument, but he shot down a straw UFO, a Markowitz design. UFOs don't use photon rocketry, at least near the ground where we get a good look at them. No one sees lakes dried up, with water vapor condensing vast clouds, or great vaporized holes in the ground. UFOs are much too efficient for all that. The UFO engineers do not use a propulsion system totally out of keeping with the surroundings of their use, one which destroys the surroundings.

E. Conclusion

We have effectively eliminated all particles (except the neutrino) as possibilities for the near-earth propulsion of UFOs, because their characteristics do not fit the observed operational facts. One thing that was perhaps not sufficiently emphasized in the discussions is the fact that, for any and all particle propulsion, as the particle speed approaches light speed the particle beam energy approaches the same prodigious energy as is characteristic of the photon beam, and the impact of its dissipation on the surroundings would be great.

In eliminating particle propulsion, little if anything has been lost. At UFO speeds that are measured in thousands of miles per hour, the energetic particles have speeds that are far too high for efficient propulsion. In fact, the efficiency, which is about equal to the ratio of UFO speed to particle speed, is near zero for low-speed operation. This is tantamount to a poor system.

Section VI
Transmission of Forces

A. The Possibilities

In order to discuss the invisible propulsive force system utilized by UFOs, we will first list all of the ways known to the engineering sciences for the transmission of forces. As long as UFOs retain mass, and extensive evidence in Section I indicates that they do, they must be propelled by a force which in engineering terms is called *thrust*. The ways in which forces can be transmitted may be put into 6 somewhat arbitrary categories:

Direct mechanical action mechanisms, such as pushing or pulling with a tow bar, wheel, screw propeller, etc. UFOs obviously don't use this method.

Pressures and pressure gradients in adjacent fluids. This includes buoyancy, explosive forces, aerodynamic lift, and other fluid-dynamic forces.

Rocketry, the reaction force from the high-speed ejection of propellants.

High-speed particle ejection. This could be classed under rocketry. However, the rocket is a heat engine, while particle acceleration is normally accomplished with force fields and the speeds are characteristically much higher than rocket exhausts.

Friction. Such forces are generally adverse to propulsion.

Force fields. The field (gradient) applies a force on all objects in the field which are affected by the field.

(1) Electric field. Applies a force on all electrically charged bodies.

(2) Magnetic field. Applies a force on all magnetic bodies, such as iron or nickel, bodies having a magnetic permeability other than that of air. If the field moves relative to (across) a conductor of electricity, it applies a voltage to the conductor. If a current flows in the conductor, the magnetic field applies a force to it.

(3) Gravitational field. A centrally directed acceleration field. Applies an attractive force on all matter, whether in the form of mass or energy. According to Joseph Weber, if negative mass exists it is accelerated and attracted exactly as ordinary matter.

(4) Repulsive force field. An outwardly directed acceleration field. Applies a repulsive force on all matter. There are two possibilities:

(a) A field other than antigravitational as yet undiscovered except as a UFO phenomena.

(b) Negative gravity, a field the same as that which presumably emanates from negative gravitational mass, i.e., an antigravitational field. According to Weber, it is still an unsettled question as to whether antiparticles have negative gravitational mass. They can't be tested by a gravitational field, as they will be attracted whether positive or negative. Negative mass and antigravity are not inconsistent with metric gravitational field theory (general relativity) and are inconsistent with quantum-field theory. In quantum-field theory, the quantum of gravitational field energy is the graviton, and the quantum of antigravitational field energy is the antigraviton. If these exist, they are zero-rest-mass quanta which travel at the speed of light and have an infinite range of action, as do photons and neutrinos.

B. Discussion

The possibilities are discussed in the order just presented.

MECHANICAL

If the transmission of forces were by mechanical devices, the devices themselves would be visible. UFOs have no visible mechanical propulsive devices.

PRESSURES

Aerodynamic forces could not support a hovering UFO. The required down drafts of air are definitely not present. Also, in level flight the saucer UFOs are clearly observed to tilt the leading edge down as required by repulsive force field propulsion, not up as would be required for aerodynamic lift (Section XI). UFO accelerations and forces are too high to be accounted for by aerodynamic forces, the magnitude of which is limited by the dynamic pressures of the air flow. UFOs are not aircraft, for they do not utilize aerodynamic forces. For the UFO machine, atmospheric forces have only nuisance value. They move it smoothly out of their path to permit the attainment of high supersonic speeds within the atmosphere (Section XIII).

ROCKETRY

Observations about why UFOs cannot be propelled by rocketry are given in detail in Section XII. Briefly, here we will say that the reason is the lack of rocket or other jet noises. For example, one witness said, "If it had just made some ordinary noise—like a car, or a train, or a jet—it wouldn't have been so bad, but that eerie light and lack of sound just got to me. It was like watching a ghost or something" (Lorenzen, *UFOs Over the Americas*, 35).

HIGH-SPEED PARTICLE PROPULSION

High-speed particle propulsion was treated in detail in Section V and was eliminated as a possibility except for the neutrinos, which are dealt with in Section VIII. UFOs are not propelled by the ejection of high speed particles in the ordinary sense of the phrase. For one thing, many particles would leave the ground radioactive, which does not happen. The only qualifier to these statements is that, according to quantum-field theory, fields may be considered to consist of particle-like field quanta (anti-gravitons, for example), and only in this sense is it proper to think of the UFO as being propelled by particles. Field quanta are sometimes called "virtual particles" to distinguish them from all others and to avoid any confusion.

FRICTION

This force was included for the sake of completeness and is sometimes important, as in human propulsion and automobile propulsion, to keep feet and wheels from slipping. It doesn't apply to UFO propulsion except in the usual negative, or obstructive sense—air-friction drag, for example.

FORCE FIELDS, OR ACCELERATION FIELDS

The names *force fields* and *acceleration fields* are interchangeable. Here we probably have pay dirt. Fortunately so, for we have almost eliminated all the other possibilities by virtue of their being inconsistent with observed facts. In contrast, force field propulsion will be found to be consistent with all reported observations that fit a general UFO pattern, no matter which type of UFO. What we are doing is paying strict attention to the observed evidence, and not prejudging by our current knowledge as to how difficult it might be, or even how possible or impossible it might seem by our standards. We strictly prescribe to fit observation.

One of the general observations about UFOs is the

lack of visible external components easily recognizable as part of the propulsion system. Force field equipment could be located within the shell of the UFO, which the field would penetrate nondestructively while the field generators remain hidden within.

Force fields appear to have a mysterious quality which used to be called "action at a distance," the transmission of forces through space without an evident means of doing so. This quality adds to the awe that the observer feels, and the aura of mystery surrounding the UFO. However, instead of thinking in terms of action at a distance, we now think in terms of field-energy distribution, with the field forces being proportional to the slope, or gradient, of the field energy. To technical people this removes the mystery. Einstein worked hard to popularize this concept. Magnetic separation process specialists and inventors vie with each other to obtain the highest magnetic flux (energy) gradients in their processes. To get a mental picture of force field action, think of the force field energy as the elevation of all points on the surface of Mount Fujiyama, chosen only because it's easy to picture. Then the steepness of the slope is the field energy gradient. The field force is the tendency for a toboggan to slide straight down the snow-covered slope when properly oriented to do so. Each of these statements is in essence literally true for gravitational energy, and is a correct analogy for other fields such as magnetic and electric.

The potential strengths of fields can be enormous, much greater than one might think. To get an idea, consider the electric charges in a copper penny weighing 3.1 gm. The positive charge of its protons is 130,000 coulombs as is the negative charge of all its electrons. This is the amount of charge that runs through a 100-watt 110-volt light bulb in 40 hours. A 200,000-ton supertanker is in an insulated dry dock. It is not possible to separate all the positive charge from the negative charge in the penny, but suppose that it were, and that the electrons could charge the tanker while the positive protons were suddenly removed to a 200-kilometer altitude. The amazing force between two such charges separated by a distance of 200 km (124 miles) would be a little more than twice the weight of the loaded tanker and a 4500-ton vehicle would be given a 100-g acceleration! The elementary calculations can be found in *Physics, Part II* (Halliday and Resnick 652-53). The reason that no such electric forces are realized in practice is that electron fields are so strong that we have not learned how to separate electrons from protons on a massive scale; our condensers only slightly unbalance the known electric fields.

It may be beneficial to summarize one more point about the use of fields for propulsive purposes. The point is that electric and gravitational field types propagate at the speed of light. Nuclear fields do not move that fast. The use of a field that moves at the speed of light could have great significance in long-range high-speed travel because of the field's increased range of action. Speed-of-light fields are said to have an infinite range of action, a point of importance in interstellar drives. The high-speed field has a better chance to maintain the important balance of action-equals-reaction over a greater range of distances and speeds, a balance of great importance to the well-known energy-conservative nature of the fields with which we are familiar. If vehicle propulsion can be accomplished by an energy-conservative field link, it is surely the best possible form of propulsion. UFOs apparently at least approximate this operating mode. With this concept before us, it is logical to predict that at some future time man will also use field-propulsion for advanced locomotion on free trajectories.

We are now ready to examine the positive evidence that UFOs utilize a force or acceleration field as their means of propulsion. Actually there is quite massive evidence that they do, as we shall see in the next section. Then we shall be in a much better position than our present situation, of only having eliminated the other possibilities.

Section VII
Direct Evidence of Force Field Propulsion

A. The Reasoning

In Section VI, we arrived at force field propulsion by a process of elimination. Other methods were not in conformity with the observations. In this section we shall try the shoe on the other foot, and we will see that things happen in the world of UFOs that only a force field action can explain.

B. The Evidence

EXAMPLE VII-B1. MAN KNOCKED DOWN

Mr. Reidar Salvesen, of Norway, was driving his car on the main road to Jaeren at 4:00 P.M. on October 29, 1970. It was twilight time, and he had just turned on his headlights when he was blinded by the approach of a bright light; he stopped the car. The following account is taken from *APRO Bulletin* (January-February 1971):

> . . . he opened the car door to have a look and saw a bright ball of fire which slowly drifted toward the car and stopped . . . Salvesen then got out of the car, whereupon the light was gone but a disk-shaped object was hovering above his car. He estimated its altitude to be about 10 meters . . . All around the circumference was a belt that shimmered a yellow color, but the material of the object was steel blue in color. . .
>
> Suddenly, with no warning, Salvesen was knocked to the ground. He felt no pain, and held out his right hand to break his fall, At the same instant he heard the sound of breaking glass. Rising to his feet, he noted that the object was leaving at a high rate of speed and that the pulverized windshield of his car was inside as if a blow from without had broken it.

Comment: Salvesen's story "hangs together" and will be shown to be very important to UFO theory. That the UFO force field knocked him down and the windshield inward as it took off (probably with a slight tilt and a sudden increase in thrust) is fairly obvious.

EXAMPLE VII-B2. TREE BRANCHES BROKEN

There have been several accounts of tree branches bending down beneath slow-moving, low-flying UFOs. The following account of branches being broken off will serve as an example (Lorenzen, *UFO, The Whole Story*, 90).

Private Jerome Scanlon was stationed at a Nike base in Maryland, 17 miles from Washington, D.C. At 5:30 A.M. on September 29, 1958, he was walking from the sentry post to his barracks to sound reveille when he heard a humming noise above him. Looking up, he saw an object shaped like a bullet with a tapered aft end, but truncated to form a blunt base; that is, it looked like what is commonly called a streamlined or boat-tailed bullet. It was about the size of a medium-sized plane, and was moving slowly away from him at about 300 feet altitude and making about 30 mph. He said it moved over trees, breaking branches in its path. "Exhaust flames" issued from the rear, and its luminous green skin lit up the surrounding terrain with a weird glow. It came in for a landing about a mile and a half away.

Scanlon encountered a friend, Riney Farris, who had also seen the object shortly, after Scanlon did. Together they went and inspected the traversed area where the object had landed. In addition to the path of broken branches, they found a half-mile strip of scorched earth and vegetation as evidence.

Note: There is an "optimum" UFO speed for maximizing the bending and breaking of tree branches, depending on the diameter of the UFO force field and the natural period of swaying of the tree branches. If one bends a tree branch down and lets go, it swings up in about half its natural period. Assuming the UFO is low and the diameter of the force field is about the same as the UFO, maximum bending occurs at the speed at which the UFO moves one diameter in the time for one swing of the branch, or, what is the same thing, in half its natural period of vibration.

If the object were 45 feet long (used instead of diameter), and the branches' half-period of vibration was about one second, then the speed for maximum bending and breaking would be 30 mph as observed, because 30 mph is a movement of 45 feet in one second. This relationship gives approximately what in engineering is called a sudden load whose deflection is twice the steady load value that would apply if the UFO were stopped, or barely moving. At higher speeds than that described, the branch hasn't time to achieve maximum bending before the load is relieved by the UFO's passing.

EXAMPLE VII-B3. UFO PARTS TREE BRANCHES WITHOUT TOUCHING

The following account of trees and bushes being deflected aside without the UFO touching them is direct evidence of force field action. Additionally, in this case riflemen standing near a dark UFO couldn't register a bullet impact (*APRO Bulletin*, September-October 1972). This could be construed in the same manner.

Mr. Bennie Smit of Braeside Farm, near Fort Beaufort, South Africa, had close contact with a UFO at 9:00 A.M. on June 26, 1972. He said that one of his laborers led him to see a ball of fire, and "sure enough, there was a fiery ball hovering at tree top height. It was about two and a half feet across, with flames shooting out . . . When I first looked it was a big red ball, but now it was green and it suddenly changed to a yellowish white."

Smit went for his rifle and called the police. He returned and fired eight shots at the object. He was sure his eighth shot hit, for he heard a thud. It moved up and down and disappeared behind the trees. Soon after the police arrived, "We saw a round black shiny object about two and a half feet in diameter emerge from behind a tree . . . Shots had no effect and when anybody approached it it shied away behind the bushes."

Smit then moved into the thick bush, looking for it. Suddenly he saw it about 20 yards away. He fired two quick shots, but with a loud whirring noise it veered off over the tree tops, cutting a pathway through the foliage.

"Smit said that the trees and bushes parted for the UFO as it sped away. He was adamant that no air blast caused this, so it appears that some type of force field may be associated with the object."

The account also mentioned that although the UFO had looked like a ball of fire and had been very close to the foliage, nothing was burned. This is further evidence that the plasma around a UFO may be quite cool. It only looks like fire because excited molecules give off light whether hot or cold.

Either there were two UFOs or, as seems more probable, it just changed color one more time, to black. It is worth a passing thought that the dark daytime color might be associated with an increase in its force field, so that the bullets couldn't get through. This would also cause the nearby branches to deflect more noticeably.

EXAMPLE VII-B4. UFO KNOCKS TRUCK OVER

The following is an excerpt from the Lorenzens' *UFO, The Whole Story* (p. 228), reporting an incident that took place on the Andean Highway of Venezuela in January 1960:

> A truck approached Pisani's jeep from behind and the driver sounded the horn to pass, so Pisani pulled his vehicle to the extreme right of the road, which was very narrow, and the truck passed and continued on ahead. Pisani took no special note of the truck until a few minutes later like a bolt from the blue, he said a brilliant, metallic, disk-shaped object which looked like polished blue steel swooped down out of the sky at incredible speed and crossed perilously close over the front of the truck.
>
> The results of this maneuver were astounding to Pisani, and the disk, after passing over the truck, rose again and was lost to sight . . . in seconds. When it rose in the air *above the hood* of

the truck, the truck also rose a few feet in the air and overturned in the direction taken by the object, falling into a sand bank at the side of the road with its 4 wheels upturned.

Comment: An A-B-C analysis of the above events is in order:

A. The italicized phrase indicates that the saucer did a pull-up, and that it tilted backward either to perform this maneuver or to deliberately knock the truck over. See the stopping illustration in Part B of Section XI.

B. The horizontal force field component knocked the truck over.

C. In the flipping-over action, the ground reaction forces on two wheels threw the vehicle a few feet in the air.

EXAMPLE VII-B5. UFO TOUCHES OR BUMPS PICKUP TRUCK

According to Mrs. Rick (Donna) Bouchard of Ottawa, Ontario, Canada, she, her husband Rick, and their three children left Embrum, Ontario, at 10:30 P.M., November 8, 1973, to go back to Ottawa (*APRO Bulletin*, January-February 1974). They were in the cab of their pickup, with Rick driving.

They had gone about 2½ miles down highway 417 when Rick saw some lights in his rearview mirror. He asked Donna to look in her rearview mirror and tell him what she saw. The lights were at hydro-pole height, 40 feet, and because the lights were spinning she could not make out what it was. Suddenly it dove at the back of the truck. Rick got the truck up to 100 mph, but the object stayed right behind. It wobbled like a saucer on a table top, and the lights around the bottom spun around the object.

The object backed off once during the chase, going up to hydro-pole height and over the bush that ran along the highway. It was gone only a matter of seconds when it came down at the truck at a "fantastic speed," as if it were coming down a steep hill, then stayed right behind into the outskirts of Ottawa. It even followed the pickup right under the Anderson Road overpass, lighting up the highway as it did so. The underpass is approximately 15 feet high by 50 feet wide.

At one point during the chase the object seemed to touch the truck, but there remained no evidence to prove it.

This report invites the following comments. Because of the lights rotating around the bottom and its limited height, the craft was probably a UFO of the saucer type. If such a vehicle, in the 10- to 30-ton class physically touched or bumped a pickup, there would remain evidence of dents or other marks. However, the vehicle could have touched the truck with its force field without leaving a trace, because a force field pushes within the material contacted, and not against the surface as in all ordinary types of push. Thus a force field push is characteristically nondamaging. Here we have a new application of "the soft touch." Perhaps "gentle push" would be a better phrase.

It could be mentioned in passing that a force field, with its gentle push, whatever its detailed nature, is an ideal agent for imparting acceleration to the occupants of a space vehicle undergoing high acceleration. With the pushing directly against each internal cell of the body, none of the structure or internal organs of the body tend to get crushed or even strained. In fact, it is easy to prove that if a uniform field gradient provides the total acceleration to a passenger, the passenger undergoes no stress whatever. He wouldn't feel a thing, even that he was accelerating.

Let us now picture an experiment that Rick might have performed. Suppose that just after Rick felt the object touch the truck (or sense that it did touch, however he sensed it) he had lightened his foot pressure on the throttle while glancing at the speedometer. What would have happened then would have given a lot of additional information on the force field, particularly on the degree of focusing or the angles of the lines of force. He might have found himself getting a free ride toward Ottawa. In a similar case, a following UFO accelerated a car to 85 mph after the driver, Mrs. Louise Smith, had removed her foot from the accelerator (*APRO Bulletin*, October 1976).

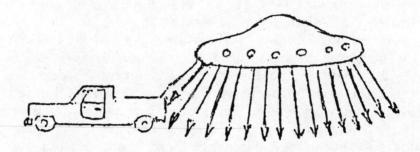

FIGURE VII-1.

Field direction lines give force directions. Force equals maximum energy gradient in both magnitude and direction. Lines intercepting truck give it a push—down and ahead. Field is focused by UFO. Divergent field gives more push.

EXAMPLE VII-B6. SAUCER ROCKS CAR

Most saucers which pace cars seem content to follow along behind, as in Example VII-B5. This is fortunate, for when one moves too close alongside, over the front, or even directly over head, the car's steering can be affected or other instabilities can be introduced. Cars without power steering have been turned 180 degrees on a dry pavement by a UFO crossing over the front end. The front wheels on the old cars turned in the direction of any substantial side load on the car because the castoring forces on the front wheels tended to jerk the steering wheel out of the driver's hands. This situation doesn't happen on a modern car with power steering unless the motor cuts out, turning off the hydraulic steering power. This instance is an intermediate case where the saucer was directly over the car for a few seconds, resulting in unstable car motions (Lorenzen, *UFOs Over the Americas*, 26).

At Hillsboro, Kansas, the night of March 21, 1967, was cloudy and dark, making any unusual lights very noticeable. Mary Beth Neufeld saw a light about a mile west of town near U.S. Route 66. It seemed unusual and out of place. Mary Beth and several friends drove over to investigate. However, it seemed to be a case of who was investigating whom, for, as they approached the light, the light also approached them. They saw that it looked like an upside-down cup on a saucer. Obviously, it was a domed saucer. The UFO, directly overhead, paced the car. "The car began to rock real bad," they said, "and the engine stopped." Within a few seconds the saucer sped away. They were able to start the car again, and they went into Hillsboro to report the events to authorities.

The car rock was probably caused by the center of the force field moving from side to side of the center of the car, or vice versa. This could be caused by the saucer rocking, or by the tense driver doing a zigzag with the same effect.

EXAMPLE VII-B7. SAUCER DISLODGES ROOF TILES

At 9:30 P.M. on an evening in February 1959, the people of two Greek villages, Digeliotica and Agiou Apostolou, heard a humming noise coming from the direction of the sea (Lorenzen, *UFO, The Whole Story*, 97). Running out of their homes, many people saw a luminous disk circling over the villages. The disk circled low overhead for about 10 minutes, while the radios failed to operate and the current in one house failed completely. When people in the street saw the disk fly low over the house of the priest, Papa Costas, there was a loud noise or clatter and the whole house seemed to shake, making Papa Costas inside think there was an earthquake. When he rushed out, people on the street told him the disk had just flown over his house as it circled about. Inspection of the house revealed that many of the roof tiles had been displaced, and others were on the ground. His first thought seemed to be that the disk had struck the roof, but by the time he talked to reporters he said that a low-flying disk had somehow dislodged some of the tile on his roof.

Papa Costas probably realized that the disk didn't actually strike his roof. For one thing, the witnesses merely said it flew over. For another, if his house had actually been struck it would have been a disaster area. Tile would have been shattered, not merely displaced. The mystery was *how?*

What happened was that the tile got the "gentle"—but effective—push of the UFO force field as the disk banked overhead. The field force direction was sufficiently aligned with the sloping tile to dislodge the looser ones.

This theory supposes that the tile was dislodged on one side of the roof, as the field force could hardly align with both sides simultaneously.

EXAMPLE VII-B8. THE ROCK-THROWING EXPERIMENT

For years, I've thought that an ideal experiment for investigating the field strength of a hovering UFO would be to hold a stick under the UFO to feel the down-force. Or to pick up a rock and toss it under to observe the change in trajectory. At last the account of an observer who performed the rock-throwing experiment has been found.

On February 14, 1967, at 7 A.M., a farmer in Miller County, Missouri, was heading for his barn, located 100 feet east of his house (Lorenzen, *Encounters With UFO Occupants*, 190). It was a clear morning just before sunrise, and the ground was partially lighted. Through some trees he saw a lighted object about 335 feet away, in the field east of the barn. He placed inside the barn the bucket of feed he was carrying and headed for the object.

He could see that the object was a disk about 15 feet in diameter and 6 feet thick, flattened on the bottom and rounded on the top. A central shaft about 1½ feet in diameter and 2½ feet long protruded from the bottom to the ground. The surface of the object was smooth, grey-green in color with a silken sheen, and was uninterrupted except by a ring of oblong ports about 6 to 8 inches long and spaced a foot apart around the lower circumference. Bright lights emanated from the ports. The lights changed color, covering all the colors of the rainbow spectrum.

He could see 10 or 12 smaller objects about 2 feet tall moving about beneath and around the larger object. The farmer's sketch of the objects or "humanoids" resembled a peanut with a proboscis-like protrusion near the top, indicated wide-set eyes, and what looked like a visor. They had slender arms which moved rapidly, and although these objects moved about rapidly no legs or feet were observed.

As the farmer approached the object, the smaller objects started to move behind the central shaft and into it, entering the craft. The last small object entered when the farmer was still about 80 feet away.

As the farmer reached a fence gate about 70 feet beyond the barn, the idea for an experiment apparently entered his mind, for later he said, "As I came through the first gate I picked up two rocks, pretty good size one of them was. I got up to about 30 feet of it and it was sitting there kind of rocking slightly and I thought, boy, here goes. I'm going to knock a hole in that thing and see what the hell it is. I cut down on it and the rock stopped along about 15 feet from it and just hit the ground. The next rock I thought I would throw on top of it and it just hit 'something' and bounced."

The farmer told the APRO field investigator, "I thought I was going right up to it; I got up to about here [about 15 feet from the object] and there it was. I just walked up against a wall [an invisible wall]; I couldn't see it at all; there was just a pressure [holding him back]."

As he stood there about 15 feet from the object, it started to rock, and oscillated about 6 times before it took off.

"When it took off it just rocked back [tilted] and moved real fast to the left of that ridge," he told the field investigator, pointing to a nearby hill, "and the shaft was pulled up into it as it took off."

This highly evidential account has many points in agreement with the UFO pattern, and probably represents accurate data. UFO data-pattern correlation is my way of separating UFO fact from UFO fiction. The UFO described is a typical "mushroom saucer." The retractable central column is frequently seen, although less frequently than multi-legged landing gear.

I offer the following comments on this experiment. The first rock falling about 15 feet short of the UFO is consistent with the farmer feeling the invisible wall of force at the same distance. What the rock and the farmer ran into, the wall of force, was the propulsive force field energy gradient discussed in Section VI. The field force *is* the field energy gradient. Such a field force is reminiscent of the thin force shields of science fiction, but quite different in that the field energy gradient must have been about 15 feet thick in this case. That the force field was turned on at the time is corroborated by the saucer's "kind of rocking slightly" as the farmer flung his first stone. The saucer crew was prepared for Earthman antics.

Probably because the first rock was deflected downward and fell short, the farmer raised the trajectory of the second one. That the second rock bounced on the force field shows that the field exhibited the energy-conservative nature of a mechanical spring; i.e., the rock "sprang" back. This is exactly what static-field theory indicates it should do because static fields conserve energy. Any energy the field absorbs from the rock it must give back on the rebound.

We all should acknowledge that the farmer, the field investigator, and the Lorenzens deserve a great deal of credit for the excellent data about this incident.

Section VIII
Force Field Evaluation: Which Type?

A. Field Types and Newton's Law

In evaluating the force fields to determine which type is used, we shall examine the static-field types: the electric field, the magnetic field, and the repulsive force field. The first two are well known, but the third is not. As we have mentioned, the latter may be thought of as a negative gravity field, or a field with similar properties as yet undiscovered. Negative gravity is the field that theory indicates is associated with negative matter and possibly with some antiparticles. This field repels all matter.

The electromagnetic field is not a static field; it travels at light velocity. It might be utilized in deep space to obtain speeds near the speed of light, because at high speeds the electromagnetic drive would seem an effective one. However, for near-earth applications which we are discussing, the electromagnetic field was eliminated in Section V as not being at all in keeping with the observed UFO facts. It was treated there as a photon beam.

We now quote Sir Isaac Newton, one of the greatest physicists of all time: To every action [force] there is an equal and opposite reaction [force]. If object A exerts a force F on object B, there is a reaction force of -F back on object A. No exceptions to Newton's (third) law have ever been found. The UFO is object A, or, more specifically, the UFO field generators will be collectively taken as object A. The reaction force -F on the field generators is the force that drives the UFO. This force on the generators is called the reaction force to be consistent with rocket terminology and other usage in which the same phrase occurs. Object B is not quite as specific as object A and may vary from case to case. Object B is collectively all objects caught in the field on which the field pushes with the combined force F, and which we can think of as applying a force base against which the UFO pushes for propulsion. Clearly we have a force field with its stresses acting as intermediary between the force on the field generators on one side, and on the force-base objects on the other, everything in balance and Newton's followers happily smiling. Newton's laws, with little modification, work on a broader base today than ever before, still forming one of the cornerstones of modern particle physics.

B. The UFO Game

We now ask two definitive questions:

(1) What objects (B) does the action force affect? (The answer comes from the case data.)

(2) Is the observed action force result possible with this type of field?

Question (1) focuses attention. Question (2) is the key that unlocks the mystery of the type of force field used by the UFO. Question (2) is also definitive for certain particle force actions—neutrinos, for example—by substituting the word *particle* for *field*. The importance of correlating UFO data with (2) has not previously been appreciated.

In each data case considered, we assume in turn the presence and use of the three field types—electric, magnetic, and repulsive force field—and ask: Could this field accomplish what actually happened? The correct field should work every time. It can't be hit or miss.

This is the UFO Game, and the rules have now been stated. We play the game with examples presented in Section VII. Other UFO students may wish to apply the methodology to their own examples.

Game 1

Example VII-B1 has two actions. The Norwegian was knocked down without being hurt, and the windshield was knocked inward. They will be treated separately.

ROUND 1 (EXAMPLE VII-B1)

(1) On what object does the action take effect?
On the Norwegian. He was knocked down.

(2a) Could an electric field knock him down?
No, because standing on the ground he carried no electric charge.

(2b) Could a moving magnetic field do it?
Conceivably, but with the high eddy currents in his body necessary to produce the force he probably would have been stunned. Doesn't fit well.

(2c) Could a repulsive force field knock him down?
Yes. It repels all matter. Then why wasn't he hurt? Because the field pushes on every cell in his body and is scarcely felt if the body is free to move. It is a soft push.

ROUND 2 (EXAMPLE VII-B1, continued)

(1) On what object did the field action take place?
On the windshield. It collapsed inward.

(2a) Could an electric field collapse it?
No. A glass windshield cannot carry an appreciable electric charge.

(2b) Could a magnetic field collapse it?
Absolutely not. Magnetic fields affect magnetically susceptible materials and conductors. Glass is neither. This test couldn't be more definitive if performed in a laboratory with a captive UFO!

(2c) Could a repulsive force field do it?
Yes, if strong or sudden, or both. The windshield is supported around the edges, but not elsewhere, and a sudden push could shatter it.

ROUND 3 (EXAMPLE VII-B2)

(1) On what did a force field act?
On tree branches. They were broken.

(2a) Could an electric field break them?
Not a chance. A tree is perfectly grounded. It won't hold a charge.

(2b) Could a magnetic field break them?
Probably not. A stationary magnetic field would of course do nothing. For a moving magnetic field, the shape of tree branches is poor for setting up eddy currents. If the magnetic field cycled at the frequency of a saucer hum (see Section IX), the result could be no greater than a high-frequency shaking of the tree leaves, if that.

(2c) Could a repulsive force field break them?
Yes, particularly because the UFO moved slowly, as already explained. If a UFO has a weight per unit planform area of a hundred pounds per square foot or more, this should bend the branches and break a few.

ROUND 4 (EXAMPLE VII-B3)

(1) What object and action?
The branches of bush and trees parted as the UFO left.

(2a) Could an electric field do it?
No, they are all grounded.

(2b) Magnetic field?
No. At least in my limited experiments, magnets won't move a twig.

(2c) Repulsive force field?
Yes. A divergent field with horizontal components would accomplish it—that is, a field not highly focused in the downward direction.

ROUND 5 (EXAMPLE VII-B3, continued)

(1) The bullets had no effect. They didn't seem to

strike. This could be due to bad marksmanship by nervous people. The bullets are therefore disqualified from the game.

ROUND 5 OVER AGAIN (EXAMPLE VIII-B4)

(1) Object?
The truck was tipped over.

(2a) Could an electric field tip it over?
No.

(2b) Magnetic field?
Yes. The truck is built of magnetic materials.

(2c) Repulsive force field?
Yes, it pushes on all ordinary materials.

ROUND 6 (EXAMPLE VII-B5)

(1) UFO bumps truck.

(2a) Could an electric field do it?
No.

(2b) Magnetic field?
Yes. It's made of magnetic materials. Could it bump truck without marring it? Yes, it certainly could.

(2c) Repulsive force field?
Yes. Without marring? Yes.

ROUND 7 (EXAMPLE VII-B6)

(1) On what was the action?
A car was rocked by a over-flying UFO.

(2a) Electric field?
No.

(2b) Magnetic field?
Yes.

(2c) Repulsive force field?
Yes.

ROUND 8 (EXAMPLE VII-B7)

(1) On what was the action?
Roof tiles were dislodged.

(2a) Could an electric field do it?
No.

(2b) Magnetic field?
No. Tiles are neither magnetic nor conductors.

(2c) Repulsive force field?
Yes, it has all of the qualifications.

SCORE SHEET

Round	Electric	Magnetic	Repulsive Force	Action
1	No	Maybe	Yes	Man knocked down
2	No	No	Yes	Windshield collapsed
3	No	No	Yes	Tree branches broken
4	No	No	Yes	Tree branches parted
5	No	Yes	Yes	Truck tipped over
6	No	Yes	Yes	Truck bumped
7	No	Yes	Yes	Car rocked
8	No	No	Yes	Tile dislodged
Score	Zero	50%	100%	

The magnetic backers may have enough to cling to by their fingernails. Otherwise, the scores speak for themselves. The repulsive force field is the only consistent winner.

This UFO game does not indicate that magnetic fields are not present, or even used in UFOs. UFOs surely utilize electric currents, each one of which always has an associated magnetic field. Besides, there have been several indications that UFOs have a magnetic field, or signature. According to the *APRO Bulletin* of March-April 1974, there is a group of Southern California scientists who have designed instrumentation to measure the magnetic field of a UFO as it passes. This is called its signature. Along with other UFO students, I am waiting to hear detailed results from that magnetic research program.

Game 1 does say that the UFO does not get a direct propulsive force from either a static magnetic field, or a static electric field. The field the UFOs do use cause a lot of things to happen that the magnetic and electric fields could not cause.

Many years ago several self-styled UFO experts said that UFOs propel themselves by generating a strong static magnetic field which pushes against the earth's magnetic field. The public seems not to have forgotten this. Clearly this could not be true for at least two reasons besides those cited in the game. One reason is that the earth's magnetic field runs parallel to the earth's surface only in the equatorial regions. If we think of the magnetic field in terms of the field lines and follow along a field line going north in the northern hemisphere, we find that the line loses altitude rapidly and plunges into the earth on an incline. This effect is called the magnetic dip. The dip occurs in the southern hemisphere also. The force between the UFO, treated as a strong magnet, and the earth-field lines can only be perpendicular to those field lines. This relationship wouldn't be entirely perfect as the earth-field lines would sag under a heavy load, but the dip would remain. The UFO would be like a toboggan pointed down an icy hill. This is a good analogy because the force between the toboggan and the ice surface is also normal. The UFO, attempting to hover, slides down the field line until it strikes the earth. It can't hover.

The second reason: If the UFO turns on more magnetic repulsion, it can stop the fall, but with more force only by gaining more velocity toward the pole. Thus we would have a sort of super-Sargasso Sea at each pole— the graveyards of derelict UFOs.

Actually, there is the possibility of a sensible magnetic

propulsion system for UFOs if one wishes to classify a magnetically propelled ion jet in this manner. This method could also be called ion propulsion or magneto-jet propulsion, as it would accelerate the ionized air sheath around the UFO, utilizing it as a reaction fluid. The scheme would be based on magnetic reactions similar to those in an electric motor, but more exactly it would be a linear motor rather than a rotary one. In the magneto jet, a current is passed through the ionized air in a direction perpendicular to the desired thrust and the magnetic field. Anyone interested in the detail of such a scheme, or a very similar one in which the electric current is passed through salt sea water, need only refer to the literature on the propulsion of submarines for deep-sea exploration, where it has already been used.

Up to this point, such an ion drive has been classified in my mind, and in Section VI, as a form of jet propulsion, even though magnetic fields be used as a means to an end. It is included here because it uses a strong magnetic field. However, the question is not how suitable such a system would be, but do UFOs use it? The answer is simple. The UFO uses nothing as unsophisticated as an ion jet; it doesn't fit the UFO pattern. Anyone knocked down by the exhaust, or jet stream, would know what hit him. That is, besides the sand and gravel he would be picking from his skin. Fast jet streams from departing UFOs are completely foreign to the observations. This propulsion scheme also has a close kinship with aerodynamics. There is absolutely no evidence that UFOs use the atmosphere to obtain any kind of acceleration forces, propulsion or otherwise.

Enough background has now been laid to play another game with a UFO and the three force fields. Let the UFO be hovering over bare ground at a place where there are no iron or nickel deposits.

Game 2

(1) On what object is the field pushing?
It's pushing on the ground with a force equal to the weight of the UFO.

(2a) Could an electric field do it?
No. The ground is neutral.

(2b) Could a magnetic field do it?
No. It has nothing to push on except a magnetic field of the earth, and it would slide to the north in our hemisphere. It couldn't do a "UFO-rock" toward the south.

(2c) Could a repulsive force field do it?
Yes. It has the properties of negative gravity.

End of game.

C. The Neutrino as a Propulsion Possibility

We now return to reconsider the neutrino beam as a propulsive method. In Section V, which treated energetic particles as propulsion possibilities, the neutrino was left in the running because it was the only energetic particle that didn't leave the ground radioactive or have other unobserved effects. Also, a sufficiently powerful neutrino beam would give the UFO the needed thrust. But the neutrino must pass the UFO Game test. We play the game with the neutrino as the single entry, in abbreviated format.

Game 3

Could the neutrino beam:

(1) Knock a man down?	No
(2) Break a windshield?	No
(3) Break tree branches?	No
(4) Deflect bushes, tree limbs?	No
(5) Tip a truck over?	No
(6) Bump a pickup truck	No
(7) Rock a car?	No
(8) Dislodge roof tile?	No
Score,	Zero

The neutrino beam is no better than the electric field at meeting the test of observed facts. It cannot account for UFO propulsion.

D. Conclusions

1. The UFO game is an effective rationale for the evaluation of possible UFO propulsion methods.

2. The neutrino has been eliminated as a propulsion possibility, along with all other known particles.

3. UFOs are propelled by a force akin to gravity, but of an opposite nature. In quantum terminology, the field can be represented by anti-gravitons.

It should be noted that none of these conclusions were premeditated or preconceived, but simply resulted from the application of the rationale given.

Section IX
The Saucer Hum and the Cyclic Field

A. Preliminary Statement

Saucers emit a characteristic noise generally referred to as a hum, buzz, or whine. According to close-proximity observers, the hum of a hovering saucer increases in intensity and pitch during the last couple of seconds before takeoff. Conversely, on starting to hover after moving, or on other power reductions, the hum decreases. This strongly suggests that the hum is power-plant connected. In fact, the data quite clearly shows that the force field cycles at the hum frequency.

By way off review, recall that during night sightings the saucer characteristically also brightens just before and during takeoff. This is actually an increase in air ionization due in turn to an increase in the UFO radiation causing it. These effects are also tied in with an increase in cycling rate as the power plant is readied for and accomplishes the increase of thrust at takeoff.

B. Typical Evidence

EXAMPLE IX-B1

On August 11, 1960, at 3:10 P.M. on a cloudy afternoon, Ray Hawks of Boulder, Colorado, had an important sighting of what was clearly a saucer repair job (Lorenzen, *UFO, The Whole Story*, 224). That part of the story will be told later where the data fits. Hawks said that just a few seconds after the operation was over the saucer hum increased in intensity until it reached a very high pitch, whereupon the disk appeared to be surrounded by a shimmering field. Then the disk elevated and disappeared back into the clouds from whence it came.

EXAMPLE IX-B2

According to a UPI story dated January 13, 1966, a Mobile, Alabama, high school student was driving home at 3:15 P.M. His car stalled on the highway when he encountered a silver ball about 15-20 feet in diameter. About 10 inches outside the ball there was a flat ring encircling it, about 8 inches in width. He said, "I was about 15 feet away from it. It was hovering about 5 feet above the highway . . . The thing was making a whining sound, increasing in intensity. Then it moved around and over the car and was gone. My car started then."

EXAMPLE IX-B3

A man, his wife, and two children were seated in their car in a drive-in theater (Edwards, *Flying Saucers: Serious Business*, 27). The children said that they heard bees. The parents attributed it to the children's imagination, but soon the father heard a buzzing also. Looking up, he saw a disk with lights on the rim approach and go by at an altitude of about 100 feet. The noise subsided as the saucer receded. The mother didn't hear anything. However, some other people in the theater described the noise as sounding like hornets. One man heard a sound like a paper clip caught in a vacuum cleaner.

EXAMPLE IX-B4

Two young Swedish men saw a light coming from a pine woods (Lorenzen, *UFOs Over the Americas*, 60). They went to investigate and found its source to be a disk-- shaped object about 5 meters in diameter and a meter thick, resting on a three-legged landing gear. Following the men's encounter with several diminutive occupants which was a real brawl, the saucer took off. "But most remarkable of all was the sound the object made—a thin, high, intense sound you felt rather than heard. When the object left we were shaken by powerful, extremely rapid vibrations that quite paralyzed us." The medical team which examined the men physically and mentally concluded that the men "had actually encountered a field force of enormous strength."

A sidelight may be of interest. The occupants ceased combat and the saucer took off when one of the men broke away, ran to the car, and blew the horn. They seemed afraid of the noise.

EXAMPLE IX-B5

Mr. and Mrs. Hatchett and daughter Valerie were heading west in their pickup near Manford, Oklahoma, at 12:20 A.M. when they noticed a bright light getting closer (*APRO Bulletin*, September-October 1973). When the object turned to an intercept course with the pickup, they stopped. The object also stopped, opposite the pickup just beyond the fence on the south side of the road and about 200 feet above the ground. The air seemed charged and oppressive as the giant object hovered there. The whole of it emitted a white light. Mr. Hatchett estimated the size as about equal to a 707 jetliner, but the lighting was intense and so ionized that they could discern no detail of its shape. Both Mr. and Mrs. Hatchett heard, or felt, or both, an intense and penetrating humming sound, and otherwise they sensed a stillness.

EXAMPLE IX-B6

A forestry lookout named Russel Hill in an isolated area about 40 miles southwest of Calgary, Canada, spotted greenish-colored UFOs on four occasions in September 1967 (Hall 34). These UFOs decommissioned his lighting system and two-way radio. When Hill got a good look at one, he described it as a saucer about 75 feet in diameter. On one occasion, Hill heard a strange pulsing sound as a green light swept the cabin. On another occasion, a hovering craft cast a garish green light into the cabin as a throbbing hum shook the cabin walls.

EXAMPLE IX-B7

The general manager and the chief engineer of a St. Louis broadcasting station went fishing on the Lake of the Ozarks (Edwards, *Flying Saucers: Serious Business*, 175). In a fog, 300 or 400 yards from shore, their outboard motor died. They heard a humming noise, and when the fog parted briefly they saw a saucer hovering about 5 feet above the water, only 100 feet away. Directly beneath it the water was dancing in thousands of sharp-pointed waves. The men paddled for shore—with their hats.

Comment: The force field was vibrating the water.

C. Discussion

Accounts IX-B1 and IX-B2 introduce the hum and the whine. The whine is, of course, a higher frequency sound than the hum. Both accounts, as do a great many others, indicate a buildup of the sound and its frequency as part of some preparation for takeoff. Interestingly enough, here at last is something a UFO can't do "instantly"—something that takes some time. It takes them a couple of seconds or more to "get their hum up" from a hum to a whine. The noise description certainly reminds one of a vacuum cleaner or a turbine engine, and indeed we are tempted to think of the time involved as being the time to build up the rpm of rotating machinery. Also there is evidence that both saucers and saturn UFOs utilize rotating machinery, as we shall see. Nevertheless, it is more sophisticated to think of the change in noise pattern simply in terms of an increase in cycling rate, as this allows for the possibility that the root cause may be from the cycling of nonmoving equipment as in, for analogy, the electric transformer, in which vibration and sound is caused by the cycling of field forces.

Example IX-B4, about the two Swedes, brought up the critical point that the noise is felt as much as heard. Example IX-B5 corroborates this, as do many others. This "feeling" the noise indicates that a vibrational force of exactly the same frequency as the sound is at work. Example IX-B6 shows that the vibrational force shakes inanimate objects, such as cabin walls, as well. In Example IX-B7, a vibrational force set the water to dancing in thousands of sharp pointed waves.

In my experience with intense sound pressures, low-frequency sound vibrations are felt as a shaking of the body, predominately in the abdominal regions, but high-frequency sound is not felt as a shaking, although it is painful to the ears. This leads me think that people who feel the whine, or even the hum, are getting some form of direct input or effect from a pulsating or vibrating force field, rather than feeling vibrations just from the air.

The existence of a considerable body of data to indicate that the UFO force field is of a cyclic nature was pointed out to me by Dr. Robert M. Wood in his visit to me at the Langley Research Center in October 1967. By a coincidence, Dr. R.M. Wood is the son of Professor K.D. Wood, from whose text I first studied—*Practical Aerodynamics*. In 1967 Dr. Wood was Deputy Director for Research and Development for Douglas Aircraft's Advance Systems & Technology Division. He is now an APRO consultant. From the weight of the evidence—the vibrations felt by people, vibrating objects like street signs, and smooth water set to dancing—I have concluded that Dr. Wood was right; the UFO field and its forces are cyclic.

When the musicians tell us the pitch of the hum, we will know its frequency, for the relationship is well known. One witness already volunteered the information that the hum rose an octave when a UFO took off. That means the frequency doubled.

D. Reader Question: Can You Define *Cyclic Field* More Clearly?

The term *cyclic field* means that the strength of the field varies with time in a periodic or repetitious manner. The field is not just a static field, but consists of the sum of a large number of waves that are sent out from the UFO. In this concept, new waves add to the strength, replenishing field energy losses. The vibrations felt are due to the passing of the field waves, which are also due to the variation of field strength with time. One of the simplest wave forms we can imagine for the variation of field strength at any point in space is a square wave superimposed on a steady-state value of field strength as shown in Figure IX-1.

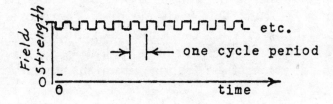

Figure IX-1. Square Wave Ripple

The frequency is the reciprocal of the cycle period shown, and vice versa.

Another simple representation for field strength variation is the saw-tooth wave, shown in Figure IX-2.

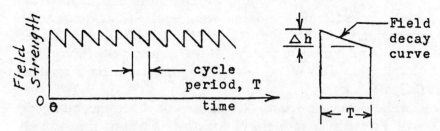

Figure IX-2. Saw-Tooth Waves

The curved top of the enlarged sketch of a single tooth represents a decay in field strength, which at the beginning of the next cycle is replenished by a pulse of strength Δh, coming out from the field generators.

Figures IX-1 and IX-2 represent time views of the wave system at a given point in space. In Figure IX-3, we look at the space distribution of field strength at a given point in time. In this schematic the height of the curve again represents field strength, but the horizontal distance, or abscissae x is the distance from the field generators to any point below the UFO.

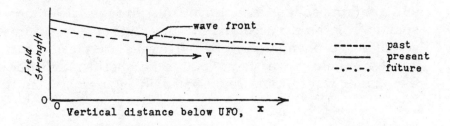

Figure IX-3. Spacial Distribution of Field Strength

The field waves are close together in a time diagram, but far apart in space because of the high velocity T of the wave. For this reason, we see only one wave in this space diagram. The solid curve gives the present field-strength distribution. The dashed curve shows what the strength was before the wave passed, and the dash-dot curve what it will be after it passes. The height between the two curves is the cyclic decay being replenished by the field wave. Even if the wave front is not vertical, it goes by any one place as a sudden, high-velocity front.

The field-strength curve is intentionally not shown to vary inversely as the square of the distance from the UFO because of force-field focusing by the UFO. We shall study this point later. Instead, the field strength varies inversely with the beam cross-sectional area. If the force field beam were cylindrical, these curves would be quite flat with distance. The air-motion analysis which follows is made for the case of a cylindrical force field beam.

E. The Cause of the Hum

I thought it important to analyze the effect of a cyclic force field on the atmosphere and on various solid bodies. Accordingly, a mathematical analysis was made of the effect of an oscillating force field on the interaction between the atmosphere and solid bodies, and is presented in Appendix 1. The general results are presented here. The simplest result is that sound waves are created at the interface between the lower surface of the UFO and the atmosphere, and travel out through the atmosphere. This nicely accounts for the hum as a basically aerodynamic phenomenon. Sound waves are created for any force field wave shape, but to be specific, consider the square wave ripple represented in Figures IX-1 and IX-4.

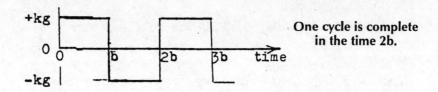

Figure IX-4. Square Wave Force Field Ripple

This force field may be considered to have a constant or steady component plus a square wave component responsible for the hum, and other vibrations. Let the square wave component have a cyclic period of 2b, and an amplitude of kg, where g is earth gravity and k is a dimensionless constant, giving acceleration magnitude in g's. The analysis shows that the corresponding sound wave pressure at the lower surface of a saucer, for example, varies with time as shown in the Figure IX-5 at time 6b (solid curve).

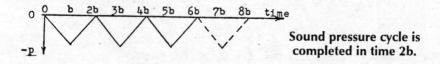

*Figure IX-5. Variation of Sound Pressure
at Saucer Surface*

The dotted line shows how the curve grows with an increase of time of 2b. The rest of the curve stands still, as it represents past history.

The sound waves extend themselves below the saucer at the speed of sound a, traveling the distance ab in the time b. Figure IX-6 shows sound pressure versus distance x from the lower surface of the saucer for two values of time t, where x is expressed in multiples of the distance ab.

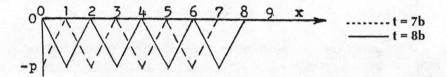

Figure IX-6. Sound Pressures Below UFO

This is a "moving picture," shown in stop-motion at two instants of time, t = 7b, and t = 8b. A single curve may be pictured as moving to the right with increasing time like a side-winding rattler. At any one place, x, the pressure oscillates continuously between zero and a negative maximum.

The analysis made also shows that if we could find an object below the UFO that is large and sufficiently rigid to call stationary, then sound pressures like those in Figures IX-5 and IX-6, but with positive pressures instead of negative pressures, would result at the air-object interface. A heavy bridge beam spanning below the UFO, or even a rocky earth surface, might answer this description, but most objects would not. Clearly, such rigid surfaces would generate sound waves, but 180 degrees out of phase with the waves from the UFO surface.

In order to investigate what might happen at the surface of and within an ordinary flexible body, an analysis was made of a body assumed to be fixed or stationary at its lower end and subjected to the cyclic field. To be specific, suppose that a cylindrical body has a height of 2cb, where c is the velocity of sound in the body, and that the bottom is well supported. Then the motion of the top surface due to the cyclic forces within the body and the internal waves set up is shown in Figure IX-7.

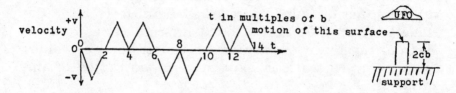

Figure IX-7. Motion of Top of Supported Body

The internal waves traverse the column 4 times before the motion is repeated. In this case, it takes the time 2b to traverse once, or 8b for a complete cycle. The free end has an interesting double-beat motion—twice up, twice down. If the height is cb there is a single beat, 3cb a triple beat, 4cb a quadruple beat, etc.

The vibrating motion shown in Figure IX-7 will act on the air like the membrane of a drum, or like the vibration of a speaker diaphragm. Thus individual objects below a UFO are potential sound sources. This will be seen to explain a lot of things.

The cases treated with the square wave ripple were also solved for a cosine $(\pi t/b)$ ripple with similar results, but representable by sine and cosine waves of sound pressure and physical vibrations, compared to the straight line segment representations in the sketches for the square wave ripple. Thus the shape of the force field ripple is not too important to the results.

Conclusion and Discussion

1. It has already been noted that the air-saucer interface appears responsible for the hum. If this theory is correct, the hum is an external acoustics effects, not an internal hum or whine coming out through the shell structure.

2. The vibrations set up within restrained bodies somewhere below the UFO also account for the important

observation that the sound can be felt as well as heard. A person standing on the ground is a pretty fair approximation to a cylinder supported at the bottom. It also accounts for the vibration of inanimate objects as when "a throbbing [interference of wave patterns] hum shook the cabin walls."

3. We now consider the case in which the buzzing noise was heard in the drive-in theater. The automobiles parked in rows would react with vibrations traversing the bodies, acting as individual sound sources. The UFO was putting out a lot of power and part of it was generating sound. With the multiple sound sources at near the same frequencies, the soundwave interference patterns would be interpreted by the ear as a buzz, for just the same reason that a swarm of bees or hornets make a buzz—there are many sources. A loose-part jingling on one of the cars reminded the occupant of a paper clip caught in a vacuum cleaner.

4. Many people have concluded that UFOs use ultrasonic vibrations as a weapon. Maybe they do. "All" that it would require would be a beamed force field with a sizeable cyclic component of the field of appropriate frequency. For this special application possibly it would be entirely cyclic with no net force. Perhaps the regular UFO power plant can assume the weapon function by raising the cyclic field frequency to ultrasonic values.

Mr. Robert Barrow wrote an interesting article pertaining to the possible use of ultrasonic (US), vibrations as a UFO weapon (*APRO Bulletin*, March-April 1971). Mr. Barrow is an ultrasonic medical technician. He says, in part:

> Significantly . . . I must acknowledge that the upcoming theories do possess a possible hinderance to their workability. And that is that ultrasound requires a medium through which to travel. In medicine, a clear jelly or even a layer of mineral oil is applied as a go-between, connecting sound-transmitting apparatus and the body area to be treated . . . This insures an easy, compatible flow of vibrations to the involved area.

Theoretically, then, US must have a medium before it can disperse forcefully enough for its characteristics to be felt.

But how could a UFO, for whatever reason, emit sound waves without a similar medium? This question is a serious drawback to the whole UFO-US theory.

According to the cyclic field sound theory developed in Appendix 1 and presented here in Part E, the US transmission question need not be a critical one, for, besides the air path between the UFO and effected body for US waves, energy is transported across space by the cyclic field, and sound, at cyclic field frequency, is generated *at the body surfaces*. No jelly is required for its transmission. Sound is generated at the interface between two mediums having different stiffness (compressibility modulus, or Young's modulus) i.e., a different ability to resist the accelerations of the cyclic field. In the human body, that interface is the skin. As is well known, if the frequency is ultrasonic the destruction of body cells and burns can result.

5. One negative finding was made. The air column below a UFO—saucer, for example—does not oscillate at its natural frequency, like a pipe organ. If it did, observers would report a note that lowered in tone as the UFO increased altitude at takeoff. This is not observed. The tone, or pitch, rises as the UFO takes off, showing that the field cyclic frequency is increasing as the power builds up.

In general, the UFO maintains more than enough hovering altitude to prevent the possible coincidence of the cyclic (hum) frequency with the natural frequency of the air column. If it didn't, quite a racket or roar might be set up. Indeed, such a roar was reported by Lonnie Zamora when the landed UFO at Socorra, New Mexico, and took off at a very shallow angle. In this and a few similar cases, the roar may be a low-altitude resonance of the force field and air column which ceases with an increase in altitude. Note that this is more the exception than the rule.

Section X
Propulsion Oddities

Although UFOs, like vagrants, have in general been noted to have "no visible means of support," a few close observations have revealed otherwise. The observers involved have seen the UFO mechanism from which I have concluded the force field emerges, in effect, the part which is to the UFO what the drive wheels are to the automobile—a power-focusing or driving link in the system. In the case of the saucer, it comprises a bladed mechanism located in the annular area just within and below the rim. Besides the direct observations, there are numerous observations a little less direct, but just as evidential, leading to the same conclusion. First we will look at some of the direct observational data along with some supporting observations. Then we will address the strong indirect evidence.

A. Where the Force Field Emerges

EXAMPLE X-A1. MECHANISM REPAIRED

We now refer back to the sighting by Ray Hawks, of Boulder, Colorado, of a saucer repair, mentioned in Example IX-B1. Hawks was operating a tractor-shovel loader when he noticed a strange craft drop out of the cloud cover and descend vertically until it hovered at a couple hundred feet altitude. He described the craft as being like two convex disks joined together at the rim in typical saucer configuration, its depth being about one fifth of its diameter. It was dull aluminum in color, and around its perimeter, a little way in from the edge, was a series of shiny metal plates with a small radial gap between each, which he could see on the under surface as it descended and on the upper surface as the saucer wobbled in coming to rest. One of the plates was giving off a bright blue smoke which oozed around the edges. The saucer hum was intermittent.

The smoking plate began to tilt until one end, and then the whole plate, was taken inside, leaving an elongated hole where the plate had been. Immediately another plate was worked into place from within, and Hawks heard a click as it came into place. Then the hum increased in intensity and the craft ascended into the cloud cover from which it came. Hawks did not say that the blades rotated.

EXAMPLE X-A2. DETAILED DESCRIPTION

On March 2, 1965, John Reeves, a retired longshoreman who lives a mile west of Weeki Wachee Springs, Florida, left his trailer park about 1:15 P.M. and walked through the nearby woods (Steiger and Whitenour 119-22). He saw something that looked like the roof of a trailer. Curious about why a trailer should be parked out in this part of the woods, he walked toward it. When he got within about 300 feet, he saw it again. In giving his account he said, "I noticed right away it was a flying saucer. Some sort of space ship."

He approached the saucer, using bushes for cover, until he was within 100 feet. He stopped there to watch when suddenly he saw a humanoid on his left who approached to within about 15 feet of Reeves. Spotting Reeves, the humanoid watched him for a couple of minutes before pointing some form of apparatus at Reeves which gave out a flash of light. Reeves thought his picture had been taken. This action with the apparatus was repeated. Then the humanoid went to the vehicle and entered it through an opening in the bottom center, as Reeves lay down on the ground to better see what was going on.

It was a saucer about 20 to 30 feet in diameter and about 6 feet thick. It stood on a four-legged gear, about 4 feet above ground level. In the outer rim there were blades that were about 36 inches long by 8 or 10 inches wide. Reeves could see into the ship through the gaps in the blades. Soon the blades opened and closed, venetian-blind style. The rim system containing the blades began to rotate in a clockwise direction, picking up speed until the vehicle lifted. A whistling noise increased in intensity as it rose. The landing gear swung or rotated outward, then slid or injected into the saucer. It went straight up, and in 10 or 12 seconds was out of sight.

The humanoid was about 5 feet tall and wore a silver-grey suit with a glass helmet. He was dark-complected, with wide-set eyes and eyebrows, normal nose and mouth, and a somewhat pointed chin. Beneath the helmet he wore a head covering over the top and sides of his head. Footprints left by the humanoid were 11 inches long, about 4 inches wide at the ball and heel, and 2½ inches wide at the middle, or instep. Photographs of the prints show that the ball and heel marks are round in planform, giving a dumbbell-print impression, and also show that the sole and heel marks left a distinct waffle-grid pattern.

Researchers estimated that the humanoid, although only 5 feet tall, weighed about 250 pounds to leave such prints. The landing gear prints were round, about 6 inches in diameter, and about an inch deep. Photos of both footprints and gear prints are reproduced in Steiger and Whitenour's book.

Besides his detailed description of the vehicle, Reeves had a comment: "But the funny thing about it was there was no exhaust or nothin' coming out of it...so whatever made it go, I don't know."

EXAMPLE X-A3. TYPICAL RED-GLOWING RIM

On July 28, 1952, at 12:11 A.M., UFO student August C. Roberts mounted the Civil Defense Skywatch Tower in Jersey City and with George Conger saw a glowing saucer-shaped vehicle which he studied with binoculars and also photographed (Stair and Gauvin 104). The part of the story of interest to us was the color change. There was a reddish brown dot in the center, and the rim was

Figure X-1

also reddish brown. When the saucer speeded up, the
rim turned a bright glowing red.

This story is just a reminder that among observers who differentiate between one part of the saucer and another, it is generally the bottom rim area that glows orange or red. Clearly showing the same thing is the sketch in the clipping presented as Figure X-1 (next page), bearing a note from my secretary Agnes Dunkley to the effect that I should combine UFO watching with rock hunting. Clearly, Dr. Kukla was very impressed. Another red-rim account is the impressive incident condensed in the following paragraph.

On August 1, 1966, at Rushville, Indiana, several girls were playing outside at 7:45 P.M. Donna Glosser first noticed the UFO hovering over a tree half a block away. It was described as round, with an angular diameter four times that of the moon, and of a bright, silvery color. Although the outline was fuzzy, it appeared to be a solid object, and it rocked a little as it hovered. (It was therefore a saucer, not a sphere.) When Donna called to her friends to look at it, the object turned a reddish orange color, mainly on the "outer edge of the bottom," and crossed to the other side of the road so fast it seemed to jump. This UFO was also witnessed by adults (Lorenzen, *UFOs Over the Americas*, 109).

For a description of an orange rim, see Example III-3B.

EXAMPLE X-A4. THE SATURN'S RING.

The following sighting is an excellent example of a typical Saturn-type UFO. The account provides evidence that UFOs with configurations other than the saucer also "do business in the rim" (Lorenzen, *UFO, The Whole Story*, 151-53).

On February 24, 1958, at 3:05 A.M., three men were traveling in a car in the state of Bahia, Brazil. Their car began missing and coughing, and came to a complete stop. As they could not locate the cause of the trouble, they decided to sleep on the side of the road until morning. Soon they noticed a huge luminous object overhead. It glowed with a strange light, between a silver and a blue (silver-blue is fully ionized). At first it was only a light, but as it got closer they could discern a solid object behind the glow. The object was two hemispheres, one above the other in normal orientation, but between them was a luminous disk spinning at high speed. The disk was the *source of the brilliant glow* surrounding the entire object. The "disk" is of course better described as the Saturn ring.

The object came silently toward the car; when it was about 240 feet from the observers and about 90 feet above the ground, the three men were able to clearly discern its contours. The bottom was slightly smaller than the top hemisphere and slightly flattened. (The reader is encouraged to see the Trinidad Island photos in Lorenzen's *Flying Saucers: The Startling Evidence of the Invasion from Outer Space*, plates 3A-3D.) The luminosity spread in a curtain of luminosity between the UFO and the ground below (excellent evidence that the UFO is focusing energy in a downward-directed beam).

By this time the men were out of the car, but the frightened driver got back in. The other two decided to investigate and walked toward the strange object. As they approached the illuminated area, which was about twice the size of the UFO diameter of 60-75 feet, the object took off in a vertical climb (demonstrating more concern for the safety of the men than the men themselves showed). It stopped at an altitude of about 600 feet and made a tight circle in the sky, its luminous focus on the ground tracing a larger circle than the object itself was tracing in the sky. Clearly, we note in passing, the UFO was banking to turn in a curvilinear path; this will be discussed in Section XI.

The UFO stopped again, and one of the men, Dr. Pereira, noted that the Saturn ring was notched like a cogwheel whose indentations appeared to be oblique in relation to the edge of the ring.

The object began to move again, in a series of high-speed maneuvers, sometimes moving vertically, sometimes horizontally, in different directions, and sometimes in tight circles about the car. These maneuvers were described in terms such as "moving faster than lightning" and "becoming a dot in the sky in a split second."

These obvious exaggerations simply show that this one-UFO circus act was performed with accelerations which were beyond the comprehension of the observers, and in conformity with our discussion in Section II.

Then the object did a dead-leaf descent, stopping 9-12 feet from the ground. When the observers again tried to approach it, the UFO left at high speed. It had stayed one and a half hours. The car then started without difficulty.

While these accounts quite clearly show a correlation between the location of certain UFO mechanisms and concentrations of ion illumination, comment is withheld until after the data on "saucer rings" has been presented in the following paragraphs.

B. Saucer Rings

EXAMPLE X-B1. CHEMICALLY ALTERED RINGS

Chemically altered rings are annular traces on the ground where a concentration of UFO radiation, of ionizing strength, has induced chemical changes to take place, at the same time drying the ground to a crystalline-powder form which will not absorb moisture. Often, as in this example, the ground remains phosphorescent for several days, meaning, of course, that the ring glows in the dark with some characteristic color. The explanation of the color glow is very similar to the explanation of the colors radiated by the atmosphere ionized by (the same) UFO radiation, namely, the light quanta generated by electrons dropping to lower energy levels; but in phosphorescent chemicals the process is a slow one.

We refer back to the sighting first mentioned in Example III-B6. On the evening of November 2, 1971, about 7:00 P.M., on a farm near Delphos, Kansas, Ronald Johnson, 16, saw a saucer either hovering extremely low or landed (APRO Bulletin, November-December 1971 and March-April 1972). It was "really bright—like a welder." He watched it for about 5 minutes before it took off, and he suffered with eyeburn for a couple of days as a result. Mr. and Mrs. Johnson, who came out at Ronald's call in time to see the UFO in the process of leaving, went with Ronald to the spot where the UFO was sighted by Ronald and found a glowing, phosphorescent, annular-ring-shaped area on the ground. They noted that portions of adjacent trees were also glowing. The soil in the ring was dried out, while inside and outside of the ring the soil remained muddy. Thirty-two days later the soil of the ring was still so dry that snow melted very slowly, thus showing the location of the ring. Figure X-2, a photograph taken from the November-December 1971 *Bulletin*, shows the position of the ring relative to the tree. It is clear that the UFO could not have been of larger diameter than the ring. Clearly the location of the saucer ring relative to the low-hovering UFO which caused it corresponds to the annular location of the bladed mechanisms described in Examples X-A1 and X-A2.

The altered crystalline grain or oxide powder nature of the soil remains, perhaps indefinitely, but the phosphorescence lasted only four days. Investigator Clarence D. Tull revealed that one of the strangest (or most inexplicable) of all UFO phenomena was also observed in this sighting—the UFO jitter. Ronald said that the base of the object seemed stationary, but that the upper portion of the object was (or seemed to be) moving or vibrating from side to side, or possibly up and down. I inserted the "seemed to be" because I maintain that the UFO jitter is more apt to be an optical phenomenon than a vibrating-mass phenomenon. It may also be a valid clue to the nature of force field generation.

EXAMPLE X-B2. GRASS RINGS

Figure X-3 shows what I am calling a grass ring. At 11:30 A.M. on September 1, 1974, Mr. Edwin Fuhr spotted a symmetrical (round) bun-shaped UFO hovering only a foot off the ground. He was riding his swather, cutting the rape (seed) crop which is the tall grass shown in the photo. He dismounted and approached on foot to within about 15 feet of the object, where he could notice that the grass beneath the object was being swirled down. The UFO was also turning, but which direction was not specified. In a couple of minutes he returned to the swather, at which time he noted four more similar UFOs, all hovering low. In about 15 minutes they all left at once, on vertical trajectories. Where each had hovered the grass was swirled down, in a clockwise direction, in an annular area, leaving the grass in the center standing upright.

Figure X-2. The ring described in the Kansas landing case.

Figure X-3. Edwin Fuhr indicates
where one of the objects hovered.

EXAMPLE X-B3. PRESSURE RINGS

Pressure rings, or Camrose rings, are the markings on the ground found near Camrose, Alberta, Canada (Lorenzen, *UFOs Over the Americas*, 30-31). Although no UFO was seen making one, 3 out of 4 local farmers had previously reported UFOs in the area, according to APRO Investigator W.K. Allen.

Briefly, the rings were annular bands or imprints pressed into the turf. The rings were about 6 inches wide, varying from 33 to 36 feet in diameter. Another feature was that where the pasture had considerable slope, the ring there imprinted was elliptical, with the long axis in the direction of maximum slope.

The turf was very firm, as Investigator Allen was unable to make an imprint on it with his heel, which he estimated gave a test pressure of 3500 pounds per square foot. Since the rings had an area of about 50 square feet, this suggests a UFO weight in excess of 175,000 pounds. Allen supposed that a UFO might have impacted the ground to have left such an impression. This supposition, however, is contradicted by the evidence of the elliptic ring which must have been made by a hovering UFO, perhaps in leaving, when the thrust is greater than the weight. Also, large-diameter circular landing gear fits no UFO pattern. My conclusion is that the rings were directly imprinted on the soil by an annular force field having a narrow focus. This concept fits this specific data as well as the saucer and Saturn UFO pattern of annular force fields.

While the predominant feature of these rings was the depression of the ground level, the expected chemical action was also present, as evidenced by the imprinted bands turning an off-white color. Exactly where we find the force field we also find the evidence of energetic waves capable of ionization and consequent chemical action. In this correlation lies the importance of the Camrose rings.

C. Discussion

The fact that a saucer ring on sloping ground was elliptical in shape with the long axis running uphill shows that it was pressed into the ground by the annular-shaped circular force field from a UFO hovering in a horizontal attitude. We therefore conclude that they were all made the same way, by force field impressions. If we judge the focusing of a saucer force field by the Delphos, Kansas, ring or the Camrose rings, which are narrow, then we conclude that the focus can be sharp, but it does not follow that this is always true, as will be demonstrated by an example shortly.

The narrow saucer ring consisting of chemically altered earth indicates that a hard wave radiation accompanies the force field and that the hard wave radiation can have the same degree of focusing as the force field. My first reaction was that perhaps the force field waves and the hard wave radiation occurring in the same place were one and the same phenomenon. This would be a neat explanation if it were true, for then we would know that the ion field about a UFO always occurs wherever the force field is above the minimum intensity required for ionization. Following a little homework on this matter, I concluded that such an explanation is oversimplified and untrue. The conclusion is based on a calculation of energy transfer from the force field wave front to a molecular electron. The calculation shows that the energy transfer fails by orders of magnitude to account for molecular ionization, i.e., projecting the electron outside the molecule. While the wave front may give a strong push, it passes too quickly to impart enough impulse and momentum to dislodge the electron.

It seems we will therefore have to be satisfied with the idea that the propulsive waves and the ionizing waves are two separate entities that (more or less) go out together. The hard waves could be ordinary electromagnetic (EM) waves of x-ray strength, as concluded in the study of UFO radiation discussed in Section IV. The hard waves could provide some form of supporting wave mechanics for the generation of force field waves, or simply be a by-product of the force field generation.

The dual-wave picture, based on the ring evidence that both wave types are pointed in the same direction, nevertheless indicates that we should expect atmospheric ionization to be greatest where the force field is strongest. This is consistent with observation. Thus it becomes evident why the red and orange ionization that is characteristic of low-power operation is so often observed to be concentrated under the rim of the vehicle where the force field apparently emerges.

The Saturn UFO cited in Example X-A3 provides an example in which a parallel observation can be made, concerning high-power operation. That vehicle was doing high-powered maneuvers, and the notched ring was cited as the source of the illumination. This probably just meant that the illumination, or ionization, was strongest near the ring. Either the observer's citation of the ring as the source of the illumination, or my interpretation of his observation, can be taken to single out the ring as the source of the force field and hard radiation, giving a consistent picture of the force field coming from an annular area in both the Saturn and saucer UFOs, and a consistent picture of the ion-illumination showing where the radiations are concentrated, as well as a strong suggestion as to whence they are emanating.

Detailed observations of saucer and Saturn UFO construction are meager, but the data available indicates that the saucer's ring of plates and the Saturn's notched ring are located where the field action is greatest, and below which saucer rings are created. If the plates in Example X-A1 were not handling a lot of power, one wouldn't have been smoking. It seems evident that these components have something to do with processing the force field, perhaps focusing it, but just what they do and how is still a mystery.

We now return to Example X-A3 to discuss the curtain of light extending from the ring to the illuminated focus on the ground, which had a diameter of nearly two UFO diameters. As most readers will realize, it is not just an electromagnetic beam, as from a search light.

It is a column of ionized air, probably activated by x-ray photons accompanying the force field. Its importance to UFO theory is that it demonstrates, by specific example, how very adequately UFOs can focus their field power.

Without the ability to focus the force field, the field would have little value to a UFO. Suppose that their propulsive field had spherical symmetry. That is, suppose that it had equal strength in all directions. Then the UFO could descend to earth on a radial vertical path, or leave earth in a radial direction, but it could not maneuver or even travel horizontally. UFOs must and can point their force field in any desired direction, an ability which requires both focusing and the ability to point the beam. Anything that is focused can be represented by an arrow showing the direction in which it is pointed. If the length of the arrow also represents the resulting beam strength, the arrow is called a vector. It is very proper to represent the UFO force field by such a pointing arrow, or vector. The UFO then has control by pointing the vector. In modern missile terminology this is called "thrust-vector control," and I assure the reader that all UFOs use it, as will be made clear in the Section XI. At this point, however, we are just establishing the prerequisite that UFOs do focus the field.

The best example demonstrating a broad range of focusing capability has been saved until last. It is taken from Jacques and Janine Vallee's *Challenge To Science* (40), which presents sketches presented in Figure X-4. The observer noted that the object had the shape of a hemisphere, or inverted bowl, and that as it hovered what he at first thought to be jets were in reality formed by a luminous cone (a), that opened up under the object like an umbrella (b), giving the impression that it was "rising, on luminous flames." Of course, the reader now knows it is rising above cold plasma, not flames. The object then tilted, base toward the viewer after takeoff (c), and while the object was going away the plasma zone was shaped as (d).

Figure X-4. UFO Focusing Sequence.
(a) As first seen. (b) Umbrella focus.
(c) Facing away. (d) Leaving.

This amazing sequence indicates that this UFO (approximately a saucer) could:

1. Sharply focus, resulting in a plasma cone (a);
2. Broadly focus, as in (b), the umbrella act;
3. Could exhibit a plasma zone shaped like an inverted gas flame (d), suggesting that the plasma is swept inward by the axially symmetric air flow about the vehicle; and
4. Point the focused field in any direction it chooses (by vehicle tilting).

This UFO indeed demonstrated versatility. For a perfect verification of the last instance in the sequence, see Photograph 1 in Hynek's *The UFO Experience*, which shows position (d) in Figure X-4 exactly. A sharp eye can even see that the plasma in the photo is swept a little to the left, indicating that the domed saucer shown has a component of motion to the right.

Section XI
Saucer Dynamics

A. Data

The UFO Experience (Hynek 100-08) gives one of the best available descriptions of the important UFO chase across Ohio and into Pennsylvania on the morning of April 17, 1966. Officers Dale Spaur and Wilber Neff, who were in one police car, and Officer Wayne Huston, who was in a second, described the appearance and actions of the saucer-type UFO after engaging in the chase. The chase was mostly pre-dawn, and the plasma cone, as well as the saucer dome, were plainly visible. Officer Huston said it was shaped something like an ice cream cone. Figure XI-1 shows three schematics of the officers' descriptions and sketches.

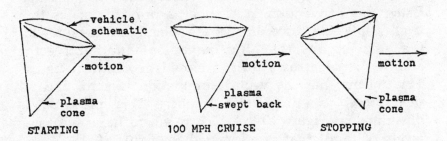

Figure XI-1

The officers said that the vehicle tilted "forward" to start and "backward" to stop. At low speed the cone was symmetric, like the kettledrum case, but at high speed they reported that the cone was swept backward, thus confirming (one more time) that the cone was a plasma, and the UFO a saucer.

B. Mechanics

"Flying" saucers, whether disks, lenticular-shaped vehicles, inverted bowls, straw hats, conical hats, or what-have-you, have an axis of symmetry normal to the plane of the saucer or disk and, of course, passing through the center of it. Suppose, utilizing as evidence the saucer cones and other symmetrically ionized regions as well as the saucer ring data from Section X, we make the totally natural assumption that the propulsive force field is axially symmetric also. In strict conformity with the laws of mechanics, then, the action of the force field can be determined by replacing it with a force vector, which is an arrow with a length equal to the force (to an arbitrary scale), drawn on the axis of symmetry and pointing upward to the center of the disk. In Figure XI-2 this force vector is labeled *thrust*. The UFO weight is another vector quantity to be drawn pointed straight downward from the center of gravity, assumed to be at the geometric center.

According to the physicist d'Alembert, there is an "inertia force," equal and opposite to the product of vehicle mass and acceleration, which resists acceleration. Using this convention, d'Alembert's principle states that if all applicable force arrows are joined end-to-end with the head of one touching the tail of another (vector addition), the arrows form a closed geometrical figure. This means that the vector summation is zero, and all the forces are in perfect balance. This principle is illustrated in Figure XI-2, which refers to the same three levels of flight that is addressed in Figure XI-1.

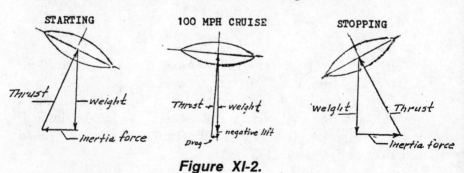

Figure XI-2.

In the starting and stopping diagrams, the speed is low and the aerodynamic forces neglected. The only advantage of force diagrams, as applied to the UFO, is that they are simple in concept and educational. For example, we see in the center diagram why the UFO cannot use the atmosphere for flight like a bird or an aircraft. The aerodynamic "lift" points downward! The saucer disk is tilted the wrong way for positive lift. We can also learn from the center diagram, which has no inertia force because the acceleration is zero, that a slight saucer tilt is necessary to overcome the small drag and maintain velocity. The UFO force diagram is practically useless in solving for the actual values of the forces, however, because we do not know the UFO weight.

The system I have used many years for the analysis of test missiles, flying platforms, spacecraft, and unconventional craft (UFOs) is to divide each force vector by the weight of the craft, transforming each to an acceleration vector in g units. Not only does this method overcome the problem of not knowing the weight, but for vehicles on a level flight path the diagram becomes a highly useful acceleration-performance diagram giving numerical results for all quantities. Instead of the weight vector, we now have a unit vector pointing straight downward from the UFO center, signifying the 1 g acceleration of earth gravity. The thrust becomes thrusting acceleration in g units, pointing upward along the axis of symmetry, and the inertia force is replaced by an acceleration vector pointing in the opposite sense. The 1-2-3 procedure is simple:

1. Draw UFO schematic at an arbitrary tilt angle; put in centerline, ₵ .

2. Draw in a unit vertical vector pointing downward from the center.

3. For horizontal acceleration, draw horizontal line from (bottom) tip of unit vector to the ₵ , putting the arrow head tip-to-tip with the head of the unit vector. The horizontal acceleration is

the length and direction of this vector, in g's. The length on the ₵ is the UFO thrust in g's and is in the proper direction.

Figure XI-3 shows a typical example with UFO accelerating horizontally, tilted 30 degrees from the horizontal.

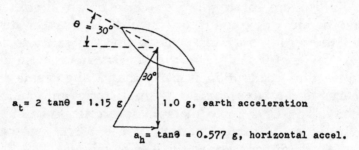

Figure XI-3.

Of course, the UFO uses a lot of thrust just to hover, but in this case for an increase in thrust of only 15 percent the UFO can accelerate almost like a drag racer, at 0.577 g. If it tilts 45 degrees it beats the racer with an horizontal acceleration of 1 g, at a thrust increase of 41.4 percent. Thus a UFO can go somewhere quickly without much more thrust than used to hover. The more extreme accelerations generally involve an upward-sloping trajectory.

C. Sudden Reversals

Consider the case of a saucer traveling from left to right at a speed of 100 mph in level flight. Let it be tilted 84.3 degrees with respect to the horizontal, as shown in Figure XI-4.

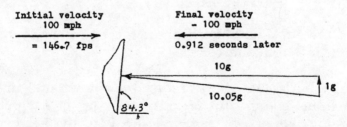

Figure XI-4. Saucer Making 10 g Reversal.

The horizontal acceleration, A_h, is

$$A_h = -\tan 84.3 \times 1g = -10 \times 1g$$
$$= -10g$$

or ten times Earth gravity. The minus value merely indicates that acceleration is opposite to initial velocity, or the vehicle is slowing down.

If we take g as 32.17 ft/sec^2, 10 g is 321.7 ft/sec^2. The vehicle comes to a stop in 146.7/321.7 = 0.456 seconds. The vehicle decelerates smoothly through the stopped position, remaining stopped no time whatever. In another 0.456 seconds, it is back up to a velocity of 100 mph going in the opposite direction. The elapsed time of 0.912 second is a bit short for the observer. In less than a second, before he fully realizes what is going on, the vehicle has gone from 100 mph in one direction to 100 mph in the opposite direction! In the same example, the time involved from 10 mph to the right, to 10 mph to the left is less than one tenth of a second. This is less than the time it takes our thoughts to follow what happens. Who can blame the observer for calling this an instant reversal, particularly since the instant of time at which zero velocity occurred was a true instant, a point in time with zero duration, dividing the forward velocity from the reverse? Yet no law of mechanics, that branch of physics dealing with force, mass, acceleration, and velocity, has been violated.

The reversal of direction catches the observer by surprise because Earth vehicles—wagons, bicycles, and motorcycles, cars, airplanes, and even helicopters—characteristically make U-turns to reverse direction. The observer is then surprised and mystified by the sudden, silent, and swift doubling back over the same course and realizes something unusual, or at least unfamiliar to him, has occurred. The sudden reversal, a maneuver becoming an increasingly familiar part of the UFO pattern, is explainable in a straightforward manner by the standard laws of mechanics, or physics if you prefer.

D. Bank-To-Turn Maneuvers

It is evident that UFOs' bank-to-turn-when-circling maneuvers suit their purpose, as we can see in the following sightings.

EXAMPLE XI-D1

The first is a sighting by the scientists of the Aeronautical Division of the General Mills Corporation, as reported by Major Edward Ruppelt. One reason for selecting this example is that I had a working relationship with the same people when the Applied Materials and Physics Division of the Langley Research Center contracted with General Mills to build the world's largest balloon, which we used as a rocket-launch platform at altitudes in excess of 100,000 feet. They related this and other sightings to me at that time (1965). I also liked the way the General Mills scientists stood up to Ruppelt, head of Project Bluebook, when he visited them in Minneapolis on January 14, 1952, in the middle of a cold wave and blizzard. Having directed the launching and tracking of all the Skyhook balloons prior to Ruppelt's visit, they were familiar with the appearance of their balloons in all weather conditions, altitudes, and lighting. They knew meteorology, aerodynamics, and astronomy, and they also were very familiar with UFOs. As Ruppelt put it, the thing that made the General Mills scientists so sure that UFOs existed was that they had seen so many of them. Ruppelt said, "Every time I suggested some natural explanation for UFOs I just about found myself in a fresh snowdrift."

In a daylight sighting on January 16, 1951, two people from General Mills and four from Artesia, New Mexico, were watching a Skyhook balloon from the Artesia airport. After watching the balloon for about an hour, one of them spotted two tiny specks on the northwest horizon. The group watched the specks move in quickly, and in a few seconds they could see that they were two round, dull-white objects flying in close formation. The two objects headed almost straight toward the balloon and then circled it. To circle the balloon, the UFOs tipped on edge in a steep banking maneuver, and the observers saw that the objects were disk-shaped. This excellent opportunity to determine the size of the saucers by comparison with the known balloon size resulted an estimate of 60 feet in diameter.

EXAMPLE XI-D2

The second sighting to be offered in evidence of banked turns is the famous one usually referred to as the Tremonton, Utah, film. The film was shot by Navy Chief Photographer, Warrant Officer Delbert Newhouse in July 1952 (Ruppelt 220). The Newhouses were on a cross-country trip; when they passed near Tremonton on a bright sunshiny day, they happened to see a group of about a dozen objects milling around in the sky. They stopped the car and got out for a good look, and Newhouse reported his immediate impression of the objects as flying disks. It should be pointed out that Newhouse, with 2000 hours flying time as an aerial photographer during his 21 years with the Navy, was in effect a professional aerial observer, a unique qualification for making the sighting.

Realizing that in all his experiences he had never seen anything like this, he turned the turret on his movie camera to a 3-inch telephoto lens and filmed the spectacle in color. In good movie style, he held the camera steady while the disks did tight circling and other maneuvers in his field of view. Then, when one left the group he stopped the camera in front of it, letting it fly through the field of view to get its angular velocity. In short, he did a perfect job.

When Ruppelt received the film, he ran it 20 to 30 times, then called in fighter pilots for their opinions. After watching the objects circle and dart about the cloudless sky, their unanimous and unqualified comment was that no airplane could do what the UFOs were clearly doing. The film had already been studied by Navy analysts, who concluded that the disks were neither airplanes nor birds, but were intelligently controlled vehicles!

I had the good fortune to see the Tremonton film way back in the 1950s. I saw it repeatedly at normal speed, slow motion, forward, backward, and stop motion, just as we studied Wallops Island movies of the research vehicles in flight. My conclusions were similar to those of the other analysts, but contained an additional, third, point:

1. The vehicle maneuvers could not be replicated by earth vehicles. The film was good evidence of the existence of saucers.

2. The maneuvers indicated impressive propulsion capability in terms of accelerations and energy expended. They appeared to use energy as though there were no allocations for tomorrow, zipping around in a playful manner like cavorting lambs.

3. They banked to turn. What Ruppelt took to be fading in and out I was sure was the presentation of broadside and edge views due to banking. In stop motion, one could see the elliptic in-between in some frames.

I had already concluded, back in 1952-53, from analysis and experiments on flying platforms, that saucers and other UFOs bank to turn. Now, here, in 1956, was the visual evidence on film.

From these examples, we can see that, in addition to doubling back on their tracks in a reversal of direction, UFOs also engage in circling and general curvilinear maneuvers. They bank to turn like an airplane, except they use a field force in place of an aerodynamic force. Otherwise, the mechanics are similar.

Everyone who has ridden airplanes knows that when they bank (one wing tip up, the other down) they turn. The force that turns them is the horizontal component of lift, at right angles to the flight path. In our triangular acceleration diagrams, it is the horizontal component of acceleration which makes them turn. The acceleration diagrams we have already used solves the problem for both the airplane and the UFO for any level flight turn. Figure XI-1 illustrates this principle for the case of a 60-degree banking turn.

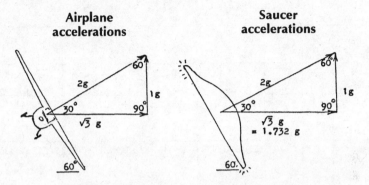

Figure XI-5. Sixty-degree banking turns.

The diagrams were constructed by drawing a 1 g vertical vector to the scale of 1 inch equals 1 g, then a horizontal line to the bottom of the 1 g vector, and a line inclined at the bank angle drawn to the top of the 1g vector completes the triangle of accelerations. As most pilots and engineers know, a level flight 60-degree banking turn must be made by "pulling" a 2g lifting acceleration (which is defined as being along a line of symmetry which tilts with the ship). As the diagram shows, this gives a 1g vertical acceleration to counteract gravity, and a horizontal acceleration of $\sqrt{3}$g or 1.732 g expressed as a decimal fraction. This number is the tangent of 60 degrees, while 2 is the secant of 60 degrees. These trigonometric relations, which are derived from the triangle of accelerations, hold for any bank angle except 90 degrees where the triangle disappears and the turning acceleration cannot be obtained.

Using θ for bank angle, the horizontal acceleration A_h and the total or lifting acceleration A_l are given by

$$A_h = g \text{ tangent } \theta$$

and

$$A_l = g \text{ secant } \theta$$

These relations are summarized for a few angles in the following table:

HORIZONTAL BANKING TURN ACCELERATIONS, g UNITS.

bank angle, θ degrees	0	10	20	30	40	50	60	70	80	85
vertical acceler.	1.0	1.00	1.00	1.00	1.00	1.00	1.00	1.00	1.00	1.00
lifting acceler. = sec θ	1.0	1.0154	1.0642	1.1547	1.3054	1.5560	2.0000	2.9238	5.7588	11.474
horizontal acceler. = tan θ	0	0.1763	0.3640	0.5773	0.8391	1.1918	1.7321	2.7475	5.6713	11.430

Simply substituting tilt angle for bank angle, this above table is also valid for low speed rectilinear (straight line) flight, as in reversals.

As an illustration of the use of turning accelerations, let us find the turning radius for a UFO with a level flight velocity of 1,000 ft/sec banking at 80 degrees. Utilizing equation (1) from Section II-C in transposed form and taking g = 32.17 ft/sec^2 the turning radius is

$$r = \frac{V^2}{A_h g} = \frac{(1000)^2}{(5.6713)(32.17)} = 5481 \text{ feet}$$

If we have a photo of a UFO that is known to be in a level flight turning maneuver, the turning acceleration, A_h, can be estimated from the apparent bank angle and the above table or, if the angle can be obtained precisely, by A_h = tan θ. However, there are problems. One problem with most UFO photographs is that the horizontal (or vertical) reference is not accurately known, or is even nonexistent. In the latter case we may be reduced to assuming one edge of the camera was held level to within perhaps 10 degrees, etc. Another problem is that the saucer has not obliged us with an edge-on view from which the angle can be measured. We may be estimating the angle merely by appearances and cannot expect to be closer than, say, the nearest 10 degrees.

Within the limitations just stated, the UFO literature contains many photos from which turning performance can be estimated. For example, *UFO, The Whole Story* contains four pages of UFOs at various tilt angles (Lorenzen 152+). If we assume these UFOs are in level flight, or in level flight turns, then within the limitations expressed in the preceding paragraph, we can estimate the horizontal, or turning accelerations as follows:

1. The first photo presents an edge-on view of a saucer tilted at 50 10 degrees, and from the above table $A_h = 1.2 \pm 0.1$ g.

2. The second photo has two saucers, one tilted about 60 degrees and the other about 80 degrees, to within 10 degrees. The corresponding accelerations are

$$A_h = 1.7 \pm 0.2 \text{ g}$$

and $$A_h = 5.7 \pm \text{ about } 1.0 \text{ g}$$

3. On the third page the UFO appears to be banked at 90 degrees, a vertical bank. This is the one case for which the system does not work.

4. The last photo is so far from an edge view that we judge the bank angle from appearances, which includes ellipticity. It looks like 40 degrees, giving a ballpark A_h of 0.8 g, which may be grossly in error.

All of this discussion indicates that at moderate accelerations airplane and UFO turning performances are much alike, following the same laws of mechanics. The difference between the two is often one of degrees, based on differences in force-to-weight capabilities, structural limitations, and occupant limitations. A passenger jet plane can pull only about 4 g before structural damage begins to occur. Acrobatic and fighter planes are designed to withstand 10 g without structural damage, but at about this point the pilot blacks out, so 10 g amounts to a practical limit for aircraft. In Section II-C, a UFO turning acceleration of 122 g was estimated from visual observation, illustrating well the superior maneuver capability of the UFO, compared to aircraft. The point is, the g's they can utilize is, at the minimum, of an order of magnitude greater than that available to aircraft.

E. UFO Takeoff Dynamics

EXAMPLE XI-E1

At 5:00 P.M. on August 24, 1967, Ron Hydes was on his motorcycle on the highway from Melbourne to Sidney when he was blinded by a brilliant light coming from overhead (Lorenzen, *UFO, The Whole Story*, 179-81). Stopping, Hydes dismounted and wiped his eyes. He saw a typical saucer-shaped vehicle hovering 3 to 4 feet above ground level about 100 feet to the left of the road. The saucer was silvery on top, showing a cupola, and was darker underneath. He also spotted two humanoids approaching him, about 5 feet tall and dressed in shiny, metallic-colored coveralls and dark yet transparent helmets.

Hydes panicked, jumped on his bike, and took off down the highway at full throttle, making about 100 mph. The UFO was soon after him. Hydes realized this when he heard it hum as it passed over his head at an altitude of 100 to 200 feet, and then preceded him down the highway a couple hundred feet in front. Not liking the situation, Hydes slowed down as did the saucer, and the both came to a stop. However, in a moment or two the saucer tilted appreciably (base toward Hyde) and left rapidly on a flight path or trajectory making an angle of about 45 degrees with the horizontal.

EXAMPLE XI-E2

In Example X-B2 (with the grass rings) Mr. Edwin Fuhr encountered 5 UFOs hovering at only one foot above ground level, and swirling down the grass in an annular pattern. They all took off simultaneously on vertical trajectories.

Steep trajectories, as steep as in Example XI-E1 or even steeper, are commonly used by UFOs in takeoff from low-elevation hovering conditions. Indeed, the most common is that of Example XI-E2, a vertical trajectory obtained by increasing the lifting g to some value higher than the 1 g used to hover, without any tilt of the UFO. There seems to be a logical reason for this, for if the UFO is hovering within a foot or two of the earth as they sometimes do and the UFO is relatively flat on the bottom like a saucer, it would need to acquire some altitude before tilting appreciably to avoid striking the ground. They can of course choose their takeoff g, A_l, and given sufficient ground clearance they can choose the tilt angle, θ, to accelerate in any vertical angular direction, ß, that they please. ß is measured with respect to the horizontal, and θ is zero when the plane of the saucer is horizontal. Clearly, for takeoff with $\theta=0$, ß= 90 degrees, a vertical acceleration, for there is no horizontal acceleration when $\theta=0$. For any combination of lifting acceleration, A_l, and θ, the assumption will be made that both A_l and θ are quickly adjusted and maintained at constant values during takeoff. Then ß is not only the acceleration direction, but the constant angle the flight path makes with the horizontal as well.

Takeoff dynamics is represented graphically in Figure XI-6.

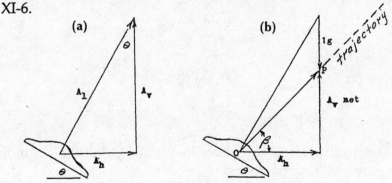

Figure XI-6. Takeoff Dynamics.

In sketch (a) of Figure XI-6, we see the triangle of accelerations at the moment of takeoff with the saucer tilted at angle θ. We also see the lifting acceleration, A_l, with its two components, A_h and A_v. In sketch (b) we subtract earth's 1 g from A_v, giving the vector A_v net as shown. A_v net and A_h are now the components of the resultant vector $\overline{OP}$ drawn in to intersect the tip of A_v net, and making the angle ß with the horizontal. The vector $\overline{OP}$ gives the vehicle acceleration in magnitude and direction. The angle ß also gives the (straight line) flight-path direction, and continues to do so as long as all parameters such as θ , Al, and earth g may be considered constants.

While solutions may be obtained by drawing sketches to scale, a simpler and more accurate method for those familiar with the definitions of trigonometry is illustrated. From sketch (a):

$$A_v = A_1 \cos\theta \quad \text{and} \quad A_h = A_1 \sin\theta$$

From sketch (b):

$$\tan \beta = \frac{A_v \, net}{A_h} = \frac{A_v - 1}{A_h} = \frac{A_1 \cos \theta - 1}{A_1 \sin \theta}$$

For example, if $A_1 = 10$, and $\theta = 30$ degrees,

$$\tan \beta = \frac{10 \cos 30 - 1}{10 \sin 30} = \frac{8.667 - 1}{5} = 1.533$$

$$\beta = 56.87 \text{ degrees}$$

The following table gives the flight-path angle for a range of values of θ and A_1.

TRAJECTORY ANGLE, ß, DEGREES
Lift-Off Acceleration, A₁, in g's

θ						$\propto$ = 90-θ
A₁ =	2	3	5	10	20	
0	90.00	90.00	90.00	90.00	90.00	90
10	70.29	75.08	77.52	78.90	79.48	80
20	52.12	60.57	65.19	67.84	68.97	70
30	36.21	46.81	53.10	56.87	58.50	60
40	28.02	33.95	41.37	46.02	48.09	50
50	10.56	22.00	30.03	35.32	37.73	40
60	0.00	10.89	19.11	24.79	27.46	30

A column of $\propto$ defined as 90 minus θ is also given. This is the inclination of the axis of symmetry, or thrust axis, from the horizontal. Now we compare the high-g values of ß with $\propto$ and find them nearly equal. This means that at high-g takeoff, where earth gravity lowers ß only slightly, the UFO goes almost in the direction its axis of symmetry is pointed.

F. Optimum Trajectory Theory

UFOs are often seen traveling on a level trajectory. At other times they take off with extreme acceleration on a steep trajectory. In the latter case, while the UFO usually goes out of sight in seconds so that its destination is actually unknown, it is my hypothesis that it is on a highly efficient ballistic arc which takes it economically from the starting point A to some destination B which is either out of sight beyond the horizon or a space point or orbit destination.

As is well known, the most efficient ballistic arc is obtained with the highest possible acceleration, adjusting the accelerating time to obtain the velocity required for the mission; that is, according to how far away destination B may be or to whatever near-earth point in space B may be located. The UFO vehicles seem exactly suited to the high acceleration requirements of the most efficient ballistic arc. In fact, they are sometimes accused of the impulsive attainment of velocity which would give the ideal ballistic arc.

Appendix 2 gives a brief study of level-path and ballistic-path travel for ranges which are small compared to planet diameter. Impulse is the product of thrust and time. It is shown that the minimum impulse requirement to go from point A to point B by level trajectory is obtained by accelerating at 1 g for half of the trip and decelerating at 1 g for the other half. This requires that the UFO tilt its thrust axis 45 degrees. For the assumptions made, such as neglecting air drag, see Appendix 2. This result applies for any planetary or lunar value of g as long as local g is used. Again, an acceleration of one earth g is greater than that of a drag racer, so even for level trajectories the high values of acceleration and corresponding high speeds are compatible with economy and time saving and with general UFO observations.

The total impulse per unit mass imparted to a vehicle in order to accomplish a mission is known in rocket parlance as ideal velocity, V_i. The mission energy cost is proportional to V_i. Letting g be local gravity, and d the trip distance, the level-path trip requirement in terms of V_i is proportional to the square root of g times d:

$$V_i = 2\sqrt{2}\sqrt{gd} \qquad\qquad \text{(A2-7a)}$$

This equation shows a tendency for the longer, faster trip to be most economical.

Of course the UFO may introduce a constant velocity mid-trip, possibly limiting speed for observational reasons. The trip is then a little off-optimum energy-wise and time-wise. In comparison with the ballistic trajectory this is then "the scenic low route."

The most economic ballistic-arc trip has a very high acceleration, giving, as nearly as possible, an impulsive start and stop. For short trips of a few hundred miles or less, where g may be considered to have a constant magnitude and direction, the optimum trajectory path angle is ß = 45 degrees. From an inspection of the trajectory-path-angle table, the thrust angle inclination is a little greater than the path angle.

The cost of the ideal ballistic trajectory in terms of V_i, from point A to point B, at distance d and at the same elevation as A, meeting the requirement that the UFO will come to a soft landing or hovering condition at ß, is shown to be:

$$V_i = 2\sqrt{gd} \tag{A2-8a}$$

Comparing this result with equation (A2-7a) we can see that the optimum short-range horizontal flight requires more impulse than the equivalent best ballistic arc by a factor of $\sqrt{2}$. The time in transit on the level trajectory is also greater than the time on a ballistic arc by the same factor, $\sqrt{2}$ (see Appendix 2).

Thus we see that the mechanistically oriented high-arc route (with peak altitude tending to be about one fourth of d) requires both less impulse and less time than the less spectacular, scenic low route. It should therefore not surprise us too much that the UFO most often takes off "like a scalded cat" on a steep trajectory. Such a trajectory is the best trajectory to go from one place to another when the vehicle is neither earth- nor atmosphere-bound.

Irrespective of path optimization, it is clear that when the destination B is a space point having an altitude greater than the range (distance along the earth's surface) a trajectory arc having an elevation angle ß somewhere between 45 and 90 degrees is needed to reach it. Thus a desire to go to a high-elevation point in space could well account for the very high-angle trajectories. This comment sees particularly applicable to a UFO traveling on a highly energetic vertical trajectory.

In summary, it may be said that the most economical UFO travel is at very high acceleration and speed. What may look like an extravagant use of energy is actually economical because the thrust duration is shortened more than the acceleration is raised, and time is saved besides. The high-arc trajectory is more economical and quicker to destination than a low-altitude, level-path trajectory.

G. Platform Experiments

In 1951 I had lunch on numerous occasions with old friend Dr. Charles Zimmerman, a stability and control scientist-engineer recently returned to the Langley Research Center from employment in industry where he had designed and supervised the construction and tests of a circular-wing airplane. However, the thing that interested me more was the invention by Zimmerman of the idea or principle that a man could balance and fly with a thrust vector (lifting force) attached to his feet. By tilting his feet he should achieve both balance and control of his motion in space. From the triangle of accelerations as discussed earlier, it was clear that control of motion would be achievable if the balance characteristics were favorable.

Intrigued with the idea, I soon started investigating. I first built a model that looked like a flying coat hanger. It was supported in flight by an air jet which served as the thrust vector, and controlled in angular attitudes by auxiliary jets. This I flew around my office by remote control.

Next, I rigged up a simple simulator involving man in the proper way. I placed a bowling ball on the floor and a piece of plywood on the ball, and stood on it—a three-dimensional rolla-rolla, although I had never heard of such a device at that time. Although it was difficult to balance, I practiced nights in the winter of '51 until I could watch a TV program while on the ball. I knew I was ready for a serious test.

I had at my disposal a vast supply of 200 psi compressed air which I normally used to operate a supersonic wind tunnel used to test ram jet engines prior to their free-flight testing. I had the shops build a supersonic nozzle with a 1¼-inch-diameter throat. This was bolted to a 19x29-inch piece of plywood to which the feet would be fastened with cleats and rollerskate straps. A borrowed parachute harness, an overhead safety line, and two lengths of over-age fire hose donated by the Langley Fire Department to connect the nozzle to the air supply completed the equipment.

The experiments were carried out first indoors, then outdoors in free flight to the extent limited by the length of the air hoses. Figure XI-7 shows the outdoor rig with me posing comfortably (with overcoat and gloves) as I hover in mid-air for this photo, which, on declassification of the results in 1955, was published July 9, 1955, on the cover of the *Illustrated London News* accompanied by the following caption and text:

A MODERN MERCURY: STANDING MOTIONLESS IN MID-AIR, ABLE TO FLY OFF IN ANY DIRECTION AT A SLIGHT INCLINATION OF HIS BODY, A PILOT TESTS NEW U.S. VERTICAL TAKEOFF DEVICE OR JET PLAT-FORM.

One of the most intriguing developments arising from the intensive modern research into vertical takeoff methods is that of directional control of wingless aircraft by means of weight-shifting. The man in the photograph above is standing on a "jet-platform," in effect a kind of aerial ski attached to his feet; a jet of air from an attached hose provides lift, and to hover in mid-air he has only to remain stationary. To move away he inclines his body in the required directions. . .

Perhaps the reader begins to see some similarities between the platform and the UFO.

Figure XI-8, a movie frame, shows me taking off on the indoor rig. The air-jet is visible for the first few seconds while the moisture is being blown from the air hoses. The safety lines immediately become slack after takeoff, so the flight is free. Another frame, Figure XI-9, shows the executions of lateral translations with sudden reversals, analogous to those of the UFO as described in Section XI-C. However, the motion pattern here is exactly the equivalent of the UFO motion variously described as a pendulum motion, the falling leaf, or the UFO rock.

With these experiments I soon began to realize that I

probably had the first valid dynamic simulation of a UFO—that the UFO, the platform, and similar thrust-vector-controlled devices operate with the same balance of forces and triangles of acceleration that we have addressed in this section. The pendulum motion was a case in point for simulation study. It dissipated energy in lateral motion and gave a fine, or vernier, yet quick-acting control of altitude, always tending to reduce it. It gently lowered altitude. This probably explained why UFOs so often approach the hover altitude while rocking. They are using the rocking motion to lower altitude while maintaining a small excess of thrust until they are satisfied with their position.

The silver-dollar wobble was also tried. This was the saucer motion observed by Ray Hawks of Boulder, Colorado, for example, when a silvery disk dropped out of the cloud cover and descended nearby, doing the wobble as it stabilized its altitude in hovering. The wobble was found to dissipate energy by an almost unnoticeable circular motion and served as a vernier altitude control also.

The effects of both the rock and the wobble may also be explained on a force basis. The effective lift force is the product of lift and the cosine of the tilt angle, θ. The effective reduction of lift therefore varies as $1 - \cos\theta$. In the rock, $1 - \cos\theta$ varies with time, and a time average is effective. In fact, $1 - \cos\theta$ passes through zero twice per rocking cycle. In the wobble, on the other hand, θ and $1 - \cos\theta$ can be constant at its maximum value. The wobble is therefore the stronger control.

Apparently the rock and the wobble both give a finer, faster control of altitude than can be obtained by an adjustment of UFO thrust by a buildup or decrease of force field intensity. The field intensity change, by all evidence such as the buildup of the hum, requires seconds to accomplish, whereas a wobble or rock can be initiated in a fraction of a second.

The reader may wonder, "Why the problem?"

To discuss this very briefly, consider the helicopter. When within one rotor diameter of the ground, the helicopter encounters extra aerodynamic lift which gives it a ground-effects altitude stability. For each power setting and wind velocity, there is a corresponding hovering altitude. The rocket platform and UFO are not so lucky. The only aerodynamic effects they experience are miscellaneous disturbances and they must continuously jockey thrust or introduce other artificial control. At least that is my experience with the platforms. Within a very small distance of ground level, say a meter, saucer-like machines behave as though they possess a degree of altitude stability, but clearly don't have it at higher altitudes.

The platform was connected with saucers in another way. The U.S. Air Force was interested in building a saucer-shaped aircraft for experimental purposes, seemingly with the philosophy of "If you can't beat them, join them." They teamed up with the Royal Canadian Air Force and AVRO of Canada to build it. An artist's sketch of the AVRO-disk can be found in Edwards' *Flying Saucers: Serious Business*. Two pilots were selected to fly the disk. They were Col. David Henderson, USAF, and Wing Comdr. Paul Hartman, RCAF. The photo presented as Figure XI-10 shows Henderson and Hartman as they arrived at the Wallops Island rocket research vehicle base to try their skill at platform flying. They did all right. In fact, Henderson was unusual. He was the first to ever fly the platform for considerable time with his eyes closed, seeming to defy the usual need for a visual reference. Later I heard that the AVRO-disk was plagued with developmental problems, including being underpowered, and was abandoned.

Figure XI-11 shows me making indoor tests of what was called a rotor-supported platform. The platform was circular, and the 7-foot-diameter rotor which supported it was powered by tiny air jets at the rotor tips. To simulate forward speed, I flew it outdoors in a hurricane. The fly-ability was good.

Figure XI-12 shows a saucer-like platform built for the U.S. Navy's Office of Naval Research by Hiller Helicopters. It was also rotor-supported, the rotors being enclosed by a circular housing, or venturi, which became the visible body of the machine. I was consultant to this project. In fact, test pilot Phil A. Johnston, shown in the photo, as well as project engineer Robertson, flew my jet-supported and rotor-supported platforms during the design phases of their project.

We now come to the last of the saucer-like vehicles we shall consider. Figure XI-13 is an artist's conception of my proposal to the NASA Apollo Management for a rocket-powered lunar flyer for lunar exploration. It was to be kinesthetically controlled by body motions in a manner already familiar to the reader. For this application this type of control has the great advantage of simplicity and reduced weight, since the only moving parts are the throttle and throttle valves. Like a saucer, this is a true space vehicle—light, handy, fast, and economical because of the bare-bones design and the low value of lunar gravity. However, the Manned Spaceflight Center elected to use a wheeled vehicle, and they didn't have room for both types on board.

Figure XI-7. Author hovering on thrust-vector in balance with gravity.

Figure XI-8. Air jet visible as author blasts off.

Figure XI-9. Author doing the UFO-rock.

Figure XI-10. AVRO-disk pilots arrive at Wallops Island for disc flight training, January 14, 1954.

Left to right: John C. Palmer, Wallops Island; Lt.Col. David Henderson, USAF; Wing Comdr. Paul Hartman, RCAF; Paul R. Hill, LAL; and Thomas L. Kennedy, LAL.

Figure XI-11. Author making rotor-supported platform test.

Figure XI-12. Office of Naval Research gets in on the action. Phil Johnston, pilot.

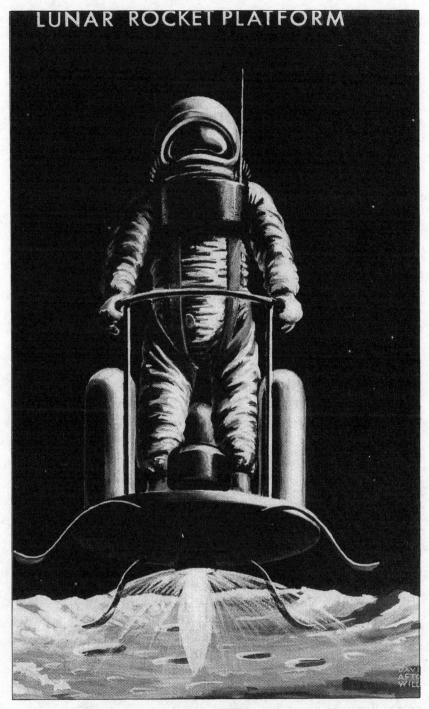

Figure XI-13. Artist's conception of lunar rocket platform.

Section XII
Silent Subsonic Operation

High-performance conventional vehicles such as racing cars, jet planes, and rocket-powered vehicles are noted for being noisy, especially during the high-powered accelerating phase of their travel. In contrast, the silent operation of UFOs is, in general, one of the unusual properties they have in common. Their silence is particularly remarkable or surprising during the high-acceleration and supersonic phases of their trajectories. Because of the difference in the nature of the phenomena involved at subsonic and supersonic speeds, the subject of silent operation has been broken into two phases: Silent Subsonic Operation, to be treated herewith, and Silent Supersonic operation, to be treated in the next section. By way of illustration, we shall consider the data and some operational theory for the big dirigible and cigar-shaped UFOs.

A. Data

EXAMPLE XII-A1

The data will partly consist of my own observations during a stormy afternoon in Hampton, Virginia, in 1962. The time was about 4:00 P.M. and the storm was clearing. A heavy cloud layer with a bottom at about 3000 to 4000 feet altitude lay over the lower end of Chesapeake Bay and over Hampton Roads, which is the body of water where the famous battle between the *Merrimac* and the *Monitor* took place during the Civil War. The rain had stopped, and the air beneath the cloud cover was clean and clear. I was heading west on Chesapeake Avenue, which is on the north shore of Hampton Roads, and was near the intersection with La Salle Avenue. Although I was a front seat passenger in an old Dodge sedan, I had a practically unobstructed view of the southern Bay and entire Roads area, which I was scanning to inspect the cloud formation.

Looking back over the southern end of Chesapeake Bay, I was surprised to see a fat aluminum- or metallic-colored "fuselage" nearly the size of a small freighter, but shaped more like a dirigible, approaching from the rear. It was at an altitude of about 1000 feet and was following a path about parallel to the ship channel and parallel to Chesapeake Avenue. It was moving slowly, possibly 100 mph or a little more. When it was first seen it was a couple of miles back over the Bay in a front-to quartering view by which one could tell it was round in cross-section. I kept staring at this unusual object as it approached. It took about a minute to reach Fort Wool, which marks the beginning of the Roads. Its shape was clearly visible in good lighting, with its bright surface contrasting the darker cloud cover, and there was ample time to study it in changing perspective.

Puzzled, I asked the driver to look for a wing or other appendages to this strange vehicle. It looked like a big, pointed-nose dirigible, but had not even a tail surface as an appendage. The puzzling thing was that the big dirigibles had disappeared from the scene many years before; in fact, the big dirigible hanger at Langley Field had even been torn down. Had this been the Blimp, I could have read GOODYEAR, but it was much longer. The driver didn't take time to look, as there was some traffic.

Soon after passing the area of Fort Wool and Fort Monroe, and when it was about opposite La Salle Avenue, it began to accelerate very rapidly and at the same time to emit a straw-yellow, or pale flame-colored wake or plume, short at first but growing in length as the speed increased until it was nearly as long as the object. Also, when it started to accelerate it changed from a level path to an upward slanting path, making an angle of about 5 degrees with the horizontal. It passed us going at an astounding speed. It disappeared into the cloud layer opposite the Newport News coal-loading docks in what I estimated to be four seconds after the time it began to accelerate. The accelerating distance was measured by the car odometer to be 5 miles.

As discussed in Section II-C, if the acceleration was uniform, to cover 5 miles in 4 seconds with a 100 mph start means an acceleration of 100 times earth gravity and a speed at disappearance into the cloud layer of 8900 mph. But just as astounding as the performance figures was the silent operation. Not a sound was heard. This was surely a sophisticated performance, to make the understatement of the year.

EXAMPLE XII-A2

The second detailed example is of a spectacular UFO sighting from a ship at sea. The data is taken from an independent account of one of the passengers (Lorenzen, *Flying Saucers, The Startling Evidence,* 18) and extracts from the ship's log (Edwards 12).

On the night of June 30, 1947, the coastal steamer *Landovery Castle* was passing the Straights of Madagascar, off Kenya, en route from Mombassa to Cape Town, South Africa. The sighting occurred about 11:00 P.M. on a moonless, star-studded night. Mrs. A.M. King, who made the independent report, was in the bow with a lady companion when her attention was attracted to something approaching the ship very rapidly. A passenger strolling at the stern also became aware of an unusual blackness, blotting out many stars, that seemed to be getting larger, or approaching. He pointed this out to a deck officer who agreed and called a superior to the deck. Altogether, the events were witnessed by 9 passengers and 3 ship's officers.

By the time the object was alongside, it had slowed to the speed of the ship, and followed alongside, but standing off. As it arrived it beamed a powerful searchlight down on the water, and the object could quite clearly be seen in the light reflected from the water.

Mrs. King described it as a gigantic cigar-shaped vehicle made of steel, about four times as long as the

Landovery Castle and four times as high, about 50 yards to one side of the vessel and maintaining a height of 20 feet above the surface of the water. The ship's officers reported in the log that it was a gigantic dirigible-shaped craft about twice the size of the *Landovery Castle*, pacing them at a half mile off the starboard side. The latter estimate put the length at roughly 1000 feet. The log said that it was made of such a polished, reflecting material that it not only reflected the light from the water, but also the stars. It stayed alongside several minutes, making no discernable sound.

Mrs. King's account furnished the following additional valuable information. Just before the object left, it cut off the searchlight. "Fierce flames" issued from the rear, shooting out a distance of half its length as it gained speed, soundlessly disappearing in seconds. It seemed to Mrs. King that there must be something like a huge furnace inside, but she thought it strange that she could not hear the flames.

B. Discussion

These two accounts of large dirigible-like vehicles with fiery-looking wakes, which witnesses and rocket-thinking commentators alike have described as flaming exhausts, are by no means unique. The encounter of Eastern Airlines pilots Chiles and Whitted with such a vehicle in July 1948 while piloting a DC-3 near Montgomery, Alabama, is a famous and classic example of the same thing (Lorenzen, *UFO, The Whole Story*, 34). Chiles and Whitted reported that their plane was rocked by the "blast" as the object passed them, slanting upward and disappearing in seconds. They also reported that they heard nothing.

Of course, everyone is inclined to describe things in familiar terms, and now that the first steps have been made in space travel from earth utilizing rocketry, people are strongly inclined to be thinking in terms of rockets. The fact that witnesses report gigantic, silent "exhausts" is just one of the reasons that some members of the scientific community, who are obviously also "rocket-thinkers," cry "defying the laws of physics," and accordingly refuse to believe such reports. They all know that a large rocket taking off nearby makes an ear-splitting, body-shaking noise, and even a military turbojet engine with afterburner on makes a thunderous noise that can be heard for miles. In my opinion, if the scoffer would reserve his scorn and disbelief for the jet-propulsion explanation rather than for the sighting he would then be correct.

Here again we come to a place where the repulsive-force field together with the accompanying ionizing radiations come to the rescue of the witnesses' stories. Fields are nearly silent. Of course, for high forward acceleration the field is directed and sharply focused toward the rear, making all parts of the jigsaw puzzle fit together: the ionized flame-like wake, the surprising silence, the high acceleration performance, and even the fact that the plume grows in length with increasing speed which is uncharacteristic of a rocket. The vehicles' upward slant during acceleration described by Chiles and Whitted as well as by me probably has the significance that the force field is more effective when directed to intersect and push against a portion of the earth as well as the earth's atmosphere.

Even the witness on the ship was surprised at the silent operation. Mrs. King knew that large flames make distinctive sounds. Of course, the answer is that no flames shot out or she would have heard them. Various accounts of dirigible-shaped UFOs have erroneously reported large "rocket exhausts," yet no sound was heard. The UFO that I witnessed was of a size comparable to the Saturn (Apollo) rocket system and if the wake had been a rocket exhaust the roar could have been heard in North Carolina. All turbojet and rocket exhausts roar (in the atmosphere).

The turbojet roars partly because of combustion chamber noise and also because of the interaction of the high-speed jet with the surrounding atmosphere at the velocity discontinuity called the jet boundary. At the jet boundary high-energy vortices and turbulence produce screaming and roaring. Rocket jets roar for the same reasons, but louder because rocket jets are faster and more energetic. Rocket jets are also supersonic, and, never being perfectly expanded to atmospheric pressure, the jets are criss-crossed with shock waves converting kinetic energy to sound energy. From all this we may conclude that no silent UFO shoots out a propulsive jet. In the relatively silent world of UFOs that is a broad statement.

To think that a dirigible UFO wake is a flame is also erroneous. A flame is defined as a gaseous exothermal (heat producing) reaction. That means a flame is hot, and radiates enough energy in the infrared and visible spectrum to be readily noticed nearby. Yet numerous UFO close encounters fail to demonstrate appreciable or even noticeable heat radiation, even when a UFO "flames up" on coming to rest as in Example VII-B1. And had the giant luminous wake, estimated to be 500 feet long, seen from the *Landovery Castle* been high-temperature gas the witnesses should have felt and reported radiant energy. But they did not.

All the confusion has resulted from the fact that, hot or cold, an ionized plasma looks like a flame. The flame-colored appearance is due to the electrons of excited molecules dropping to lower vacant energy levels and emitting photons of visible light. This process is substantially independent of whether the gas is hot or cold, and, by the same token, substantially independent of how it was ionized, i.e., by chemical reaction (flame) or by hard radiation (UFO).

The flame-like (in appearance) wake of the dirigible-shaped UFO is just the air which has flown smoothly over the body and is flowing smoothly and silently into the wake. The air gets a shove backward by the tremendously strong propulsive force field, but there is no jet boundary or velocity discontinuity as in jet propulsion (because the field was a gradient, not a discontinuity) and therefore no noise. However, the propulsion system radiation ionizes the air that passes into the force field cone and makes it visible. Note how parallel this is to the saucer cone, as in Figure X-4, for example.

Aerodynamicists have a name for smooth, silent, loss-free flow. They call it *potential flow*. Subsonic flow of air over a dirigible whose axis is aligned with the airstream is an excellent approximation to potential flow. This was first demonstrated early in this century by a German scientist, G. Fuhrmann, who compared wind tunnel experiments on dirigible models with potential flow theory and found excellent correlation.

The wake that I saw (Example XII-A1) was axially symmetric and plume-shaped, growing in length with speed as would be expected from a relatively long ion-relaxation time. Its appearance is shown in Figure XII-1, together with rocket jets for comparison:

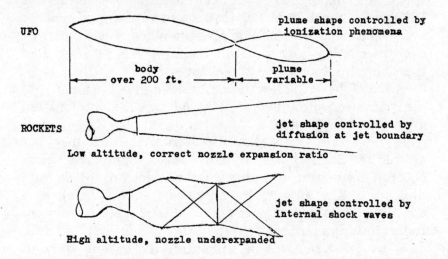

Figure XII-1. Dirigible-UFO Plume and Rocket Jets

Section XIII
Silent Supersonic Operation

"It was shaped like . . . a streamlined fat cigar. There was a red light on the front. The leading edge glowed red."
—Capt. Laurence Coyne,
Army helicopter pilot.

A. Supersonic Aerodynamics

Silent operation at supersonic speed is a more involved subject than we have dealt with in other sections and, to be meaningful, will have to be convincing to technical specialists. In order to establish the position that shock-free airflow about bodies moving through the atmosphere at supersonic speed should be possible with sufficiently advanced technology, the discussion will have to involve quantitative analysis. If this sounds like an apology, it is, but I will try to address the general reader to the extent possible. It is assumed that the reader has a nodding acquaintance with elementary algebraic representations; more complex analysis is put in the appendices.

Most of the energy loss at supersonic speed arises from what is called the *bow shock wave* (pronounced like the bow of a ship, from which the name is derived). In the central section this shock wave is shaped like the bow of the vehicle. It then extends outward and backward into a huge cone, so big that it often reaches the human ear and is recognized as a sonic boom. The elimination of the shock system is the heart of the problem. To have silent supersonic flight requires what the aerodynamicist calls potential flow—a loss-free flow, with no energy dissipated as shock or sound waves or in any other form. In the simplest case of potential flow, for low and medium subsonic speeds, the air is not much compressed and the applicable theory is called constant-density flow theory. Strangely, even paradoxically, constant-density potential flow theory is adequate to study the flow field in a region ahead of and around the UFO at supersonic speed because, as I soon discovered, the use of a force field to control the airflow can eliminate air compression as the air approaches the body.

In subsonic flow the pressure impulses from the vehicle travel ahead at sonic speed, letting the air know that the vehicle is coming. The air, feeling the pressure build up, is slowed accordingly, and even obligingly begins to move aside to let the vehicle pass in a phenomenon called streamline flow. The problem at supersonic speed is basically one of information. When the vehicle is advancing faster than the speed of sound, the air out front does not receive the incremental pressure signal to slow down, move aside, as in subsonic flow. The first signal the air receives is when it slams into the bow shock, suddenly converting the flow in the near vicinity of the nose to subsonic flow. Then, behind the shock wave, the air receives the pressure messages from the body, and obligingly moves around it.

By now the reader may have guessed the basic answer. The signal that the supersonic vehicle is coming will be given by a force field having a probable action velocity equal to the speed of light. There can then be no signal-speed problem as is normally the case. The air will be asked to slow down and move aside at all velocities, no matter how fast.

At this point a long story could be made short by stating, or claiming, that for all streamlined bodies the proper use of a force field to signal the air and persuade it to slow gradually would eliminate the shock system. What follows is a series of arguments to back up this statement. Additionally, it will be shown that if the force field is adjusted to give constant pressure and density around the entire body, potential loss-free flow will result and there can be no shockwaves anywhere in the flow field. In the meantime, the reader will doubtless assimilate something of the nature of force field controlled airflows, as compared to conventional airflows,

Perhaps because of his wind tunnel experience, the aerodynamicist uses a convention which in practice is normally contrary to the facts. He considers that a vehicle which moves with a velocity V_o is really standing still, and the undisturbed airstream is approaching the vehicle at the velocity V_o. In the discussions of aerodynamic theory which follow, this convention will be used.

B. Relation Between Pressure, Kinetic, and Field Energies

In ordinary, incompressible aerodynamic theory, the air approaching the vehicle is slowed down by the rise in air pressure encountered as it comes closer to the nose. The slowing may be seen as the direct result of the pressure gradient, which is the rise in pressure across unit volume of air, and this pressure rise or difference constitutes a force retarding the air. I have long held the belief that a force field could provide an equivalent force to retard the air by properly adjusting the field energy gradients to replace the aerodynamic forces. Thus, while the pressure gradient signalling system fails at supersonic speed, the force field system would not.

We digress to define stagnation point. For a symmetrical body of revolution, like a dirigible, cigar, ellipsoid, or football-shaped vehicle, whose long axis is aligned with the airstream, air coming in along the axis extended and slowing due to the rising pressure comes to a complete stop when it reaches the intersection of the axis with the body surface. For this reason that point is called the *stagnation point.*

It is very instructive to examine the problem in another way—that is, to apply the principle of energy conservation to the approaching airstream. In constant-density aerodynamic theory, the ratio of pressure to density, p/ρ represents the pressure energy per unit mass of air. The kinetic energy per unit mass of air is half the square of the velocity, $V^2/2$. Applying the conservation principle, for every incremental increase in pressure energy there is an equal incremental decrease in kinetic energy, or, symbolically, for each increase in p/ρ there is an equal decrease in $V^2/2$. This is true for large changes as well as small. The change in pressure energy to free-stream pressure energy, p_o/ρ, and the change in kinetic energy to free-stream kinetic energy, $V_o^2/2$, the increase in pressure energy equals the decrease in kinetic energy, symbolically stated:

$$\frac{p - p_o}{\rho} = \frac{V_o^2}{2} - \frac{V^2}{2} \qquad (13\text{-}1)$$

At the stagnation point where $V = 0$, this becomes

$$P_s = P_o + \rho\frac{V_o^2}{2} \qquad (13\text{-}1a)$$

which means that the stagnation pressure is equal to the free-stream atmospheric pressure plus a term called free-stream dynamic pressure because it is convertible to pressure in conventional aerodynamics. Such pressures can run high.

Before comparing force field theory to ordinary aerodynamic theory, let me mention that I was prepared to employ, if necessary, shaped or focused force fields for use in airflow control, just as is necessary for force field propulsion theory. However, when I reviewed the requirements for flow control, it became evident that spherically symmetrical fields should do the job. Accordingly, spherically symmetrical fields are all that are considered. Other field shapes are obtainable by using a distribution of spherically symmetrical fields, or field centers. If φ_1 and φ_2 represent the field energies of 2 separate spherical fields, by superposition the total field energy is $\varphi = \varphi_1 + \varphi_2$, which is nonspherical. For the moment we shall consider only a single spherical inverse-square force field. The fields considered are repulsive and attractive force fields which act on the air because the air has mass, but if the reader prefers to think of the field as an electrical field which acts on an electrified atmosphere, any other combination, the theory is the same.

Let us now review the nature of a spherically symmetric repulsive force field. The field potential energy at any point P in the field, φ_p equals the amount of energy necessary to bring unit mass from far away (infinity) to the point P. Owing to the symmetry of the field, the path followed doesn't matter, or the energy, φ_p, depends only on the location of P. The field potential energy varies inversely with the radial distance of P from the field center and may be represented symbolically by $\varphi_p = K/r_p$. Here K is a field-energy constant and r_p is the distance of P from the field center. The slope or gradient of φ with respect to r is the field force on unit mass (of anything) and is equal to $F = -K/r^2$, or the force varies inversely with the square of the distance to the field center, the minus sign signifying repulsion.

Earlier we discussed the equivalence of pressure field and force field by relating pressure gradient to field force (now more neatly stated as the equivalence of pressure-energy gradient to field-energy gradient in controlling airflow). We now consider their equivalence on a total energy basis, which is closely related. In pressure-field-controlled aerodynamics, an increase in pressure energy is accompanied by an equal decrease in kinetic energy. In force-field-controlled aerodynamics, an increase in field energy as the air approaches the field center is accompanied by an equal decrease in kinetic energy, assuming for the moment that air pressure remains constant.

Ahead of the body where the flow is supersonic, the pressure signals are not coming through, and the equivalence of force field energy change to kinetic energy change (as just stated) satisfies energy conservation. For simplicity of ideas, consider for the moment a single repulsive force field centered at r = 0, and of potential energy $\varphi = K/r$. At a great distance away (r very large) the value of φ may be taken as zero, but its value may be large at small values of r. Because of the zero value of φ at great distance, the increase of φ from far to near is the near value minus the far value (minus zero) or just K/r. To comply with energy conservation, this increase in K/r is equated to the decrease in kinetic energy giving

$$\frac{K}{r} = \frac{V_o^2}{2} - \frac{V^2}{2} \qquad (13\text{-}2)$$

Note the similarity of this equation to equation 13-1 for the pressure controlled case. At the stagnation point $V = 0$ and $r = r_s$, or

$$\frac{K}{r_s} = \frac{V_o^2}{2} \qquad (13\text{-}2a)$$

gives the value of K needed to stop the air at the stagnation point. With this value of K the field absorbs all the kinetic energy; there is no energy left for a pressure rise, our first result. Air arrives at the stagnation point at atmospheric pressure.

For complete real-body cases the energy distribution needed would be more complex, and φ would be represented by a group of K/r terms, some positive, some negative, but all zero at large r's. Equation (13-2) is then written

$$\varphi = \frac{V_o^2}{2} - \frac{V^2}{2} \qquad (13\text{-}3)$$

at the stagnation point

$$\varphi_s = \frac{V_o^2}{2} \qquad (13\text{-}3a)$$

and again there is no energy available for a pressure rise. These equations are important to field-control theory and are used repeatedly.

From equations (13-2) and (13-3) it is seen that K/r and φ have the dimensions of velocity squared, while inverse square force terms represented by $-K/r^2$ for repulsion force per unit mass and K/r^2 for attraction have units of acceleration. It is therefore perfectly proper to think of these fields as acceleration fields, and I often use the terms *acceleration field* and *force field* interchangeably. The possible kinship of this theory with warped-gravity theory also becomes apparent.

C. Corroboration

A nice corroboration of these basic ideas was obtained when I reviewed some old textbooks on fluid mechanics and aerodynamics, such as Tietjens' *Fundamentals of Hydro and Aeromechanics* and Kaufmann's *Fluid Mechanics*. Apparently as far back as Euler, whose differential equations of fluid motion form the basis of theoretical fluid mechanics, the equations of fluid motion were set up containing what they called a body force F per unit mass of fluid, that is due to the direct action of conservative force field. Presumably they had the gravitational field of the earth in mind, but no mention is made of this until they come to hydraulic applications, and the equations allow for the inclusion of an inverse-square repulsive force field as well as any other.

On page 118 of *Fundamentals of Hydro and Aeromechanics*, for example, Tietjens could have been discussing the UFO problem when he said, "We postulate the existence of a force function, φ, for the body force, F, so that F equals gradient of φ." Tietjens then integrates Euler's differential equations of motion along a streamline to obtain the following steady-state, constant-density result, derived originally by Daniel Bernoulli in 1738 and named after him:

$$\frac{V^2}{2} + P + \varphi = \frac{V_o^2}{2} + P_o \tag{13-4}$$

The subscripts, o, refer to initial values, which in our case are free-stream values. The symbols are the same as we have been using except that P stands for the ratio of pressure to density, p/ρ, or the pressure energy per unit mass of fluid. Across the centuries, the message to us from Daniel Bernoulli in the form of equation (13-4) is that pressure energy and field potential energy, P and φ, can be interchanged on a one-to-one basis. They may be used together as shown, or if either one is zero the other can take over. This is the corroboration.

The hydraulic application, for which Bernoulli is best known, is made by letting φ in (13-4) equal gz, where g is the acceleration of gravity and z is an elevation above an arbitrary datum. Then gz is the gravitational energy of the water at elevation z.

Letting $P = p/\rho$, making a few algebraic manipulations, and representing free-stream dynamic pressure by its standard symbol q_o gives the following nondimensional form of the equation, handier for applications.

$$\left(\frac{V}{V_o}\right)^2 + \frac{P - P_o}{q_o} + \frac{\varphi}{V_o^2 / 2} = 1 \qquad (13\text{-}4a)$$

In the field air-control theory for the UFO we represent complex field shapes by summing the individual potentials $\varphi_1 + \varphi_2 + \varphi_3$ etc. due to a number of elementary spherical fields whose individual centers have a spacial distribution and whose individual strength coefficients are K_1, K_2, K_3, etc. Then, with r_1 being the distance from field center (1) to any point in the airstream, r_2 the distance from field center (2) to the same point in the stream, etc., we have for that airstream point (ellipses mean *and so on*):

$$\varphi = \varphi_1 + \varphi_2 + \varphi_3 + \dots$$

$$= \frac{K_1}{r_1} + \frac{K_2}{r_2} + \frac{K_3}{r_3} + \dots$$

$$\varphi = \Sigma \frac{K}{r} \qquad (13\text{-}4b)$$

where Σ is mathematical language meaning "the sum of."

With this symbology and meaning, equation (13-4a) becomes

$$\left(\frac{V}{V_o}\right)^2 + \frac{P - P_o}{q_o} + \frac{\Sigma K/r}{V_o^2 / 2} = 1 \qquad (13\text{-}4c)$$

The first term is the fraction of free-stream kinetic energy existing as local kinetic energy, the second term, called "delta p over q," is the fraction of the same energy stored by any pressure rise, and the third term is the fractional energy stored by the field as field energy.

With a perfect field design the field absorbs the whole reduction of kinetic energy so that the pressure everywhere remains at p_o and the second term of (13-4c) drops out. Equation (13-4c) then gives us a powerful and sweeping method for specifying the field distribution and therefore the field design for constant-pressure, constant-density airflow. Letting $p = p_o$, and rearranging,

$$\varphi = \Sigma \frac{K}{r} = \frac{V_o^2}{2}\left[1 - \frac{V^2}{V_o^2}\right] \tag{13-5}$$

While this equation is general, specific consideration will only be given to UFOS which are bodies of revolution such as dirigibles, ellipsoids, and spheres. How to obtain V for equation (13-5) will be discussed in what follows.

D. Significance of Acceleration-Field Flow Control

Now for the surprise! With flow at constant pressure the density must be constant. But it is shown in Appendix 3 that for constant-density potential flow over a given body shape there is only one possible flow pattern. This means that for many UFO shapes we already know V/V_o from incompressible flow theory, often thought of as subsonic theory. If UFOs use this method of flow control, nullifying the pressure field around the entire body by equivalent acceleration-field energy, then the supersonic flow over a UFO is cast in the same mold as our old and well-known friend the subsonic flow field for the same body shape. While the streamlines and V/V_o are the same, supersonic values of V_o result in V also being supersonic over much of the flowfield. All this means there is a great store of conventional potential flow theory to draw on for establishing V/V_o, the required φ, and the $\Sigma K/r$ to do the job. The design of the field $\varphi = \Sigma K/r$ gets into detailed design involving considerable mathematics and is discussed in Appendix

3. The methodology for such a design is given there and illustrated.

If UFOs faithfully follow this idealized system, there is no room for doubt about the elimination of supersonic shockwaves. The essence of a shockwave is an abrupt increase in pressure, density, and temperature. In a constant-pressure, compression-free zone there is no shockwave. In fact, such a UFO would create no pressure waves at all, either of compression or expansion. This is more than can be said for aircraft, even at subsonic speed. Instead, the UFO sends out its force field (acceleration field) which would be interpreted by stationary objects as a wave of force.

There is another interesting point about acceleration-field flow control. Drops of moisture or rain, dust, insects, or other low-velocity objects of any kind would follow the streamline paths around a high-speed UFO rather than smash into it. Particles on the central streamline which reaches the stagnation point are brought smoothly to a stop without impact. Theoretically, a fly on this central streamline could put his feet forward and land on the nose, but he couldn't stick because the field is insistent that everything moves along on schedule. If the UFO compromised the plan and used only a single repulsive field center to eliminate or reduce the intensity of a bow shock, then particles in the airstream would no longer follow the streamlines but would fly off to the side on a hyperbolic path, just as a high-speed electron does when it approaches an isolated proton. These aspects may have practical significance relative to surface erosion. Even with sand in the air, the UFO surfaces would not be sandblasted.

The air-control field is a conservative field. It stores air kinetic energy as the air approaches and slows, but passes the energy back in other areas as it speeds the flow up again. Finally, the air leaves with the same velocity it had initially, and, in theory, at no cost to the UFO. The action is slightly similar to a mass being stopped by a spring, and rebounding with its initial velocity.

The remainder of this section will be devoted mainly to some possible practical variations of the method that has been described and to the illustration of results for specific cases. The question should also be asked: Is an altogether different method for airflow control possible?

E. Slender Nose Investigation, Simplest Possible Field Control

In my first investigation of an alternate variation of airflow control, I attempted to solve the problem in reverse: to shape the body and aerodynamics to fit the simplest flow-control field. Could a nose shape be designed for which a single spherical repulsive field would eliminate the bow shockwave? It seemed to me that a slender nose would be the best, and this coincided with some slender-nosed dirigible sightings, including mine, so this seemed a good choice.

Consider two equivalent flows over the same nose shape, one controlled by a pressure field $(p-p_o)/q_o$ of equation (13-4c) with $\Sigma K/r = 0$, and the other controlled by a single force field of energy distribution $(K/r)/V_o^2/2$ with $p-p_o = 0$. Solving (13-4c) for V/V_o for the two cases, first for pressure control, gives

$$\frac{V}{V_o} = \sqrt{1 - \frac{(p-p_o)}{q_o}}$$

(13-4d)

and for the single repulsive field

$$\frac{V}{V_o} = \sqrt{\frac{1 - (K/r)}{V_o^2/2}}$$

(13-4e)

If the velocity ratio computed by (13-4e) corresponds to that of conventional theory, (13-4d), the force field is doing a perfect job and the pressure difference $p-p_o$ has been nulled to zero. Conversely, if the velocity ratios are not equal, p is not equal to p_o.

This simple velocity-ratio comparison test, which I dubbed the "velocity match," was my first step in the dark in the investigation of the field-control problem.

Equation (13-4d) is usually used to find the pressure variation from the velocity ratio and was introduced here to clarify ideas. Actually, the nose shape and its constant-density (subsonic) V/V_o, is developed from conventional potential-flow theory derived for the purpose discussed in Appendix 3.

The nose shape developed and three streamlines are shown to scale in Figure XIII-1. The nose is a body of revolution about its axis of symmetry, and of course the flow around it is three-dimensional. The top and bottom streamlines are mirror images and together form a typical 3-D streamtube of air with axial symmetry. The air within a streamtube is trapped, and no flow crosses its boundary. The other streamline lies on the axis of symmetry ahead of the nose, which at the stagnation point branches out into the body contour, the longitudinal elements of which are also streamlines.

The line source referred to on the figure (one of the tricks of conventional aerodynamics) has a length, T, and runs along the nose centerline from the point 0.0 to the point 1.0 of the horizontal axis. Note that the front end of the line source is the center of the coordinate system, and lies 0.01 T behind the point of the nose.

In the comparisons to follow, T will have a length of 50 ft., corresponding to a big dirigible UFO. The field center will also be located at the coordinate center, 0.0, now 1/2 foot behind the point of the nose. For supersonic flow with force field control, the free-stream air speed is taken as 2000 ft/sec, and the field- strength constant, K in equation (13-4e), is $K = 1,640,000$ ft^3/sec^2 to make the supersonic and subsonic velocity ratios match over the widest area. The V/V_o for incompressible (subsonic) flow is taken from equation (A3-16) of Appendix 3.

The resulting velocity ratios along the streamlines are shown in Figure XIII-2, which is a plot of V/V_o against axial distance in feet from the coordinate center. For conventional flow calculations, the solid line gives V/V_o, along the axis, and the dashed line the values along the other streamlines (streamtube). The circle and triangle symbols give the matching force-field-controlled values of V/V_o.

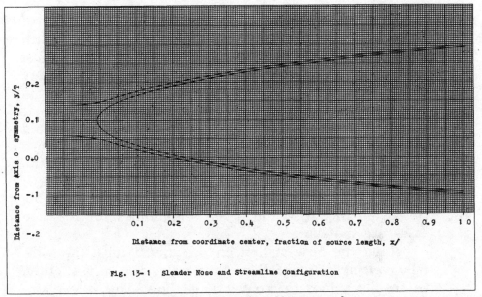

Fig. 13-1 Slender Nose and Streamline Configuration

Figure XIII-1. Slender Nose and Streamline Configuration.

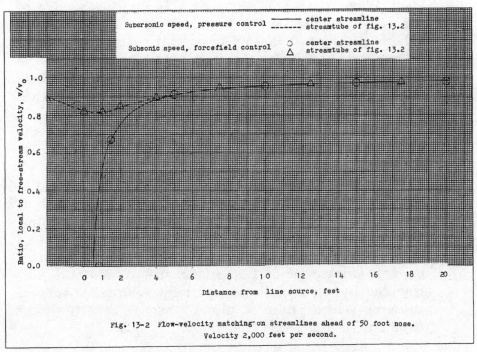

Fig. 13-2 Flow-velocity matching on streamlines ahead of 50 foot nose.
Velocity 2,000 feet per second.

Figure XIII-2. Flow-velocity matching on streamlines ahead of 50-foot nose. Velocity 2,000 feet per second.

In general, the match is impressive. For stations ahead of the stagnation point (at the 1/2-foot station) the match looks nearly perfect. In the entire flowfield there is just one appreciable discrepancy. Owing to the arbitrary choice of K the force field appears to bring the flow to rest 4 inches ahead of the nose, forming a tiny dead-air region. (If such should actually happen this region would probably be highly ionized, looking like a neon light.)

The purpose of this simple control is to prevent the bow shockwave in the region ahead of the nose. This it certainly does, as indicated by the flow-match. Matching flow velocities also mean the streamlines for the two cases are the same.

Behind the nose station on the stream tube, the force field velocity ratios fall progressively, but very slightly, below the values for conventional flow. This is explainable in that by placing $p-p_o$ equal to zero in equation (13-4c) we have assumed the pressures to remain constant. Where the small discrepancy begins, at the side of the body, the pressure is beginning to fall below atmospheric pressure as the air speeds up again. This was to be expected. To make the flow velocities match everywhere would require the addition of more field centers on the nose axis, and could easily be done for this case with the methods I have now developed. But the results of this first investigation were so favorable, meeting the objective, that we shall "let well enough alone" and rest the case.

While this simple example demonstrates the acceleration-field elimination of a bow shockwave, perhaps it is just as important to realize that matching velocity ratios also give substantiation to the general theorem (developed and first presented here) that UFOs which maintain constant-pressure flow at supersonic speeds are surrounded by a subsonic flow-pattern of streamlines, and subsonic velocity ratios. Naturally such a flow is shock-free. This is the broad viewpoint.

F. Airflow Over a Spherical UFO

THE PROBLEM: AERODYNAMICS OF THE SPHERE

The sphere is a bluff aerodynamic body, not a body that could be called streamlined. All streamlined bodies have tapered afterbodies with a length of several diameters. The sphere, with its length equal to its breadth, has a blunt afterbody. As a result, the airflow separates from the afterbody, creating a broad turbulent wake at all speeds. This gives it a high drag even at subsonic speed. At supersonic speeds, its blunt shape gives it an exceptionally strong bow shockwave, and it also carries a strong stern shockwave, or trailing shock, originating about where the flow separation takes place.

At subsonic speeds, the speed of the local airflow alongside where its width equals the diameter (the sphere's equator, taking the stagnation point as the north pole) is half again that of flight speed, giving it a negative pressure around that circumference of $-1.25 \, q_o$ compared to a positive pressure at the stagnation point of $+1.0 \, q_o$. This is a severe pressure distribution. In short, the sphere has bad conventional aerodynamics and offers the UFO a challenge to improve the aerodynamics as well as eliminate the shockwaves.

THE SOLUTION

The spherical UFO can solve its flow problems by generating the necessary acceleration fields. The field generators must be physically located within the UFO to meet the requirement of rotational symmetry about the sphere diameter aligned with the airstream. This diameter will be called the axis of rotational symmetry. Fore-and-aft symmetry is also observed, meaning that all systems and fields in the rear half are mirror images of systems and fields in the front half. Ideally, the field generating systems would be located just within the spherical shell, with capacity distributed and strength adjusted to give the required field. In theory the field generators could be distributed along the axis of symmetry to meet symmetry requirements, but this location might have practical drawbacks.

The field requirement given by the value of φ from equation (13-5) is perfectly general, applying to the sphere as well as any other shape. The equations needed to give velocity ratio, V/V_o, anywhere in the sphere's flowfield are derived from potential flow theory and given as equations (A3-6a, 6b, and 6c) of Appendix 3. The resulting velocity ratios and the required values of acceleration field potential φ computed from equation (13-5) are given in Table A3-1 for the nine typical flowfield points illustrated in Figure A3-2 (see Appendix 3). It is more convenient and general to give φ in its nondimensional form $\varphi/\left(v_o^2/2\right)$, and φ is so given in the last column of Table A3-1. The nine points serve for illustration, but a few more are needed to adequately describe the field. If the field generators meet requirements at an adequate number of points in the flowfield they have accomplished the task.

Appendix 3, part C, describes the mathematical procedure for laying out a system of spherical field centers on the axis of symmetry, each of proper strength. This may be considered as a mathematical equivalent to a real distribution of field generators within the shell, just as in aerodynamic theory the distribution of sources and sinks on the axis of symmetry are mathematical equivalents to the real thing. (No one would think air really flows from an aerodynamic source.) This field layout has nine field centers to exactly satisfy the field strengths specified at the nine illustrative points of Figure A3-2. Part C also gives the values of the nine strength coefficients to illustrate procedure. Five are positive and four negative. Part E of Appendix 3 presents the equation (A3-9) describing the streamlines for the resulting controlled flow over a sphere at supersonic speed.

Figure XIII-3(a) shows the computed streamlines for the flow over a sphere at supersonic speeds with acceleration-field (force field) control. The corresponding figure (b) shows the bow and trailing shockwaves, flow separation, and resulting broad turbulent wake normally encountered by a sphere in supersonic flight (Russian manned space capsule re-entering, or cannonball). The mechanism of flow separation is that the higher pressure in the aft region leaks forward toward lower pressures in that part of the boundary layer close to the body where the flow is subsonic and the resulting steep pressure rise stalls the low-speed boundary layer air. The stalled air piles up in the flow-separation phenomenon, creating a large dead-air region which becomes a turbulent wake.

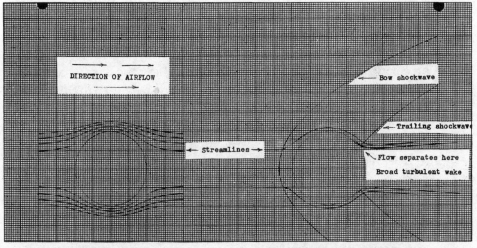

(a) **UFO With Airflow Control.**
   No shockwave system;
   Streamlines, drawn to scale,
      are speed-variant;
   No separated-flow region;
   Small turbulent wake;
   Very low drag.

(b) **Space Capsule or Cannonball.**
   Strong shockwave system;
   Streamlines vary with speed;
   Flow separates on stern, causing
   Large turbulent wake;
   Very high drag.

Figure XIII-3. Flow over spherical bodies at supersonic speed with and without acceleration-field airflow control.

It is now no secret why the constant-pressure flow over the UFO cures the stalling of the air in the boundary layer and the flow separation. The unfavorable rising pressure region is eliminated and the constant-pressure control has changed the bluff body into a streamlined body as if by magic. The base of an artillery shell creates a turbulent wake which in part accounts for its noisy passing. Spherical UFOs are not reported to make this noise.

The acceleration-field air control accelerates the air around the body in a subsonic pattern at all speeds. Mach-1 no longer has any significance with this control. The body is surrounded by a potential flow at all speeds. The field strengths required vary exactly as $V^2/2$. That is why φ is presented as $\varphi/(v_o^2/2)$. No adjustment of field strength is required for the changes in air density with altitude because accelerations remain unchanged.

A grain of sand or a small insect will follow the streamline path of Figure 13-3(a). They will not centrifuge out of the air path as in pressure-controlled flow (windshield wipers not needed). To imagine that the air and insect are hurled around like a roller coaster on a track is misleading, for if the insect is small enough that it doesn't feel the difference in acceleration between one part of its body and another it won't feel anything. It is on a free-fall path like a satellite in orbit.

The particular streamline paths of Figure 13-3(a) are the natural paths, for if the field is adjusted to encourage some other paths constant-density air won't fit in the streamtubes and must be compressed and expanded in different parts of the flow, causing changes in air pressure to occur, and shifts in the streamlines. (Such a flow is then partly pressure-controlled and free-fall trajectories no longer coincide with the streamlines.) The changes in air pressure re-introduce the possibility of a shockwave somewhere in the flow. Such flows must be inspected for shockwaves on an individual basis.

In the following discussions of the flow over ellipsoidal bodies of revolution, we will consider a case with very large changes of pressure in the flow.

G. Aerodynamic Control for Ellipsoidal UFOs

GEOMETRY

The ellipsoidal UFO is one which looks roughly like an egg or a football. The ellipsoid has three axes, a major axis and two minor axes at right angles, which are equal. An ellipsoid may be generated by revolving an ellipse about its major axis, which is the axis of rotational symmetry. According to most UFO reports, ellipsoidal UFOs travel with the long axis pointed into the wind. The ellipticity depends on the ratio of the long to the short axes. When the ellipticity is zero, the axes are equal, and this member of the family is a sphere.

THEORETICAL FORCE FIELD ARRANGEMENTS

As for the sphere, the energy distribution centers for the surrounding acceleration field might be located just within the shell, and would have fore and aft symmetry as well as rotational symmetry about the long axis. However, as with the sphere, we introduce a conceptual equivalent with spherical field centers on the axis of rotational symmetry as in Figure XIII-4. In general, more field centers than the three illustrated are needed to obtain an approximation to constant-pressure flow, but this simple diagram serves as an aid in discussing some of the physical principles involved. Field centers (1) and (3) are equal repulsive centers and center (2) is negative, or an attractive center. Clearly, we assume the UFO builders have appropriate field technology.

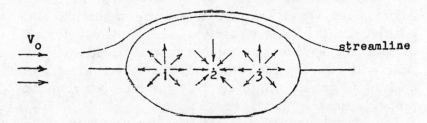

Figure XIII-4. Simplified field arrangement for ellipsoidal UFO.

The three fields provide the following air-control functions:

No. (1), repulsive force field
  a. Stops flow at forward stagnation point

b. Slows all oncoming air
c. Turns air outward to go around body
d. Returns energy to leaving air
e. Strongly tends to lower pressure at vehicle sides (adverse effect)

No. (2), attraction force field
a. Turns air around body
b. Maintains air pressure in central region, counteracting the opposite effects of (1) and (3)
c. Maintains flow density, limiting velocity increases

No. (3), repulsive force field
a. Slows air near stern
b. Turns air parallel to body axis
c. Maintains stern pressure near p_0
d. Speeds air to free-stream velocity as it leaves

In principle, this field arrangement seems an ideal one. With a few more positive and negative field centers, the ideal constant-pressure field control could be installed in a straightforward manner. But what if the UFO designers could not supply negative force fields? Or suppose they placed a premium on having the air-control field exert no acceleration forces on the passengers. Let us suppose that both these stipulations are in force. The first stipulation means we are reduced to the use of the two equal positive fields. These two alone can probably eliminate the bow shockwave, but without negative fields the pressure will go very low alongside the ellipsoid and our analysis is grossly complicated by the occurrence of compressible flow.

The second stipulation is easy to meet by proper design, which distributes the field sources uniformly just within the shell, so that the field potential at the shell is constant. With the shell potential constant, borrowing from electric-potential theory which is exactly the same, the force potential everywhere in the UFO would be constant and the force on passengers and internal equipment would be zero. (This follows from the fact that accelerations are the field potential gradient, which is zero.)

For our two equivalent spherical fields centered on the axis of symmetry (a fictitious but highly useful mathematical construction) the specification of a constant-potential shell is the simple statement

$$\varphi = \frac{K}{r_1} + \frac{K}{r_2} = \text{constant} \qquad (13\text{-}6)$$

where the two K's are equal, r_1 is the distance from the first field center to any point on the shell, and r_2 is the distance from the second field center to the same point on the shell. This equation specifies the shell shape (not an exact ellipsoid). For the shape specified, the equation can be used to determine the value of φ anywhere in the flowfield by letting r_1 and r_2 be the radii to any point in question. This is necessary for flow study.

HOW TO LAY OUT A CONSTANT-SURFACE-POTENTIAL UFO

A constant-potential UFO surface of revolution corresponding to a pair of force field centers on axis can be laid out utilizing equation (13-6) and a compass in a 1-2-3 procedure as follows:

(1) Lay out a longitudinal centerline and cross it with an axis D-D having, to some scale, a length equal to the desired UFO diameter. Lay out two force field centers on the longitudinal axis, equidistant from the axis D-D. The distance chosen determines the ellipticity. Compute r_D by the Pythagorean theorem. For example, let semi-diameter = 4 meters, field centers at ±3 meters.

$$r_D = \sqrt{3^2 + 4^2} = 5 \text{ meters}$$

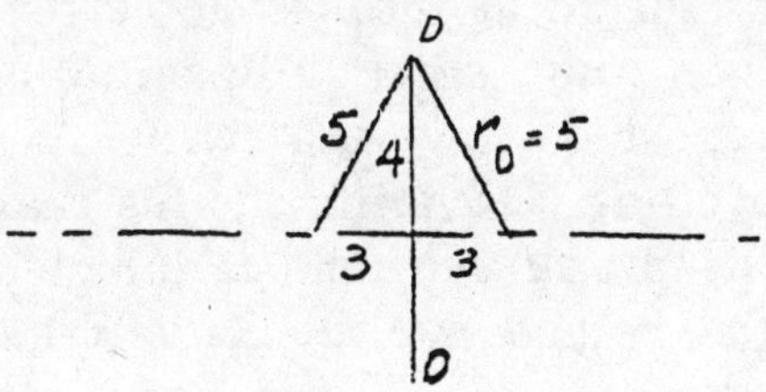

Figure XIII-5.

(2) Choose a nominal surface half potential, say $\varphi_s/2 = 10$. Then since $\varphi_s/2 = K/r_D$,

$$K = \frac{r_D \varphi_s}{2} = (5)(10) = 50$$

Now compute the stagnation radius:

$$\varphi_s = \frac{50}{r_s} + \frac{50}{(r_s + 6)} = 20$$

from which $r_s = 3.405$, and the major axis length is

$$L = 2r_s + 6 = 12.81 \text{ meters}$$

(3) Choose a series of equally spaced potentials with a half-step at either end, such as 5.5, 6, 7, 8, 9, 10, 11, 12, 13, 14, 14.5, and compute r for each from $r = K/\varphi = 50/\varphi$:

φ	5.5	6	7	8	9	10	11	12	13	14	14.5
r	9.09	8.33	7.14	6.25	5.55	5.00	4.55	4.17	3.85	3.50	3.45

Draw a series of partial circles using these radii and both field centers as centers. Label each arc with its value of φ, as 10, and 10 for the two circles drawn with a radius of 5. These two intersect where $\varphi = 20$. Where circles 10+1 and 10-1 intersect gives $\varphi = 11+ 9 = 20$, 12+ 8 = 20, etc. Clearly the intersections are on the desired equipotential surface.

The resulting constant potential surface is shown in Figure XIII-6. It is not a true ellipsoid because the sum of the focal radii is not constant. However, it does look like some small ellipsoidal-class UFOs that have been reported hovering with the long axis in a vertical attitude. Hovering in this manner seems to indicate that the propulsive field is oriented toward one end, and that the vehicle would convert its attitude by nearly 90 degrees for high-speed horizontal flight.

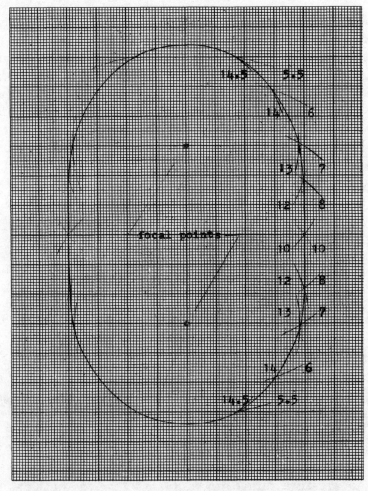

Figure XIII-6. Constant-Potential-Surface Layout

Data: Construction arcs are drawn from focal points (force field centers). Paired numbers give the potential of constructing arcs. Paired numbers add to 20, the nominal surface potential.

COMPRESSIBLE FLOW AROUND ELLIPSOIDAL UFOs

The energy equation for compressible (variable-density) flow for force field control is derived from first principles in Appendix 4 and is given by equation (A4-10). This equation corresponds to the Bernoulli equation for constant-density flow. If the force field were left on when a UFO came to a stop, the force field would pump a low atmospheric pressure in its vicinity, lowest at the surface where φ is highest. The corresponding value of pressure ratio without airflow will be called the static pressure ratio; it may be obtained by putting $V/V_o = 0$ in equation (A4-10), or by using equation (A4-5), which was derived for the purpose. For a constant potential UFO surface, the normal value of φ_s corresponds to $V_o^2/2$ [equation (13-3)] and c_o in equation (A4-5) is the speed of sound in undisturbed air which is approximately 1116 ft/sec. Some typical values of φ_s and the corresponding static pressure ratios, p_s/p_o, at the surface are here given:

Static Pressure Ratios at UFO Surface

V_o, ft/sec	$\varphi_s = V_o^2/2$	p_s/p_o (Eq. A4-5)
1500	1,125,000	0.2082
2000	2,000,000	0.0274

The pressure ratios away from the surface are also obtained by the same equation using the K/r's.

The ram-pressure effects in front of the UFO traveling at supersonic speeds keep the pressure ratio near 1.0, but for reasons explained in Appendix 4, parts C and D, the pressure ratios gradually fall toward the sides to values close to the static-pressure ratios. As the air moves to the side in a streamline path, the pressure ratio at some point becomes equal to the static-pressure ratio and a comparison of equations (A4-10) and (A4-5) shows that where this happens the local velocity is exactly back to the free-stream velocity, V_o. Thus we see that the force field does not prevent the air from moving by the vehicle at supersonic speeds. If the flow alongside were slow (as claimed by magnetic-field-flow-control advocates and others) there would be a gigantic blockage of the airflow.

EXAMINATION FOR SHOCKWAVES

Flow around the sides at the mid-body offers no problem with respect to shockwaves. The reason can be tied to a divergence of the Mach lines as shown at points a in Figure XIII-7. (Note: A Mach line represents a weak pressure wave traveling at sound speed in a supersonic flow, and swept back at an angle which makes the component of supersonic velocity normal to the wave equal Mach 1.)

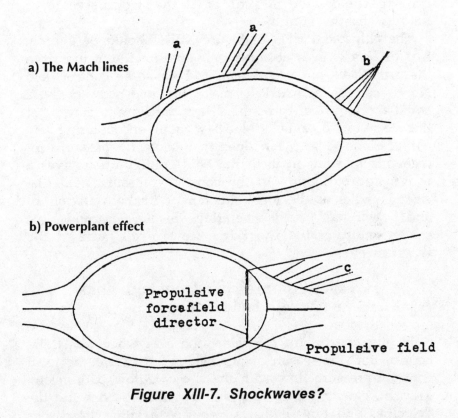

Figure XIII-7. Shockwaves?

The divergence of Mach lines is accepted in aeronautical circles as a sign of shock-free flow. To judge a flow by the Mach lines, just remember that the faster the flow the more the Mach line is inclined or swept back, so that a flow which is speeding up tends to be stable according to this criterion. Conversely, converging Mach lines as at b indicate trouble. If the flow at b is going against a pressure buildup, each Mach line represents a small compression, and by converging they form a trailing shockwave. Without aid from the propulsive force field the flow around a constant-surface-potential ellipsoid or sphere would probably shock at b.

Figure XIII-7(b) shows the effect of the propulsive force field. When the flow comes into the domain of the propulsive field, it is strongly accelerated and the converging compression lines at b are changed to nonconverging expansion lines as at c. The result is that a trailing shockwave is avoided if the propulsive force field is strong enough.

The ellipsoidal UFO of Figure XIII-4 should be entirely free of shockwaves at supersonic speed without aid from the propulsive force field. This is because air-control field No. 2 can be adjusted to make the mid-body pressure equal to freestream pressure. Then the flow is slowed at the stern by force field No. 3 without encountering any compression. The Mach lines then have no pressure increments to sum. In fact, this field configuration gives a rough approximation to the constant-pressure field discussed earlier as the ideal situation. With both air-control and power plant fields operating, this UFO should have exceptionally stable shock-free flow in all parts of the flowfield.

H. Exact Compressible-Flow Equations with Field Control

Finally, we briefly reconsider the case where the flow-control, for one reason or another, fails to yield the ideal constant-pressure flow with the subsonic-flow pattern and known velocity ratios. It is still possible to compute the velocities and flow paths, as well as the fluid properties of pressure, density, and temperature throughout the flowfield by numerical methods. However, the conventional differential equations for compressible flow must be extended to include the proper force field terms. This I have done.

In Appendix 4, part C, are developed the complete differential equations for the acceleration-controlled airflow about any body of revolution which moves with its axis of symmetry aligned with the airflow (goes the way it is pointed). Technically, the flow analyzed is axisymmetric, compressible, potential flow in a space with an arbitrary acceleration field. The theory contains three systems of equations (continuity, gas law, and energy) which are combined into a single equation suitable for solution by standard, but advanced, numerical methods and computer technology. The methods are similar to those necessary when no acceleration field is present.

Postscript: Is There a Possible Alternate to Acceleration Fields?

It is reasonable to ask if there is a possible alternate to acceleration-field control of airflow for silent supersonic operation. If UFOs had the incredible ability to de-mass matter in their vicinity, including air, the answer would have to be yes, for if the UFO could neutralize the mass of the surrounding air the speed of sound would be raised to a high value while at the same time the deviations from atmospheric pressure due to air dynamics would be negligible, and the air would follow the well-known subsonic, shock-free flow pattern illustrated elsewhere in this Section. However, there is next to nothing in this century's science to indicate such a possibility.

Speculation about zero mass is encouraged by reports that automobiles, animals, and even humans have been floated above ground level by UFOs. But such levitations could be accomplished by a counterfield to the earth gravity field and do not constitute convincing evidence that mass is controlled.

Section XIV
The Aerodynamic Heating of UFOs

A. The Problem as Seen by Earth Technicians

For many years technical people have been astounded by and often incredulous of reports of UFO speeds of 5000 miles per hour or more, as reported in Section II. How could they travel at such speeds without burning up, or even showing severe signs of heating? Perhaps today, with the accumulated experience of projects Mercury, Gemini, Apollo, and the Shuttle they may be less inclined to be surprised and skeptical. Still, surfaces of the Shuttle reach a blinding-white heat, of the order of 1300 degrees centigrade or 2300 degrees Fahrenheit, while UFOs apparently do not. Why is this?

Of course the aerodynamic technician's and material expert's viewpoints are colored by experience. The flight technologies needed for the projects mentioned above took years of intensive research and development. Earth vehicle aerodynamic heating problems were first encountered in the late 1940s and early 1950s. Beginning about 1945, the Langley Research Center set up and operated a secret flight-research missile base at Wallops Island. When the vehicle speeds reached Mach numbers between 3 and 4 some of them began disintegrating in flight, not only because the construction materials were weakened by the heat, but (as I discovered) they were actually catching on fire and burning up. The first laboratory studies on the vehicle ignition problem (not the fuel, the vehicle) were reported in *High Temperature Oxidation and Ignition of Metals* (Hill, Adamson, et al). The problem at those and higher speeds was overcome by the use of more heat-resistant materials.

In Section XIII, the reader was introduced to the concept of the aerodynamic stagnation point as that point on a nose, or leading edge, where the air is brought to a complete stop. It is at the stagnation point that the heating is characteristically the greatest because it is there that the most kinetic energy is converted to thermal energy by the process of compression. The air-temperature ratio at the stagnation point in degrees absolute, either Kelvin or Rankine, is given closely by a simple energy relation: one plus two tenths of the Mach number squared (Equation A4-llf in Appendix 4). Suppose the atmospheric temperature is 70 degrees Fahrenheit or 70 plus 460 equals 530 degrees Rankine. Then according to the above relation at the following Mach numbers stagnation temperatures in degrees Rankine (R), Fahrenheit (F), and centigrade (C) are given in the following table:

Table XIV-1. Typical Stagnation Temperatures

Mach no.	1	2	3	5	7
T_s, R	636	954	1484	3180	5724
T_s, F	176	494	1024	2720	5264
T_s, C	80	257	551	1493	2907

The values for Mach 7 are a little too high because the stagnation-temperature energy relation cited makes no allowance for the energy required to dissociate molecules of air into atoms as happens at this temperature. Still, the trend toward extremely hot air at high Mach numbers is clearly shown by the table.

The nose (and leading edges if there are any) of a supersonic vehicle operating within the atmosphere is normally heated by both radiation and convection, while the rest of the vehicle is heated only by convection, sometimes referred to as air-friction heating. The heat transfer is proportional to the difference in the effective boundary layer temperature and the temperature of the vehicle surface. (The other factors are lumped into a heat-transfer coefficient.) Not wishing to make this a course in heat transfer, it will just be said that the rise in effective turbulent boundary layer temperature is about 88 percent of the rise in stagnation temperatures listed in the table, so it can be seen that the boundary layer surrounding the vehicle is extremely hot at high Mach numbers also. The factor just given is called the boundary layer recovery factor.

So severe can the heating be that in 1955 it was generally believed impossible to put a man in earth orbit without having him be burned up on re-entry. These ideas were so firmly fixed at the time that the man who was to become the first Director of the Manned Space-flight Center, Dr. Robert Gilruth, said, "Anyone who thinks a man can be put into orbit just doesn't understand the problems." Needless to say, he changed his mind following advances in heat-shield technology.

UFOs, on the other hand, can come in from a high-speed flight and be relatively cool. Witnesses can tell if a nearby vehicle is hot by the heat radiated to their faces and hands. My first graphic experience with radiation heating was when, as a boy, I went to see an oil well fire and found I could not approach within a couple hundred yards without discomfort from radiant heating. Much later, in studies related to the heat protection of hypersonic vehicles, I witnessed the wind tunnel test of a 4x4-inch piece of graphite plate electrically heated to incandescence at a temperature something above 3000 F. The test was observed through a tunnel window of quartz plate mounted in a rim of asbestos, about a foot from the graphite. Even though the supersonic tunnel air was cold, in a few seconds after the graphite specimen was up to temperature the asbestos window mounting began to melt and run down the tunnel wall! The skin of the observers, viewing through dark glasses at a distance of about 10 feet from the specimen, felt uncomfortably hot. This observer backed up.

This information can be interpreted and extrapolated as follows. If the plate were 4x4 feet in dimension, the radiated energy would seem severe at 12 times the observer distance of 10 feet, or 120 feet. If the dimension were 40 feet, corresponding to an ordinary or big UFO, the radiation would seem severe at 1200 feet distance, etc., the distance at which a given rate of radiant heating can be felt being proportional to the size.

This extrapolation simply means that if UFOs were thermally very hot, the close observer would be driven away by radiant heating. Yet in Example III-B1, the Saturn-type UFOs near Ponta Poran, Brazil, which had been traveling cross-country and stopped to pace and maneuver around a jeep, were reported by the witnesses to be without heat, odor, or perceptible noise. In the similar case of Example X-A4, in which a Saturn-type UFO in Bahia, Brazil, maneuvered at extreme speed and acceleration about the witnesses and approached to within 300 feet, no radiated heat was mentioned.

Even when a UFO looks like a ball of fire it is still not hot, as was pointed out in Section III. The fiery look is an illusion due to ionization of the surrounding air.

One of the hottest UFOs yet reported was the one encountered by the Canadian prospector Michalak (Example IV-B4). The saucer was seen flying at high speed before it landed nearby. It "was radiating heat in rainbow colors," but was not hot enough to prevent Michalak from approaching and touching it with his rubberized glove.

The glove promptly melted enough to slip off the surface; however, this is not the intensity of heat to be expected from supersonic aerodynamic heating. The aeronautical engineer is puzzled as to why UFOs traveling continuously at Mach numbers of 4 or 5 do not generate temperatures sufficiently high to be destructive to known materials. Commentators often begin to speculate about supermaterials capable of withstanding the rigors of UFO flight. The facts are, however, that UFO surfaces are not reported to be even red-hot. This is in contrast to high-speed Earth vehicles, such as missiles, for which red heats are common. UFOs somehow *prevent* the high aerodynamic heating rates, instead of permitting a heating problem, then surviving it with heat-resistant materials. A few UFO investigators have realized this. Notable among them was the Brazilian investigator Dr. Olavo T. Fontes, who wrote the chapter on Physical Evidence in *Flying Saucers: The Startling Evidence of the Invasion From*

Outer Space, for he came into convincing evidence that a particular UFO was made of magnesium, one of the least heat-resistant of all the metals.

B. The Force Field Control of Aerodynamic Heating

As a prerequisite for reading this subsection, the reader should become somewhat familiar with the concepts of supersonic airflow control by means of force fields as set forth generally in Section XIII, especially the subsection on Aerodynamic Control for Ellipsoidal UFOs. The part on compressible flow is pertinent. Since the control for the prevention of aerodynamic heating is essentially identical to the control for the prevention of shockwave drag, there seems little point in repeating the control descriptions and theory here. The technical reader who studied Section XIII and Appendix 4 doubtless realizes that the hypothesized control system could prevent the heating problem as well as the shockwave problem. It is easy to imagine how a force field which absorbs the free-stream kinetic energy from the air as it approaches and comes close to the vehicle, then passes it back as it leaves, would resolve both the heating and the drag.

I would like to emphasize again, as I did in Section XIII, that because of the wide variations in design possibilities I don't pretend to know just how the UFO controls the airflow. What I have attempted to do is to show possibilities and to present a theory with sufficient breadth to have a chance of including the real solution. I am also trying to undermine the concept that UFOs "defy the laws of physics," and replace it with the more constructive idea that we still have much to learn about those laws and their applications.

In treating the force field control of aerodynamic heating, we shall consider only two points on the UFO surface as being sufficiently representative. One is the stagnation point and vicinity. The other is a typical point on the side of the UFO which can be taken as representative of the remainder of the UFO surface. With the force field control system we have visualized, the stagnation point and vicinity, which is normally the most severely heated part of a supersonic vehicle, gets no heating at all. The field brings the air to rest at the stagnation point without any compression (equation A4-10) and since it is the energy of compression that causes stagnation heating, there is no heating. This is also verified by the flowfield thermal analysis of Appendix 4 and equation A4-11g. Another way to look at stagnation point heating is that it is caused by the conversion of the kinetic energy of the air into thermal and pressure energy. Since the force field absorbs the kinetic energy along the stagnation point streamline, there is no energy left to heat the air or the vehicle. This statement also holds approximately for streamlines adjacent to the stagnation streamline and hence the no-heating result applies to the general vicinity of the nose near the stagnation point. This concludes the stagnation heating discussion.

In discussing the heating of a typical point on the side of a UFO we emphasize the same class of ellipsoidal UFO that was emphasized in Section XIII, the ones having a force field potential energy that is constant over the surface. These are the ones that would generate the control field near the vehicle surface without putting unwarranted forces on interior components or passengers, in close analogy with electric theory.

When the force field strength is adjusted according to flight speed to stop the air at the stagnation point the force field pumps the air alongside to relatively low pressures. Typical values of the pressure ratios are given in the table in Section XIII for two flight speeds. While the pressure ratios in the table are what was called static pressure ratios, they also represent the pressure ratios under dynamic-flow conditions exactly at the point on the side where the velocity re-achieves freestream velocity as a result of the partial vacuum. The static temperature ratios corresponding to these pressure ratios will now be obtained from equation A4-11c of Appendix 4, but the reader is reminded that the vehicle is not cooled by the static temperatures but by the difference in the boundary layer temperature and the wall temperature. The static temperature is the temperature outside the boundary layer, while the boundary layer temperature is the effective air temperature where the air meets the wall. To obtain the boundary layer temperature, we use a typical turbulent boundary-layer recovery factor of 0.88, which means that the boundary layer recovers 88 percent of the drop in static temperature.

The table from Section XIII is here extended to give the static temperature ratio, T_{st}/T_o, and the boundary layer temperature ratio, T_b/T_o, for constant surface potential airflow control at a point on the sidewall. Again, the temperature ratios are in degrees absolute, either Rankine or Kelvin.

Table 14-2. Typical Pressure and Temperature Ratios on a Sidewall

V_o, ft/sec	p/p_o	T_{st}/T_o	T_b/T_o	T_b, °F
1500	0.2082	0.6387	0.9566	47
2000	0.0274	0.3577	0.9229	29

The first column gives both flight speed and local speed just outside the boundary layer, since they are the same. The last column gives the boundary layer temperature in degrees Fahrenheit on a day when the ambient atmosphere is 70°F or 530°R. The faster the UFO goes, the lower the boundary layer temperature to whatever speed the UFO can maintain the force field strength needed. At a vehicle velocity of 2000 ft/sec, the temperature is below freezing.

C. Cooling: A Fallout From the Heating Problem

When I read Frabush's account of the UFO in the gravel pit (Example III-B2), I was completely baffled by the strange occurrence of the pond being frozen over when the UFO left. However, as I wrote the word *freezing* in the last paragraph, I was reminded of the incident and realized that I had a valid possible explanation for the phenomenon. It could be accounted for if a UFO should leave its air-control force field active while hovering.

Consider the physical situation surrounding a UFO which has left its air-control force field turned on after it stopped. In that event the air pressure ratios are very low. These were termed static pressure ratios in Section XIII-G, and the equation governing these ratios in the entire space around the UFO is equation A4-5, in Appendix 4. The corresponding static temperature ratios are also low, and can be obtained from equation A4-11c.

The high-speed boundary layer discussed above is nonexistent and heat transfer is governed by the static temperatures and air convection. The term *convection* just means that the air is moving, either due to a breeze blowing or to thermal draughts. I favor the breeze hypothesis because the atmosphere is practically never dead calm.

The atmosphere around a UFO under the influence of a continuous force field with an approximate inverse first power energy distribution has strange yet simple properties. Any unit mass or unit volume of air experiences no net force because (in this static case) the field forces are exactly counterbalanced by air-pressure-gradient forces. Any slight additional force on the air can move it. It follows at once that a breeze can move air into and out of the zone without appreciable impedance, and the refrigerator is at work! It is the adiabatic expansion to low temperature of the air going into the zone that is responsible, just as it is the adiabatic expansion of the freon going into the freezing coils of a refrigerator that is responsible there.

In case the reader is wondering why the propulsive force field does not generally act in the same manner, it is because the propulsive field is generally focused, not continuous. Of the two field types, the propulsive field may be thought of as being long-range and narrow, and the airflow-control field as short-range, continuous, and having components which are uniformly distributed with respect to direction.

In this particular case, the UFO was described by Frabush as being a lenticular-shaped saucer, and, as we noted in Section X, the saucer is very adept at adjusting the field focus from narrow to wide and vice versa. It may be possible that with a very wide focus a continuous field would be approached and low pressures and temperatures occur; I don't know.

It is well known that UFOs emit radiations which heat their surroundings. This is particularly true with respect to the ground over which a UFO has been hovering for some time. Heating is the norm rather than cooling. No particular contradiction exists, however, since we assume that the UFO's air-control fields are generally inoperative while the UFO hovers.

In the Frabush case, we have an example where the theory is perhaps stronger than the data, because the case data is unique. Throughout this work on UFOs it has been the rule to deal only with phenomena which have been repeatedly witnessed, which conform to a pattern, and which must logically be accepted as something real. An exception has been made in this case because it so neatly supports the air-flow control field-potential theories laboriously developed and applied in the previous section, and applied with success in this section. That the UFO can freeze ice now seems reasonable, but we should find more case data before accepting the UFO "chill" as a definite part of the pattern.

D. Other Possibilities: Slip Flow

No discussion of the relief from aerodynamic heating would be complete without some consideration of a phenomenon known as *slip flow*. According to theory, the air-friction drag and heating of moving vehicles is due to the fact that air molecules cling to any surface; that they cling in clumps, making the surface somewhat rough, makes matters worse. That is why it does no good to polish an aerodynamic surface beyond the point at which the surface proper is smoother than the adsorbed layer of air molecules with its clumps. The clumps contribute to air drag in this manner. A fast-moving air molecule strikes a clump and is stopped, giving up its momentum and kinetic energy. This gives drag plus heating. Molecules leave clumps in random directions, giving no drag alleviation. This process is analogous to diffuse reflection in lighting. Laboratory wind tunnel tests showed that at a combination of low enough pressure and high enough speed and temperature, much of the adsorbed layer of air is knocked off the surface. In this condition the fast moving air molecules can bounce on a smooth surface and reflect off again without losing much energy, in a process analogous to the specular reflection of light from a mirror surface. This desirable operating condition, in which drag and heating are dramatically reduced, is known as slip flow.

In the supersonic flight vehicle research of the Langley Research Center carried out at Wallops Island in the early 1950s, a research vehicle known as the RM-10 was developed under my direction and completely equipped with surface and boundary layer survey instrumentation to measure supersonic friction drag and heating rates over a range of speed and altitude conditions and under conditions of realism impossible to obtain in the tunnels. The normal range of investigation was an altitude of from 1000 to 30,000 or 40,000 feet and over all Mach numbers up to 3.5. On some models an extra rocket was added to conduct the tests at altitudes above 80,000 feet, well into the range where slip flow was predicted by wind tunnel test. We were very disappointed to find that the measured skin friction and heating showed no evidence of slip flow, which had very significant implications with regard to both missile and aeroplane flight at supersonic speeds and high altitude. The failure to obtain slip flow was something fundamental, and no fault of the research program, which was conducted with meticulous care and repeated tests. For example, the test models were polished with all the care used in polishing the facets of a fine diamond, and the surface roughness was confirmed by various methods of measurement to be less than 15 millionths of an inch, even though the construction material was an aluminum alloy.

In the early 1960s, William J. O'Sullivan, our Division Head Scientist, and I collaborated on a laboratory experiment in an attempt to get slip flow by artificial means. My special interest at the time was to see if what looked like a blue corona discharge on some of the UFOs could explain their lack of supersonic heating by an artificially induced slip flow. O'Sullivan's avowed interest was that if we got a slip flow breakthrough, a light plane could go 500 mph on 100 horsepower. However, he would not touch the experiment unless we kept it off the record, which I felt was due to its UFO connection. To keep the experiment off the record, we did all the design, assembly, and operational work ourselves, without the aid of laboratory technicians, and used borrowed equipment, working nights and weekends at no cost to the government. It was hard work, but without red tape.

The idea behind the experiment was to try and knock the air clumps off an aerodynamic surface by a corona discharge. We assembled a motorized rotating drum inside a hollow, stationary cylinder so that the flow of air in the air gap simulated a boundary layer, and the measured input electric power and rpm of the calibrated, variable-speed motor gave us the aerodynamic drag. We connected an adjustable, high-voltage direct current supply across the air gap so the electrons would flow from the rotating drum to the cylinder. The whole assembly was placed in an oversized glass bell jar, with electric and instrumentation leads and vacuum lines going in through the base.

With all equipment operating, the pressure was pumped down until the corona started, the beautiful blue glow of the spectral lines of nitrogen, showing that the air in the air gap was ionized. The ammeter showed that electrons were crossing the gap. Colorwise we had a beautiful UFO experiment, but to our chagrin the power to the motor didn't decrease an iota. The electrons were not carrying those stubborn, sticky, molecular clumps from the surface. We learned two things:

(1) We weren't going to have 500 mph Piper Cubs.

(2) This was not how the UFOs solve the heating problem!

High-Acceleration Loading On Occupants

A. The Problem

It is often claimed, usually by doubters, that UFO occupants would never be able to stand the crushing accelerations they are subjected to by the UFO maneuvers. Then the commentator usually qualifies the remark by adding at least if they are anything like us. Of course the latter remark offers a possible answer. If the UFO occupants are very different from us they may be able to stand 100 g better than people can stand 10 or 15 g, which is in the vicinity of their limit for conscious activity. The amount people can stand without blacking out depends on the direction of the g-loading, etc,, and is known to be less than the linear accelerations and maneuver g of UFOs. As we have seen, these can be of the order of 100 g and possibly higher. Of course a partial answer could be that some of the UFOs are unmanned, just automated vehicles for data recording and other intelligence gathering functions, like a snooper-missile. However, for the following discussion we shall assume, without verification, that there are UFO occupants and that they cannot withstand the high accelerations either: they need relief.

At this point it must be made perfectly clear that, while UFO fields have been called force fields because of their effect on mass, UFO fields are actually acceleration fields. This is directly analogous to gravity fields which cause weight because they are acceleration fields. To be specific, the inverse-square force field term K/r^2 is force per unit mass, which must have units of acceleration.

B. The Superposition of Fields

Acceleration field strengths, like all other field strengths, can be added algebraically (added or subtracted), or, better stated, they can be added vectorially. This is called the principle of superposition. This principle, together with the equivalence (interchangeability) of acceleration and gravitation, is one of the foundations of general relativity. What we do is perfectly analogous; we note the equivalence of vehicle acceleration and force field acceleration and that they can be added vectorially. What it means, practically, is that if the occupants of an accelerating vehicle can be properly located relative to a UFO acceleration field (force field), the effect of UFO-maneuver acceleration on the occupants can be neutralized. Since we have emphasized the use of repulsive force fields, this can be taken to mean that the field centers would be behind the occupant in a UFO with forward acceleration, although in principle there would be nothing wrong with a negative field centered ahead of the occupant. The repulsive field used to neutralize the effect of vehicle acceleration on the passenger can also be a leakage component of the propulsive field.

From a practical standpoint, it may be desirable to adjust the neutralizing field to neutralize most, but not all, of the vehicle acceleration. Then the operators would know by the feel approximately what was going on when not looking at the accelerometers or speedometer. If the vehicle accelerates in a straight line, the vehicle acceleration is spacewise constant. Since the neutralizing fields have an acceleration which is a space variable there may be some feel to the acceleration in any case.

C. An Example: The Dirigible-Shaped UFO

To crystalize ideas, consider the following hypothetical schematic of a dirigible-shaped spacecraft:

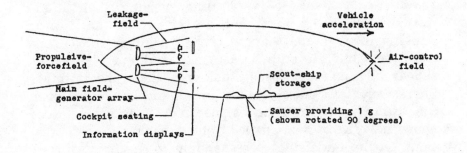

Figure XV-1. Acceleration Neutralization in Dirigible Spacecraft. (Leakage field strength in cockpit approximates vehicle acceleration.)

Assume this vehicle is accelerating at 100 g, and that most of the propulsive field generated is directed as shown to provide propulsion. Let the remainder leak forward toward the cockpit seating area as a 3-dimensional diverging field. Because of the inverse-square field strength, the seating can be located at a distance from the field generators where the forward acceleration of the leakage field is 100 g or 99 g. This cancels the 100 g "field" of the vehicle acceleration, or leaves one percent for "feel." At other vehicle accelerations, the field leakage is a constant percent. Then at a 10 g vehicle acceleration, for example, the seating area will receive a 10 g or 9.9 g forward acceleration, canceling all or most of the vehicle 10 g. Therefore, the same seating location is suitable for any vehicle acceleration. The seated occupants feel the acceleration only to the extent that they choose; to feel more or less of the vehicle g they have only to adjust their seats in a fore and aft direction.

The storage of saucers along or within the undersurface of large dirigible- or cigar-shaped vehicles has its basis in many reports. One is detailed in the *APRO Bulletin* for September-October 1973. It relates a sighting by Mr. Buzz Montague and his partner, who were on a hunting trip in the Sellway wilderness of Idaho, in the early 1960s. They were camped on the bluff of a hill overlooking a mine dump half a mile away.

When they awakened at six one morning, their attention was attracted to something shiny on the dump. Looking through the scopes on their hunting rifles, they could see that the shiny object was a domed lenticular saucer having four hoses stuck into the mine tailings. There were four such vehicles in all, each hovering over the dump with their hoses inserted. A thousand feet above hovered a cigar-shaped vehicle having four depressions on the underside corresponding to the four saucers. One by one the saucers elevated to the parent vehicle and on entering a depression neither the depression or the vehicle was visible! Each soon returned to the mine dump, presumably for another load of tailings, and the witnesses estimated that each made a total of four trips in roughly an hour's time. Then, with the saucers in place, the large vehicle climbed away to the northwest.

Following Aime Michel's lead in *The Truth About Flying Saucers*, I believe it is a likely possibility that one or two saucers furnish hover power for the larger vehicle as suggested by Figure XV-1. With one or more saucers furnishing hover or slow cruise power, the occupants would feel about one g. While the sketch shows both the hover field and the main propulsive field, only one would be turned on at a time, depending on the mode of operation. With the main field operative, a slight nose-up tilt takes care of planetary gravity, as we have learned from the triangle of accelerations in Section XI. This is also in accordance with my observations, for the vehicle I witnessed slanted upward at the same moment its forward acceleration leaped to immense values (Example XI-A1).

Neutralization of the vehicle acceleration is probably a practical necessity for the occupants during the initial and final phases of interstellar travel with field propulsion. This is because the vehicles would use their highest g capability for several days to achieve interstellar speeds, directing their field at the sun or other star that they are leaving. Relatively low-thrust systems may be used in deep space. With these, no acceleration neutralization would be needed.

D. Acceleration Neutralization During Maneuvers

The saucer UFO is a good example on which to focus ideas, for it is among the most common unconventional craft reported to make maneuvers which amaze the observer with a dazzling performance. There is such a modicum of data on the internal arrangement of saucers that it is pointless to speculate on the placement of field equipment. Nevertheless, the principle of the field neutralization of vehicle acceleration is clear and just as straightforward as in the case of the big dirigible vehicles. Also, the saucer is just one of a class of vehicles which have their propulsive field in fixed alignment with the axis of symmetry, and tilt the field axis to accomplish their maneuvers by tilting the entire vehicle. The Saturn vehicle is another of this class (Section X).

A key point in this discussion is that when the vehicle tilts to maneuver, except for the relatively minute accelerations due to the insignificant aerodynamic forces, the only acceleration the vehicle occupants can feel is directed parallel to the axis of symmetry. They never feel a component of earth gravity directed perpendicular to the axis of symmetry, no matter how much the vehicle is tilted. It follows that directing the short-range acceleration-neutralizing field in the direction of the vehicle axis of symmetry does a nearly perfect job. This amounts to a great simplification as the counter-field equipment can be fixed in orientation relative to the vehicle. Thus the field needed to neutralize the vehicle acceleration during a steep bank-to-turn or during a horizontal linear acceleration is the same as that required to make a high-g vertical takeoff.

It has been my experience in association with technical people on rocket projects that even technical people sometimes become confused about the point made in the preceding paragraph regarding earth g being imperceptible aboard the vehicle. However, in rocket vehicles it is usually accelerometers that feel the accelerations. Insufficiently experienced people have been known to erroneously make a correction for the acceleration of gravity when reducing the accelerometer data. The reason that earth g is not felt on board is, again, that the principle of superposition of fields is in effect. Except for the thrust or external forces, if any, the vehicle is properly considered to be in a state of free-fall with the falling acceleration canceling out the earth gravity field.

The total result is that the theory of acceleration neutralization is both simple and accurate, even for those unconventional vehicles whose maneuvers are the most varied.

Section XVI
UFO Artifacts

The study of UFO artifacts should be of paramount importance to the determination of the nature of UFOs. However, it has so far not worked out that way, for several reasons, a couple of which we will touched on here.

First of all, the UFO is such a reliable machine that broken or discarded parts are extremely rare. Then too, the recognition of a UFO artifact is not a simple matter, partly because we don't yet know what a piece of a UFO looks like, or what other properties to expect.

The very importance of UFO artifacts has stood in the way as a stumbling block to investigation. The main interest that has been taken in the subject by the average citizen and scientist alike has been with regard to the proof-of-existence theme. It is generally believed that if we can't obtain possession of a complete UFO for proof, a piece of one is the next best, and might constitute proof. This is unfortunate, because in the inevitable clash of opinion which follows, the atmosphere is such that no one learns anything of value. One aim of this book has been to help foment a studious atmosphere on UFOs, and that, of course, includes the subject of UFO artifacts. In short, what can we learn from UFO artifacts is a better question to ask than what proof do they offer.

Besides possible structural pieces, UFO artifacts include physical refuse discarded by them. A consistent pattern of refuse, as determined and documented by the civilian UFO investigating agencies, is the ejection a fine, white, translucent filament that has come to be known as angel hair. No investigation of this substance commensurate with its potential importance has ever been made. Some of the shortcomings of past investigations will be pointed out.

Another type of UFO evidence is nearly borderline with respect to constituting artifacts. That evidence is the imprinted tracks left by the UFO, particularly by the landing gear, and we should include the possible footprints or other tracks said by witnesses to be made by UFO occupants. Such tracks are highly perishable, and are not really artifacts. But it seems this evidence could be converted to the nature of artifacts by the simple expedient of making plaster casts of the prints. A public museum would be the logical repository for the casts, which probably would form a high-interest display, along with photographs of the area where they were made.

A. The Ubatuba Magnesium and the Isotope Ratio

One of the most believable of the UFO artifact stories is the one concerning what have come to be called the Ubatuba magnesium fragments. The believability stems from the supporting facts developed by Brazilian government laboratory tests showing the sample tested to be nearly 100 percent pure magnesium and entirely without the metallic trace elements characteristic of Earth manufacture. Another strange result that simply baffled the laboratory scientists was the finding that, although pure, the magnesium was 6.7 percent heavier than ordinary pure magnesium. On reading the elegantly given account of this story in *Flying Saucers, The Startling Evidence of the Invasion From Outer Space* (Chapter 9) about a decade ago, I was impressed by the possibility that a non-universal isotope ratio might be the cause of the weight discrepancy. If so, it would also explain the purity from other elements. This would be strong evidence of extraterrestrial manufacture because, even now, the only isotopes to have been separated on a significant scale are those of uranium 235 and 238. I ran through some trial computations. Sure enough, if the magnesium tested was the pure isotope magnesium 26, mg^{26}, its density would check the measured value to within about one fourth of one percent. This small discrepancy could be experimental error, while the 6.7 percent couldn't be. I was amazed at this finding, and was even more surprised that the materials experts had not come out with it.

Confusion was added to fact when the third fragment, tested in the United States, turned out to be of a less impressive composition. But to understand this story, it is necessary to start at the beginning.

On September 14, 1957, the Rio newspaper *O Globo* published a report by the columnist Ibrahim Sued stating that there had been eye witnesses to a UFO explosion over the sea near Ubatuba, Sau Palo, Brazil. The eye witnesses were on the beach when they saw a "flying disc" approach at fantastic speed and pull up to avoid striking the water. Still traveling rapidly, it exploded into thousands of fiery fragments which fell into the sea. A number of small fragments fell near the beach and some were recovered. A witness sent 3 small fragments in a letter to Mr. Sued. The capable and productive Brazilian UFO investigator Dr. Olavo T. Fontes, in a fast bit of footwork, interviewed Mr. Sued on the day the story broke. Letting the columnist know he had connections for the scientific analysis of the samples, Fontes walked out with them.

The three fragments, weighing a few grams each, were gray in color and had very irregular surfaces. Their appearance suggested that they were fragments of a much larger piece or object. The surfaces were covered in scattered areas with a thin layer of a white powdery substance, adherent to the surface. They appeared burned with fire or heat, and had many small cracks in the surfaces. The fragments were numbered 1, 2, and 3, and then fragment 1 was cut into a number of subpieces for testing. All the irregular surfaces were cut away, leaving little pieces with polished surfaces weighing about 0.6 gm each.

Subpieces of sample 1 were analyzed by the Mineral Production Laboratory, a division of the National Department of Mineral Production in the Agricultural Ministry of Brazil. This laboratory is the official Brazilian laboratory for the analysis of minerals. The analysis was done under the direction of the laboratory's chief chemist, Dr.

Feigl, from Germany. Following a simple test on one of the pieces to prove the sample a metal, he decided on a spectrographic analysis to determine the composition. Each metallic element has a characteristic set of spectral lines which are uniquely its own and the tests, while destructive, can be extremely sensitive.

The first spectrographic analysis was made by Dr. Louisa Maria A. Barbosa. One of the pieces was burned in an arc in a routine test to show the metal was magnesium. Then a second piece was burned in a large Hilger Spectrograph to determine the metallic impurities (trace elements) present. Surprisingly, there was no trace of any other metallic element—a very spectacularly pure magnesium. A test by another operator confirmed this finding. However, six faint lines not belonging to any metal showed the presence of a mere trace of a non-metallic substance.

Since the magnesium purity was so unusual, even unheard of, it was decided that an x-ray crystallography test should be made both as a confirmation and to determine the non-metallic constituent. Dr. Elysiario Tavora Filho, head of the Laboratory of Crystallography, carried out the sophisticated x-ray diffraction tests needed. The results again showed pure metallic magnesium with a faint trace of the hydroxyl radical, as in magnesium hydroxide. The x-ray diffraction tests not only confirmed the purity of the magnesium, but clearly explained the nature of the white powder on the fragment surfaces as being magnesium hydroxide formed when the pieces hit the water. They also showed that the trace of hydroxide was something probably not present before the material hit the water. To complete the picture, it was clear that the fragments had dropped into the water in an incandescent state as the witnesses said, because only at elevated temperatures could the hydroxide have migrated to the interior of the samples. Finally, the six faint lines previously unidentified on the spectrographs were checked out as being due to the slight trace of magnesium hydroxide.

It only remained to check the material density in gm/cc, taking the density of pure water at 4 degrees centigrade as unity. The density of fragment 1 was determined for a small, carefully polished piece taken from the center of the fragment. The standard procedure of suspending the chip from a Jolly balance and taking the ratio of the weight of the chip in air to the loss of weight when suspended in water was followed. Operators and spectators alike were in for a big surprise. Three successive tests all showed a density (specific gravity, if you prefer) of 1.866. The expected density of magnesium was 1.741!

Repeated measurements in agreement showed accidental errors to be negligible. However, systematic errors are doubtless present and are difficult to analyze. No mention was made of the corrections needed or made for the buoyancy of the fine wire generally used to suspend the sample in such a test, nor of the effects of water surface tension on the wire. Such systematic errors and their calculated corrections might account for a fraction of one percent error in the density, but by no stretch of the imagination for the difference between 1.866 and 1.741. Nor could the minute trace of hydroxide account for it.

Everyone was baffled. Fontes discussed isotope ratios and the possibility of their great importance. He also considered the possibility of a previously unknown closely packed crystalline structure. Of the three possible explanations, he concluded:

1. The crystallography tests showed standard hexagonal close-packed crystals.
2. Hydroxide was present in too small an amount to account for the discrepancy.
3. The density ratio gave no ground for reliance on an unusual isotope ratio.

Fontes felt that a program to search for a low-density sample should be undertaken, but it wasn't. The situation was left as a baffling mystery. Fontes felt well satisfied by the extreme purity result in itself; at least his words seem to say so.

I totally disagreed with the third conclusion. The following elementary computations are based on the fact that the volume of a given number of atoms of magnesium is fixed by the outer electron shells, which is the same for each isotope, within close limits; hence the density is proportional to the isotopic weight. The (equivalent) atomic weight of magnesium is computed in the table:

Table XVI-1. Computation Table

(1) Isotope	(2) Relative abundance	(3) Atomic weight	(4) = (2) x (3) Relative weight
Mg^{24}	0.786	23.99189	18.85763
Mg^{25}	0.101	24.99277	2.52427
Mg^{26}	0.113	25.99062	2.93694
	1.000	Sum =	24.31884
			= atomic weight magnesium

Then the proportion is: The density of a pure isotope of magnesium is to the normal density of magnesium as the atomic weight of the isotope is to the (normal) atomic weight of magnesium. We thus obtain the density of pure mg^{26}:

$$\text{Density pure } Mg^{26} = \frac{\text{Atomic Wt } Mg^{26}}{\text{Atomic Wt } Mg} \times \text{normal density } Mg$$

$$= \frac{25.99062}{24.31884} \times 1.741$$

$$= 1.861 \, \frac{gm}{cm^3} \quad \text{to four figures}$$

The experimentally measured value of fragment 1, 1.866, is only 0.005 higher than the theoretical value for pure magnesium 26! This amounts to O.005/1.861 = 0.27 percent, say a quarter of one percent higher than theory. As already mentioned, the most probable source of such a small discrepancy is the procedure for weighing a very small specimen submerged in water, plus the inclusion in the test of foreign material, such as the trace of migrated magnesium hydroxide.

These computations give a strong indication that fragment 1 was the pure isotope magnesium 26. This not only solves what is otherwise a density mystery, but explains the phenomenal purity at the same time, for there is no surer way to obtain purity than by the separation of isotopes. Still, it is just an indication, not a measurement. Fragment 1 absolutely should have been tested in a mass spectrometer. This gives the last word on isotope ratios and on chemical contaminants present as well.

As soon as the magnesium of fragment 1 was determined to be of rare purity, the interested parties should have reacted like diamond merchants with three rare diamonds to cut. Instead they made a double error: they didn't test fragments 2 and 3 at all, and they tested fragment 1 to extinction.

There was no ground for assuming that the fragments were basically identical, for they probably came from different parts of the disk. They might have had totally different uses and been of different compositions to suit. Fontes' discussion indicates that the laboratory personnel, Professor Filho in particular, knew the full implications of finding a specimen of such rare purity, a "Star of India" among metals. Didn't they want to know if fragments 2 and 3 were crown jewels also? Fontes had given one subpiece of fragment 1 to the Brazilian Army at their request, and another to the Brazilian Navy at their request. The last of the subpieces went to Prof. Filho, who powdered them one by one as he repeated his pet diffraction tests to measure the magnesium hydroxide content. These relatively unimportant tests could have been accomplished with subpieces of fragments 2 and 3 as they all contained the hydroxide from the reaction with sea water. Had he done so, he would have had a preliminary reading on the composition of the other two fragments. Instead, the last pieces of fragment 1 just went down the drain. One or two of these should have gone to the United States or Europe for tests in a mass spectrometer. One or two should have been preserved in a bottle of dry helium and offered to major world museums as relics.

According to *UFO, The Whole Story* (Lorenzen 213), Dr. Fontes sent the remaining fragments to APRO to be tested in the United States. Public record is a bit nebulous as to who tested which fragment. Oak Ridge and Dow Chemical both tested subpieces of one fragment. The only highly unusual result to be reported from this pair of tests was that the fragment contained possibly as much as a thousand parts per million of aluminum. As can be seen in Table XVI-2, aluminum in such a quantity is not expected in a commercially produced pure magnesium. A fragment subpiece was also given to the U.S. Air Force even though they would not see to the presence of an APRO representative during the tests. When the Air Force reported that they had burned up the sample in a spectrometer test without result, and asked for more, naturally Mrs. Lorenzen refused.

The remaining fragment was turned over to the University of Colorado UFO project. This fragment weighed just under 5 grams and was about the size of the last joint of your little finger (Saunders and Harkins). Since it was an irregular piece, it must have been the original fragment 3, as Dr. Fontes reported fragment 2 was cut and polished before it was sent to APRO. Appropriately, the project's physical chemist, Dr. Roy Craig, assumed responsibility for the test program. He decided on a neutron-activation procedure which can be effective yet economical of material. In this procedure, the subsample to be tested is placed in the center of an atomic reactor where it is radiated with neutrons, making the material radioactive. Removed from the pile, the sample is placed in a gamma-ray spectrometer which can identify the various elements to within a few parts per million. More detail of the test procedure is given in Chapter 3, written by Dr. Craig, of *UFOs? Yes!* The tests were conducted by the FBI's Alcohol Tax Div. Laboratory in Washington and were personally witnessed by Dr. Craig.

Only a small chip of the main sample was used, and it was tested for the presence of the eight metals listed in Table XVI-2. The quantity of each was determined in parts per million to the percentage accuracy shown. The middle column gives the results for the Brazilian UFO, and the right-hand column the corresponding results for Dow commercially pure magnesium.

Table XVI-2. Elements Found in Comparative Magnesium Samples
(Concentrations in parts per million)

Element	Brazilian UFO	Dow magnesium
Manganese	35 ppm ± 14%	4.8 ppm ± 10%
Aluminum	not detected	not detected
Zinc	500 ppm ± 20%	5.0 ppm ± 20%
Mercury	not detected	2.6 ppm ± 19%
Chromium	32 ppm ± 31%	5.9 ppm ± 20%
Copper	3.3 ppm ± 30%	0.4 ppm ± 50%
Barium	160 ppm ± 12%	not detected
Strontium	500 ppm ± 20%	not detected

Dr. James A. Harder of the University of California Civil Engineering Department (*Symposium on Unidentified Flying Objects*) makes the additional point that no trace of silicon or calcium was disclosed by the tests, either. He also adds that, of all the elements, calcium is the most difficult to remove when a serious attempt is made to achieve pure magnesium by earth technologies.

In view of the absence of elements difficult to control, and the presence in greater amount of elements easily removed if desired, such as barium and strontium, one can gather the impression that the composition is intentional, well controlled, and unique. In the official report, Dr. Craig said, "Although the Brazilian fragment proved not to be pure, as claimed, the possibility remained that the material was unique. The high content of strontium was particularly interesting, because strontium is not an expected impurity in magnesium made by usual production methods." Need more be said?

In *UFO, The Whole Story,* the Lorenzens made one of the most significant comments about the Ubatuba magnesium fragments: "The really strange facet of this particular incident and the subsequent investigations is the fact that three different analyses performed on three different fragments yielded completely different results." Agreed! Yet all of the analysts are probably correct in their physical findings.

Anyone experienced in missile development can explain the quoted result. When a supersonic developmental missile fails by disintegration it usually breaks into what looks like hundreds of fragments which seem to fill the sky like confetti. All parts of the vehicle get scrambled together. On reaching Earth they are better shuffled than a deck of cards on the deal. Any complex Earth machine is composed of dozens of metallic alloys, a different alloy for every special purpose. UFOs may well use special purpose materials also. The point is that the differences may be intentional. David Saunders also makes this point.

Thus the best overall view of the Ubatuba magnesium fragments is that each one is unique to its special purpose. Fragment 1 was the most intriguing of them all, for according to the tests of some of the world's most experienced metallurgists that fragment was absolutely pure of all metals other than magnesium. This is as would be expected if it were the pure isotope magnesium 26. Fragment 1 was also the only fragment with the density to be expected of this pure isotope.

B. Frank Edwards' Tale of Wilbert Smith

Frank Edwards has a most interesting Chapter 4 in his *Flying Saucers: Serious Business,* entitled "Pick Up the Pieces." The particular stories told, while fantastic in their implication of the possession of UFO artifacts by various world governments, nevertheless appear to be well documented. To anyone much interested in artifacts, "Pick Up the Pieces" is recommended reading. Frank Edwards' position that world governments such as those of the U.S.A. and Great Britain have made high-level

UFO studies, aided by the possession of certain artifacts, has a ring of truth to it.

This short discussion will be limited to remarks credited to Wilbert B. Smith, a Canadian scientist-engineer who headed the Canadian investigation program to study UFOs. Edwards quotes Smith in a talk on UFOs before the Illuminating Engineering Society, Canadian Regional Conference, at Ottawa on January 11, 1959: "Various items of hardware are known to exist but are usually clapped into security and are not available to the general public."

Edwards continues:

The riddle absorbed the time and attention of countless interested parties, but apparently none of then made any real attempt to solve it. That job was finally taken on by . . . C.W. Fitch of Cleveland, Ohio, and George Popovitch of Akron, Ohio. They arranged an interview with Mr. Smith, and they had the foresight to record what was said. Thanks to them I have a copy of that tape and it is from that source that the following material is taken.

Some quotes from the interview in November 1961 follow:

Fitch: I have been told by a mutual friend that in 1952 you showed Admiral Knowles a piece of a flying saucer. Is that statement correct, sir?

Smith: Yes. It is correct. I visited with Admiral Knowles and I had with me a piece which had been shot from a small flying saucer near Washington in July of that year—1952. I showed it to the Admiral. It was a piece of metal about twice as big as your thumb which had been loaned to me for a very short time by your Air Force.

Fitch: Is this the only piece you have handled which definitely has been part of a UFO, Mr. Smith?

Smith: No. I've handled several of these pieces of hardware.

Fitch: In what way, if any, do they differ from materials with which we are familiar?

Smith: As a general thing they differ only in that they are much harder than our materials.

Fitch: What about this particular piece from that UFO near Washington—did it differ from conventional materials? Was there anything unusual about it, sir?

Smith: Well, the story behind it is this: The pilot was chasing a glowing disk about two feet in diameter.

Fitch: Pardon me, sir. But did you say two feet?

Smith: That is correct. I was informed that the disk was about two feet in diameter. A glowing chunk flew off and the pilot saw it glowing all the way to the ground. He radioed his report and a ground party hurried to the scene. The thing was still glowing when they found it an hour later. The entire piece weighed about a pound. The segment that was loaned to me was about one third that. It had been sawed off.

Fitch: What did the analysis show?

Smith: There was iron rust—the thing was in reality a matrix of magnesium orthosilicate. The matrix had great numbers—thousands—of 15 micron spheres scattered through it. [Author's note: A micron is a millionth of a meter, and 15 microns equal 0.00059 inch.]

Fitch: You say that you had to return it—did you return it to the Air Force, Mr. Smith?

Smith: Not the Air Force. Much higher than that.

Fitch: The Central Intelligence Agency?

Smith: (Chuckles) I'm sorry, gentlemen, but I don't care to go beyond that point. I can say that it went into the hands of a highly classified group. You will have to solve that problem—their identity—for yourselves.

COMMENT

It would be helpful to know the material of the 15

micron spheres. Since small particles scatter E M waves by refraction, the spheres might act as a wave reflector for some purpose, or as absorption re-radiation centers. One would not expect a two-foot saucer to be a scaled down model of a big one. It would be totally automated, for one thing (probably no occupants).

C. Angel Hair

EXAMPLE XVI-C1

According to the March 1974 *UFO Investigator*, under the headline UFO ANGEL'S HAIR STILL REMAINS A MYSTERY, the following series of events occurred in Sudbury, Massachusetts, beginning at 2:00 P.M. on October 22, 1973. A child ran into the house calling, "Mommy, come see the biggest spider web in the world." The mother accompanied her son into the yard and there, covering bushes and hanging from wires, was a silvery-white web-like material. Looking upward for the source, she spotted a shiny, silvery, spherical object moving off to the west and disappearing behind some trees. She also saw more of the web still falling from the sky. It continued to fall until about 4:00 P.M.

The witness reacted very intelligently. She returned to the house for a piece of construction paper, which she rolled into a cone. Samples of the material were placed in the cone, and the cone into a jar which was capped and placed in her refrigerator. (She couldn't have done better.) The witness said the material felt sticky to the hands and stuck together when handled.

The witness took a sample of the material to the University of Massachusetts for examination. Under a microscope, the material was white and translucent. Its diameter diminished rapidly (under the heat of the microscope illumination) and no diameter was given. However, the refrigerated supply was diminishing also. The only finding by the laboratory was that the material was not spider web.

The local newspaper took an interest in the proceedings and the diminishing supply. It ran an article telling of the tests being run in the local laboratory and of the diminishing supply. Anyone with an available sample was asked to donate it to the laboratory.

EXAMPLE XVI-C2

A multiple-witness, multiple-UFO case occurred on August 6, 1961, near Meekatharra, Western Australia (Lorenzen, *UFO, The Whole Story*, 232). It was reported by sheep-shearing contractor Edwin Paine and witnessed by Paine and his employees. Twelve metallic-white disks were seen by an equal number of witnesses between 3:00 and 9:30 A.M., against a clear blue morning sky. The disks discharged a substance resembling snowy-white filaments. It was obvious to all witnesses that the material came from the disks. They saw it on the trailing edges of the disks, then watched it detach and float to the ground. Mr. J.L. Steere retrieved samples which disappeared as he held them in his hands.

EXAMPLE XVI-C3

At 3:00 P.M. on October 22, 1954, in Marysville, Ohio, Mr. Rodney Warrick of Raymond, Principal of Jerome Special School, was called into the school yard by his students (Lorenzen, *UFO, The Whole Story*, 60). They watched with astonishment a large, silvery, cigar-shaped object which was hanging motionless in the sky. Soon it took off, traveling majestically on a horizontal trajectory. In its wake the big cigar left a trail of a whitish web-like substance which floated down and began to hang from wires along the road by the school. It descended both in strands and in balls. Soon wires, bushes, and trees were covered with the stuff.

Samples were examined by Warrick and one of the teachers, Mrs. Dittmar. They said it felt like asbestos. When a single strand was taken by the ends, it could be stretched into a long thread which was broken with difficulty. Like all angel hair that has been reported, it tended to sublime rapidly when handled, soon disappearing entirely. Anyone who handled the material would immediately see a greenish tinge appear on the hands. The tinge would disappear immediately on washing, but otherwise would remain 30 or 40 minutes.

EXAMPLE XVI-C4

UFO, The Whole Story (p. 61) also reports a sighting over Florence, Italy, on October 28, 1954. This sighting involved both a silvery cigar and disk-like objects which shed wispy trails of angel hair that settled to the ground. The unusual part of this story is that someone evidently analyzed the substance, as the "chemical composition was found to be boron, silicon, calcium, and magnesium." That was the extent of the information.

GENERAL COMMENT

The importance of angel hair, like all UFO artifacts, is that a better understanding of it may help to understand the operation of the UFO. Some have speculated that the objective use of angel hair may be to hide the UFO, citing the known instances where saucers have been seen spiraling around cigar-shaped vehicles, enveloping them in a mist or shroud. I disagree with this conjecture, thinking it is more apt to be a particulate vapor or chemical smoke that surrounds the cloud-cigar because these have the proper light refraction property. Also, in most cases where angel hair is formed no envelopment or hiding has been observed. The other common conjecture is that angel hair is a power plant by-product or residue. Perhaps, as this suggests, it is the product of some UFO process. If so, it seems to be a process that the cigars (or dirigibles), spheres, and saucers have in common—something general and perhaps fundamental.

OBJECTIVE

The obvious thing to everyone is that we should first

find out what angel hair is, then we can make more educated conjectures about how it fits into the UFO jigsaw puzzle. In consideration of the scientific possibilities, the experimental results on angel hair are a disappointment. Taken together, the field and laboratory handling of angel hair is a disaster area.

When we know, or suspect, that a substance is a complicated molecular compound, it is very little knowledge to know that some of the atomic constituents are boron, silicon, calcium, and magnesium. If this analysis were valid, angel hair would resemble fine wire and would not sublime at ambient temperatures. Among other things, the negative-valence atoms are missing from this formulation. What is needed is an analysis of the molecular composition, so that we will know the molecular compounds which form angel hair. Then we will know what it is.

APPLICABLE BACKGROUND EXPERIENCE

While nothing of a chemist, I have had some applicable experience. From 1958 to 1968, my prime functional endeavor at the LRC was to stimulate and direct research aimed at space travel and space living. Space laboratory (often called space station) planning served as a focal point for supporting research. Advanced regenerative life support systems were one objective, and to study integrated systems a large, hermetically sealed sphere was used. Manning the systems by personnel also sealed within the sphere involved an element of risk to the operators' lives, because it sometimes happened that during the malfunction of equipment noxious or even poisonous gases would be released to the atmosphere. Yet the presence of the inboard personnel was required to release carbon dioxide, sweat, and flatus into the atmosphere, to provide urine to be reprocessed into drinking water, etc., as well as to make on-the-spot repairs to malfunctioning equipment. Therefore, the most rigorous monitoring of the atmospheric composition and purity at all times was required and was accomplished.

The monitoring of atmospheric purity was accomplished by a combination of gas chromatography and mass spectrometry. To obtain checks on our own laboratory work and to obtain preliminary results before our own chromatograph- and mass-spectrometer combination were ready, the project scientist had sample bottles prepared and contracted with a small but capable chemical laboratory to test the samples. The contract was for less than 10,000 dollars. Sampling bottles were formed of metal tubing, two or three inches in diameter, about eight inches long, and fitted with end caps. Each end cap had a tubing fitting and petcock. Through all this the atmosphere was aspirated and the petcocks closed when the sample was in the bottle.

First tests showed that the main difficulty was getting the sample bottles clean to begin with. In fact that is the only trouble encountered. Our experience was that we never ran into a gaseous chemical compound too complex or too rare to be analyzed. The chromatographs narrowed the possibilities down to two or three choices and the mass-spectrometer made the final decisions.

For example, when the Boeing Aircraft Co. of Seattle reached readiness with their closed-ecology life support system, we requested to participate by sampling their atmosphere periodically and having the samples analyzed by our contractor, who also happened to be located on the West Coast. Boeing agreed. The head project scientist for the Boeing experiment was also a medical doctor. To the best of my recollection, he manned the test alone, so that only his life was at stake. Sure enough, within a few days he got sick. He finally came out at the insistence of company executives, and none too soon! The poison gas involved was quickly determined by our contractor to be a complex and deadly compound of fluorine resulting from the overheating of a piece of linoleum that had been placed under hot equipment. According to medical opinion, with a few more hours of exposure the good doctor would not have recovered.

THE METHOD TO USE

Surely by now the reader has made the connection.

In the days when wet chemistry was supreme, the problem was often how to get a compound into solution. Now the problem is apt to be how to get a sample in volatile form. With angel hair this problem solves itself. If angel hair is in a suitable bottle we won't worry if it sublimes. So much the better! A glass or plastic bottle with removable cap and seal on one end (to get the sample inside) should be suitable, but glass or metal tubing connections with petcocks should be fitted in order to connect to the gas chromatograph and later to the mass spectrometer. A transparent bottle is suggested so one can observe the degree of sublimation that has taken place.

Let me digress for a moment to define a gas chromatograph, for no doubt some of my readers need clarification. It is a semi-automated means of analyzing gases by the color of chemical reactions; it is a sort of glorified and vastly extended litmus test. It consists of a long glass tube filled with a sequential assortment of chemicals in granular form. The tube is usually coiled to make it compact. It reminds one of a bottle with layers of colored sand taken from the painted dessert. The gas sample is passed into one end of the tube. When the gas reacts with one of the chemicals the change in color is noted. This tends to classify the gas. When that reaction nears completion, unreacted gas goes down the tube to the next test, etc. In the older wet-test procedures, the color of reactions and precipitates was important to the test interpretation. In chromatography this technique has been extended to a continuous test that is highly effective.

PHYSICAL TESTS

The first physical test that should be undertaken on angel hair is to determine the temperature below which it no longer sublimes at one atmosphere of pressure. This knowledge would be of practical importance in the storage and transportation of angel hair. For example, if angel hair does not sublime at carbon dioxide ice temperature, it could be transported to the laboratory in a box of dry ice, or stored indefinitely. But the experiment should start at the lowest practicable temperature in order to avoid waste of material, not at dry ice temperature. One possibility is to select a laboratory which is equipped to operate a microbalance at liquid nitrogen temperatures or lower. Temperatures are adjusted upward until a measurable weight loss rate is encountered. If this program is too sophisticated and costly, a snip of hair can be put in storage at each of several temperatures for periodic observation. Much pioneering research is accomplished with simple procedures and shoestring financing.

All chemical compounds have three phases: solid, liquid, and gas. Water is a good example. When a material goes directly from the solid to the gaseous phase, as does dry ice, it is said to sublime. Angel hair sublimes. This is a low-pressure characteristic of materials. Any material that sublimes at one pressure will instead melt at some higher pressure. That is, the material will assume the more typical three phases of state at the higher pressure. The fact that angel hair is tacky and very plastic at normal temperature and pressure probably means that at pressures not far above one atmosphere a liquid phase will be encountered. Thus the pressure storage of angel hair material in the liquid phase is an excellent possibility.

The physical properties of angel hair under pressure can be practically determined by sealing a good-sized sample of angel hair in a very small bottle where it will generate its own pressure. The bottle should be transparent, to facilitate observation of the phase states. It also should be fitted with strain gauges, cemented on the outside, for determination of the internal pressures. The amount of angel hair is determined by weighing the bottle before filling and after sealing. A great deal of physical data can be determined from this sample by varying the equilibrium temperature: the vapor pressure versus temperature, crude calorimetry using a calorimeter, and melting-freezing data. If we know the bore of the bottle, the amount of liquid formed can be estimated. The vapor pressure referred to is also the pressure of the liquid, for I expect the material to act like a partly filled bottle of liquid butane gas. The more we learn about this material, the more educated we will be about the UFO and the possible significance of angel hair.

This line of reasoning suggests that angel hair may be a liquid on board the various UFO types, stored under pressure and released to the atmosphere through small orifices, solidifying when it hits the lower pressure and temperature conditions of the atmosphere. The vehicle would thereby avoid discarding it as large liquid spills or as large chunks, either of which would be relatively crude procedures. Since the fine strands soon volatilize, the UFO operators get an A for nonpollution of the ecology. This is a higher grade than we can give his artifact-throwing (artifact being a new name for beer cans) human counterpart.

Last but not least, the bottle of liquid and gaseous "Essence of Angel Hair" is sold to the highest-bidding museum for a minimum price equal to the cost of the test program. At this time, the laboratory gets paid for services rendered, if they are to be paid.

CONCLUSION

UFO investigators and laboratory personnel alike have been caught short when their angel hair samples converted to the gaseous phase. Research, like any other business, requires management. Until such management is applied to the details of UFO chemical and physical research, we shall continue to read "UFO Angel Hair Still Remains a Mystery." Here is a case where a little knowledge, a little organization by a project scientist, and a few contract dollars should get the job done. If it doesn't, if this material by chance should defy the world's best chemical brains and techniques, then we should indeed be humbled.

Section XVII
The Humanoid Occupants

Only a couple of major points will be made about the humanoid UFO occupants. This section will therefore be brief. However, the subject is well worth more study than can be devoted to it in a single section or in an entire book. The reader is advised to make a study of this subject on his own for the double reward of basic education plus fascinating entertainment. Here is surely a case where truth is stranger than fiction. Only by the digestion of considerable occupant data can anyone get the proper feel for, and a balanced view of, the entire UFO panorama.

A. Sample Data

EXAMPLE XVII-A1. THE SCARECROW

Anatomy of a Phenomenon (Vallee 77) reports the following story that took place in the French countryside on September 26, 1954:

> The little dog began to bark and howl miserably. [A woman] saw it standing in front of something that looked like a scarecrow. But going closer she saw that the scarecrow was some sort of small diving suit, made of translucent plastic material. Behind the blurred transparency of the helmet, two large eyes were staring out at her. The suit began to move toward her with a kind of quick, waddling gait. She uttered a cry of terror and took to the fields.
>
> Looking back, she saw a big metallic object, circular and rather flat, rise behind some nearby trees, move off toward the northeast with considerable speed, gaining altitude as it did so.
>
> Neighbors gathered quickly and at the spot where the object had risen, they found a circle, ten or so feet in diameter, where

the shrubs had been crushed. Trees at the edge of this imprint had some branches broken and bark rubbed off, and the wheat in the direction of takeoff was flattened out in radiating lines. The original witness was found in a state of nervous collapse. She was put to bed where she remained for two days. . .

EXAMPLE XVII-A2. DWARF BESTS TRUCK DRIVER

The following incident took place in Caracas, Venezuela, at 2:00 A.M. on November 28, 1954 (Edwards, *Flying Saucers: Serious Business*, 101). Panel truck driver Gustavo Gonzales and his helper Jose Ponce were leaving Caracas on their way to Petare for a load of food for the Caracas morning markets. Jogging along a street on the outskirts of Caracas, they found their way blocked by a glowing disk-like object hovering about six feet above the street. It was about ten feet in diameter.

Gonzales stopped the truck and the two sat and stared, dumbfounded. On a common impulse, they got down from the cab and walked forward to investigate. When about 25 feet from the hovering craft, they found they were being approached by an occupant, a small (about 3½ feet tall), hairy, dwarf-like or animal-like biped whose fierce eyes glowed yellow in the truck's headlights. Gonzales grabbed the creature, lifting it off the ground. He later said it weighed about 35 pounds. Showing great strength, it twisted out of Gonzales' hands, somehow giving him a shove that sent him sprawling in the street. Ponce turned and ran for a police station a couple of blocks back.

Gonzales managed to get up on one knee and get his knife out as the little fellow leaped into the air and returned to the attack. He could see that instead of hands the creature had webbed extremities with claws about an inch long. With these he raked his human antagonist, while Gonzales tried to drive the knife blade into the creature's shoulder. The blade glanced off as though it had struck steel. When a second hairy occupant emerged from the vehicle and blinded him with a beam of light from a small shiny tube, Gonzales thought he was finished. But the fight was over. When Gonzales regained his vision, he saw the vehicle rise above some trees and quickly disappear from view.

Gonzales made for the station, arriving not long after his companion, torn, bleeding, and terrified. The first reaction of the police was one of disbelief, but they summoned a doctor who determined that both men were in a state of shock and that neither had been drinking. The doctor treated Gonzales for a long deep scratch down his left side and gave him a sedative.

Fortunately there was another eyewitness. A well-known Caracas physician out on night calls had also seen the UFO. With the understanding that his name would be kept confidential, he came forward and submitted a corroborating report to the police.

EXAMPLE XVII-A3. THE HOPPERS AND FLYERS

The stories about the Hoppers (and Flyers) are among the most charming of the humanoid anecdotes. The following triply-witnessed, essentially single incident, fits a pattern of little humanoids who characteristically proceed on the ground by hopping motions rather than by placing one foot ahead of the other as in walking. Another interesting class is the gliders, who are more scary than charming, but that is another story.

The following incident was reported in the September-October 1973 *APRO Bulletin*; the October 23, 1973, Hartford City (Indiana) *News Times*; and Blum's *Beyond Earth: Man's Contact With UFOs*. We first quote from Blum's book, which in turn quoted the story from the *News Times* article. The case was investigated by APRO field investigator Don Worley.

> When it comes to UFOs there are believers and disbelievers. An incident last night made real believers out of two Blackford Co. men. . .
>
> Last night the eastern portion of Blackford County was visited by two tiny, silver-suited men, according to Gary Flatter and DeWane Donathan.
>
> Flatter, who operates Chaney's Corner, is not a man to joke about something as serious as what he witnessed about 1 o'clock

this morning. And Donathan, a young married man, said he didn't believe in such things—until it happened to him. . .

When Donathan was contacted this morning and told that Flatter had also seen the creatures, the young man was relieved that he and his wife were not the only ones to see the strange beings.

It all started when the Donathans were headed home about 9:45 P.M. As they traveled east they saw what at first appeared to be a reflection from a tractor. As they got closer they could see two figures who looked like they were dancing to music.

Donathan said, "They were kind of dancing around in the middle of the road in a circle. It didn't look like they wanted to get very far apart from each other. When they turned around and looked at our car, they acted like they couldn't get (walk) off the road. They looked like they were skipping, but didn't have their feet in front of them and couldn't move very fast. They had their arms in front of them."

What Flatter saw was even more hair-raising, and might explain why the creatures appeared to be skipping. . .

At this point we go to the *Bulletin* data, which is more complete. Mrs. Donathan was driving and stopped the car only 30 feet away. The creatures were of slight build, straight of form, and about 4 feet tall. She describes the feet as having boxes on them, somewhat larger than a shoe.

Gary Flatter turned out to be the star investigator of the case. He was in the police station chatting with Deputy Sheriff Ed Townsend and a state policeman when the Donathans' call came in. He rode with Sheriff Townsend to the designated area, but they saw nothing. However, he heard a high-pitched sound at one point on the road. The state policeman also drove out and back. Later, Flatter drove out the second time, in his wrecker, as did the state policeman in his patrol car. The officer drove on east of the sighting area, while Flatter tried a south turn, then an east turn. As he approached an area due south of the Donathan sighting, he was interrupted by an exodus of small animals crossing the road from north to south. Stopping the wrecker, he counted 6 or 7 rabbits, a possum, a raccoon, and several cats. The same high-pitched sound was in the air.

Flatter then looked carefully around and spotted the

silver-suited beings standing in the plowed field just to the north, illuminated by the edge of his headlights. They were about 75 feet away and facing him. He estimated their height at 4 feet, and they were dressed in tight-fitting silvery suits that glared in the light. Illuminating them further with his spotlight, he was almost blinded by the reflection. The creatures didn't like it either, for with a hop, they immediately turned their backs to the beam. He turned it off.

Their heads were egg-shaped and fitted with what looked like gas masks fitted with a garden-hose-size hose connection to the lower chest. Naturally, he could not see their facial features behind this (breathing) equipment.

Flatter noted that the feet were "square with the heel a little over the back" (rectangular parallelopiped) having the approximate dimensions of 6x3x2 inches.

As they continued to hop, they moved up and down in slow motion. They seemed to use no muscular effort when they jumped, but moved as though skipping rope. He said *the motive power seemed to be in the feet.* "They would move up about 3 feet off the ground, then go back down, all in slow motion . . . they might move an arm, but not much." The fourth time up, they simply flew off! Flatter said, "They *flew like a helicopter in feet-down position.* They just flew off into the darkness and I couldn't find them with my spotlight. I did see some red trace-like streaks coming down and that was all."

The next day seven imprints were found in the hard ground of the field near the Donathan sighting. They looked as though made with a nearly square heel, 3 inches wide, and ¾ inch deep. Investigators' feet left no marks. It would seem that interesting prints should have existed at the Flatter sighting location, but no mention was made of an investigation.

EXAMPLE XVII-A4. THE COLLECTORS

The January 1974 *UFO Investigator* reported the following incident that took place in New Hampshire on November 3, 1973.

The account withheld the names of witnesses.

At 7:30 the witness's neighbor called him to see a glowing object through their telescope. He saw an object which he described as "a silverish saucer-shaped craft with 4 red glowing windows at one end." He thought it hovered above a radio tower a mile away.

The witness went home later on, and retired. Shortly after midnight the witness's dog seemed restless and he got up to let him out. Going into the kitchen, he saw a light coming from outside. When he looked out the door, what he saw gave him a shock! The light was a diffuse glow coming from two silver-suited creatures. They had oversized pointed ears, large noses, and dark, egg-shaped eyes that resembled holes. Their boots were without heels, and had curled-up toes. The creatures, or their suits, appeared to be self-luminous. They were picking up things from the ground and collecting them in a sack.

The witness went to the bedroom and returned to the kitchen with his .38-caliber automatic pistol, putting more shells in the clip. He had advised his wife what was going on, but she wanted no part of it. (Scratch corroborating witness.)

At his master's command, the snarling, vicious German shepherd leaped to the attack. On reaching the intruders, he stopped in his tracks and returned whining into the house. The humanoids went on collecting. By this time our witness was trembling so he could hardly hold the gun, much less use it effectively, but he vowed he would shoot if the beings came closer.

Meanwhile, he had been giving a running commentary to his wife. She did not respond until she got the word the creatures were leaving. She reached the kitchen only in time to see their glow disappearing in the woods.

The police had been called and arrived at 12:30 A.M. Since the ground was hard and covered with pine needles, no tracks were found.

B. Physical Characteristics and Significance

CATEGORIES

In *UFO, The Whole Story* (p. 184), the Lorenzens have neatly classified the UFO operators into three categories as follows:

Operator Categories
(part of a UFO pattern outline)

Category	Description	Height, feet
1	Human-sized humanoids	over $4\frac{1}{2}$
2	Small humanoids	about 3
3	Animal-like bipeds	about 3

They further state that there are dozens of reports of human-sized humanoids, while there are hundreds of reports of the much smaller entities. Nine-foot-tall beings are occasionally reported. Their skin may be light or dark, but green is seldom reported.

Of the illustrative examples given in the preceding paragraphs, Examples XVII-A1 and XVII-A3 clearly belong to category 2; Example XVII-A2 belongs to category 3; and, while Example XVII-A4 does not give the estimated height of the humanoids, they would clearly belong to category 1 or 2.

Mainly in category 1, an element of confusion at times comes in, although apparently not often, as to whether or not some of the entities may be robots. For example, in what is known as the Pascagula case, Blum quotes Charles Hixon as saying both he and Calvin Parker decided the entities which carried them aboard their craft were robots. Since they had no recognizable facial features (and few others) and did not wear space suits, they may have been robots.

In our two examples of category 2, the entities wore either a space suit or an equivalent breathing mask. Therefore there must have been live beings inside. The animal-like bipeds of category 3 seem not to need space suits in our atmosphere, but they certainly are not robots. They fight most unmechanically. A goodly percentage of those in categories 1 and 2 wear close-fitting suits which are usually, often without a transparent helmet. Some use a simple head covering instead.

It is my impression that a very low percentage of the reported humanoids would pass for human. There seem to be as many variations among the humanoid features as there are variations in the detailed design features within the main classes of UFOs. They have various distinguishing features such as big round or wide-set slanting eyes, oddly shaped and placed ears, long noses or no noses, and sometimes a slit for a mouth. I recently came across one of my old margin notes at the end of a chapter on humanoids. It read "Miscellaneous Galactic Types." After much additional perusal of the subject, I have seen no reason to change this opinion.

The humanoid entities cannot possibly be Earth creatures. Earth has no more produced them than today's human technology can produce a UFO. If they are real and factual biological creatures, they have to have originated somewhere else. Nor can the numerous well-witnessed humanoid sightings be swept under the rug. If we face up to it, the presence on Earth of a variety of nonhuman entities practically spells *extraterrestrial*.

We might ponder why this is so difficult for many to accept. The reasons are certainly not the technical difficulties of space travel. With their large cigar- or dirigible-type UFOs, these entities are precisely equipped for it. The stumbling block to acceptance seems to be an emotional one, better left for discussion by psychologists.

The parapsychologists also have their ideas on the subject. It has been proposed by one or more parapsychologists of stature that both UFOs and their operators are projected here by superior minds somewhere in space. One could logically ask, why strain the mind teleporting the giant dirigible-like vehicles? Why should they be needed? However, with this idea the parapsychologist is really proposing an alternate means of transportation, rather than questioning the extraterrestrial point. It is therefore a discussion of teleportation as a possible means of space travel. This concept does not offend me; in fact, we have one point in agreement. One way or another, superior minds and knowledge are behind the mission.

Various commentators on the UFO scene propose the manipulation of time, either forward or backward as needed, by the space traveler. This idea has appeal and even reasonableness, as in principle it cannot be less than half right, as will be very briefly discussed shortly. Relativistic principles indicate that extremely high speed catapults the subject into the future, and when we examine a distant star with large telescopes and scientific equipment are we not examining its past history? The manipulation of time is a legitimate province for any discussion of space travel. However, any such discussion, as this paragraph, is merely a discussion of technique.

Finally, a few visionaries confuse the evidence and the more obvious explanations by bringing in the ancient dual-universe hypothesis: we are living with these creatures and their vehicles all the time, but they are visible only under the right conditions. This point of view, which has been used for centuries to explain the spirit world, supports the duality everywhere and holds that interstellar travel is accomplished virtually instantaneously in the other plane, as time does not exist there. This is essentially the view of the believing contactee. But we are still discussing transportation mode, or perhaps *plane* is the more appropriate word.

The only way to kill or deny the extraterrestrial idea is to kill or deny the data. This gets harder and harder to do. As the old saying goes, perhaps we should just hitch our wagon to a star.

Clearly, the point to be made is that here are beings—with their space vehicles—from other worlds. How they managed it is of course debatable. It is nearly obvious that they came in their vehicles, for they are seen jumping in and out of them. This seems to leave open only the question of the techniques used to negotiate interstellar space. The most common view with regard to technique is the reasonable one that they have managed to develop able star ships.

We move now to consideration of the question "What are they doing here?"

C. The UFO Occupant As a Scientist

WHY ARE THEY HERE?

The reason for visitations by UFOs and their occupants, consistent with the data and most appealing to human logic, is that they are on a mission of cosmic exploration. The part of this exploration to which we are witnesses is planetary exploration, namely the examination of planet Earth.

The humanoids in Example XVII-A4 above fit a consistent pattern showing that our humanoid visitors collect samples of virtually everything in sight. Typical things collected include rocks, minerals, water samples, wild animals such as elk, domesticated animals such as cattle and chickens, wild plants, domesticated plants such tobacco and lavender, and also humans for physical and possibly mental examinations. There was even one well-known observation of a saucer-like UFO with a vacuum hose attachment which was lowered to suck up leaves, dirt, and trash from a roadside ditch as it moved along the roadway making a sound like a vacuum cleaner (Lorenzen, *UFO, The Whole Story*). Clearly, they have covered not only the natural earth sciences of geography, mineralogy, etc., but have included a sampling of our plant, animal, and human ecological factors. Their inclusion of human refuse along roadways and in yards seems closely parallel to the study by archeologists of prehistoric peoples from their refuse and discarded artifacts.

This activity in exploring our planet and its inhabitants may explain, in part, the aloofness of these planetary visitors, who appear to seek no contact with humans on an intellectual level. We might amount to a continuing observational experiment on the part of some of the visitors who observe rates of technological growth, changing socioeconomic patterns, etc. Others may be looking us over for the first time. It is one of the known tenets of science that the experimenter should conduct the experiment with a minimum of disturbance to the subjects. This may be why they are standoffish, and would even account for the alleged post-hypnotic suggestions to not remember the contact. It is another tenet of science that it is an impossibility to conduct an experiment with no disturbance to the subject. Even visual inspection includes the use of rays of light, which are often reciprocal. Thus, at the same time we often get to see what is going on, obtaining visual, audio, and other sensory data. The standoffish nature of the UFO operator is also consistent with the typical UFO "chase" description. When a UFO (operator) shows enough curiosity to follow an isolated vehicle it usually breaks contact when that vehicle nears an urban area.

WHY SUCH AN INTEREST IN EARTH?

As planets go, Earth is probably a very good one. At least it does not display some of the hostile features of its neighbors: Venus with its oven-roasting heat, Jupiter with its hydrogen ice, and Mars with its rarefied, oxygen-less atmosphere. Earth has a distribution of land and sea, mineral variety, an oxygen-rich atmosphere, botanical and zoological abundance, sunshine and rain, even blue skies and scattered clouds. Perhaps planets with the quality of Earth are either not too plentiful or have no-vacancy signs out. At this point in history, think what a race there would be to plant flags and colonies on Mars and Venus if those planets were similar to Earth. This is not meant to insinuate that our visitors may have plans to settle down. They are the explorers gathering data—the traveling scientists and their crews. But they have scrutinized us to an almost embarrassing degree, and to what use the data is put would seem an important question.

THE COSMIC SCIENTIST AS A SPACE TRAVELER

It is clear that I am in agreement with John Northrup, founder of the Northrup Aircraft Co. and co-founder of

Lockheed Corp., who said in a talk to faculty and students at Cal Tech that he believes UFOs are manned by scientists from an advanced civilization. I would simply put that in the plural number—civilizations—based on the variety of humanoids, animal-like bipeds, and robots reported. (For a scientific-looking humanoid, see cover drawing of the January-February 1975 *APRO Bulletin*.)

My reasoning that the cosmic scientist is a space traveler is based on the principles of relativity and the large distance between stars. With UFO performance available (here it is assumed that this means high acceleration to near light speed) the years and years of waiting for information about the galaxy are necessary only for the scientist who stays at home. To show this we assume data is required of planets which are x light years from the cosmic scientist's home base. Then the scientist left at home base must wait the "observer" time for the outbound trip, which is slightly over x years. Then he waits exactly another x years for the radio-data message to return at the speed of light, making a total time of a little over 2x years. To make matters worse, if he decides additional data is needed, there goes another 2x years. According to relativity, when the distances run to 50 or 100 light years or more, the interstellar research process of exploration is virtually impossible to manage or control from home base. For the stay-at-home scientist, there is an abysmal separation between interstellar worlds, as we are constantly reminded by the stay-at-home astronomer and other stay-at-home commentators.

But for the ship's officers and visiting cosmic scientist, the outlook is rosy, entirely different. For example, let the cosmic scientist leave Tau Ceti in a slow ship bound for the sun 12 light years away, accelerating for 13 days at 100 g by their own clocks and accelerometers, bringing the ship to a speed of 0.999c, where c is the speed of light. At this speed, they just coast along until time to decelerate, also 13 days. Earth arrival occurs just 7 months after departure. As another example, let a starship science expedition leave Zeta 1 Reticuli on a faster direct trip to Earth, 37 light years away. For this distance, let them use acceleration and deceleration periods of 2½ weeks at 100 g, giving a top speed of 0.9999c. This mission profile brings them an Earth-fall just 7.2 months after departure. Meanwhile, universal time has catapulted 37 years into the future. For these stars, check your Marjorie Fish UFO star map. Since the latter trip is over three times as far as the first, the importance of a little extra speed may be appreciated.

Our traveling scientist can begin to collect planetary data in a relatively short time after leaving home base, and he could spend some of that time with interstellar star gazing from new angles. He is now in a perfect position to manage the research program. If he needs to change data-gathering techniques or objectives he does it *now*, not 2x years later.

This discussion shows that it is very advantageous for the cosmic scientist to have a place in the cosmic scientific expedition. The interstellar vehicles (cigars or larger dirigibles) are large enough to constitute a small city, and should be both comfortable and equipped with the things a scientist would need, including scout vehicles. If the scientist wants his wife to stay young he takes her along. If not, their wave of goodbye may be their last, for he is about to leap into the future.

COLONIZATION AND TRADE?

If UFO operators are representatives of races or species both technologically and sociologically advanced, they may have learned to control population pressures. In most cases, this may mean that interstellar colonization is more a logical process than a forced one (their logic, of course). But when the star of an inhabited planetary system approaches the nova stage all logic would point to colonization. For any advanced civilization this would be reason enough to apply their talents to the development of space ships and interstellar exploration, perhaps with millions of years of lead time.

It seems that we have escaped colonization thus far— unless by remote chance we are the colony. Most people agree, however, that anthropological discoveries constitute convincing evidence that we are real, genuine, evolved natives. Also, if we are a colony we certainly got short-changed on knowledge and technology, notwithstanding the demonstrated ability of the ancients at stone constructions. We simply note that cosmological changes occur on a cosmic time scale. Probably we shall "escape" colonization a great deal longer.

Strictly speaking, UFO occupants have never been known to trade anything. Whatever they have wanted they have taken, giving nothing in return. They are even meticulous on this point, as tokens of mutual contact seem to be nonexistent. UFOs have been known to take on water and minerals, and some observers are convinced that they take electric power from power lines. All three could be supplies, or possibly only samples. Even if we define their "trade" as a one-way street, if they take very much of anything it is without our knowledge.

D. The Hoppers

BALANCE AND CONTROL

In Example XVII-A3, witness Gary Flatter won the UFO gold medal for sleuthing, observing, and instant analysis. Having read my account of platform research in Section XI, the reader will realize why I am so enthusiastic. The similarity between my research (and old research plans) and the flight of the hoppers goes somewhat further than the platform or helicopter similarity.

Although I didn't get to carry out the project for safety reasons, in the early 1950s I planned a sort of advanced platform in which a small rocket would be attached to the inward side of each foot at the instep, in such a manner that the rockets would not touch the ground or interfere with normal foot and leg action when turned off. The main difference between this and the single-rocket platform is that moving one foot toes-up and the other toes-down gives right- or left-hand rotational (yawing) capability which the first platforms did not have. The plan was to have a system in which the wearer could walk normally, with trouser legs hiding the rockets, and take off by actuating the rockets with the flip of a switch. Then, if the wearer wishes to escape muggers he flips on the switch, or to cross a heavily traveled street he hops across. He has joined the hopper-flyers.

Platform flying was my hobby for several years. This work on personal rocket flight was carried out well before the publicized competition's shoulder-pack rocket experiments. I believe that taking the lifting thrust at foot level is inherently superior to other means because it allows for balance and control by instinctive principles, while at the same time leaving the hands free for miscellaneous tasks. For example, I found that I could do target shooting from the platform with almost the same accuracy I had when standing on the ground. Having the lifting principle attached to the feet probably gives superior stability and control than either the Buck Rogers rocket belt or the more recent shoulder-pack rocketry. The reason is that ever since man walked on two feet (a couple million years?) he has been practicing balancing his weight on his feet. That is a lot of practice. It means man can instinctively balance on his feet (as can animals). I tried stooping, squatting, and all manner of body positions while airborne on my feet, with no balance or control difficulty. I found, as apparently do the hoppers, that sometimes a little arm motion is instinctive, or part of the articulation. When I tried sitting down on an airborne platform, I had practically zero balance and controllability. This demonstrated the superiority of applying the forces to the feet.

Actually, the best means of balance and control was determined by experience to be an almost imperceptible amount of body-English. One moves his waist and hips to the side the weight should be on. After a brief period of catching on, it is all automatic, the motions imperceptible. To move off in any direction one simply wills it, but thinks no more about the detail than he thinks about which foot he will put forward when he starts to walk. The body continues to balance while in a leaning position for travel. There is no upsetting moment or other instability.

It can be seen that being supported by the feet in flight is an easy, instinctive, and natural way to locomote. As Flatter said, it is akin to going by helicopter—without the helicopter. It is going by a pair of flight shoes!

THE POWER SOURCE AND HOP DYNAMICS

Gary Flatter said the motive power seemed to be in their feet. Right on! Perhaps it would be technically more accurate to say their motive power was in those shoebox affairs that probably housed the equipment as well as their feet, being in effect a pair of flight shoes. As long as there is a levitating force in each foot it makes no difference in effectiveness whether the forcing principle is rocketry or force fields, but since there was no dust or flying stones it was not rocketry.

If the force fields are negative gravity, and if gravity is a warp in space-time, when these little fellows hop they are giving space-time an opposite warp that is locally stronger than that given by the Earth. It is of great interest that the noise hoppers make is a high-pitched whine, very much like the noise which characteristically accompanies various UFO types at takeoff. Assuming the similarity is a fundamental one, it seems to mean that the force fields of both are cyclic fields which set up the whine as described in Section IX. One is reminded of some form of powerful oscillating circuitry. (Possibly positro-gravitic instead of electromagnetic?)

The slow-motion feature of the hopping is easily explained by thrust adjustment. First we recognize that the hoppers, like all of us, are held to Earth by the inevitable 1 g. Suppose, for example, that when ready to hop they have their thrust adjusted to 0.9 g (ready for a quick takeoff if danger threatens). Then to hop suppose they flick on a 0.2 g thrust increment, making their upward acceleration equal to 0.9 + 0.2 - 1.0. The result is plus 0.1 g, which carries them upward in slow motion. On the way up they flick off the 0.2 g increment, allowing them to stop and descend at 0.1 g, also slow motion. While hopping they can turn or move about easily.

The weighty-looking footprints could be partially due to the weight of the field-generating equipment, augmented by ground-impact conditions.

Time Requirements
For Interstellar Travel

A. Time Is Not a Constant Factor

CONFUSION IN THE INTERPRETATION OF RELATIVITY

Much of the general public and a segment of the technical world have misconceptions about the theory of relativity. As an example of the typical confusion existing among the public a portion of an article on the subject of space travel, entitled "Extraterrestrial Visitation?" is quoted from the *UFO Investigator* of September 1974. The excerpt had as a subhead "Travel Problems."

> Since Einstein's theories tell us that the speed of light is as fast as anything can travel, extraterrestrial origins presents a problem. How could "they" reach us? We could speculate that Einstein was wrong. A somewhat risky speculation since most of modern physics is based on his theories. However we learn much more each day and it would be "foolhardy" to think that we know everything there is to know. If the speed of light could be exceeded the time necessary for such a trip would not be such a barrier.
>
> If we are right in our evaluation of the laws of the universe, the proof of the theory that UFOs are of extraterrestial origins would seem to lie in one of two areas, i.e., we are dealing with an intelligent civilization which (1) has learned to travel by means other than accelerating through normal space, or (2) has a life span far greater than ours which, combined with advanced technology, would make a round trip of 10-15 years seem relatively short in comparison to such a lengthy trip by someone with our life span.

An example of confusion in the technical world is

given by the violent reactions to a paper entitled *Flight Mechanics of Photon Rockets*, given by Eugene Sanger before a congress of leading physicists and engineers in 1956. Professor Sanger was the top-rated German scientist of pre-World War II, one of the world's outstanding physicist-engineers who included among his credits the invention of the swept-wing airplane as embodied in the German rocket planes of World War II vintage. (The swept-wing airplane was invented independently in the United States at the Langley Research Center by Robert Jones.) Sanger's scientific critics nearly crucified him on two points. One was his statement that, when an interstellar vehicle accelerates at 1 g for over a year's time and the on board integrating accelerometer (a type of speedometer which multiplies acceleration by time) reads a velocity greater than light speed, in the on board reference frame the reading is correct. The other thing was Sanger's calculations that an interstellar vehicle accelerating and decelerating at 1 g (for maximum passenger comfort) could cross the known universe, stopping at the most distant galaxy in less than 50 years in passenger or occupant time. Somebody was wrong. I always thought it was the critics.

TIME RATIO

Everyone has heard of relativistic time effects, but whenever UFO travel times are discussed it seems that these effects are overlooked or forgotten. Anyone who didn't spot the errors in the excerpt from the article on Travel Problems should review what happens to travel time from the traveler's point of view when he nears that well-known limit of light velocity. Such a review is now given.

The effect of speed on travel time can best be understood by first ignoring the acceleration and deceleration portion of the trip and considering what happens to on board time at any given travel speed. The Lorentz equations of relativity show that relative to the time of all stationary observers the time on board a spacecraft approaching the speed of light is dramatically foreshortened. This is a case where the time relation can best be tied down by a simple formula. If v/c is the velocity of the spacecraft compared to the speed of light determined by a stationary observer with kilometer posts and a timer, and t'/t is the ratio of time increments on board to time increments on stationary clocks, then

$$\frac{t'}{t} = \sqrt{1 - \left(\frac{v}{c}\right)^2} \qquad (18\text{-}1)$$

This time-ratio relation, originated by H.A. Lorentz and incorporated by Einstein as a cornerstone of his Special Theory of Relativity, says to square the velocity ratio, subtract from one, and take the square root to obtain the ratio of on board time to the time for the stationary observer. The trip proceeds just as the stationary observer expects: observer time is distance divided by velocity. If the velocity is near light speed the time in years is slightly over the distance in light years to the observer.

Meanwhile, on board the traveler is enjoying the time-ratio benefits. For him the trip time is drastically slashed, in an attractive manner. Consider the total range of v/c and the resulting time ratios computed by the Lorentz relation and given in the following table.

Table XVIII-1. Dependence of Time-Ratio on Speed-Ratio, v/c

$\dfrac{v}{c}$	$\dfrac{t'}{t} = \dfrac{\text{traveler time increment}}{\text{observer time increment}}$
0.0	1.0
0.866	0.500
0.900	0.436
0.990	0.141
0.999	0.0447
0.9999	0.01414
0.99999	0.00447
0.999999	0.00141
1.0	0.0

Among the indications of Table XVIII-1 are the following:

1. Traveling at the speed ratio of 0.866 cuts the travel time in half compared to a non-relativistic computation.

2. Comparing time ratios for v/c's of 0.99, 0.9999, and 0.999999, we see that every two decades increase in velocity ratio cuts passenger trip time by a factor of 10! For example, traveling at a speed of v/c = 0.999999 covers one light year of distance in 0.00141 year or in 12 hours and 35 minutes on board time, a piece of cake for the UFO operator who can make that speed.

3. In the theoretical limit of v/c = 1.0 we have the actual speed of the photon, the graviton, and the four neutrinos. Nothing else known can go that fast. At that speed the ratio of on board time to Earth time is zero, or time stands still. In the popular literature on relativity, this relation gives rise to the "photon ride" analogy. If we could ride on a photon any part of the universe could be crossed in no time at all. This is equivalent to a one-way time-space machine, which turns "universal" time one year forward for each light year of distance traversed. The relativistic theory doesn't tell us how to turn time backwards. That is why our space-time machine is one-way. While no vehicle can achieve light speed, approaching very close gives almost the same on board results, for the vehicle moves through a light year of distance and a year of observer time in the fractional year given in the t'/t column of Table XVIII-1. Furthermore, demonstrated UFO accelerations through normal space are such as to make practicable the achievement of speeds approaching light speeds.

A little thought shows that the time of importance to space travel is the time the space traveler spends on board his vehicle during the trip, the time shown by his own clocks. This is the time that determines the wear and aging of equipment, how long the traveler must await his arrival, how much he ages during the trip, and the amount of food and all other consumables needed for the voyage. In short, it is the time of importance for planning and executing all operational phases of the trip. Conversely, the elapsed time to an Earth observer or other stationary observer is of little consequence to the feasibility of making such a trip. Outstanding is the fact that the high-speed space trip keeps the traveler young, his wait short. What does he care that, in making a trip of nearly a hundred light years, Earth history moves ahead 100 years if the trip only takes six months of his time? It's our wait, not his. Where is the problem for the traveler that people have been propagandized into believing?

The prohibitive-interstellar-distance propagandists have for decades been getting away with using the inconsequential limiting stationary observer time, the interstellar distance in light years, as the limiting time of importance to the trip. The fallacy is that they never mention the on board time for a fast trip. For self-consistency most assume that interstellar vehicles travel at chemical rocket speeds. At such a low v/c, on board and observer times are equal, so they don't differentiate. But when they start talking limits, and limits must be v/c's approaching unity, then to give stationary observer limit time and not mention that on board time is approaching zero is a gross miscarriage of argumentative justice.

It must be made perfectly clear that the article on Travel Problems quoted is not such a propaganda article. Incidentally, the author is an astute businessman and able manager. Like so many of us he is an innocent victim of "scientific" propagandists, and is only trying to make sense of various conflicting inputs from the world around us. He has written an interesting, thought-provoking article. It served as an excellent focus for shaping my own relativistic explanations. As that author suggests, anyone who speculates that the principles of relativity are wrong is making a risky speculation. The main comment to be made has already been made. If the UFO can accelerate to near light speed, as is perfectly reasonable, there is essentially no problem. Unique spaces are not required.

We must now consider the time required for a UFO to accelerate to speeds approaching light speed.

B. Acceleration and Mission Profile

Most writers, and physicists too, in estimating the time for interstellar travel, neglect the effect of the accelerating portions of the trip on the trip time, making the simplifying assumption that the vehicle makes the entire trip at constant velocity. This is probably done because the requisite equations are scarce items in the literature. This practice involves a nonconservative error which can be small or large, depending on the case. The assumption of a constant speed trip puts the trip calculations squarely in the realm of the Special Theory, which deals only with nonaccelerating frames of reference. However, since the vehicle reference frame undergoes acceleration and deceleration the Special Theory requires some extensions.

It was characteristic of Einstein's work that he spent most of his time in a quest to advance the far frontiers of relativity, leaving many special cases and applications to be worked out by others. The equations for space travel is a case in point. They have been worked out piecemeal by authors here and there and presented piecemeal in technical periodicals, often incomplete in substance and derivation. For this reason, I include as Appendix 5 a derivation of the equations needed to calculate interstellar travel time. The presentation at least has the merit of being all in one place. Not only do the equations agree with the published works of others, but the derivations have been checked by a number of relativity experts at the Langley Research Center.

The mission profile is a plot of speed versus time. The profile considered is one with a constant on board acceleration period followed by a constant velocity coast period, and terminating with a constant deceleration period which is a mirror image of the acceleration period, as shown in Figure XVIII-1. The mission profile shown is laid out in terms of quantities read by on board instrumentation, on board speed and on board time. Then, since the on board acceleration is constant, as is the deceleration, the plot consists only of straight line segments.

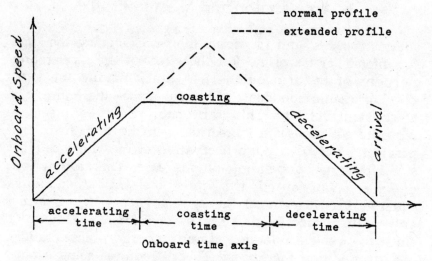

Figure XVIII-1. Interstellar Mission Profiles

The mission profile can be thought of as involving a lot of possible accelerations, accelerating times, coasting speeds, coasting times, and distances covered. Thus this mission profile is suitable for making parametric studies, wherein the variables are systematically changed to note the effects. When the accelerating time is increased to half the trip time, the mission profile takes on the triangular shape indicated by the dotted lines. This is the limiting case of the more general trapezoidal mission profile drawn in solid lines. The parametric study results, which we shall examine, always include this limiting case.

We now examine the vertical axis of the mission profile, the on board time. Using primed symbols for on board parameters, v' is the on board speed, which is equal to the product of constant on board acceleration, a', and the elapsed on board time, t'; that is, v' = a't'. The on board speedometer is a simple computer that multiplies the accelerometer reading by clock-time increments and keeps a running tally or summation. The computer can also divide by the speed of light to give the speed readings as decimal fractions of light speed, that is v'/c = a't'/c. This identity will henceforth be called the on board speed parameter. Since the computer is simple-minded (?) as well as simple, it knows nothing about the speed of light as a limit; it just does its job. When a't'/c exceeds 1, it just keeps summing away, no matter how many times unity its output registers. V-e-r-y interesting! Of course, we stay-at-home observers know that the vehicle is traveling at less than light speed, or in our symbols v/c is less than 1. The relation between v/c and the on board speed parameter a't'/c can be obtained by equations A5-2 and A5-2a of Appendix 5. This relation is graphically displayed in Figure XVIII-2 and will be discussed in the next subsection.

C. Parametric Studies

Using the applicable equations developed in Appendix 5 in order to take acceleration into account in the relativistic computations, a parametric study was made of the time for interstellar travel. Both on board and stationary observer times were computed. The parametric variables are interstellar distance, in light years, v/c in decimal decades as in Table XVIII-1, and vehicle acceleration in earth g's.

A COMPUTATION CHART FOR SPEED

Figure XVIII-2 shows the speeds resulting from any combination of on board acceleration and acceleration time. The vertical time scale, at the far left, can also be read on the graph grid, where the smallest division is 2 days. To use the chart, choose an accelerating time on the time scale and project horizontally to a chosen g-line, project the intersection up to the v/c curve, reading the v/c on the vertical v/c scale. Vice versa, choose a v/c on the curve, using the tagged values as necessary at extreme speeds, and project down to any g-line, reading the time on the scale to the far left. For example, chose v/c = 0.999 and acceleration = 100 g. At the intersection of these two quantities read on board accelerating time is 13.5 days.

Any v/c can also be projected down to its equivalent on board time parameter, a't'/c. Again projecting down from v/c = 0.999, we read the on board time parameter is 3.8. The on board instrumentation and computer combination is indicating 3.8 times light speed in its non-relativistic computation.

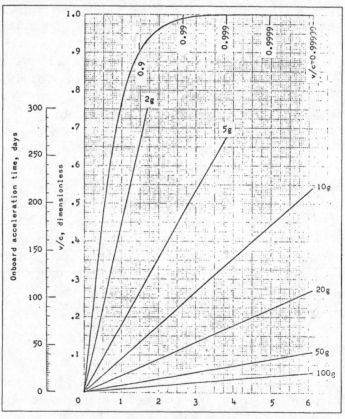

a' t ' / c
On board time parameter, dimensionless

Figure XVIII-2. Variation of v/c and on board time with on board time parameter.

The product of time and acceleration is decisive in the determination of on board and observer speed reached. Again, at the time parameter of 3.8 and v/c = 0.999, it makes no difference in speed whether the vehicle accelerates 13.5 days at 100 g, 27 days at 50 g, 67.5 days at 20 g, or 135 days at 10 g, as may be verified from the chart.

The nearly equal spacing of the v/c tics is important. It shows that each successive decade in v/c achieved requires nearly equal accelerating time. Since every two decades in v/c slows the on board clocks by a factor of 10, each decade slows the clocks by a factor equal to the square root of 10, about 3.16

RESULTS OF STUDY

Figure XVIII-3 shows the effect on the on board trip time of varying the acceleration from low values to 140 g. We note:

1. There is a pronounced knee in the upper curves, showing g to be critical in the 10-20 g range of acceleration; that is, the UFO needs to use at least this much g to avoid wasting time.

2. For the lower curves corresponding to higher speed trips, the use of higher g is even more important to trip time.

3. The top speed (coasting speed) of the trip is more important to trip time than acceleration. For example, the 100 light year trip made by accelerating to v/c = 0.999 at 140 g takes 4.5 years, while the same trip made by accelerating to v/c = 0.99999 at 140 g takes 0.52 year, an overall ratio of about 9. For the latter speed, cutting the g's back to 5 gives a trip time of 2.5 years, a ratio of about 5.

4. It is possible for an interstellar trip to be very short. The trip from our nearest neighbor,

Aloha Centuri, a triple star system 4.3 light years away, made by accelerating at 140 g to a v/c of 0.9999 is accomplished from a standing start to a standing finish in 6 weeks, 0.115 year.

5. All the trips include a coast period at the labeled speed except the trip corresponding to the left terminal of each curve, which has a triangular mission profile. The curves necessarily terminate at the value of g which gives the listed speed at the mid-point of the trip. A glance at the curves shows it is always a waste of time to use a triangular mission profile. Higher acceleration with a coast gives a quicker trip.

Figure XVIII-4 shows how long it takes to travel to the Sun from a few well-known F, G, and K type stars within a hundred light years distance, at what I consider to be reasonable values of g toward the lower end of the range. These are just typical nearby stars not too unlike the Sun to support planetary life as we know it. However, there is some doubt about the stars of spectral types less than F5 having planets, but the probability is very high that the G and K stars have them. From Figure XVIII-4 we note:

1. The slow trip, with a v/c of 0.9, requires an on board time equal to half the distance in light years for distances above 10 light years.

2. At a speed of v/c = 0.99 the interesting (from the viewpoint of proximity, probability of life and intelligence, and possible technological development) stars ε Eridani and τ Ceti are only about 2 years away to the UFOnaut.

3. The fast trip, v/c = O.99999, cuts all the travel times from stars within 100 light years to less than one year.

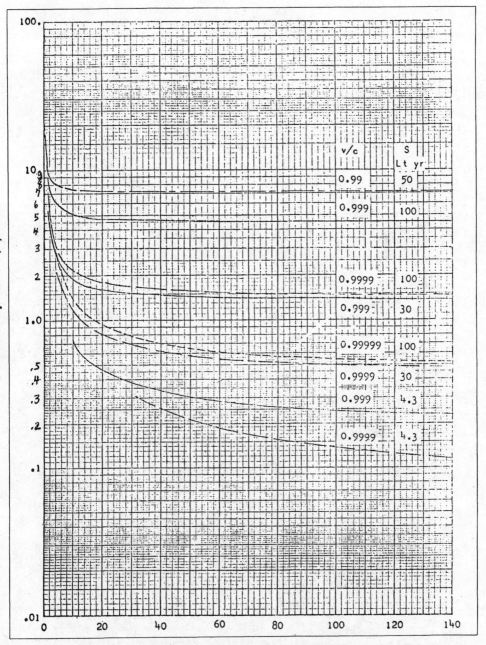

Figure XVIII-3. Trend of on board total elapsed time with acceleration rate.

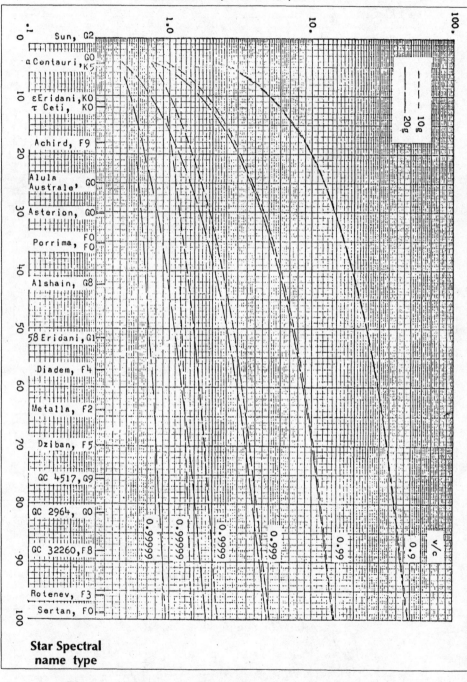

On board trip time T ' , years

Figure XVIII-4. Dependence of on board time on stellar distance.

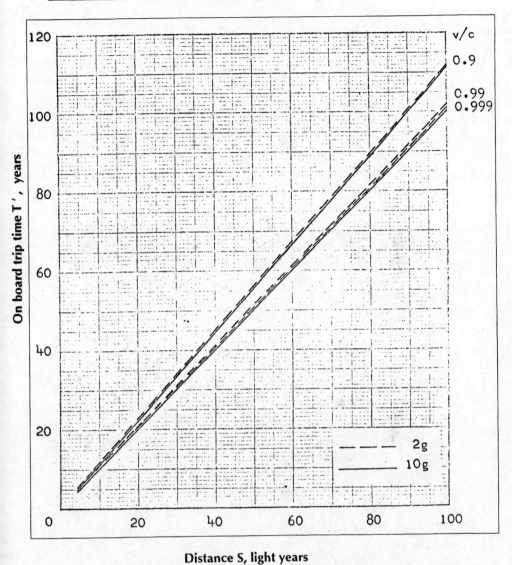

Distance S, light years

Figure XVIII-5. Dependence of observed time on stellar distance.

4. At the highest speeds considered, the travel time is not at all proportional to the distance. For example, at 20 g and v/c = 0.99999 we read a distance of 25 light years takes 0.6 years on board, while a distance of 100 light years is covered in almost a year. The reason is easy to visualize. Once the vehicle is up to speed, vast amounts of additional distance may be covered during the coast period with but little increase in time and, obviously, with no increase in energy expenditure. For the case just cited, each additional light year covered while coasting takes only an additional 39 hours on board (see Table XVIII-1 and calculate that 0.00447 times 8760 Earth hours per year equals 39 hours on board time).

The time for extending any trip to cover greater distances by extending the coast time can be simply determined by this method. Just add the extended time to the times given in Figures XVIII-3 or XVIII-4, in which the complications of relativistic acceleration and deceleration are already accounted for.

Thus far the trip times illustrated have all been in terms of the time of primary importance to the traveler, the on board time. We now present the (highly propagandized and much overrated) trip time as it appears to the stationary observer. Figure XVIII-5 shows the dependence of observed trip time on the stellar distance for values of v/c = 0.9, 0.99, and 0.999 and for 2 and 10 g. The main result is strikingly simple. Except for a v/c of 0.9, all speeds and accelerations give an observed trip time only very slightly greater than the stellar distance expressed in light years. For the slow trip, v/c = 0.9, the observed times are roughly 12 percent greater. It is clear from the figure that going to higher values of g or higher values of v/c than those shown would result in negligible decrease in observed time.

D. The Effective-Speed Concept

Those interested in the idea that in their own reference frame spacecraft may have an effective speed greater than light speed should read Appendix 5. In the effective-speed concept, effective speed v_e' is equal to the Earth-reference distance traveled per unit of on board time. The effective-speed ratio is the effective speed divided by light speed, or v_e'/c. The effective-speed ratio may have any value. As v/c approaches unity, the effective speed ratio approaches infinity.

At constant travel velocity the equivalent definition of effective-speed ratio is the distance traveled in light years S (S equals distance/c) divided by on board travel time, or

$$\frac{v_e'}{c} = \frac{S}{T'}$$

and, conversely, the on board travel time at constant velocity is

$$T' = \frac{S}{v_e'/c} \quad \text{years}$$

(A5-13c)

The effective speed for a vehicle with constant acceleration may be computed by the following simple non-relativistic computation. Multiply the on board acceleration in g's by the acceleration of Earth gravity and Earth accelerating time in seconds, and divide by c. For example, for a vehicle accelerating at a hundred g for one Earth day (86,400 seconds) the effective speed-ratio is

$$\frac{v_e'}{c} = \frac{(100)(9.8)(86,400)}{(3 \times 10^{8})}$$

$$= 0.28224 \quad \text{per day}$$

The time to achieve an effective-speed ratio of 1.0 is obtained by taking the reciprocal of 0.28224 which is 3.543 Earth days. By proportion, the time to achieve an effective-speed ratio of 0.1 is 0.3543 days, of 0.5 is 1.771 days, of 2.0 is 7.086 days, and of 10.0 is 35.43 Earth days. That the method is correct is demonstrated in Appendix 5. These values of speed ratio will be used in the following table.

The following columns give the time to travel one light year at the speed ratios just cited. Use the equation A5-13c and perform the division mentally:

$\dfrac{V_e}{c}$	T' years
0.1	10.0
0.5	2.0
1.0	1.0
2.0	0.5
10.0	0.1

These simple non-relativistic calculations of effective speed and of on board time at constant vehicle speed follow the methods of low-speed computations yet give answers that are valid at all speeds. The computed on board times, using this concept and methods which I originated, are exactly the same as those obtained by the more complex relativistic computations.

E. Conclusion

I hope I have made it clear that there is an important distinction to be made between the time experienced by the space traveler and the time which passes meanwhile on the home planet and on the planetary destination. The tremendous acceleration, speed, and energy capabilities displayed by UFOs make them well suited to capitalize on this distinction by the attainment of greatly reduced on board times realizable by approaching the speed of light. Even an approach to 90 percent of light speed gets the job done for the nearer stars. Higher fractions of light speed give attractive time reductions for longer trips.

Don't be misled by the countless statements in the literature that interstellar distances and the speed of light constitute some kind of barrier to space travel. There are only two paths to this conclusion:

1. Nobody in the universe has the technology to approach light speed.

2. Observer time is significant, and on board time is to be ignored.

Both paths are false ones. The confused second view is the more common. Its proponents are using the observed time for light to travel as the shortest possible time for passage. Totally false.

Section XIX
UFO Operational Capabilities

A. Pushing Against a Solid Footing

PROPULSION MODES IN CONVENTIONAL
VEHICLES—WASTED ENERGY.

In all jet propulsion devices, and even in airplanes and boats using screw propellers, energy is wasted in the wake because the vehicle does not have a solid traction. It is necessary to throw the working medium backward (air, water, or combustion products in the propeller slipstream or jet wake) to get the forward thrust. The wasted energy is the kinetic energy of the slipstream or jet as seen by a stationary observer. Consider the jet, either turbo or rocket jet. Only when the speed of the vehicle is so high as to approach jet speed, so that the difference in the two approaches zero, can the system mechanical conversion efficiency approach 100 percent. Conversely, at low speed most of the mechanical energy ends up in the wake and the system efficiency is very low.

In traction devices which push directly against the Earth, as in the case of a diesel locomotive rolling on a steel track, the drive wheels transmit the driving force to the track in a direct, efficient manner. While there is a small rolling and bearing friction, no kinetic energy is thrown away as in jet propulsion systems. The drive wheel transmits mechanical energy to the train with a high energy conversion efficiency.

Another good example is that of a hand-powered boat. The boatman has a small, undersized paddle, but he is in a hurry. He throws a lot of water backward with his paddle, but he cannot get a good purchase or "bite" on the water to drive the boat ahead. His energy is being wasted. By good fortune the boatman also has a wooden pole in the boat. He tries it and, finding a good hard bottom, pushes the boat forward with ease. His propulsive efficiency has gone from very low to very high.

Birds, airplanes, and helicopters get their lift by pushing air downward. The downward moving air, called the downwash, has kinetic energy which is the cost to the bird, airplane, or helicopter of holding it aloft. As the downwash nears the ground, the kinetic energy converts to air pressure against the ground, and in the last analysis everything that stays aloft in the atmosphere is supported by the ground, however indirectly. The energy of the downwash is energy wasted in comparison with more direct systems. Direct systems are relatively new to mankind, occurring in the form of magnetically suspended experimental trains and in the force field suspension of UFOs.

DIRECT FIELD SUSPENSION

The operation of the static fields with which we are familiar is a marvel of efficiency. They transmit energy with almost perfect efficiency. Now that the age of space travel has arrived to buttress the already existing science of astronomy, there is hardly anyone not familiar with the energy conserving nature of the solar, planetary, and lunar gravitational fields. The gravitational field energy together with objects such as spacecraft coasting through them are said to form an energy conservative system; energy is transferred from the field to the spacecraft or from the spacecraft to the field without losses. As everyone now knows, the energy transferred from a departing spacecraft to the Earth's gravitational field is called the escape energy, and corresponds to a speed of almost 25,000 miles per hour or about 11 kilometers per second. On the other hand, a satellite in circular orbit operates without energy exchange because it is in a constant field energy path.

The point to be made of all this, from a vehicle operational viewpoint, is that if an idealized (perfect) static force field were utilized as a propulsive device or link, the suspension of a hovering vehicle above the Earth by the static field would occur without an exchange of energy, for the vehicle is at a constant gravitational energy level, and the Earth is at a constant force field energy level. The forces are balanced and no energy is exchanged because one doesn't move relative to the other. This is analogous in result to the satellite in a constant energy circular orbit. Note that it was not stated that no energy is expended, for the UFO force field is not an ideal (perfect) static field. As visualized in Section IX, the UFO force field has a field strength ripple or pulsation, and doubtless requires vehicle supplied energy to support its existence. The statement is that if the field were perfectly static it would form a perfect link between the hovering vehicle and the ground. If the field is a good approximation to a static field, the energy exchange necessary between the hovering vehicle and the ground should still be low, and the efficiency good. That this is approximately so is attested to by the low heating rate of the ground beneath a UFO; additionally, part, if not most, of the ground heating can be attributed to hard radiation rather than to the force field strength ripple (Section X).

In theory, it is necessary only for the UFO to supply and trade force field energy to support three types of energy requirements:

1. potential energy, as it moves up against the pull of gravity;
2. kinetic energy accumulated as it accelerates away; and
3. energy to overcome whatever air drag exists.

All this operational energy it can supply at the good efficiency of field propulsion because the UFO is directly geared to the Earth by its force field as our coasting spacecraft in elliptical orbit is geared to the Earth by the Earth's gravity field. Thus we visualize the principle that the UFO supplies energy through a linkage in a manner analogous to an electric field propelling an electron, or to a motor connected to a load through a gear train; i.e., energy is exchanged in the conservative (or nearly conservative) manner inherent in field processes.

Note how completely different this is from a rocket or turbojet engine which burns up a fixed quantity of energy per second to supply a nearly constant thrust, independently of whether it is moving slowly and developing little usable power or moving fast and developing a great deal. A helicopter is another good example. A helicopter takes so much power to hover that it can move forward at 30 to 40 miles per hour on less power than it takes to hover. Its link to Earth is a tenuous one even at low altitude.

SIDE EFFECTS

Another way to visualize the operation of the UFO force field is to note that the force field pushes on everything in the field in proportion to the local field strength and in proportion to the material density of the substances being pushed. Thus its push against the atmosphere is very much less than its push against the Earth because of the greater than 1000-to-1 density ratio of Earth to atmosphere. This in turn means, and is completely consistent with observations, that air velocities about hovering and slowly moving UFOs are small, but sometimes sufficient to be noticeable. The kinetic energy lost to pushing air downward is therefore small in comparison to the corresponding downward airdraft losses of aircraft, which are large enough to be given the special name of induced losses.

The first two of the three energy requirements listed above have a converse. When the UFO descends to Earth from altitude, it beams its field down with sufficient strength to absorb the vehicle's potential and kinetic energy. Whether or not the UFO can absorb some of the energy, as an electric train can feed energy into the system going downhill, is an extremely moot point. Still, the field is absorbing energy, which may account for the not-infrequently observed air ionization flare-up when UFOs come in for a fast stop. Certainly the UFO wobble and the UFO rock are intentional energy dissipating maneuvers most often displayed at the end of descent.

INTERNAL HEATING

Much space has herein been devoted to the discussion of losses and efficiency. This attention is justifiable because efficiency is a double-edged sword, determining both the useful energy output and the internal heating problems.

If our family car gets excellent gas mileage we think of it as commendably efficient. Early in the century, however, the family car had a low-compression motor, and a larger percent of the energy went into the high-temperature exhaust gases and into the cooling system to the radiator. Not many readers will remember how the old cars used to overheat on a long hill, the driver dashing off to the nearest horse-watering trough for a pail of water.

A much more recent example of cooling problems was uncovered in the space laboratory studies carried out jointly by NASA and the aerospace industry. These first studied the experimental programs to be accomplished in space, and then designed a space laboratory to carry them out, including the electric power system to operate the laboratory. When all the required volumes for working and living aboard were added up, the volume and dimensions of the laboratory were established. Then came the surprise. The space laboratory so designed didn't have enough surface area to get rid of the waste heat generated while maintaining a reasonable internal atmospheric temperature. It was area critical, rather than volume critical. This study result was substantiated when Skylab almost had to be abandoned due to overheating.

Saucers, spherical UFOs, and other types have very limited surface areas for the rejection of internally generated heat. This fact seems to be giving us a message. Among the other marvels of the UFO, they have to be setting a record for internal operating efficiency, minimizing all losses which might turn to heat. This is particularly true of the propulsive system—the force field generators—which according to observed UFO performance handle prodigious amounts of energy.

To make the relation between efficiency and energy losses clear, we note that the conservation of mass energy requires that useful output equals input minus losses. Then the definition of efficiency, output divided by input, gives the internal efficiency, η as

$$\eta = \frac{\text{Input} - \text{Losses}}{\text{Input}} \qquad (19\text{-}1)$$

Assuming that the internal losses are equal to the internal heating, equation (19-1) can be restated in the following form:

$$\text{Internal heating rate} = \text{Power input} (1 - \eta) \qquad (19\text{-}2)$$

The mere fact that the UFO doesn't burn itself up indicates that the internal heating is small due to η being near 1.0. It is interesting to note that of all of man's prime movers, only hydraulic turbines, which really operate on the Earth's gravitational power, have an internal efficiency of near 0.9, or 90 percent. Could this be a clue? I believe it is.

B. Heading For the Stars

USE OF THE FORCE FIELD

We have seen the basic advantage to propulsion efficiency of pushing against a solid, non-yielding body with a force field propulsive link which is basically energy conservative. It is an advantage in near-earth operation, but becomes even more important when the time comes to impart the tremendous energies to a vehicle which it needs when leaving for the stars. It is in this case, in gaining speed while still near enough to a planet to realize the advantage of a direct force field link, and still at a low fraction of light velocity, that the advantage over jet, high-speed particle, or photon systems is paramount. According to the theory here discussed the field stress at the areas of generation impart kinetic energy to the vehicle; the generators push against the field, and the field pushes against the generators as well as against the Earth or other large body, maintaining the balance of forces.

As we noted near the end of Section X, the UFO must be able to focus its field to achieve thrust-vector control; at the end of Section X an example was given showing great versatility in that respect. A crude degree of focusing would suffice for near-Earth maneuvers, but as the UFO machine pulls away from the planet in a high speed departure the focus of the field becomes more important as the angular size of the planet diminishes. It is then that the UFO strives to focus sharply and keep the planet in its rear sights. This is probably the real reason the UFO has developed its field focusing capability to such a high degree.

Of course, the large dirigible- or cigar-shaped UFOs are most apt to be involved in the departure maneuver, the scout ships being packed aboard like so many lifeboats on a transatlantic steamer. Some others, such as the giant conical hat UFOs (Section III), are also probably large enough for an interstellar mission. As can be judged by the narrow, plume-shaped wake which they lay down while accelerating, visible in both daylight and dark, the big dirigibles and cigars demonstrate the high degree of focusing needed for the purpose.

PULL-UPS INVOLVED

It is indeed interesting that in the classic case of the large dirigible UFO which rocked Chiles' and Whitted's airliner (Section XII) as it flashed by displaying a brightly illuminated wake, the vehicle was doing a pull-up as it accelerated away into the cloud cover. This would cause its rearwardly focused field to intersect the ground as well as the atmosphere. It, too, was "poleing the boat." Similarly, the dirigible UFO that I observed (Section XII) slanted upward about 5 degrees at the very moment it began to accelerate. That was also the moment it showed its plume. Coincidence? Hardly. At its low altitude of about 1000 feet, the 5-degree upward slant was sufficient to make the lower end of Chesapeake Bay a base to push against in the action-equals-reaction nature of force fields.

When the starship has left the Earth, what is next? Assuming that the destination is a star, the logical next step, navigation permitting, is to pass closer to the Sun to get a big accelerating run as it points tail-to-the-Sun on a hyperbolic type trajectory whose asymptote points to the vehicle's destination. As an added maneuver the vehicle might shape the first hyperbola to pass close to one of the giant planets such as Jupiter or Neptune, using it as an additional thrusting base as it shapes its trajectory toward its final destination.

By coincidence or design, the dirigible UFO that I saw as it blasted off was heading westward, not too far from the direction of the late afternoon sun to be of importance to the application of the navigation and force-base scheme described. Since the vehicle gained such tremendous speed even in the dense lower atmosphere, it seemed to be going somewhere. I have wondered for years whether this was coincidence, or a piece of the jigsaw puzzle fitting neatly into place.

THE DISTANCE FACTOR

Somewhere there is a distance from planetary and stellar bodies, the distance being as yet unknown, beyond which the UFO force field can no longer function as a static field. Naturally this critical distance depends on the size of the body. This distance factor gives the UFO starship an incentive to make use of the highest acceleration possible in order to get to a high speed before it is out of range for the most efficient operation. Since UFOs use 100 g's just zipping around, perhaps they can accelerate at 1000 g or more when they are really serious.

Let us try an example to get a feel for the situation. Suppose an interstellar craft accelerates continuously at 1000 g starting from Earth and passing to within 23 million miles of the Sun. It then pushes against the Sun until it clears the solar system at the orbit of Pluto. An hour and a half and about 90 million miles (Pythagorean theorem) after leaving Earth, the craft makes nearest approach to the Sun at a v/c of 0.18, or 18 percent of light speed. Pointing tail toward the Sun, it passes the orbit of Pluto in another 8 hours, making about 70 percent of light speed.

If the UFO can do that well, it is doing very well, for it has reached a speed where the switch to momentum propulsion will result in efficient, effective operation. Probably it would have to switch at some lower speed unless aided by still higher acceleration. Because of the decreasing angular size of the Earth the UFO might elect to introduce a coast period before closest approach to the Sun in order to avoid a temporary switch to momentum propulsion at low v/c. Picking up a giant planet on the outbound leg would surely help.

After the distance factor becomes critical, the field generators can be considered to be driving the vehicle by the reaction from the momentum of a shower of quantum particles of energy. If the generators eject a dense shower of antigravitons plus x-ray photons, it is their momentum reaction driving the vehicle. These both eject at light speed, so the (jet) efficiency would be identical to that of a photon rocket moving at the same speed. The propulsive mode is changed without the need for a second type of power plant for high speed operation. The propulsive theory for this mode of operation is developed in Appendix 6. For a given energy input rate, the switch-over means that the thrust and acceleration are reduced in the middle-speed range, but the reduction inappreciable at near-light speeds.

C. Alternate Energy Supply Possibilities

CARRYING ENERGY VERSUS GATHERING ENERGY

There are two distinct energy bases on which the UFOs might operate. One is to carry their entire energy supply on board. The other is to gather energy from the surrounding energy fields as they go. In between are other possibilities, such as picking up part of their energy supplies at stopovers. The scout vehicles may refuel at the interstellar vehicles, and the interstellar vehicles may feast on the earth's gravitational field while the scouts are working.

If UFOs can gather energy from the surrounding energy fields while underway, the speed of light is the only performance limitation known to twentieth-century physics (relativity). As we have seen, this is not much of a limit to on board scientists and crews. Their range of action would be essentially unlimited. In the other extreme, if UFOs carry their entire energy supply on board there exist speed limits beyond which they cannot go. For example, the limitation theory developed in Appendix 6 shows they might reach a speed on the order of v/c equals 0.999, but probably not 0.99999.

Such limits depend on the fraction of the total mass of the vehicle which is convertible to useful energy. As an extreme example, a chemical rocket with a heating value of 10 million joules per kilogram of propellants converts about one part in 10 billion of propellent mass to energy, a fraction so small it can't be weighed. But if a particle collides with its antiparticle, all of the mass can be converted to energy.

It should be pointed out that the particle-antiparticle reaction is not a matter-antimatter reaction in the usual definition of the terms. Antimatter is a combination of antiprotons and antineutrons to form a nucleus, which is surrounded by positrons to form an antiatom. These have never been observed. On the other hand, positrons are common in the high-energy physics laboratories, and electrons extremely common. The annihilation reaction of the two have been frequently observed. Each reaction converts 1.8×10^{-30} kilograms of mass to one million electron volts of energy.

HIGH EFFICIENCY MASS CONVERSION

Next, in the following subsection we will consider the very best that can be done by any vehicle carrying its entire energy supply along, using a propulsion mode which converts the total energy expended into vehicle relativistic kinetic energy. This mode could represent the conversion of on board mass to force field energy and the force field energy to vehicle kinetic energy. Since we don't know the proper conversion efficiency to assign, we investigate the limiting case of 100 percent. Also investigated is the case of the momentum reaction cycle, or rocket cycle, with full energy conversion to the beam. These two together will illustrate typical limiting cases of performance under the assumption that the total energy supply is carried aboard.

This propulsion exercise, along with the parametric study of the time for interstellar travel at various accelerations and speeds, was carried out on a spare-time basis at the time that the Condon Committee was in session, in order to check on the validity of their results. The Committee, however, seemed to prefer to study mirages, radar ghosts, ball lightning, etc., rather than anything as fundamental as UFO propulsion.

Finally, we will discuss the case for gathering energy en route, including the engine cycle mechanism from a particle-reaction viewpoint.

D. Mass Ratios and Speed—All Energy Stored On Board.

MASS RATIO

All vehicle performance equations are worked out in terms of the ratio of initial to final mass, called the vehicle mass ratio. This is conventional for conventional vehicles. However, it is convenient to present UFO performance in terms of the reciprocal of the mass ratio, which will be called reciprocal mass ratio.

To give the reader a feel for the mass ratios of spacecraft, we note that in modern rocketry, both in liquid fuel and solid fuel practice, the rocket structural weight of a single stage unit is about 10 percent of the rocket gross weight, leaving 90 percent of the gross weight as propellent. We say the propellent fraction of the rocket is 0.90. Thus the ratio of initial to final mass is 10. This is for the motor only. If we add a payload whose weight equals the weight of the structure, then the final mass at burnout is 0.2 compared to a rocket gross of 1.0. The initial mass is the rocket gross of 1.0 plus the payload of 0.1 for a total initial mass of 1.1. Then clearly the initial-to-final vehicle masses are in the ratio 11 to 2, giving a vehicle mass ratio of 5.5.

The first ICBM, the old Atlas rocket, was structurally one of the most efficient rockets ever built. Its structural mass fraction was 0.05 compared to the 0.1 quoted above for more modern practice. This light weight was achieved by applying an internal pressure to the propellent tanks. Otherwise the rocket would have collapsed under its own weight on the launch pad. Since weight in orbit is zero, this design would be adequate for space work.

We wish to determine, as a reference, the best that people can do with mass fractions. Since there is no limit to the amount of propellent that can be put into orbit, the payload fraction can be reduced toward nothing by adding propellent and tankage. The inert weight of a big space system with Atlas construction can therefore approach 0.05 of the total, giving a mass ratio of 20. One would suspect that UFO designers could do as well.

SPEED PERFORMANCE (ALL ENERGY STORED ON BOARD)

Figure XIX-1 shows the relation between reciprocal mass ratio and speed computed according to the equations developed in Appendix 6. The results are given for three cases:

1. The short-dashed upper curve is for complete conversion of expendable mass energy to vehicle kinetic energy. This case is limiting, the best that any vehicle can possibly do carrying its own energy.

2. The solid lower curve is for an idealized anti-graviton and/or photon rocket with all converted energy going into the jet.

3. The middle curve is for a combination, illustrating a switch-over from mode 1 to mode 2 at half of light speed, v/c = 0.5.

The vertical scale is the ratio of final-to-initial mass. There are two speed scales for a simple reason. Logarithmic scales can't start from zero as does v/c. The data is therefore plotted against 1 - v/c. The data can be easily read at the even decades of v/c. Otherwise use the 1 - v/c scale and convert to v/c by subtracting from 1. A log plot is necessary to cover the big speed range of interstellar vehicles. No allowance has been made for stopping. That requires a second stage, or an allowance can be made by doubling 1 - v/c.

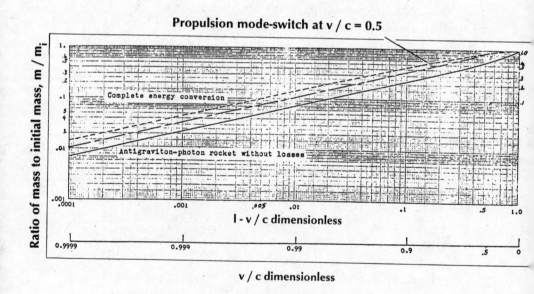

Figure XIX-1. Idealized Propulsion Mass Ratios

At our comparison reciprocal mass ratio of 0.05, complete energy conversion shows 1 - v/c equals 0.0012, or v/c is 0.9988. At that speed the time ratio is 0.049, or about 20 light years are traveled per year on board. Evidently UFOs could manage carrying the entire energy supply. Whether they do or not is another matter.

The antigraviton/photon rocket curve shows the possibilities utilizing propulsion mode 2 described above from a standing start. In comparing this case with 1, note that the rocket curve descends more steeply at low speeds where it is inefficient, while the curve for energy conversion with field traction descends very slowly at low speeds. At high speeds, between v/c = 0.99 and v/c = 0.9999, the curves are straight and parallel with a constant ratio of 2 to 1.

It is possible that mode 1 is applicable only at modest distances and speeds. Inspection of the top and bottom curves suggests the desirability of mode switching at a v/c of 0.8 or beyond where it would make little if any difference. The middle curve illustrates mode switch-over at v/c = 0.5. The resulting speed penalties can be seen to be modest.

In utilizing these curves to evaluate UFO performance limitations, it should be remembered that all results are for loss-free operation except for losses basic to a rocket cycle operating with a jet velocity equal to light speed. Inevitable additional energy losses will lower the reciprocal mass ratios given.

Admitting that fantastically advanced technologies are necessary to approach the given results, this review of propulsion possibilities and limitations indicate that UFO propulsion systems should drive the craft toward and close to that ultimate velocity, the velocity of light.

FORCE FIELDS FOR LAUNCH?

My background in a broad range of vehicle launch systems makes me conscious of certain launching possibilities. If UFOs can focus a powerful force field beam from a moving craft, a huge, fixed installation near home base should make it possible to direct an even larger and more powerful force field beam into space. Such a beam could not be located on a home planet, for the power of the beam would create atmospheric storms, not to mention stripping the planet of some of its atmosphere. A moon should be satisfactory.

A large, directed force field beam would be an ideal launch mechanism. It would be virtually impossible to get the field strength and vehicle acceleration too high, for every atom and molecule would be pushed in proportion to its mass, all accelerating equally. This avoids acceleration stresses. The acceleration forces that people fear would occur only if tie-down-and-release mechanisms were attempted. The passengers, instruments, stowables, and the vehicle itself would feel no g stresses. All would be in freefall the moment of lift off, the accelerometers reading zero.

Depending on the power and length of the beam, the vehicle would approach the speed of light in a few hours, or at least be off to a beautiful start. Conversely, returning vehicles could decelerate in the force field beam pointed to intercept them. The use of this method would avoid any need for staged vehicles as previously mentioned.

E. Performance Unlimited—Energy Gathered en Route

PROFESSOR HERMAN OBERTH'S CONTRIBUTION

Professor Herman Oberth was the first to conclude that UFOs convert gravitational field energy to propulsive purposes. Professor Oberth was the guiding light in Germany's early rocket programs. To distinguish between Oberth and Dr. Werner von Braun, von Braun as a younger man in German scientific circles was project engineer for the V-2 rocket development program. I can recall him later quipping about his work, "To observe V-2 accuracy, I used to stand on the target. It was the safest place."

According to Frank Edwards (*Flying Saucers: Serious Business*, 126; *Flying Saucers: Here and Now*, 124), after

World War II the West German government hired Prof. Oberth to head a commission for the study of UFOs. He reported the gist of their conclusions in a press conference in 1954. He and his colleagues concluded that UFOs are factual, and are propelled by the conversion of gravitational field energy. Prof. Oberth said:

> [UFOs] are conceived and directed by intelligent beings of a very high order, and they are propelled by distorting the gravitational field, converting gravity into usable energy.
>
> There is no doubt in my mind that these objects are interplanetary craft of some sort. I and my colleagues are confident that they do not originate in our solar system but we feel that they may use Mars or some other body as a sort of way station.

Frank Edwards' own comment is pointed and succinct:

> If UFOs are propelled by conversion of gravity it would simplify space travel, since it would eliminate the necessity of carrying a fuel supply. Gravity pervades the universe; where it is weakest, less of it should be needed for propulsion; where it is strongest, more of it would be available.

This writer simply agrees.

WHAT IS A FIELD?

At this point we digress to consider the particle aspects of a field. The particle aspects of a field pertain to particles which are unobservable while performing their task, and therefore called virtual particles. In Section V, where 34 particles were eliminated as a means of UFO propulsion, observable particles in an external particle beam were being considered. That had no bearing on the virtual particles now being discussed, which form an alternate view of field activity and therefore could be directly pertinent to UFO propulsion.

In reasoning about the detail or fundamentals of UFO propulsion, it is helpful to examine the evolution of field concepts from the pre-twentieth century to the present. As a reference we note that all the known subatomic particles have been discovered within 100 years. Correspondingly, the ideas of a field have totally changed. In my view, the explanation of fields has gone from "instantaneous action at a distance" to a "strain in the ether" to a "strain in spacetime" to a separate fluid with granular properties or "quantum field," something which can be destroyed and created in lumps with the concurrent birth and annihilation of particles, to the rather unifying idea that field effects are "really" the exchange between particles affected by the field of the energy and momentum of some other particles, which are therefore called exchange particles. The exchange particle is born and dies in the process. Along this evolutionary route of ideas, the only concepts abandoned have been instantaneous action at a distance—as being impossible—and the concept of the ether—as being unobservable and therefore meaningless. The other concepts are able to coexist as multiple aspects of the same phenomena, much like the dual wave and particle aspects of the photon.

For the non-mathematical reader, an excellent reference on this and related subjects is Chapter 27 of Ford's *Basic Physics*. In fact, the entire book is a surprisingly good reference on twentieth-century physics, having a self-imposed non-mathematical style of presentation.

The most familiar of the exchange particles is the virtual photon. It accounts for the electric field and the magnetic field, and of course a photon is an electromagnetic field. Fermi and Dirac showed that the electric force between two charged particles is due to the incessant exchange of virtual photons between the two particles. Thus a "field" force has been simulated, explained or done away with, as one chooses to view it. The forces in the everyday world around us are electric in nature. When the ball bounces off the bat, it is the virtual photon exchange particle between the electrons of the bat and the electrons of the ball that sends the ball on its way. Other photons enable us to watch the ball.

In 1941, Hideki Yukawa won the Nobel Prize in physics for his prediction in 1935 of pion particles in the atomic nucleus whose exchange among the protons and neutrons would provide the nuclear glue or "strong field" to hold them together. His theory was based on the Heisenberg uncertainty principle which permits particle energy violations for a very short period of time. This theory permitted a cloud of pions to escape from a proton core for the extremely short time of about 10^{-23} sec, and therefore an extremely short distance, about 10^{-15} meters, even though they don't have enough energy to escape. According to these quantum ideas, the energy law enforcement officer is willing to look the other way as long as the violation doesn't last longer than 10^{-23} seconds. When a neutron approaches to within the critical distance of the proton, the pion may make it to the neutron before the time limit is up, and the escape is achieved. If the pion exchange particle is carrying a positive charge, the proton it leaves becomes a neutron, and the neutron it joins becomes a proton, so their roles are constantly changing. The exchange of pions and other mesons in the atomic nucleus produces a strong attractive force now called an exchange force. These short-range exchanges occur with great frequency, holding the atomic nucleus together in spite of the electric (virtual photon) forces tending to blow it apart.

Two other recognized fields remain to be experimentally explored by the exchange particle route. These are the gravitational and antigravitational fields by the exchange particles called gravitons and antigravitons. They remain undiscovered and difficult to involve experimentally. Still, these particles are needed to give a reasonably rounded out picture of exchange particles accounting for all the fields of nature. The basic idea in natural processes is that a mass such as the earth showers out gravitons at a rate proportional to its mass, symmetrically in all directions at the speed of light. On reaching the moon, for example, they "interact" to accelerate the moon toward the Earth. Meanwhile, the moon also showers out gravitons at a rate proportional to its gravitational mass, and on arriving at Earth interact to produce the expected Earth acceleration, the tides, etc. Therefore graviton exchange is the equivalent of a gravitational field. The catch is that now Yukawa has stepped forward to explain the detail of the exchange interaction (what happens when the graviton reaches the mass particle).

The discovery of the antigraviton, which is presumably produced only by the antiparticles in the laboratory, is even more remote because of their scarcity. Even the negative gravitational mass of antiparticles is in doubt. Prof. Joseph Weber (*General Relativity and Gravitational Waves*, 6) shows a comparison of theory and experiment indicating that the gravitational mass of a positron is not negative; i.e., it would not be expected to radiate antigravitons. Also, it is well known by watching the behavior of positrons in the magnetic field of cloud chambers that their inertial mass is positive, their path curving opposite to the path of the electron.

On the other hand, metric gravitational theory shows that if negative matter exists, its field repels all matter, positive or negative (Weber 5). Such a field would need an antigraviton exchange particle to be in keeping with exchange-particle field theory. The theory is there, but to put it frankly, experimental confirmation seems remote, even hopeless.

Granting the possibility of antigraviton existence, the next question is what happens or would happen when it encounters an ordinary mass particle of the earth, or anything else in its path? What is the exchange-particle interaction? The simplest idea is that an antigraviton carries energy and momentum in the usual ratio for particles traveling at the speed of light (the ratio is light speed itself) and delivers momentum, but little energy, in a sudden change in course at the interaction. In our part of the universe, the antigraviton would be a loner, from a lone source. To fulfill the two-way function of exchange particles, the course change would have to approximate a 180-degree reversal of direction to carry particles back to the source. That is, to carry out its role the antigraviton would have to reflect. If nature is willing to do this, the UFO could be in business using the antigraviton. Reflection would nicely account for the theoretical repulsion of ordinary mass particles, and all others for that matter.

THE UFO FIELD EXCHANGE PARTICLE, THE UON

From the point of view of the exchange-particle theory that all acceleration (or force) fields are really exchange-particle interactions, it is clear that the UFO must obtain its acceleration field action and reaction through the intermediary of a virtual exchange particle, be it what it may. Since the exchange particles clearly haven't all been discovered, there seems to be an excellent probability that UFOs operate by means of an exchange particle as yet unknown, or at least undiscovered. We could call it the Uon. (Uep doesn't have an agreeable sound.) If so, to fulfill its two-way exchange function nature it would have to reflect from ordinary matter, just as explained for the antigraviton acting in the role of Uon. We may call this the Uon-reflection hypothesis. We characterize the Uon specifically to account for the UFO propulsion field characteristics. This does not mean that the Uon is or is not the antigraviton. It leaves the point open. Whatever particle qualifies is acceptable.

A hovering UFO would beam vast numbers of Uons toward Earth and these would reflect back to the UFO, whereupon most would re-reflect from the UFO for a second round trip. This multiple reflection emulates the field quality of energy conservation. The opposite attribute, absorption, would vaporize the ground with excessive heating, which clearly the UFO does not do. In parallel or common with all other field virtual exchange particles, the reflections are really absorptions and re-emissions in the proper direction. The action here described is analogous to photon-reflection in a mirror.

Suppose, for analogy, that a hovering UFO beamed down photons onto a level plane mirror at ground level, the beam reflecting intensely back to the UFO, which would in turn re-reflect some of the photons back down, etc. When one of these photons encounters the mirror, it doesn't turn around at the surface of the metal with which the mirror is silvered. It may pass by, or through, a dozen atoms of metal before it interacts with an electron. This electron is set to vibrating (accelerating) laterally which absorbs the photon, but the lateral accelerations also create an equal photon on the reverse path, called a reflection.

To the Uons, the Earth is a thick mirror. Uons penetrate much further into the earth than photons do into a mirror or metallic surface. The Uons are concerned with mass and mainly do business with the neutrons and protons which average about 1837 times as massive as the electron. Since the nucleons are smaller and more widely spaced targets, naturally penetrations would be much greater and, by the same token, surface smoothness less important.

DOES SCIENCE AGREE (WITH OBERTH) THAT UFOS CAN CONVERT GRAVITY INTO USEABLE ENERGY?

Since, in general, scientists have not studied the UFO, this question is interpreted as meaning, do today's scientific concepts and theories tend to support Professor Oberth? The reader can judge for himself from the following quote from the Russian physicist D.D. Ivanenko. Ivanenko, speaking of the leading American physicist J.A. Wheeler, says, "Wheeler entertains the hypothesis, as we do, that it may be possible for electron-positron pairs to be transformed not only into photons, but also into gravitons; moreover, he believes conversely, that it may be possible for the gravitational field to be transformed into ordinary matter" (Ivanenko and Vladimirov 28).

Although couched in cautious language, that is certainly an impressive one-sentence yes to the question. Ivanenko not only says yes but also suggests the route: field energy to ordinary matter, and electron-positron pairs into gravitons.

Of course, UFOs may have been the farthest thing from Ivanenko's mind, and we have no right to infer that he meant us any form of encouragement relative to a power plant application. Also, I see tremendous problems with the application of this energy conversion idea to propulsion, and with no more than I have to go on I would never say a particular route is the way the UFO does it. With that understanding, suppose we discuss some of the problems and some methodology.

Every physicist will know that Ivanenko and Wheeler must be referring to the possibility of low-yield reactions, that is, low probability of occurrence. To be a useful propulsive mechanism, control to give yields of near 100 percent would be needed, more like the sure-fire behavior of electrons in an electronic circuit. Then too, at least four of the basic conservation laws are involved in possible violations in the particle reactions. These are: conservation of charge, spin, momentum, and mass energy. This means that in any reaction the sum of each quantity before the reaction must also equal the sum of each quantity afterward. Otherwise, the reaction is forbidden.

In going from the gravitational field to matter, I don't know enough about it to make more than one constructive comment. Since the gravitational field is electrically neutral, if we convert some of its quantum grains of energy to a charged particle such as an electron, at the same time we must convert others to a positively charged particle such as a positron. Then charge is conserved. This is favorable, for now we have the mass energy needed for the second step.

The spin of the electron is $\frac{1}{2}$ and of the positron $\frac{1}{2}$ and can be oriented to suit, adding to 0 or 1. Now, how can Ivanenko's graviton having a spin of 2 result from a reaction having a spin of 1 or 0? Since other particles artificially created come in pairs, better we should create a graviton-antigraviton pair with a combined spin of 0, selecting 0 spin before and after. This selection may have a slight ring of favoritism, for without the antigraviton, or other "repulsive" Uon the UFO can't make it with this particle approach. Conversely, the antigraviton is just what the doctor ordered. Assuming that the antigraviton carries positive momentum and the graviton negative momentum, to be effective the antigraviton must be sent downward (from a hovering UFO) and the graviton upward. This requires an appropriately balanced reaction.

This reaction could possibly have a spin prohibition. Spin direction is defined in accordance with the direction of motion. If an advancing particle turns in the direction of an advancing wood screw, it has right-hand spin; if in the other direction, left-hand spin. All discovered particles except the neutrino and antineutrino can spin in either direction. The neutrino is unique in that it always has left-handed spin, while the antineutrino is always right-handed. If gravitons can spin either way, there is no problem. Or if gravitons and antigravitons are both right-handed or both left-handed, there is no problem. But if, like neutrinos, one is born right-handed and the other left-handed, we pitch this theory in the round file and are out looking for another Uon. For those who wish to mull over it, a little reflection will show that to get 0 spin after the reaction, particles going in opposite directions have to both go right-handed, or both left-handed to be rolling in opposite directions, their spin canceling.

The simultaneous balancing of momentum and energy can be achieved by mechanical means. Since the reaction output has a big downward momentum, the input must have the same. Either the electron or positron can be accelerated downward in an electric field to obtain the required input momentum. To fix ideas, let the electron be accelerated downward in vacuum and directed to strike a relatively quiescent positron (as in a television tube). The power to operate the electric field accelerator is taken from the reaction photons which are assumed to come from the reaction in opposite-directed pairs as ordinarily observed in the laboratory. If opposite-directed, they do not affect the momentum balance, and none is provided for them in the electron beam.

Assuming an ideal cycle for the theory, we now make a simultaneous solution of the equation for mass energy conservation, and the equation for momentum conservation to determine the electron beam energy for a perfect balance all around. This can be done by any student physicist (equations in Appendix 7). The answer turns out that the electrons are accelerated to

$$\frac{v}{c} = \sqrt{\frac{4}{5}}$$

or to 89.44 percent of light speed. When this is done, all the gravitons can go parallel to the UFO axis of symmetry (straight up for a vertically accelerating saucer) and all the antigravitons in the opposite direction as required. With the electron beam at this speed, excess photons not needed for beam power are obliged by the momentum principle to accompany the antigravitons in a downward direction. The theory cannot predict the percentage of residual photons accompanying the antigravitons because photons and antigravitons both travel at light speed and have the same ratio of momentum to energy. The ratio of gravitons and antigravitons to photons would have to be determined experimentally. In general, a high yield of gravitons and antigravitons compared to photons would be necessary to make the theory viable; otherwise a photon rocket would result. This is the real problem with the application of Ivanenko's pronouncement, as quoted, to UFO propulsion.

The high momentum input of the electrons at the velocity mentioned predicts good antigraviton focusing characteristics, or good UFO acceleration field focusing, and predicts that the main residual hard photon radiation will be in the same direction, much as the saucer-ring chemical alteration evidence indicates it should be. At lower electron beam velocities, the lowered momentum input allows gravitons, antigravitons, and photons to go in more random directions in a de-focused manner. This property of the calculations tends to explain UFO field focusing.

The calculated photon radiation energies also fits observations. If the random photon pair energy equals the beam kinetic energy per electron (energy conservation) and the electrons move at 89.44 percent of light speed, the kinetic energy per electron is 1.236 times its rest mass energy of 0.51 Mev (million electron volts). Each of these photons then has a strength of $(\frac{1}{2})(1.236)(0.51$ Mev$) = 0.3152$ Mev. Those escaping with this energy would have a frequency of $f = 7.6 \times 10^{19}$ cycles per second. Anything between 10^{19} and 10^{20} cycles/sec can be classed in the region of x-ray gamma-ray overlap. If, by chance, all of the energy of an individual reaction should go into a downwardly directed photon pair, the photon energy would be $(\frac{1}{2})(3.236)(0.51$ Mev$) = 0.825$

Mev. While this is definitely a gamma ray, and would cause ionization and chemical reactions to proceed, it is still not strong enough to leave the ground radioactive.

As explained earlier, if antigravitons are the Uon exchange particles, they must reflect back from the ground to the UFO. Some of these would enter the reaction zone where their behavior might be controlled by the particle reaction adage: if conservation laws allow the creation of a particle, they will also allow the destruction of its antiparticle. A reflected antigraviton arriving in the reaction zone at the right moment to enter the reaction could balance half the reaction momentum, either eliminating an upward moving graviton or making necessary an extra downward antigraviton. Either one would be all right. With enough of these events, the upward graviton flux would be reduced and the antigraviton flux increased. Other reflected antigravitons re-reflect toward the ground while some pass up through the UFO as losses. If reflection is good, the input power for a given acceleration field strength is reduced, and the UFO can "run cool."

The following paragraphs are intended to give some perspective, particularly with regard to reservations. The previous paragraphs have some of the aspects of a highly speculative theory for the internal workings of a UFO. Its foundation, Ivanenko's assertion of the possibility of an electron-positron reaction releasing gravitons, seemed so weak that I have come close to just saying so and omitting the discussion. Finally I decided I don't know enough to throw it out either. The reservation arises mainly from the likely low probability of occurrence, or low cross-section of the reaction. If the reaction really proceeds with an appreciable probability, either with a high-speed electron striking a low-speed positron, or vice versa, why hasn't an experimental physicist noticed that the energy of the resulting photon pair is insufficient to account for the input energy, as would have to be the case if a graviton-antigraviton pair is created also? Thus, a laboratory check does not require the identification of the new particles, just the finding of a pair of annihilation photons with substandard energy.

Another misgiving goes as follows. Our particle science is in a sort of embryonic stage, with hundreds of short-lived particles being discovered in the laboratory without too much sense having been made of many of them. Perhaps the UFO uses two other particles. Or perhaps wave theory is a better approach. UFO maneuver mechanics can be explained by the physics of 150 years ago, and the ionization of the atmosphere by the physics of 50 years ago. But can the inner workings of the UFO in the production of fields really be explained by today's physics? My feeling is that while we may make plausible attempts, the answer is no. We cannot reliably leap centuries of knowledge with imagination.

In situations like this I am often reminded of the Rutherford atomic model, which was based on classical mechanics. It had to be abandoned in favor of the Bohr atom, whose wave-like quantum mechanical electrons could be shown to have orbit stability. Still, Rutherford's atom had an outstanding feature. It was the first atomic model to have the nucleons all concentrated in a compact nucleus, in the correct fashion. All was not black and white. The Rutherford model had correct features and explained several things, especially electron scattering. It was useful, and it also formed a good stepping stone to a better model.

With such thoughts in mind, we note that the conversion of electron-positron pairs into antigravitational field energy along the lines suggested does a creditable job of explaining:

(a) UFO propulsion as a field capability.
(b) The ability of the UFO to sharply focus its field.
(c) Field de-focusing with decreased momentum and power input.
(d) UFO radioactivity without ground being left radioactive.
(e) The focusing of radioactive photons along with the field.
(f) Ionization of the atmosphere and ground chemistry changes.
(g) Pulsed ionization which would have strobo-

scopic-like effects and would also tie in with the observed cyclic nature of the UFO field.

F. The Control of Matter by Quark Seeding

THE POSSIBILITY OF MASS REDUCTION

During discussions that I had with Dr. James Harder, Dr. Harder suggested that the preponderance of evidence of massiveness pertains to the UFO scout ships rather than the UFO starships, which have never been observed to land, and that the latter may use low-mass materials of construction to aid interstellar flight. He further suggested negative-mass quark seeding of material, as proposed by Dr. F. Winterberg, as the possible means. From his files, Prof. Harder gave me copies of several supporting articles (see Bibliography), including Winterberg's article. In one, Arthur L. Robinson relates how a magnetic-monopole particle was recently identified in a cosmic ray balloon experiment; in another, the author explains why recently found baryons, nuclear exchange-force particles, can best be accounted for as quark-anti-quark pairs in a configuration resembling a hydrogen atom. The quark theory of matter dates back to P.A.M. Dirac's work and has exponents throughout the modern world of particle physics.

Although, in general, antiparticles do not have negative mass, the mass of the antiquark is indeed negative for reasons ably given in Winterberg's article. According to quark theory, the minimum electric charges are not those of the proton and electron, but come in units of ⅓ that amount which are the minimum charges carried by the quark and antiquark. In the smaller units the charge of the proton is 3 and of the electron -3. The three antiquarks of the proton each contribute a charge of 1 in smaller units. In the neutron the antiquark charges are 2, -1, -1. Quarks and antiquarks are also magnetically charged in quantum units that are 137 times greater than the electrostatic units of the electric charge. In the larger magnetic monopole units, the magnetic charge of the quarks may be 2, 1, or -1 and always occur in quark combinations making the summation or net magnetic charge 0. Thus the proton or neutron antiquarks would contribute magnetic charges of 2, -1, and -1.

The reader is doubtless wondering how the protons and neutrons having positive mass could be composed of antiquark particles each of negative mass. According to Winterberg, particles such as protons are three antiquarks bound together by large magnetic-charge exchange currents giving exchange forces and energy sufficient for the task. Winterberg uses a solution of the Schrodinger wave equation to predict the binding energy of a three-antiquark system. This binding energy is positive and is sufficiently larger than the negative rest-mass energy of the three antiquarks to give an energy summation that is equal to the rest-mass energy of the proton.

Winterberg suggests a new type fission, a fission of the proton to set the antiquarks free. An estimate of the interquark magnetic field strength is 10^{17} gauss. It would take a minimum of this amount of externally applied field strength to promote fission. Winterberg computes that a hard x-ray laser beam of 10^{13} erg with a pulse length of 10^{-9} second concentrated on an area of 10^{-20} sq cm or an energy of 10^{42} erg/sq cm should give the necessary magnetic field strength. Such a fission process would release prodigious amounts of binding energy, but Winterberg writes the following:

> There would be an even more exciting prospect in regard to the ash of that reaction, that is the negative mass quarks. For this let us consider what would happen when we dope a crystal lattice of solid matter with quarks by gradually replacing electrons by quarks. . .
>
> One may ultimately consider the case where a substantial fraction of the electrons is replaced by negative-mass quarks. Here, of course, a complicated balance of attractive and repulsive forces in between the quarks and the nuclei would have to be considered since in the absence of charge exchange currents the negative mass quarks with opposite magnetic charge would repel, and quarks with equal (like) magnetic charges attract. In spite of this unsolved question let us see what would happen if such a solid stable state incorporating quarks would exist. Since $m_p \cong |3m_q|$ [$\cong$ means *is approximately equal to*; | | means

change sign to plus] and since three quarks can make up for one negative electron charge, average electric and magnetic charge neutrality combined with the balance of positive-mass nuclei against negative-mass quarks could lead to a macroscopic body arbitrarily close to 0 rest mass but having a nonvanishing high tensile strength. It is furthermore conceivable that the body could have either positive or negative mass depending on the balance in between positive mass nuclei, negative mass quarks and mutual binding energy.

If by this method a macroscopic body with approaching-zero rest mass can be actually built it would be ideally suited for the attainment of relativistic velocities as they have been contemplated for interstellar flight. . .

But it is conceivable, at least in principle, to reduce the rest mass of the ship . . . such that almost no energy would be required to accelerate the ship to relativistic velocities (to near light speed). Furthermore, in approaching the state of vanishing rest mass the acceleration could be made arbitrarily large.

I and many readers will agree that Dr. Winterberg's theories pose a powerful and effective solution to the main problem of interstellar flight, that of quickly accelerating and achieving speeds close to light speeds on a minimum-energy budget. Even if the structural mass of a starship were zero, presumably the "payload" in the form of occupants, energy supply, and other cargo would have positive mass. Therefore total mass would be positive, but small. In case the interstellar craft carries its entire energy supply, the mass ratios corresponding to given speeds as given by the equations of Appendix 6 and in Figure XIX-1 are still valid, but give more favorable results, as Winterberg has stated, in that all masses—the mass at the beginning of an acceleration period, the mass at the end of the acceleration period, and the mass of the energy supply—are all unproportionately reduced. Either the storage space for the energy supply is reduced or, conversely, higher mass ratios and speeds closer to light speed can be achieved. An excellent result!

STRUCTURAL STRENGTH; MELTING POINT

According to Winterberg, the spacing of mass in an electric force field is determined by the Heisenberg uncertainty principle as depending on the magnitude of the masses independently of whether the masses are positive or negative. In a crystal lattice, the lattice spacing will be significantly reduced as electrons are replaced by antiquarks owing to the much greater, although negative, quark mass than electron mass. Winterberg gives the theoretical strength of materials as

$$\sigma = \frac{e^2}{r^4}$$

where e is the electron charge and r is the Bohr radius, which varies inversely with the mass of the particles. For a replacement of one electron in 300 by antiquarks (mass ratio of roughly 1000) Winterberg estimates an average lattice spacing decrease of a factor of 10 and therefore a strength increase by a factor of 10,000, a tremendous increase.

Not only the strength, but also the melting point depends on the factor e^2/r^4. Therefore, for the same percent of quark doping as before, a solid material with a normal melting point of 1000 degrees Kelvin would have its melting point increased to 10 million degrees, according to Winterberg. While I do not think that average lattice spacing would tell the story so simply, the trend is most interesting!

As the doping proceeds toward zero mass, Winterberg appears to lose faith in the superstrength properties due to decreased lattice spacing. This is reasonable because of the previously mentioned problem of the balance of forces between the quarks and the nuclei at small lattice spacing. Back at the factory some materials might be given superstrength and others made to zero-mass specifications.

ENERGY BY-PRODUCT

At the supermaterials factory a by-product of the proton fission is enough power to run a vast industrial complex. According to Winterberg, the binding energy Eb set free by the fission of a nucleon of mass mp into 3 antiquarks of mass $3|m_{aq}|$ is by Einstein's mass-energy relation

$$E_b = \left(m_p - 3m_{aq}\right)c^2$$

and since for antiquarks $m_{aq} = -|m_{aq}|$

$$E_b = \left(m_p + 3|m_{aq}|\right)$$

Also since $m_p \approx 3|m_{aq}|$, $E_b = 2m_pc^2$

for each proton or neutron fission. This fantastic energy release is double the amount per unit mass in the complete annihilation of matter as in, for example, a proton-antiproton annihilation.

If proton/neutron fission could be used on board during space travel, the effect of double energy release on mass ratio versus speed would be as derived in Appendix 6 and given by equation A6-14. Mass ratios needed at high speed are almost cut in half (reciprocal mass ratios almost doubled) compared to full energy conversion with complete matter annihilation.

Section XX
Summary and Conclusions

1. The UFO as a Craft and Machine

Analysis of the structural properties of UFOs shows that they are some form of craft having weight, mass, solidity, high density, and a hard or tough structural shell. All are normal physical properties of craft or machines. Because of the number of occasions on which they have been observed to carry occupants, the UFO may be tentatively classified as a transportation vehicle or craft. They display the usual features of transportation craft—windows, doors, retractable steps and ladders, rotating antenna, and a range of designs of retractable landing gear, as well as high performance. Because of the functional variable-geometry features as well as the machine-like physical properties, the UFO should also be classified as a manufactured machine, which may be defined as an assembly of parts designed for a useful purpose. The useful purpose presumably includes transportation and the inspection of planets. Educated people who accept the data of the UFO pattern at face value usually concede the probability that UFOs are produced by civilizations having at their disposal technologies far in advance of those available to man. The advanced technologies relate mainly to vehicle propulsive fields. Being knowledgeable of U.S. Government secrets on propulsion, I have known from the start that UFOs could not possibly be of Earth-technology manufacture.

2. UFO Performance

The surprise and awe felt by the witness on seeing a UFO stems in part from the superior performance, in spite of the fact that no obvious means of propulsion is in evidence and that the accustomed power plant noises are not heard. The more knowledgeable the witness is about Earth craft, the more quickly he realizes that something very unusual is going on.

The outstanding speed and maneuverability of the UFO is based on its equally outstanding acceleration capability. I have shown that the acceleration capability of UFOs equals or exceeds 100 times Earth gravity, or 100 g. This is synonymous with saying that UFO thrust can equal or exceed 100 times the UFO weight. High thrust-to-weight can be achieved either by a high thrust or a low weight. While some observers conclude that UFOs reduce mass, the scout ship landing print and flight propulsion data indicate that both their mass and propulsive forces are large. The data indicates that the fields used for propulsion are strong enough to knock people and cars over, bend and break tree branches, etc. Reduced mass is more apt to occur in the giant interstellar craft on which no landing data is available although the plumes emitted during high acceleration seems evidence of high thrust. Dr. Harder's suggestion is that the starships may reduce mass by quark seeding (Section XIX-F).

The UFO engineers have found a better engine to develop thrust than the heat engines (Rankine, Otto, diesel, jet, nuclear) used by man in one form or another for two centuries. This engine, new to man, is the field engine. The essence of the field engine is a static field link between the UFO and the Earth or other large mass, planetary or stellar.

3. Some Field Engine Properties

In a rationale for the systematic examination of force data, herein called the UFO game, it is shown that the UFO field is not of the static-electric or static-magnetic type. Rather, it appears to be a quasi-static field of a negative-gravity type. This is concluded because the data examined shows that the UFO field repels all mass, not just electrically charged or magnetic materials.

To be of any use for propulsion, the static field link has to have some degree of field focusing; that is, it puts the field out predominately in one direction in order to give control. Since polarization is one of the properties of magnetic fields, this is probably why early UFO investigators jumped at the false conclusion that UFOs use a magnetic drive.

The modern explanation of static fields is the energy quanta known as virtual exchange particles which swarm back and forth between objects affected by the field. The graviton and antigraviton are the two prepared by quantum field theory to explain gravity and antigravity. If the antigraviton has a reflection property it can explain UFO fields very well. The amazing thing about static fields is that the exchange particles transport prodigious amounts of energy without losing or wasting any. The totally energy-conservative nature of gravitational fields, for example, is among the miracles of nature. This feature is certainly what the UFO needs to explain its prodigious yet cool capability. Additions to field energy may be thought of as coming in cyclic pulses. Thus the field has a cyclic component, or ripple, superimposed on the steady component.

There exists ample direct evidence that the UFO can focus its field into a narrow beam as an aid to efficient maneuver and as required for propulsion at a considerable distance from a planet or a star. The UFO needs a good force base against which it can "pole the boat" and thus capitalize on the energy-conservative nature of static fields. When, on interstellar flight, the UFO is so far out that it loses its force base, it automatically goes into a particle-beam mode.

In Appendix 7, the mathematical details of the focused UFO beam are studied. The field intensity varies inversely with the square of the distance from a field "focal" point and the field potential energy inversely with the first power of the distance in a manner quite analogous to spherical fields, all for geometrical reasons. The field pushes on the field generators to give propulsive thrust, and equally in the opposite direction on masses in the field beam such as Earth, satisfying

Newton's law of action equals reaction. Most importantly, the total kinetic energy of all the virtual exchange particles in the beam of a hovering UFO is shown to be small, and about equal to the product of the UFO weight and its height above ground level. This is only the amount of energy it would take to lift the UFO from ground level to hover height.

4. Propulsion by Energetic Particles

Before I was sure that UFOs are propelled by a field engine, I eliminated the idea of UFO propulsion by the acceleration of particles to high fractions of light velocity. For example, for all anyone knew before this study, UFOs might be propelled by a beam of neutrinos, as suggested in Congressional hearings, or by a beam of photons, as suggested by Markowitz. Therefore, I considered all the particles of the "34-particle universe," and in Sections V and VIII eliminated them all as possibilities. The neutrino was eliminated in Section VIII because these particles would have none of the noted effects when UFO propulsion, treated as a neutrino beam, is pointed at various objects. For example, a neutrino beam could not bend and break tree branches in a UFO fly-over. The others are all eliminated in Section V as having gross effects inconsistent with observations. For example, photon propulsion for a 30-ton UFO (the actual estimated weight of a small one) hovering over water would evaporate 118 thousand tons of water per second. Since no one sees clouds of steam formed by UFOs hovering over water, they don't use photon propulsion. Virtual field-exchange particles are not included in this elimination.

5. UFO Radioactivity

The UFO field engine, like our atomic power plants, has the property of being radioactive. If as an energy source the field engine annihilates matter in mass units equal to the mass of an electron and a positron, UFO radioactivity of the class and energy range brought out the following analysis of instrumented readings is just as would be expected.

UFOs have made enough people sick with the typical symptoms of radiation poisoning (in Example IV-B4, for example, Michalak's physical condition was estimated by a radiation specialist to be equivalent to a full-body dose of 100-200 roentgen) that it is fruitless to deny that UFOs are radioactive. Saucer ring data indicates such radiation can be focused in the shape of an annular ring, and comes down from the rim along with the force field. That the rays are radioactive is also attested to by the ionization and chemical changes which occur to some depth in the soil. That residual radiation is generally not observed is not a contradiction but means the rays are not hard gamma rays.

It is concluded that the observer is hit or missed by the radioactive rays depending on his proximity and the sharpness of focus of the harmful rays, as well as whether the UFO tilts so that the rays strike the observer. For example, in the significant Bahia, Brazil, sighting (Example X-A4), the Saturn UFO, in a fantastic 1½-hour display of its power, always maneuvered so that the illuminated focus on the ground missed the observers. The illuminated focus is the radioactive area, the ionized area, and the force field area as well. The force field generation creates the radioactive rays, and the radioactive rays create the ionization, which in turn gives the light.

Bill Rogers' repeated Geiger counter readings of a quarter roentgen at nearly a mile from a UFO is instrumented proof that UFOs can be highly radioactive. The analysis of this and other Geiger counter reports tie the radioactive ray energy to between 25 electron volts and 3 million electron volts. This range coincides with the total range of x-rays plus some overlap into the lower end of the gamma ray spectrum. The same tests prove that the rays are waves, not particles (Section IV) and therefore probably are actually x-rays. Thus we may say that force fields have an electromagnetic component in a frequency range high enough to account for their radioactive property.

6. Ionized Air Zones

UFOs are surrounded by a zone of ionized and excited air molecules. Ionized molecules are electrically unbalanced, while excited molecules have one or more electrons at energy levels above their ground-state energy levels. Around a saucer the most intensely ionized zone is an annular space below the rim, as is most easily seen at low power settings, but this ionized zone may extend downward in various configurations such as a cone, top, or umbrella shape, depending on the focus of the radioactive rays which excite the ionization. Some evidence (Section X) and some theory (Section XIX) indicate that the radioactive rays are about coincident with the force field which is focused also. The radioactive rays and the ionization are therefore by-products of the field engine, whose function is to generate the field in a more or less focused beam. There also seems to be considerable leakage or random radiation because the UFO is sometimes completely surrounded with an ion zone, particularly with the ion flare-up after a quick stop.

At night and to a lesser degree at twilight, the ionized zone lights up like a neon light, usually in one or two colors. The colors red and orange, which take the least energy to excite, generally correspond to low-power operation such as hovering or moving slowly. Blue and blue-white, which take most energy to excite, generally correspond to a high-power setting in which the UFO is either traveling or getting ready to travel with high performance. The theory is that at low power the UFO is putting out soft x-rays and at high power harder x-rays. Just before and at takeoff, as the hum builds to a whine, the brightness of the ionized zone increases, showing that the intensity of the invisible ionizing rays is increasing. This could be either because the UFO is building up its power output in readying for takeoff or because it is concentrating the focus for takeoff or both.

The big dirigibles and cigars focus their force fields and electromagnetic fields to the rear in their high-thrust accelerating mode of operation. The result is a well-defined trailing plume, so highly ionized that it is visible day or night. The plume is a cold plasma of ionized air, not the flaming propulsive jet it has always been reported to be in the UFO literature. Such an explanation is untenable because these vehicles operate silently (Section XII). Hot and cold plasmas look alike because both are highly ionized and have similar light emission properties. Hot plasmas are often combustion products, or flames, which is why UFO observers have jumped to the false conclusion that dirigibles and cigars are jet-propelled. Cold ionization may be caused by energetic particles, as in Figure III-5 where the cause was energetic electrons, or by photons such as x-rays, where each photon has sufficient energy to knock almost any electron out of an oxygen or nitrogen molecule. Thus it appears that, like their smaller counterparts the saucers and Saturns, etc., the big dirigible and cigar force fields have a high-energy electromagnetic component.

In close-up night sightings, the plasma always tends to obscure the edges of the vehicle. If the plasma zone is intense and thick, the UFO edges become completely invisible. This is because plasma has a critical thickness beyond which a ray of light cannot penetrate. Behind this fact is the principle that an excited gas has an absorption spectrum about equal to its emission spectrum. The ray of light by which we would see the edge of the UFO, going from the edge to the eye, is absorbed by excited molecules and re-radiated in random directions. It doesn't reach the eye or the camera lens, as the case may be. While many observers have correctly tied the UFO illumination to a surrounding ion plasma, I have had the pleasure of contributing to the subject the explanation of the indistinct and invisible edges being due to the capability of excited molecules to absorb light of the same frequencies at which they emit. I was taught this bit of physics in an undergraduate course in thermodynamics and heat transfer at the University of California, Berkeley, in 1935—so what's new?

7. Why UFOs Tilt To Maneuver

The force field focus discussed in Conclusions 4, 5, and 6 is of extreme importance to UFO propulsion. It would avail the UFO almost nothing toward maneuverability if the propulsive field were spherically symmetric, for it would then effectively only repel the Earth. It could only go up by increasing field strength and descend by decreasing it, something like a balloon!

When the field is focused, like a searchlight beam for example, it pushes on all objects in its path in proportion to the mass of the objects within the beam, and in proportion to the field strength where the objects are located. We sum the axial component of all the individual pushes and call this the beam force. We represent the beam force by an arrow located on the beam centerline, pointed in the direction of the beam and having a length proportional to the beam force. According to Newton's third law, which is still valid, the thrusting force on the UFO is equal and opposite to the beam force. The thrusting force can therefore be represented by a second arrow of equal length also located on the beam centerline, but pointing in the opposite direction as the first; it points at the center of the UFO. This arrow is called the *thrust vector*. The thrust vector remains aligned with the UFO axis of symmetry while the UFO maneuvers. When the UFO tilts, the thrust vector tilts with it. By properly orienting its body tilt, it is orienting the thrust vector to obtain a component of force and acceleration in the direction in which its commander wishes it to go. This is why the saucer tilts leading-edge-down (a common observation) to go forward, leading-edge-up to stop or reverse, banks-to-turn, etc. In common missile parlance the tilting of the body to tilt the thrust vector is called *thrust vector control*, and there seems to be no reason why we should not apply the same terminology to UFO control. They certainly use it.

As explained in detail in Section XI, the rather simple principles of thrust vector control, whereby the UFO assumes an appropriate series of attitudes to point its thrust vector as required, can be used to successfully explain all the maneuvers that UFOs make.

The best tool with which to study the UFO maneuver in detail is based on dividing thrust by weight and forming *acceleration diagrams* which are used to solve for UFO accelerations. Some simple results are here given as examples:

- Saucers accelerate horizontally in any direction in which they tilt with a magnitude in g units that is equal to the propulsive acceleration (expressed as thrust-to-weight ratio) times the sine of the tilt angle.
- The net vertical acceleration equals the propulsive acceleration times the cosine of the tilt angle, less 1 g.

The dazzling maneuver performance of UFO scout ships seems to result from their being over-designed for the investigation of planet Earth. If the UFO mission is stellar and planetary exploration, the high-g capability they demonstrate would enable them to explore giant planets with gravitational fields on the order of 100 times Earth gravity. Exploring Earth is UFO play.

I am reasonably sure of the correctness of my maneuver analyses based not only on a lifetime of experience with missile dynamics, but more importantly on the actual simulation of UFO- type maneuvers while personally engaged in flying platform research piloting (Section XI).

Because of my career as a research scientist, in several instances such as the present one pertaining to UFO maneuvers, I have had advanced knowledge of UFO technology but was effectively muzzled by the NACA policy laid down by its Director, Dr. Hugh L. Dryden, that UFOs are nonexistent. This policy impacted me in the form of specific orders from the front office to say nothing implicating the NACA with the UFO.

Finally and most importantly, it must be said that in all UFO maneuvers the laws of physics with which we are familiar are adhered to. *The laws of physics are not defied.* Most statements to the contrary are the result of the observer not understanding the acute-angle turn, the sudden reversal, etc. Some observers have failed to differentiate between things happening quickly and things happening instantly. When events happen in fractional seconds, human observational capabilities are quite limited (Section II). The stage magician can make things disappear instantly for those who choose to believe it, using elastic bands and accelerations much smaller than the UFOs use.

8. Acceleration Loading on Occupants

We often hear that observed UFO accelerations would be expected to crush and kill the occupants, at least if they are like us. Well, the little fellows—say half our height—do have a two-to-one advantage over us because at a given acceleration their acceleration stresses are only half as large as ours. If something the size of ants were driving the UFOs they could stand thousands of times as many g's as we can. But I am not suggesting such extremes seriously, just noting that the trend is there, and that half-sized UFOnauts make sense from several viewpoints. One is that they need a machine only half as big, weighing one eighth as much if simple scaling factors hold good.

Since UFO operation requires acceleration field technology for propulsion it may be assumed that this potent technology is capitalized on wherever it suits the purpose in a superior manner. The use of field superposition, wherein one field is used to either augment or to cancel another, is in order. If the "field masters" direct a local field into the cabin area which is equal and opposite to the thrusting acceleration of the UFO (thrust-to-weight ratio) the two fields will cancel and the cabin occupants will feel no acceleration whatever. They may prefer to feel some of the acceleration in order to know what is going on without looking at the instruments. Suppose that they adjust the local field to 95 percent of the thrusting acceleration. They will feel the difference, or 5 percent. If the UFO accelerates at 40 g, the occupants and all cabin contents will be stressed by a 2 g acceleration, which would not stress half-sized occupants any more than 1 g stresses us.

In this entire connection it is important to realize that a free vehicle and those on board *never* feel planetary gravity. After a UFO breaks ground contact with a planet it is in free fall. Occupants and accelerometers feel *only* the thrust-to-weight propulsive acceleration in both magnitude and direction. This leads us at once to appreciate why the UFO designers have selected the particular form of thrust vector control (TVC) that they have chosen, the kind described in which the vehicle and thrust vector tilt together. In the other form of TVC, the thrust direction is swivelled relative to the body, and at high g loadings the cabin occupants would be lashed this way and that as the local g forces changed direction. Whiplashed or broken necks would be the order of the day. This form of vehicle TVC would cause cabin and occupant accelerations very difficult to compensate by local fields because of the continual change in directions during maneuvers. Conversely, with the form of TVC that we can see the UFOs are using, a single local-field compensation (on a percentage basis) is always in the right direction and correct no matter whether the UFO is in a straight-away acceleration, banking-to-turn maneuver, sudden reversal of direction, or any other maneuver. The occupants have a smooth ride without appreciable strain.

9. Analysis of the Sound—the Hum and Whine— and Vibrations Initiated by the UFO Cyclic Force Field. The Field as a Weapon.

In 1968, Dr. Robert Wood pointed out to me that evidence of vibrations existed showing that the UFO force field either was cyclic or had a cyclic component. He said people could feel themselves shaken or vibrated by the field. In the following years, whenever I ran across an example of something around a UFO being set to vibrating, I thought, "How right Bob was!" A small collection of condensed anecdotal accounts of such incidents is given in Section IX, wherein such items as people, walls, cars, and water are set to vibrating. Several witnesses mention the UFO hum or whine as a sound felt as well as heard. With this clue of connection between the vibration and the sound—they apparently had the same frequency—it was logical to investigate the connection.

In Appendix 1, I set up the mathematical equations for the effect of the cyclic field forces of a hovering UFO on the nearby atmosphere, solved them,, and found a dual effect:

First effect: When the cyclic force component is down, the air below the UFO accelerates or falls downward. This happens because the field reaches out both far and near and makes the air all move down together. When the cyclic force is upward, it makes the air stop falling downward and accelerate or fall upward. The air falls down and up, down and up. This mass movement of air is mathematically described by the first row of terms in equation A1A-9.

Second effect: The mass movement of air down and up alternately rarifies and compresses the air at the air-UFO interface. The individual and local sequence of rarefactions and compressions travel out from the UFO surface at the speed of sound. They are sound waves which were generated at the UFO surface as an external acoustic effect. The displacement of the air by the sound waves is mathematically represented by the second row of terms in equation A1A-9.

A similar analysis was made for the interface between the air and deflection-resistant objects below the UFO. It shows that sound waves are also set up at these inter-faces, 180 degrees out of phase with the sound coming from the UFO. Interference of the two sounds as they reach the ear could account for the buzz sometimes described.

Another analysis presented in Appendix 1 shows the type of internal sounds and vibrations that would be set up by the UFO cyclic field in a cylinder standing on a relatively rigid base somewhere below the UFO. This could approximate the vibrations set up in a human being and account for the sounds "felt as well as heard."

If the field frequency is raised to ultrasonic values in a focused beam, this form of internal vibration would amount to a heat weapon. If UFOs use this form of heat weapon, the energy is not transmitted by the atmosphere, but across space by the UFO force field and directly deposited in objects (or people) having a different resistance to the field vibrations than their surroundings or supports. The greatest energy release occurs at the interfaces or contact surfaces, accounting for surface burns.

I do not believe that UFO sounds are a direct effect on the human brain of microwaves emanating from the UFO.

10. The Control of Airflow by Acceleration-Field Technology

UFO technology apparently includes a means of airflow control at supersonic speed which suppresses the shockwaves normally in evidence on manmade vehicles. The elimination of supersonic shockwaves results in a large drag reduction as well as silent supersonic operation. This is another case where the UFO can capitalize on field technology.

As every aerodynamicist learns, at subsonic speeds the air gets a message from an oncoming vehicle in the form of pressure increments transmitted forward at sonic speed. The incremental pressures combine to slow the air and move it aside for the body to pass. At supersonic speed, the pressure increments collect in the bow shockwave. If the UFO controls the air by a field whose velocity is the speed of light, the signal-speed difficulty is overcome. The control field replaces the incremental pressures and absorbs all the surplus kinetic energy of the air, bringing the air smoothly to a stop at the point of the nose with no rise in pressure, no compressive heating, and no shockwave. The tailoring of the acceleration field to replace all the pressure increments in the flowfield results in an ideal constant-pressure, constant-density flow about the UFO at any speed. This has far-reaching effects.

One effect of the constant-pressure flow goes beyond the elimination of all shockwaves, for the UFO makes no pressure waves at all, either of compression or rarefaction. Instead, the field sent out by a passing UFO may be interpreted by a stationary object or person as a passing wave of force. Constant pressure or no, the symmetry of the control field makes it energy-conservative, and it regulates the velocity of the air to its original velocity as it leaves the vicinity of the UFO. In theory, this action is accomplished not only at no cost to the UFO, but at great savings to the propulsive field because the UFO has been converted to a shock-free, low-drag body.

The resulting constant density of the flow dictates the flow pattern for a UFO of any particular shape. This flow pattern is none other than our old friend the low-subsonic-speed potential-flow pattern which existing technology enables us to construct. The flow over a spherical UFO illustrated in Figure XIII-3 is such a constant-pressure flow, and the flow over a pointed-nose dirigible-shaped UFO in Figure XIII-2 is a close approximation to constant pressure. The ideal constant-pressure solution requires both repulsive and attraction components to the field. interestingly, and unlike ordinary flows, small objects in the flow such as drops of water or grains of sand are constrained by the field described to follow the same streamline paths followed by the air, and so miss the UFO.

Various deviations from the control field described are possible and still effective in the elimination of shockwaves. Several possibilities have been suggested. Also, field design specification is broadly covered. What deviations or simplifications the UFOs actually use, of course, I do not know. What I have demonstrated is that, premised on the possession of advanced acceleration field technology, the effective control of supersonic airflow is possible.

11. Jet Noise and UFO Silence

The fiery-looking wake of the giant dirigible- or cigar-shaped UFO reported to have been seen from the deck of steamship *Landovery Castle* (Example XII-A2) was reported by Mrs. King to consist of fierce flames shooting out to half the length of the vehicle. Yet she noted that she could not hear them. Two other cases are reported in Section XII in which big dirigible-UFOs had giant, flame-like wakes yet nothing was heard. Such wakes, flame-like in appearance, are commonly reported as jet exhausts but silent.

Yet this is impossible! The most obvious characteristic of propulsive jet exhausts in the atmosphere is noise. At the jet-boundary discontinuity where the fast-moving jet contacts the more slowly moving surrounding air, myriads of vortices are formed. The small vortices scream, and the big ones roar. The sound pressures generated are tremendous. Giant ships such as these, if driven at high acceleration by a jet exhaust, would be heard for a hundred miles.

Here again the theory of the field with its ionizing radiation component comes to the rescue of the witness's story, and at the same time to the rescue of scientific rationale as being applicable to the UFO. The field beam reaches out and mainly pushes on the ground which is several thousand times as dense as the atmosphere. The air moves slowly without jet discontinuities in a relatively loss-free, silent flow known as potential flow. What looks like a flame is a cold zone of ionized air whose plume shape is controlled by the ionizing process and the ion-relaxation process.

The plume length and reported increase in length with speed is as it should be if the ion-relaxation time is slow due to air impurities, chemical actions, etc. The plume consists of air which the UFO has flown through and which it has ionized as it passed by. In a given time (ion-relaxation or plasma-extinction time) the dirigible or giant cigar passes more air at high speed than at low speed, hence the plume length increases as the speed increases.

All reports of jet exhausts issuing from *silent UFOs* are erroneous interpretations of the data and facts.

12. High-Speed Aerodynamic Heating or Cooling?

The theory for the force field control of airflow about a UFO moving through the atmosphere at supersonic speed offers a possible explanation of how UFOs stay cool at these speeds. In Appendix 4, the thermal version of the airflow energy equation is developed, showing how the local temperatures depend on local Mach number. The equation shows that with the force field strength adjusted to stop the air at the stagnation point of the nose, the temperature at the stagnation point is exactly the same as the temperature of the free atmosphere far ahead of the UFO. This is because the force field absorbs all of the kinetic energy of the air and the air arrives at the stagnation point with no compressive heating. (Stagnation point is defined in Section XIII.) The force field then passes the kinetic energy back to the air as it leaves, seemingly at no cost to anyone. By the elimination of stagnation point heating the potentially most severe heating has been eliminated.

If the air is controlled to flow around the sides of the UFO at constant pressure, the boundary layer heating on the sides could be quite severe. However, if the UFO uses only a repulsive field for airflow control, the opposite would be true; the side heating could be mild or nonexistent. For this case, air flowing around the side and near the vehicle surface encounters a big pressure drop and the expansion makes it very cold. The force field acts like a vacuum pump, lowering the pressures (Appendix 4). The temperatures get so low that even with boundary-layer friction the air at the UFO surface is below ambient atmospheric temperature. For example, according to the table in Section XIV, on a day when the ambient air temperature is 70 degrees F the temperature of the air touching a representative point on the side of the vehicle is 47 degrees F at a vehicle speed of 1500 ft/sec, and 29 degrees F at a speed of 2000 ft/sec. Under these circumstances, the UFO is cooled at various flight speeds, not heated. This would be true at any speed for which the UFO can maintain the high field strengths needed.

In a surprise fallout, it was found by this theory that if a UFO left such an air-control mechanism turned on while hovering low over water, air temperatures near the machine could get cold enough to create ice.

13. The Time Required for Interstellar Travel.

Some people are taken with the idea of traveling faster than light speed as a means of crossing interstellar spaces more quickly. Others look for some other space than our "normal" space as a means of getting around the space-time barrier locked in their minds. Then UFOs can visit us in the "other" space which has any properties they wish to imagine. Many forget what can be accomplished with light speed as a limit, or choose not to believe it (the real barrier). Suppose that we had a vehicle that could nullify mass and could travel at light speed, and that we were on board at takeoff with one eye on the clock. Before the clock ticked a second, we would be out of the galaxy and out of the universe, into the totally unknown. In fact, the clock never ticks a second because time would be standing still.

These fantasies make interesting conversation, but solve absolutely nothing in terms of twentieth-century science. To conform to science we back off to any speed this side of light speed, say $v/c = 0.99999999$, at which speed we go a light year of distance every hour and 15 minutes. You are now wearing your science cap, so don't forget the "real barrier." At this speed we could reach the surface of our Galaxy 1250 light years away in 66 days. You are afraid of overshooting? All right, reducing the v/c by two g's *speeds up the clock* by a factor of 10, so we go a light year every 12.5 hours, or about two light years per day, and that's substantial progress per working day.

Next we must see if the time to accelerate and decelerate affects the overall picture appreciably. All of the equations needed are developed in Appendix 5. Consider a UFO starship which leaves Zeta 1 Reticuli bound for Earth 37 light years away at a velocity $v = 0.9999c$. If they made the trip at full speed all the way (see table in Section XVIII) it would take 6 months, 8.5 days of on board time. More realistically, let them accelerate at 100 g for 2.5 weeks to get up to speed, coast at top speed until 2.5 weeks out from Earth, decelerate at 100 g for 2.5 weeks, landing on Earth in 7 months and 6 days. The approximately 1-month time difference between the superficial and the realistic computations is worth taking into account, but does not change the basic picture that on board the ship they are doing immensely better than the 37 years we think of light as taking to make the trip.

In this summary statement the comparison with the time it takes light to travel is emphasized because so many people are confused by the idea that it takes light x years to go x light years and "nothing goes faster than light" so they think that the limiting time for the space ship is also x years. In the above example we see that the only time of real importance, the on board time, is not x years, or 37 years, but 0.60 years, which totally changes the picture from gloom to zoom. We should extend the above quote to read "Nothing goes faster than light, but spaceships can go more quickly as reckoned by their own time."

14. The UFO Energy Supply—Is It Enough?

Unconventional objects may gather their energy supply en route, they may carry their energy supply from home base, or, as I suspect, they may do both. The last possibility could be analogous to motoring. As we go motoring along, how many of us remember that for each gallon of gasoline consumed the motor also consumes about 100 pounds of oxygen from the air, free for the taking as we go? Or so it seems.

Professor Hermann Oberth, an astute rocket pioneer in pre-World War II Germany, is generally credited with the idea that UFOs convert stellar and planetary gravitational energy to propulsive uses. He said UFOs "are conceived and directed by intelligent beings of a very high order, and they are propelled by distorting the gravitational field, converting gravity into useful energy" (Section XIX).

The pertinent comments of UFO investigator Frank Edwards are worth reiterating: "If UFOs are propelled by conversion of gravity, it would simplify space travel, since it would eliminate the necessity of carrying a fuel supply. Gravity pervades the universe; where it is weakest, less of it would be needed for propulsion; where it is strongest, more of it would be available."

Ten to 15 years ago scientific UFO opponents, quoting chemical rocket speeds as their basis, were taking the position that crossing interstellar space was virtually impossible. Today, the group has backed off from the impossibility idea. Their new spokesmen merely claim that interstellar trips are uneconomical; the trip planners cannot send out many vehicles because their energy resources are limited. If the UFO can "convert gravity into useable energy" they have an energy supply everywhere and need not overtax the home planet. The "uneconomical" argument becomes weak.

Even if unconventional objects had to carry their entire energy supply along from one interstellar stop to the next, with the complete conversion of mass to energy, as in an electron-positron mass annihilation, and the conversion of the released energy to propulsive energy, the restriction on space travel would not be overly severe. We must also remember that the distance between interstellar stops can be very large as long as the UFO is coasting at near light speeds, because the coast phase costs essentially no energy. My contribution to the energy supply subject is the conception of equation A6-8 of Appendix 6, which gives the highest possible ratio of final (rest) mass to initial mass when the UFO or any other vehicle carries its entire energy supply aboard. This is a relativistic "speed limit" equation for this case. The equation is plotted in Figure XIX-1 and labeled "complete energy conversion." This and other limit curves on the same figure show that for vehicles carrying their own energy supply, if the supply is efficiently converted to vehicle kinetic energy, or even to jet energy, the vehicle may still be expected to approach closely to the speed of light in the $v/c = 0.99$ to 0.999 range.

Analysis in Appendix 6 shows that a stationary observer watching a vehicle with complete energy conversion approach light speed sees no change in mass. To him the loss of mass as fuel exactly equals the gain in kinetic mass due to approaching light speed. The vehicle approaches light speed with its starting mass, which remains constant. This is an interesting philosophical departure from the case we often hear quoted of the mass increasing without bounds for an object accelerated toward light speed by an external energy source.

15. Speculative Theories of the Force Field—What Is It?

The UFO field is unique in that it is a directed field that appears to have static field properties. The energy-conservative electric and planet gravitational fields, for example, are spherically symmetric. To establish a theory for a shaped conservative field, I turned to the quantum-mechanical exchange-particle theory. Modern physics is slanted to the theory that all static fields are explainable on the basis of the exchange-particle: electric fields are accounted for by the exchange of photons, the strong nuclear field by the exchange of pions, the weak field by the exchange of neutrinos, the gravitational field by the exchange of gravitons, and antigravitational fields, if they exist, by the exchange of antigravitons. According to this general picture, the UFO field must have its exchange-particle which we shall call the Uon. The field is untold numbers of Uon emissaries, each carrying positive momentum.

Perhaps for various reasons, all known exchange-particles travel a two-way street. For example, the same number of gravitons from Earth reach the Moon as reach the Earth from the Moon, preserving Newton's law that action equals reaction. Photons, on the other hand, have an interesting property called reflection, which may be pictured as the absorption of the photon by an accelerated electron and the re-radiation of another photon back along the same path. The construction of a viable Uon theory requires that the Uon have a reflection property, which we shall call the Uon-reflection hypothesis. Uons are concerned with mass and will be principally reflected by atomic nuclei. On average they would penetrate to considerable depth in the ground or other target before reflecting, and surface roughness would not matter. The reflection hypothesis allows the Uon to travel in a beam and still have the two-way street properties of a static field. If the reflection is accurate, the Uon will stay in the beam and go back to the UFO where they can re-reflect, balancing out Earth gravity. Note the g-loading cancellation on the occupants!

The reflection-property hypothesis conserves Uons and field shape whatever the degree of focus or flare of the field beam. This is easily visualized by thinking of the path of each Uon as a ray, and when the Uon reflects, it goes back along the same ray or parallel to it, thus preserving the shape of the force field beam as set up by the focusing mechanism.

The Russian physicist D.D. Ivanenko said, " . . .it may be possible for electron-positron pairs to be trans-formed not only into photons, but also into gravitons" (The Earth in the Universe, 212). Using this statement as a basis, and equating graviton-antigraviton pairs to the Uon, with considerable trepidation the following theory was generated. An ideal operational cycle was visualized, in which an electron is accelerated downward (as in a TV tube) to the maximum velocity which the energy from the annihilation collision with a positron can sup-port, momentum input and output remaining balanced. This speed turned out to be $\sqrt{4/5}\, c$.

This momentum input sends antigravitons and residual photons straight down, and gravitons straight up and, interestingly, completely accounts for the parallel-beam focus of both the force field component and the x-ray strength E.M. component of the field. Smaller electron input velocities to the reaction zone would de-focus both the force field and x-ray components. Experimental ver-ification of the foundations for this theory is lacking.

16. UFO Artifacts

UFO artifacts are difficult to find and even more difficult to prove genuine. The UFO occupants seem to almost never leave anything behind, and the UFO machine is sufficiently reliable that pieces or wreckage are extremely scarce, even after 30 years of searching by interested parties.

The most available material evidence which might be called artifacts would be plaster casts or other replica made of UFO landing prints by research organizations such as APRO. Originals and copies could be donated or sold to museums of worldwide stature such as the Smithsonian. Print collections, with site photographs and eyewitness accounts, would be impressive and popular public displays.

The next most available UFO artifact is called angel hair. It is a fine white filament that looks like long strands of coarse spiderweb, and has been observed descending from virtually all types of UFOs in vast quantities. Angel hair has been gathered by many eyewitnesses, and found to be a strong, tough filament. The problem is that at room temperature angel hair sublimes rapidly, changing directly from the solid to the gaseous state of matter. This disappearing act has so far frustrated attempts at analysis. In Section XVI, I suggest methods for handling angel hair so it won't disappear, some tests to determine physical properties, and methods of turning sublimation into an asset by analyzing its chemical composition by means of gas chromatography and mass spectrography, both of which require the subject material to be in gaseous phase. Field handling can be aided by CO_2 ice or a liquid-nitrogen container.

The story of the three "Ubatuba magnesium fragments" is given in Section XVI. The first fragment tested was the UFO artifact "most provable" to be a genuine piece of a UFO. Professional spectrographic tests of this fragment showed only pure magnesium with no traces of other metallic elements present, an unheard-of purity which could not be matched by Earthly production methods. An elementary calculation shows that fragment

1 had a unique density which can only be accounted for if it was the pure isotope magnesium 26, the heaviest of the stable magnesium isotopes. Tests in a mass spectrometer could have proven this point one way or the other—an affirmative answer clinching the extraterrestrial origin of the piece—but such tests were not made. There is still a remote chance that a piece of fragment 1 is still in existence, as a piece was given to the Brazilian Army and another to the Navy.

The other two fragments had normal density and traces of other metallic elements present. Fragment 2 was found to have an unusually high trace of aluminum content, not present in Earth-made commercially pure magnesium. Fragment 3 was well-tested under the supervision of Dr. Roy Craig for the Condon Committee. Even his section of the Condon Report admitted "the possibility remained that the material was unique"! I conclude that each fragment of Ubatuba magnesium was from a different part of the fragmented UFO, each piece unique to it own special purpose and function in the UFO. Fragment 1 was surely the most unique of them all, the pure isotope magnesium 26!

17. A Summary of Astronomical Facts for UFO Students

(1) Stars are formed from vast clouds of interstellar gases and dust which are condensed by the forces of gravity. The condensing cloud breaks up into hundreds of separate gas clouds of random sizes, each of which continues to condense until it becomes incandescent and its core temperature sufficient to ignite the hydrogen core-fuel. The energy systems stabilize as the new stars are born.

(2) The most massive (white) stars are hottest and burn up their core-fuel in a few million years. There is a continuous gradation of mass, temperature, and lifetime until at the other extreme some small, cool, red stars burn their core-fuel so slowly as to last 100 billion years. When the core-fuel of a star is exhausted the star col-

lapses, igniting the hydrogen in the mantle. It swiftly grows to become a giant.

(3) Heavy elements are formed continuously in the stellar cauldron.

(4) Stellar gases are spewed out by fast-spinning binaries, giants, novas, etc., so that cycle 1-4 is a continuous, repeating one.

(5) Because new stars have been born continuously since the origin of the galaxy about 12 billion years ago, it follows that the stars of our galaxy are of *all ages* up to about 12 billion years.

(6) Astronomers classify stars according to their spectral lines into spectral classes: 0 (white), B (blue), A (?), F (yellow), G (yellow), K (yellow), and M (red) with decimal subdivisions in each from 0 to 9.

(7) Evidence is lacking that 0, B, A, and F0 to F4 stars have planets. However, F5 to F9, G, H, and M stars have obviously passed their angular momentum on to a *planetary system*. The Sun is type G2.

(8) Stellar spectrograms, interstellar gas analyses, and meteoroid examination show that the materials, chemistry, and quantum mechanics of the universe is the same everywhere.

(9) Exobiologists believe that the same forces tending to create carbon-cycle life are at work everywhere in the known universe. They are strongly supported by signs of carbon-based life in meteoroid materials and by recent discoveries of chemical compounds such as ammonia in interstellar gas clouds. Life should appear after about 3 billion years in a suitable environment.

(10) O, B, and A stars are too short-lived to develop intelligent life, but the F5 through M stars which in all probability have planets also have a lifetime sufficient to

develop it, and more. Baker's *Astronomy* gives the life of the Sun as 12 billion years, of which nearly half is in the past. (What will we do with our 6-billion-year credit card???)

(11) One of the most important aspects of statements (1) through (10) is that stars and intelligent life have been born and developed on a continuous basis since the formation of our galaxy. Of course, the same is true for other galaxies. Life in our galaxy should have practically all ages up to about 8 or 9 billion years, and intelligent life perhaps a billion years less. Since life on Earth has existed for about a billion years, and we have just stepped over the threshold of science, think how far ahead of us in scientific development innumerable civilizations in our galaxy could be. *Billions* of years—too far to *imagine!*

(12) A point worthy of note is that sooner or later all advanced civilizations are evicted from their homes as their star nears or reaches the giant or nova stage, going willingly by space travel or by extinction. Space travel is not naive—it is inevitable!

18. UFO Occupants, Our Alien Visitors

Of all UFO aspects, the study of the UFO occupants is the most fascinating. If we follow the Lorenzens' lead, we generalize that the occupants come in three sizes: diminutive, about a meter tall (the majority); human size, 5 to 6 feet (the second most populous); and giant, 8 or 9 feet (relatively few). The meter-sized occupants come mainly as humanoids, with a minority of hard, tough, hair-covered, animal-like creatures with claws and large, glaring yellow eyes that are really frightening. I often wonder if these "animals" are smarter than humans. At least they have better transportation.

The great majority of the occupants could not pass for human beings. This always makes me wonder why people like to quibble over whether UFOs are extraterrestrial. When nonhuman aliens are seen de-boarding from strange spacecraft, who do they think they are? With high-performance starships and scout ships for local runs, they seem very well equipped to get here from any home base within a thousand light years, and no telling how much further. The fact that our humanoid alien visitors come in such a variety of sizes and types, and that the detailed design of the scout ships vary so markedly, points to the conclusion that our visitors are from no one place, but that we are seeing a parade of visitors from various and numerous stellar civilizations.

The high sighting rate of UFOs gives the impression that stellar civilizations are closer together than estimated by exobiologists. Exobiologists come up with numbers like an advanced civilization every 100 light years or more. Of course, they are referring to planetary environments both so favorable and so old that intelligences developed there. They say that with stellar explorations issuing from these centers we should be visited less often than reported. On the opposite hand, if we assume that most of the suitable planets of the F, G, and K stars have been *colonized* by the UFO parade if not otherwise occupied, we might put the average distance between civilizations in our part of the galaxy an order of magnitude less than the experts estimate, including Alpha Centuri (widely-spaced triplet including a star nearly identical to the Sun) at 4 light years, Epsilon Eridani at 11 , Tau Ceti at 12 light years, and so on. A related point is that many aliens seem very sensitive to light. If these have colonized and adapted to planets of the highly numerous red stars, this would change the whole civilization distribution picture, but would be consistent with UFO data.

The main evidence as to the alien's purpose here (unless you choose to believe those who go out in the other dimension to chat with our visitors and report that they are here to save us) is that our visitors are collecting samples of everything imaginable. They collect soil, minerals, water, wild and domesticated plants, wild and domesticated animals, even people on occasion. This makes me think that UFOs are manned by scientists and their staffs on cosmic exploration. If good planetary living sites are becoming scarce, aren't the aliens apt to be gathering data on which to base the choice of new homesites?

The aliens have been very aloof. Now that the Air Force has stopped intercepting, and if others would also be more cordial (stop shooting), attitudes might change. If friendly aliens encountered an inquisitive scientist instead of Mr. John Doe, just think what he, and we, might learn! One world, yes. One universe, too! Such contact is probably our only chance for a quantum jump in knowledge.

Analysis of the Sound (Hum) and Vibrations Initiated by the UFO Cyclic Force Field

A. Sound Generated at UFO Lower Surface (with Square Wave Force Field)

Assume that a flat-bottomed saucer with a cylindrically focused force field starts to hover in a given position in quiet air at time zero, Figure A1-1(a). Assume further that the force field has a square wave ripple as shown in Section IX, Figure IX-1, and in Figure A1-1(b), also starting at time zero. Sound wave vibrations in the atmosphere below the UFO are due to the square wave portion of the acceleration field. For vibration analysis, we draw the horizontal acceleration field. For vibration analysis we draw the horizontal line Cg-Cg in Figure A1-1(b) separating the field into a steady state field of intensity Cg and a superimposed square wave of amplitude kg (g units), where g is Earth gravity and k an appropriate factor.

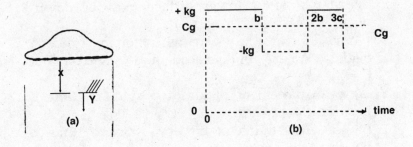

Figure A1-1.

The force field wave velocity is so high as to be considered to act instantly over the distances being considered. The force field square wave acceleration acts on every unit of air mass in the column below the UFO with the acceleration +kg (downward) from time 0 to b, and then the acceleration -kg (upward) from b to 2b, then repeats continuously. If the column of air were not restrained at areas such as the air-UFO interface, it would simply be pumped down and up in rapid succession. It is the air-restraining surfaces which create waves. In the following subsection the corresponding case for a sinusoidal variation of the acceleration will be briefly reviewed.

In this analysis, the hovering (or slowly moving) UFO is assumed to be so massive and rigid relative to the air that the UFO surface is not deflected by the cyclic component of the field. If it were so deflected, we would find that the sound waves created would be increased in intensity, not diminished.

For the present we are concerned with the motion of the air near the saucer and the generation of sound waves at the UFO-air interface, and exclude ground reflections from the analysis. These will be considered later. Of particular interest is the vertical motion of the air at any distance x below the bottom surface of the saucer (or the flat base of a cylinder or below the ring of a Saturn).

The following symbols are used:

x is distance below lower surface, positive downward.

t is time after arbitrary zero when forcing function begins. Air is undisplaced and stationary at t = 0.

$Y(x,t)$ is displacement of air at position x, time t, positive downward.

$Y_{tt}(x,t)$ is acceleration of air at position x, time t, positive downward.

b is square wave half period, seconds.

a is speed of sound in air.

ρ is air mass density.

M(b,t) is the square wave acceleration of air below the UFO.

    equals +kg (downward) for t between 0 and b.

    equals -kg for t between b and 2b and repeats indefinitely.

g is the acceleration of Earth-surface gravity.

v in part C is velocity of free end of cylinder, negative downward.

The method used is operational mathematics. It is the simplest yet most powerful method known for solving the partial differential equations of mathematical physics.

The applicable one-dimensional wave equation is a statement that acceleration equals the sum of the forces per unit mass (Churchill, 108-10). The equation is:

$$Y_{tt}(x,t) = a^2 Y_{xx}(x,t) + M(b,t) \qquad \text{A1A-1}$$

(and A1A-1 means, of course, Appendix 1, Section A, equation 1). The double subscript tt means the second partial derivative with respect to t, and xx means the second partial with respect to x. Boundary conditions are:

$$Y(x,0) = Y_t(x,0) = 0 \qquad \text{A1A-2}$$

$$Y(0,t) = Y_t(0,t) = 0 \qquad \text{A1A-3}$$

$$Y(x,t) \rightarrow 0 \text{ as } x \rightarrow \infty \qquad \text{A1A-4}$$

Equation 2 means air displacement and velocity are zero at t = 0.

Equation 3 means the air remains stationary at x = 0.

Equation 4 means we shall ignore ground reflections, which are probably diffuse and scattered.

The Laplace transform with respect to t of equation 1, aided by conditions 2 is [see Churchill 55-56 for transform of M(b,t)]:

$$s^2 y(x,s) = a^2 y_{xx}(x,s) + \frac{kg}{s} \frac{1-e^{-bs}}{1+e^{-bs}}$$

wherein t has been replaced by the parameter s. Dividing by a^2 and equating to zero gives:

$$y_{xx}(x,s) - \frac{s^2}{a^2} y(x,s) + \frac{kg}{a^2 s} \frac{1-e^{-bs}}{1+e^{-bs}} = 0 \qquad \text{A1A-1a}$$

The transforms of the boundary conditions are:

$$y(x,0) = sy(x,0) = 0 \qquad \text{A1A-2a}$$
$$y(0,s) = sy(0,s) = 0 \qquad \text{A1A-3a}$$
$$y(\infty,s) = 0 \qquad \text{A1A-4a}$$

Since $\dfrac{kg}{s^3} \dfrac{1 - e^{-bs}}{1 + e^{-bs}}$ is a particular solution of equation 1a, the general solution is

$$y(x,s) = C_1 e^{-\frac{x}{a}s} + C_2 e^{+\frac{x}{a}s} + \frac{kg}{s^3} \frac{1-e^{-bs}}{1+e^{-bs}} \qquad \text{A1A-5}$$

Equation 4a makes $C_2 = 0$. Substituting 3a ($y=0$ when $x=0$) in equation 5 gives

$$C_1 = -\frac{kg}{s^3} \frac{1 - e^{-bs}}{1 + e^{-bs}}$$

and

$$y(x,s) = \frac{kg}{s^3}\left(1 - e^{-\frac{x}{a}s}\right) \cdot \frac{1-e^{-bs}}{1+e^{-bs}} \qquad \text{A1A-6}$$

Since $(1 + z)^{-1} = \sum\limits_{n=0}^{\infty} (-1)^n z^n$ if $0 < z < 1$, A1A-6 can be written:

$$y(x,s) = \frac{kg}{s^3}\left(1 - e^{-\frac{x}{a}s}\right)\left(1 - e^{-bs}\right) \sum_{n=0}^{\infty} (-1)^n e^{-nbs} \qquad \text{A1A-7}$$

Expanding and multiplying gives the double series

A1A-8

$$y(x,s) = \frac{kg}{s^3} \left\{ 1 - 2e^{-bs} + 2e^{-2bs} - 2e^{-3bs} + \ldots \right.$$
$$\left. -e^{-xs/a} + 2e^{-(b+x/a)s} + 2e^{-(2b+x/a)s} + 2e^{-(3b+x/a)} \ldots \right\}$$

The inverse transform of $1/s^3$ is $t^2/2$, and all of the exponential terms give the time delays. Therefore

A1A-9

$$Y(x,t) = kg \left\{ + t^2/2 - [t-b]^2 + [t-2b]^2 - [t-3b]^2 + \ldots \right.$$
$$\left. -1/2 [t-x/a]^2 + [t-(b+x/a)]^2 - [t-(2b+x/a)]^2 + [t-(3b+x/a)]^2 \ldots \right\}$$

where the value of each term [ ] is zero until it becomes positive. The first row of terms is the displacement of the air due to the direct action of the periodic acceleration field. Superimposed on the direct action effect, the second row of terms gives the displacement due to sound waves, generated at the UFO surface, and moving past any point x at time t.

To see what the sound pressure waves look like, we note that the pressure in any medium is given in terms of the medium stiffness factor (Young's modulus) E, by the following relation:

$$p = E \partial Y / \partial x$$

Since the velocity of sound is,

$$a = \sqrt{E/\rho}$$
$$p = -\rho a^2 \partial Y / \partial x \qquad \text{A1A-10}$$

Differentiating equation 9 with respect to x as indicated by equation 10 gives the equation for the sound pressure waves:

$$p = kg\rho a \left\{ -\left[t - \frac{x}{a}\right] + 2\left[t - \left(b + \frac{x}{a}\right)\right] - 2\left[t - \left(2b + \frac{x}{a}\right)\right] + 2\left[t - \left(3b + \frac{x}{a}\right)\right] - \ldots \right\}$$

A1A-11

At the UFO surface, x=0, equation 11 gives the sound pressure as a function of time as in Figure A1-2, where time is expressed in multiples of b. Each bracket term is a time delay; the quantity within each bracket is only allowed positive values as can be seen by Figure A1-2.

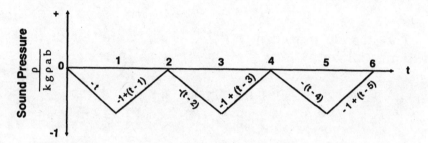

Figure A1-2. Sound Pressure at UFO Surface. (The unit of time is b.)

We see that a sawtooth type sound wave comes out from the surface, spreading downward, and doubtless outward as well, until it reaches a human ear and is interpreted as a saucer hum. The sound frequency is equal to the reciprocal of 2b, ½b, which is exactly equal to the cyclic force field frequency. This gives us our clue as to why things are shaken at the hum frequency, and why the hum can be "felt as well as heard"; the shaking vibration is the result of direct force field action, and the sound waves coincide because the air is being shaken at the same frequency. However, as this analysis indicates, the acceleration of the air by the field is not the sound; rather, the sound is generated at the air-UFO interface and at other interfaces as well, as we shall see. This point will be given additional analysis in subsection C.

I ran through an analysis similar to this, assuming the surface below a hovering UFO to be a flat, rocky-stiff or perfectly stiff surface (highly improbable, but a useful concept) and found that the resulting sound pressure generated at the interface of the air with such a surface is given by equation A1A-11 if the sign of the resulting pressures is reversed. If portrayed in Figure A1-2, the saw teeth would be above the zero line. In other words, air rarefaction waves come from the UFO surface and positive-pressure surface can be thought of as the surface of a bridge of rigid material with edge support all around the circumference of the field beam.

B. Sinusoidal Forcing Function

Instead of a square wave as in the preceding examples, let the forcing function be sinusoidal and given by $F(\omega,t) = kg\sin(\omega t)$. Otherwise, all physical conditions specified in subsection A are to remain unchanged. The boundary equations as written there still apply. Since the period of the forcing function is to remain 2b, the value of ω is π/b. The wave equation remains the same except for the substitution of $kg\sin(\omega t)$ for $M(b,t)$.

Since the transform of $kg\sin(\omega t)$ is $kg\omega/(\omega^2+s^2)$, equation A1A-1a can be written as

$$y_{xx}(x,s) - \frac{s^2}{a^2}\, y(x,s) + \frac{kg\omega}{a^2\left(\omega^2 + s^2\right)} \qquad \text{A1B-1a}$$

Taking the boundary equations into account, the solution of this ordinary differential equation is

$$y(x,s) = \frac{kg\omega}{s^2(\omega^2 + s^2)} \cdot \left(1 - e^{-\frac{x}{a}s}\right) \qquad \text{A1B-2}$$

This is a standard form whose inverse transform can be obtained from *Operational Mechanics* (Churchill 325, no. 20). The resulting air displacement is

$$Y(x,t) = \frac{kg}{\omega^2}\left\{(\omega t - \sin\omega t) - (\omega[t - \frac{x}{a}] - \sin\omega\,[t - \frac{x}{a}])\right\} \qquad \text{A1B-3}$$

As before, the pressure of sound is $p = -\rho a^2 \partial Y/\partial x$, giving for all distances below the UFO surface

$$p(x,t) = -\frac{kga\rho}{\omega}\left[1 - \cos\omega\left(t - \frac{x}{a}\right)\right] \qquad \text{A1B-4}$$

At the UFO surface x = 0 and the sound pressure is

$$p(t) = - \frac{kga\rho}{\omega} (1 - \cos\omega t) \qquad \text{A1B-5}$$

At a hypothetical rigid flat surface below the UFO the sound pressure is

$$p(t) = + \frac{kga\rho}{\omega} (1 - \cos\omega t) \qquad \text{A1B-5a}$$

If we give ω its value of π/b and let t=b in equation A1B-5, the peak sound pressure at the UFO surface is

$$p = - \frac{2}{\pi} kg\rho ab \qquad \text{A1B-6}$$

The corresponding pressure at the UFO surface for the square wave at time t=b was

$$p = - kg \rho ab$$

The fact that the results are the same except for the factor $2/\pi$ shows that the shape of the forcing function is not very important.

C. Vibration of Cylinder by Square Wave Force Field

To investigate the vibration of objects (including people) standing on the ground consider a cylindrical object of height h, standing on end on a base of much higher rigidity which is also too large to be vibrated much by a hovering saucer (Figure A1-3). The speed of sound in the cylinder is c. Calculate the history of the displacement Y(h,t), and velocity $Y_t(h,t)$ of the free end x=h set up in the cylinder by direct action of a square wave field [Figure A1-1(b)] on the material of the cylinder combined with the motion due to any internal wave action. Assume that all is at rest until time zero, and that the foot of the cylinder at x=0 is restrained from moving by the more rigid base. Since the material of the cylinder is a thousand times as dense as air, the air loading on the cylinder will be neglected; i.e., the motions of the cylinder will be considered to overpower the motions of the air.

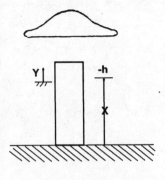

The wave equation is the same as before except that the speed of sound is now c, and the forcing function M(b,t), being directed opposite to x, is preceded by a negative sign.

Figure A1-3.

$$Y_{tt}(x,t) = c^2 Y_{xx}(x,t) - M(b,t) \qquad \text{A1C-1}$$

The boundary conditions are

$$Y(x,0) = Y_t(x,0) = 0 \quad \text{stationary at t = 0} \qquad \text{A1C-2}$$

$$Y(0,t) = Y_t(0,t) = 0 \quad \text{stationary at x = 0, any t} \qquad \text{A1C-3}$$

$$EY_x(h,t) = 0 \quad \text{no stress at free end} \qquad \text{A1C-4}$$

The transformed equations are

$$y_{xx}(x,s) - \frac{s^2}{c^2} y(x,s) - \frac{kg}{c^2 s} \frac{1 - e^{-bs}}{1 + e^{-bs}} \qquad \text{A1C-1a}$$

$$y(x,0) = sy(x,0) = 0 \qquad \text{A1C-2a}$$

$$y(0,s) = sy(0,s) = 0 \qquad \text{A1C-3a}$$

$$E \, y_x(h,s) = 0 \qquad \text{A1C-4a}$$

Since a particular solution of A1C-1a is $-\dfrac{kg}{s^3} \dfrac{1 - e^{-bs}}{1 + e^{-bs}}$

the general solution is

$$y(x,s) = C_1 e^{\frac{x}{c} s} + C_2 e^{-\frac{x}{c} s} - \frac{kg}{s^3} \frac{1 - e^{-bs}}{1 + e^{-bs}} \qquad \text{A1C-5}$$

Substituting condition 3a in equation 5

$$C_1 + C_2 = \frac{kg}{s_3} \frac{1 - e^{-bs}}{1 + e^{-bs}} \cdot \frac{kg}{s^3} f(bs) \qquad \text{A1C-5a}$$

and applying 4a to equation 5 gives

$$C_1 = C_2 e^{-2\frac{h}{c}} \qquad \text{A1C-5b}$$

Combining 5a and 5b gives

$$C_2 = \frac{kg}{s^3} \frac{f(bs)}{1 + e^{-2hs/c}} \qquad C_1 = \frac{kg}{s^3} \frac{f(bs)e^{-2hs/c}}{1 + e^{-2hs/c}}$$

and $\qquad\qquad\qquad\qquad\qquad\qquad\qquad\qquad\qquad$ A1C-6

$$y(x,s) = \frac{kg}{s^3} \frac{1 - e^{-bs}}{1 + e^{-bs}} \left[\frac{e^{-2hs/c} e^{\frac{x}{cs}} + e^{-\frac{x}{cs}}}{1 + e^{-2hs/c}} - 1 \right]$$

The problem is neater if the time it takes a wave to travel the length h is a multiple of b, say $t = h/c = 2b$, which is one force field cycle period. Then, for the free end, where $x/c = h/c = 2b$,

$$y(h,s) = \frac{kg}{s^3} \frac{1 - e^{-bs}}{1 + e^{-bs}} \left[\frac{2e^{-2bs}}{1 + e^{-4bs}} - 1 \right] \qquad \text{A1C-6a}$$

The best form for the results is obtained by expanding the terms of the denominator in series:

$$\left(1 + e^{-bs}\right)^{-1} = \sum_{n=0}^{\infty} (-1)^n e^{-nbs} = 1 - e^{-bs} + e^{-2bs} - e^{-3bs} + e^{-4bs} - \ldots$$

then

$$\frac{1 - e^{-bs}}{1 + e^{bs}} = 1 - 2e^{-bs} + 2e^{-2bs} - 2e^{-3bs} + 2e^{-4bs} - \ldots \qquad \text{(a)}$$

$$\frac{2e^{-2bs}}{1 + e^{-4bs}} = 2e^{-2bs} - 2e^{-6bs} + 2e^{-10bs} - 2e^{-14bs} + 2e^{-18bs} - \cdots \quad (b)$$

Substitute series (a) and (b) in equation 6a and perform the indicated multiplication to give

$$y(h,s) = \frac{kg}{s^3}\left[-1+2e^{-bs}+0e^{-bs}-2e^{-3bs}+2e^{-4bs}-2e^{-5bs}+0e^{-6bs}+2e^{-7bs}-\cdots\right]$$

A1C-7

The inverse transform of equation 7 gives the displacement at $x = h = 2bc$.

$$Y(h,t) = kg\left[-\frac{t^2}{2} + (t-b)^2 + 0 - (t-3b)^2 + (t-4b) - (t-5b)^2 + 0 + (t-7b)^2 - \cdots\right]$$

A1C-8

where the value of each parentheses ( ) is zero until positive.

To obtain the velocity history of the free end of the cylinder take the derivative of equation 8 with respect to t:

$$v(h,t) = kg[-t + 2(t-b) + 0 - 2(t-3b) + 2(t-4b) - 2(t-5b) + 0 + 2(t-7b) - \cdots]$$

A1C-9

where again each ( ) is zero until positive, to satisfy time delays. This is the motion we set out to find. It is plotted as Figure IX-7. Not only does the cylinder have its own peculiar vibrations running up and down, but the top end acts like a diaphragm sending out its own hum or buzz. We are now at the root of both hearing and feeling the hum. Simultaneous sources create a buzz. The text addresses the effects of various cylinder lengths.

A Comparison of Level and Ballistic Trajectories

A. Assumptions

When UFOs rapidly leave a given area they often leave with tremendous acceleration on a very steep trajectory. On other occasions they leave at high speed in a horizontal path. Assuming that these are two different modes of getting from point A to point B on the surface of Earth (or any planet), optimized control for each trajectory type is first derived or given. Then the energy cost and time cost for each are computed and then compared.

In Section XI the trajectory dynamics presented does not depend on whether the UFO thrust is based on an impulse-momentum principle, or on energy-conservative field forces, or lies somewhere in between. In Section XIX, reasons are given why the UFO can be expected to operate with some approximation to a conservative field, a field with losses. In brief, the reason is that an impulse drive (analogous to a rocket drive) would consume orders of magnitude more power in near-Earth, low-speed travel than a field drive, and since a UFO burns up neither itself nor its surroundings (the ground) it is presumed to handle power commensurate with the more energy-conservative field drive, which pushes against the solid footing of the Earth. Even so, there would be (field) losses, as UFOs are observed to do some heating of the ground and ionization of the atmosphere.

In this elementary analysis, the losses, which are a cost to the UFO in making the journey, are assumed to be proportional to the thrusting force level used and to accumulate on a time-of-use basis, rather than on a total energy basis. Thus the losses are assumed proportional to the thrust times the time of use. I don't know how accurate this assumption is for the level path case, but it cannot be far off for a near-impulsive ballistic path.

Another assumption made is that air drag can be neglected. Since UFOs travel at supersonic speed without shock waves (Section XIII), this prime source of air drag is eliminated. Since they also travel at supersonic and hypersonic speeds without noticeable overheating, air-friction drag must also be low. Negligible air drag is therefore probably an accurate assumption as well as a simplification of the theory.

For optimum horizontal flights with a range which is small compared with Earth dimensions, the velocity obtained by the UFO will be small compared to orbital speed and centrifugal acceleration will be neglected. The same pertains to the short-range ballistic trajectory treated. For short ranges, the Earth can be considered as being flat.

It is assumed that the optimum trip results when the energy losses are minimized.

B. Symbols Used

C	cost of trip in energy losses per unit mass of vehicle
a	acceleration, in g units
g	acceleration of gravity, length/t^2
t	acceleration time
v	velocity
V_i	ideal velocity, $V_i = a_t g t$
d	horizontal range
T	vehicle thrust
θ	vehicle angle of tilt
k	energy loss proportionality constant
m	mass

Subscripts:

t	total
h	horizontal
v	vertical

s	starting or initial value
d	pertaining to destination
i	ideal
max	maximum

C. Level Trajectory

In a horizontal trajectory, besides acceleration costs, the UFO must pay the losses involved in supporting itself against the force of gravity during the entire flight. To reduce this cost, it pays the UFO to hustle along to get where it is going. Accordingly, we visualize the optimum (minimum cost) trajectory of range d as one in which the UFO tilts itself and its thrust axis to some angle θ and accelerates over the half-range d/2, then tilts to an angle - θ and decelerates over the remaining range. The trip is carried out with balanced triangles of acceleration as shown in Figure A2-1.

We have assumed that the trip costs are proportional to the thrust and to the time that is applied or to their product. Then the cost per unit mass of vehicle is

$$C = k(T/m)\, t_t \qquad\qquad \text{A2-1}$$

and since $T/m = a_t g$,

$$C = k a_t g t_t = k V_i \qquad\qquad \text{A2-1a}$$

In horizontal trajectory, a_t is resolved into its vertical and horizontal components, a_v and a_h, as in Figure A2-1.

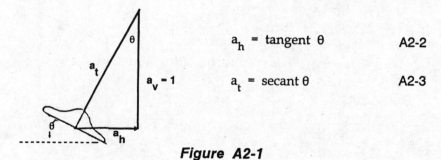

$$a_h = \text{tangent } \theta \qquad\qquad \text{A2-2}$$

$$a_t = \text{secant } \theta \qquad\qquad \text{A2-3}$$

Figure A2-1

To balance gravity $a_v = 1$ and a_h sends the UFO toward its destination. From the symmetry of the problem it is optimum for v_{max} to occur at the midpoint of the trip. Since this is obvious, it is not proven.

Maximum velocity is the product of acceleration and time:

$$v_{max} = g a_h t \qquad \text{A2-4}$$

Distance is average speed, $v_{max}/2$, times time

$$\frac{d}{2} = \frac{1}{2} g a_h t^2 \qquad \text{A2-5}$$

Solve for t, and double for total time

$$t_t = 2 \sqrt{\frac{d}{g a_h}} \qquad \text{A2-6}$$

Substitute equation 2 into equation 6

$$t_t = 2 \sqrt{\frac{d}{g \tan\theta}} \qquad \text{A2-6a}$$

Substituting relations 3 and 6a into 1a gives

$$C = k \sec\theta \; g \; 2 \sqrt{\frac{d}{g \tan\theta}}$$

which simplifies to

$$C = 2k \sqrt{\frac{d \, g}{\sin\theta \, \cos\theta}} \qquad \text{A2-7}$$

Sinθ cosθ is a symmetrical function having a maximum (to make C minimum) at θ = 45 degrees, where the product sinθ · cosθ has the value of 0.5. This gives the minimum level path trip cost as

$$C = 2k \sqrt{2\ gd} = kV_i \qquad\qquad \text{A2-7a}$$

More important, the optimum horizontal trajectory is a very energetic one, for from equation 2 we see that with tanθ = 1, the horizontal acceleration is 1 g. Therefore, when a UFO leaves with high acceleration on a horizontal trajectory it seems more appropriate to think of this as being economic rather than wasteful.

Little is lost by operating slightly off-optimum. Putting numbers in equation 7 for θ = 60 degrees or for θ = 30 degrees gives an increase in cost of 7.5 percent. Since the cost varies as the square root of d, longer flights are cheaper per unit distance. These relations are equally valid for any planet, but accelerations would vary as the planetary g, and the symbol g would stand for the local planetary value.

It will next be shown that, by our cost definition, ballistic-arc trajectories are more efficient than horizontal trajectories.

D. Ballistic-Arc Trajectory

As in the level trajectory, we will consider a short-range ballistic arc for which we may consider the planetary surface to be a plane, and gravity to have a constant magnitude and direction. Under these assumptions, the coasting trajectory is parabolic. The theory for ballistic (coasting) trajectories is well known, and we will just hit the high points. A ballistic trajectory is efficient when the acceleration is very high with short duration and maximum speed is obtained very quickly. This a UFO seems well able to do. In the limiting or ideal case the velocity needed to obtain the range d is delivered impulsively at a trajectory angle of 45 degrees, for the short-range parabolic trajectory with negligible air drag.

The starting velocity is

$$v_s = ga_t t$$

and, consistent with our cost assumptions, the starting cost per unit mass of vehicle would be kv_s. However, unlike an artillery shell, a UFO must pay for stopping also. Therefore the ballistic cost is

$$C = 2 k v_s = kV_i \qquad \text{A2-8}$$

We now compute v_s. The trip time equals twice the time it takes to fall from the vertex of the parabola to ground level

$$t_t = 2 v_v / g \qquad \text{A2-9}$$

The range is $\qquad d = v_h t_t \qquad$ A2-10

Substituting the value of t_t from 9 into 10 and noting $v_h = v_v$

$$d = 2 v_h^2 / g \qquad \text{A2-10a}$$

Solving (A2-10a) for v_h gives

$$v_h = \sqrt{gd/2} \qquad \text{A2-10b}$$

The initial velocity is

$$v_s = \sqrt{2} \, v_h \qquad \text{A2-11}$$
$$= \sqrt{gd}$$

Substituting this value of v_s into equation (A2-8) gives the trip cost

$$C = 2k \sqrt{gd} = kV_i \qquad \text{A2-8a}$$

To obtain the ballistic trip time, eliminate v_v from equation 9 in favor of v_s and eliminate v_s with equation 11. The result is

$$t_t = \sqrt{2\,d/g} \qquad \text{A2-12}$$

E. Comparison of Level-Path and Ballistic-Arc Trajectories

Within the accuracy of the assumption that trip costs are proportional to the impulse per unit mass, a comparison of equation (A2-7a) with (A2-8a) shows that the level-path trip costs $\sqrt{2}$ times as much as the ballistic-arc trip.

We now compare time. By comparing equation (A2-6a) with $\tan\theta = 1$, with equation (A2-12) we see that the level-path trajectory also takes $\sqrt{2}$ times as long. Thus the energetic high route is both faster and cheaper than the scenic low route. When we see a UFO take off like a scalded cat on a steep trajectory it may well be on an optimum trajectory to an earth destination we have called point B.

If point B is far away, say over 500 miles, it is proper to consider the UFO to be on an elliptical path. The initial path angle then tends to fall under 45 degrees. The longer the range, the lower the optimum initial angle. On the other hand, if the UFO is going to a high-altitude rendezvous, takeoff angles greater than 45 degrees can be expected. When a UFO goes quickly out of sight on a nearly vertical trajectory, it might pay to get out the binoculars and look for a rendezvous.

Appendix 3
UFO Aerodynamics: Incompressible Potential Flow Theory

A. Basics

Potential flow is a flow without losses. It has no losses from heat transfer, shockwaves, or skin friction (vorticity and turbulence). In this theory, a "velocity potential," φ exists, with the velocity of flow being the directional derivative of φ. From this fact the name is derived. If u, v, and w are the velocity components in the x, y, and z directions, and if subscripts x, y, and z denote partial derivatives with respect to x, y, and z, it follows that u = φ_x, v = φ_y, and w = φ_z. Thus, if an algebraic expression for φ is found for the flow around a particular body shape the flow velocity problem has been solved.

The simplest case of potential flow theory is the case where density remains constant. This is referred to as incompressible flow. Incompressible flow is always obtained around streamlined bodies (including UFOs) at low subsonic speeds where the pressure increments due to the airflow are so small that the change in density is inappreciable. In addition, if the UFO can replace the pressure field of incompressible flow by a force field potential, $\varphi / V_o^2 / 2)$, as indicated by equation (13-4a) of the text, constant density flow can be obtained at supersonic speed. To let the reader know where this leads, with constant-pressure, constant-density flow there are no shockwaves. Indeed, no pressure waves are created, either of compression or expansion. Obviously this is a sweeping and highly desirable result, fully consistent with observation of silent supersonic UFO operation.

Proof that constant density potential flow leads to unique flow solutions is demonstrated below. With appropriate φ/distributions the solutions are speed independent.

B. Bodies of Revolution

The following derivation of the partial differential equations for incompressible, potential flow about bodies of revolution follows the methodology of *Fluid Mechanics* (Kaufmann 185). Many UFOs, such as dirigibles, ellipsoids, and spheres, have bodies of revolution. The coordinate system to be used is shown in Figure A3-1.

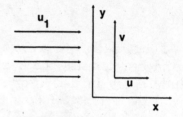

**Figure A3-1,
Coordinate System**

We here consider the case where the UFO or other body is a body of revolution with its axis of symmetry on the x-axis. For example, the long axis of an ellipsoid would be coincident with the x-axis. The free-stream velocity u_1 may be visualized as coming in from the left in the plus-x direction as shown. Because we treat a body and flow field having axial symmetry the third dimension, z, perpendicular to x and y, can be suppressed so that the 3-D problem may be treated with equations of two space dimensions. From Kaufmann's continuity equation for constant-density, potential flow around any body of revolution is:

$$u_x + v/y = v_y = 0 \qquad \text{A3-1}$$

No flow rotation means

$$u_y - v_x = 0 \qquad \text{A3-2}$$

With irrotational flow there is a velocity potential φ for which

$$u = \varphi_x \quad \text{and} \quad v = \varphi_y \qquad \text{A3-3}$$

as can be verified by taking the partial derivatives u_y and v_x and substituting in equation (A3-2). Double subscripts represent second partial derivatives. Noting that $u_x = \varphi_{xx}$ and $v_y = \varphi_{yy}$ equation A3-1 becomes

$$\varphi_{xx} + \varphi_y/y + \varphi_{yy} = 0 \qquad \text{A3-4}$$

Equation (A3-4) is a unique result for *all* axisymmetric, incompressible, irrotational flows without heat transfer, and its derivation does *not* depend on the fact that a body force, i.e., an acceleration field or force field, is present, but rather on the fact that for any good reason the air density remains constant. The replacement of the pressure distribution by field energy supplied by the UFO would be a perfect reason. The field energy required is easily specified for all flows which are solutions of equation (A3-4). Starting with the energy equation (13-4) of the text,

$$\left(\frac{V}{V_o}\right)^2 + \frac{p - p_o}{q_o} + \frac{\varphi}{V_o^2/2} = 1 \qquad \text{13-4}$$

letting $p - p_o = 0$ and solving for $\varphi\,(x,y)$ gives

$$\varphi = \frac{V_o^2}{2}\left[1 - \left(\frac{V}{V_o}\right)^2\right] \qquad \text{A3-5}$$

where V, the velocity anywhere in the flowfield, is obtained from a solution of equation (A3-4).

Note that large φ in equations (13-4) and (A3-5) is the force field potential, and small φ of equation (A3-4) is the velocity potential from which V is obtained. There exists a lot of conventional technology for obtaining the velocity potential for various bodies of revolution. Once the velocity potential is obtained it is a simple matter to obtain V, and then φ from equation (A3-5). The process will be illustrated for a spherical UFO.

C. Force Field Specification: Spherical UFO as Example

According to Tietjens, the velocity potential for a sphere of radius R in a uniform flow field of velocity u_1 in the plus-x direction is

$$\varphi = u_1 x + \frac{u_1 R^3 x}{2\left[x^2 + y^2 + z^2\right]^{3/2}} \qquad \text{A3-6}$$

From equation (A3-3) the velocity components in the x direction are

$$u = \varphi_x = u_1 + \frac{u_1 R^3}{2\left[x^2 + y^2 + z^2\right]^{3/2}} - \frac{3u_1 R^3 x^2}{2\left[x^2 + y^2 + z^2\right]^{5/2}} \qquad \text{A3-6a}$$

and in the y direction are

$$v = \varphi_y = -\frac{3u_1 R^3 xy}{2\left[x^2 + y^2 + z^2\right]^{3/2}} \qquad \text{A3-6b}$$

In the x-y plane, the value of V is

$$V = \sqrt{u^2 + v^2} \qquad \text{A3-6c}$$

Using (A3-6a), (A3-6b), (A3-6c), and (A3-5), the force potential φ is computed for the representative points of the flowfield shown in Figure A3-2, and the results are given in Table A3-1. The points are at ± 1.4R and ± R on the x-axis and 30, 60, 90, 120, 150, and 180 degrees around the circumference.

Figure A3-2

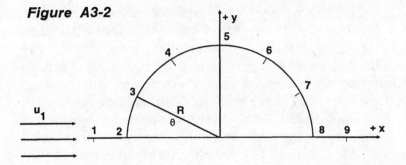

point	u/u_1	v/u_1	V/u_1	$\varphi(u_1^2/2)$
1	.6355685131	0	.6355685131	.5960526652
2	0	0	0	1.0
3	.375	.649519053	.75	.43750
4	1.250	.649519053	1.408678459	-.98437500
5	1.500	0	1.5	-1.25
6	1.250	-.649519053	1.408678459	-.98437500
7	.375	-.649519053	.75	.43750
8	0	0	0	1.0
9	.6355685131	0	.6355685131	.5960526652

Table A3-1. Specification of φ

Of course, the dimensionless values of φ are the same as the dimensionless pressure rations of ordinary flow. Note the fore-and-aft symmetry of all quantities in Table A3-1 except v/u_1.

D. Acceleration-Field-Potential Design

While it is a simple matter to specify the field-potential distribution at select points, the determination of a field compounded of numerous spherical fields whose individual centers have some spatial distribution is tantamount to a partial design of the UFO. I know of no sweeping exact method for accomplishing this, but an approximation procedure is given for bodies of revolution which tailors the field to give the correct values of φ at an arbitrary number of spacial locations in the flow. These locations will be called control points. Between control points it is hoped that the continuity of the functions involved will give a sufficiently good approximation, and this may be tested afterward. In the suggested system field centers of initially unknown strength and sign are distributed along the axis of symmetry, their number being equal to the number of control points chosen. This will result in the number of unknown values of K being equal to the number of equations we can write for φ.

A UFO which is a body of revolution would likely distribute the force field sources on an inner shell just within the visible shell, distributing the "charge" and inter-shell distance as required. It is possible to break such an inner-shell charge into infinitesimal units and find the effect on each point in space by integration procedures. From the symmetry of revolution the φ requirements are such that the field charge per unit area would be constant around a ring at a given longitudinal station. Even so, the computational labor seems great for it turns out that elliptic functions are needed to express the results of integration relative to arbitrary space points. For relative ease of computation, a nearly equivalent system can be set up by distributing a series of force field centers uniformly along the axis of symmetry as in Figure A3-3.

Figure A3-3. Acceleration-Field Component Centers and Radii to Point P

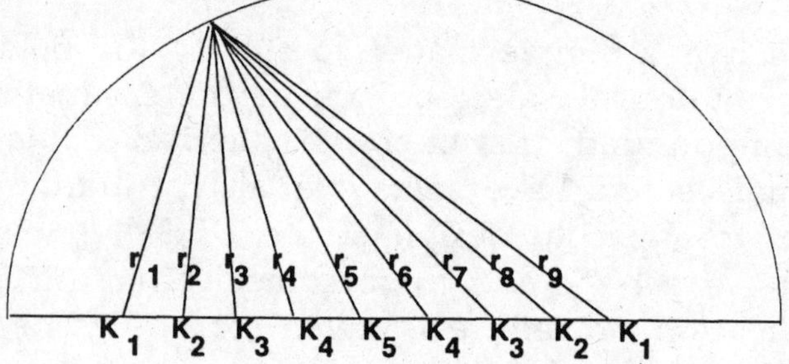

Example for sphere:

The nine points or rings of constant latitude indicated in Figure A3-2 will be used as control points. This is an insufficient number of points, but will serve nicely to illustrate the method.

The field-component centers of strengths K_1, K_2, K_3, K_4, and K_5 are located on the sphere diameter aligned with the airflow as in the sketch. Because of fore-and-aft symmetry the nine field component strengths are represented by five values of K, just as the values of φ at the nine control points have only five independent values. Finding the five values of K requires the solution of five equations for φ at five control points. Referring to Figure A3-3, the form of the equations will be:

$$\varphi = K_1/r_1 + K_1/r_9 + K_2/r_2 + K_2/r_8 + K_3/r_3 + K_3/r_7 + K_4/r_4$$
$$+ K_4/r_6 + K_5/r_5 = \text{constant from Table A3-1 times } u_1^2/2$$

$$\text{A3-8}$$

Making use of the fact that point 1 is at a distance of 1.4R from the sphere center, the equation for potential at point 1 is

$$\varphi_1 = \frac{K_1}{1.4R-.8R} + \frac{K_1}{1.4R+.8R} + \frac{K_2}{1.4R-.6R} + \frac{K_2}{1.4R+.6R} + \frac{K_3}{1.4R-.4R}$$

$$+ \frac{K_3}{1.4R+.4R} + \frac{K_4}{1.4R-.2R} + \frac{K_4}{1.4R+.2R} + \frac{K_5}{1.4R} = 0.5960526652\,(u_1^2/2)$$

Simplification yields

$$2.121212121K_1 + 1.75K_2 + 1.555555556K_3 + 1.458333333K_4$$

$$+ K_5/1.4 = 0.59605266\,Ru_1^2/2$$

$$\text{A3-8a}$$

Similarly, the equations for control points 2 through 5 yield

$$5.555555556K_1 + 3.125K_2 + 2.380952381K_3 + 2.083333333K_4$$

$$+ K_5 = 1.0\,Ru_1^2/2$$

$$\text{A3-8b}$$

$$2.557686069K_1 + 2.411246004K_2 + 2.197701006K_3 + 2.05002539K_4$$

$$+ K_5 = 0.4375 \ Ru_1^2/2 \qquad \text{A3-8c}$$

$$1.731273851K_1 + 1.861364383K_2 = 1.947719438K_3 + 1.989115961K_4$$

$$+ K_5 = 0.984375 \ Ru_1^2/2 \qquad \text{A3-8d}$$

$$1.561737619K_1 + 1.714985851K_2 + 1.856953383K_3 + 1.961161351K_4$$

$$+ K_5 = -1.25 \ Ru_1^2/2 \qquad \text{A3-8e}$$

The solution of the five simultaneous equations (A3-8a) to (A3-8e) by standard methods yields the following values of K

$$K_1 = -1.193987277 \ Ru_1^2/2$$

$$K_2 = 7.65893577 \ Ru_1^2/2$$

$$K_3 = -7.277456824 \ Ru_1^2/2$$

$$K_4 = 0.2679835833 \ Ru_1^2/2$$

$$K_5 = 0.46806739 \ Ru_1^2/2$$

These values of K in equation (A3-8) yield values of φ which are correct at the specified control points, fall off properly upstream and downstream on the x-axis, but owing to an insufficient number of control points approach zero too slowly (remain too negative) along the y axis at the sides of the vehicle. A control point should have been specified at x=0 and y about 1.4R.

E. Streamlines About Spherical UFO

To obtain the streamlines for the constant-density flow over a sphere of radius R we consider the volume of air per second, Q, flowing at station x within a streamtube of outer radius, y_1, and inner radius zero, where

$$y_1 = \sqrt{y^2 + z^2}$$

To obtain Q we must integrate the product of differential area, $2\pi y \cdot dy$, by the x-component of velocity, u:

$$Q = \int_0^{y_1} 2\pi yu \cdot dy$$

It makes no difference whether the lower limit is the boundary of the sphere or zero as shown, for there is no net flow across a slice through the sphere normal to the x-axis. Substituting the value of u from equation (A3-6a) into the integral and performing the integration gives

$$Q = R^2 u_1 \left[\frac{y_1}{R}^2 - \frac{1}{\left[\left(\frac{x}{R}\right)^2 + \left(\frac{y_1}{R}\right)^2 \right]^{\frac{1}{2}}} + \frac{(x/R)^2}{\left[\left(\frac{x}{R}\right)^2 + \left(\frac{y_1}{R}\right)^2 \right]^{\frac{3}{2}}} \right]$$

A3-9

Values of Q are constant along a streamtube or streamline. For the four streamtubes in Figure XIII-3(a) the values of $Q/\pi R^2 u_1$ are 0.2, 0.4, 0.6, and 0.8, or $0.2\pi R^2 u_1$ is the volume per second flowing in the annular spaces between the streamtubes.

F. Pointed-Nose Body of Revolution

This body shape is developed by using a line-source to make it slender. This subsection gives the methods of obtaining the streamlines and flow velocities of Figures XIII-1 and XIII-2 of the text.

The undisturbed flowfield moves from left to right at the velocity u_1 and the line source is oriented in parallel, as in Figure A3-4.

The pointed-nose body will be used to compare velocity fields with those due to a repulsive force center located at the center of the coordinate axes. If they are the same the streamlines are the same, and the aerodynamic pressure gradients have been replaced by the force field. The coordinate system used is shown in Figure A3-4.

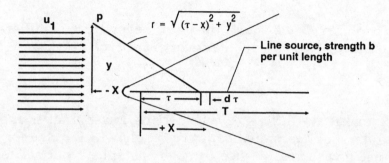

Figure A3-4. Slender-Nose Coordinate System

The center of coordinate axes is at the forward end of the line source of length T and strength per unit length of b. The coordinate z is normal to the page, but because of symmetry the variable z can be suppressed. Positive values of x, τ , and fluid velocity are all to the right. For a small part of the nose and ahead of the nose the values of x are negative.

We first write the velocity potential for a point P, keeping in mind that the potential for the source element bdτ is -bdτ/r and that $r = \sqrt{(\tau - x)^2 + y^2}$

$$\varphi = u_1 x - \int_0^T \frac{b \cdot d\tau}{\sqrt{(\tau - x)^2 + y^2}} \qquad \text{A3-10}$$

Integration with respect to τ puts the potential in algebraic form:

$$\varphi = u_1 x + b \ln \frac{\sqrt{x^2 + y^2} - x}{T - x + \sqrt{(T - x)^2 + y^2}} \qquad \text{A3-11}$$

The horizontal component of velocity u at any point P is obtained by taking the derivative of φ with respect to x:

$$u = \frac{\partial \varphi}{\partial x} = u_1 - \frac{b}{\sqrt{x^2 + y^2}} + \frac{b}{\sqrt{(T-x)^2 + y^2}} \qquad \text{A3-12}$$

At the point of the nose (stagnation point) u and y are zero and $x = -x_1$. Substituting these values in (A3-12) gives

$$0 = 1 - \frac{b}{u_1}\left(\frac{1}{-x_1} - \frac{1}{T-x_1}\right)$$

where x_1 is a negative quantity. On rearranging, this equation gives an expression for dimensionless source strength which we shall call N:

$$\frac{b}{u_1 T} = \frac{-x_1}{T}\left[1 + \frac{-x_1}{T}\right] \equiv N \qquad \text{A3-13}$$

Since x_1 is a negative quantity, N is a positive number. Substituting $b = u_1 N T$ in (A3-12)

$$\qquad \qquad \qquad \qquad \qquad \qquad \qquad \qquad \text{A3-14}$$

$$\frac{u}{u_1} = 1 - N\left[\frac{1}{\sqrt{\left(\frac{x}{T}\right)^2 + \left(\frac{y}{T}\right)^2}} - \frac{1}{\sqrt{\left(1 - \frac{x}{T}\right)^2 + \left(\frac{y}{T}\right)^2}}\right]$$

which gives the velocity ratio anywhere. Note that the value of N depends only on a geometric parameter, the nose length ration.

The vertical component of velocity can be obtained by taking the derivative of φ with respect to y which yields

$$\qquad \qquad \qquad \qquad \qquad \qquad \qquad \qquad \text{A3-15}$$

$$\frac{v}{u_1} = \frac{NTy_{/x^2}}{1 + \frac{y^2}{x^2} - \sqrt{1 + \frac{y^2}{x^2}}} - \frac{NTy_{/(T-x)^2}}{1 + \frac{y^2}{(T-x)^2} + \sqrt{1 + \frac{y^2}{(T-x)^2}}}$$

The total velocity V is obtained by summing components:

$$\frac{V}{u_1} = \sqrt{\left(u/u_1\right)^2 + \left(v/u_1\right)^2} \qquad \text{A3-16}$$

CONTINUITY

We shall utilize Tietjens' method to determine the streamlines. One of these will generate the nose shape. Consider a stream surface of revolution (tube) transporting a quantity of fluid Q_1 per second coming from the left with the air stream plus the fluid generated by the line source, Q_2, to the left of station x under consideration. Let y_o be the streamtube radius far to the left and y_1 its radius at any other point x, as in Figure A3-5.

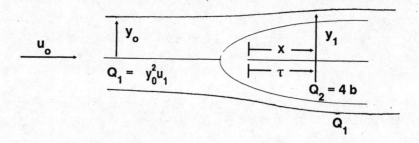

Figure A3-5. Streamline Nomenclature

Q_1 has the value $Q_1 = \pi y_o^2 u_1$ and the source emits a quantity of air 4π times the product of strength and length (to station x), or $Q_2 = 4\pi b\tau$). The sum $Q_1 + Q_2$ must equal the quantity of fluid crossing the y-z plane at station x inside the tube of radius y_1. Therefore

$$u_o \pi y_o^2 + 4\pi b\tau = \int_0^{y_1} 2\pi y u \cdot dy \qquad \text{A3-17}$$

Substituting the expression for u from equation (A3-12) with $b = u_1 TN$ and integrating with respect to y gives the general equation of continuity from which all streamline ordinates, y_1, can be computed:

$$\left(\frac{y_0}{T}\right)^2 + 4N\frac{\tau}{T} = \left(\frac{y_1}{T}\right)^2 - 2N\left[\sqrt{\left(\frac{x}{T}\right)^2 + \left(\frac{y_1}{T}\right)^2} - \sqrt{\left(1 - \frac{x}{T}\right)^2 + \left(\frac{y_1}{T}\right)^2} + f(x)\right]$$

A3-18

Integration with respect to y makes the constant of integration a function of x, $f(x)$. For x/T zero or negative $f(x) = 1$. For x/T lying between zero and 1, $f(x) = 1 - 2x/T$. In this equation $\tau/T = 0$ when x is negative or zero, builds up linearly to $\tau/T = 1$ at $x/T = 1$, and maintains the value of unity for values of x/T greater than 1 because none of the fluid generated by the source escapes from the tube.

To find the particular streamline which lies on the body surface, set $y_0 = 0$, and the flow comes in along the negative x axis to the stagnation point, then moves along the body surface given by y_1.

The body-surface and streamtube contours of Figure XIII-2 were calculated by setting $-x_1/T = 0.01$ in equation (A3-13) making $N = 0.0101$ and using this value of N in equation (A3-18). For the streamtube the value of $y_0/T = 0.03892601$, giving the streamtube contour points of $y/T = \pm 0.05$ at $x/T = 0$.

Appendix 4
Compressible Gas Dynamics with Force Field

(Compressible gas dynamics are needed only if the air-control fields allow pressure and density to vary appreciably from atmospheric values.)

A. The Static Case

Before considering the flow equations, it is instructive to calculate the air pressure around a stationary body in the presence of one or more force field components; that is, we first consider the case where the air is not moving.

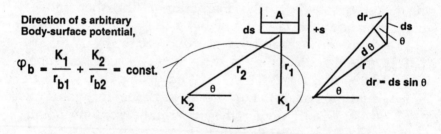

Direction of s arbitrary
Body-surface potential,

$$\varphi_b = \frac{K_1}{r_{b1}} + \frac{K_2}{r_{b2}} = \text{const.}$$

$dr = ds \sin \theta$

Figure A4-1. Coordinates Used for Static Pressure Calculations

We are solving a problem somewhat analogous to the determination of atmospheric pressure at various altitudes as affected by the earth's gravitational field. Consider a tube of air of cross-sectional area A as shown in Figure A4-1, under the influence of force field components having potentials of K_1/r_1, K_2/r_2, etc. The repulsive force the field exerts on the infinitesimal volume A ds is $(K_1/r_1^2 + \left(K_2/r_2^2\right) \sin \theta) \rho$ A ds. This quantity must equal the pressure force difference A dp across the same volume element, or

$$A \, dp = \left(K_1/r_1^2 + \left(K_2/r_2^2\right) \sin \theta \right) \rho A \, ds \qquad \text{A4-1}$$

and since $ds = dr_1$ and $dr_2 = ds \sin\theta$, we have

$$dp = \left[\left(K_1/r_1^2\right) dr_1 + \left(K_2/r_2^2\right) dr_2 + \ldots \right] \rho \qquad \text{A4-1a}$$

The assumption is made that heat transfer processes are negligible or the decompression is adiabatic. With γ being the ratio of specific heat of air at constant pressure to specific heat at constant volume, the adiabatic decompression pressure-density relation is

$$\frac{P}{\rho^\gamma} = \text{constant} = \frac{P_o}{\rho_o^\gamma} \qquad \text{or}$$

$$\qquad \text{A4-2}$$

$$\rho = \rho_o \, p^{\frac{1}{\gamma}} / P_o^{\frac{1}{\gamma}}$$

The subscript o refers to values at a distance, unaffected by the field. Dividing both sides of A4-1a by ρ and substituting expression A4-2 for ρ gives

$$\frac{P_o^{\frac{1}{\gamma}}}{\rho_o} \frac{dp}{p^{\frac{1}{\gamma}}} = \frac{K_1}{r_1^2} dr_1 + \frac{K_2}{r_2^2} dr_2 + \ldots \qquad \text{A4-3}$$

in which the variables are separated. Integration gives

$$\frac{P_o^{\frac{1}{\gamma}}}{\rho_o} \frac{p^{(1-\frac{1}{\gamma})}}{1 - \frac{1}{\gamma}} = -\frac{K_1}{r_1} - \frac{K_2}{r_2} - \ldots + C \,(\text{a constant})$$

Noting that the potential terms vanish at a great distance away, where $p = p_0$ and $\rho = \rho_0$ the constant of integration is evaluated as

$$C = \frac{p_0^{\frac{1}{\gamma}} P_0^{(1-\frac{1}{\gamma})}}{\rho_0 (1 - \frac{1}{\gamma})} \quad \text{or} \quad \frac{\gamma}{\gamma - 1} \frac{P_0}{\rho_0}$$

Dividing through by the value of C gives

$$\left(\frac{p}{P_0}\right)^{\frac{\gamma-1}{\gamma}} = 1 - \frac{\gamma - 1}{\gamma} \frac{\rho_0}{P_0} \sum_1^n \frac{K}{r} \qquad \text{A4-4}$$

Raising both sides to the $\frac{\gamma}{\gamma - 1}$ power, noting that $\gamma P_0 / \rho_0 = c_0^2$ the square of the speed of sound in the free atmosphere, and letting $\gamma = 1.4$ gives

$$\frac{p}{P_0} = \left[1 - \frac{0.4}{c_0^2} \sum_1^n \frac{K}{r}\right]^{3.5} \qquad \text{A4-5}$$

This equation shows that there would be a marked reduction in air pressure all around the body if the force potentials were acting in the absence of air flow. While this is doubtless a hypothetical circumstance, the concept will be found to help with the understanding of shock-free flow. For example, if the surface potential $\phi_b = \Sigma K / r_b$ is a constant equal to one million and c_0 is 1116 ft/sec, the pressure ratio at the surface is 0.258 or the surface pressure would be about a quarter atmosphere.

B. Gas Dynamics

PRESSURES

Bernoulli's equation for incompressible flow, which is presented in Section XIII, holds good only in cases where pressure changes are so small that the density may be considered constant. In order to make general calculations of force field influenced flows we must develop a compressible-flow equation for flow along streamlines taking into account the force field energy as well as the kinetic and pressure energies usually considered. As is customary and because the air flows by with little heat transfer (Section XIV), it is assumed that the flow is adiabatic; that is, no heat is transferred from one streamtube to another. In the general case here considered, there may be big changes in pressure and density in certain areas of the flow and these will be taken into account. In the vernacular, the flow is said to be compressible.

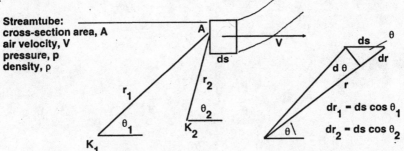

Streatube:
cross-section area, A
air velocity, V
pressure, p
density, ρ

$dr_1 = ds \cos \theta_1$

$dr_2 = ds \cos \theta_2$

Figure A4-2. Dynamic Pressure Coordinates

Consider the flow of air along the streamtube shown in Figure A4-2, distant r_1 and r_2 from the force potential centers of strengths K_1 and K_2. The rise in pressure force A dp in the distance ds is due to the following components. One force potential contributes a force on the volume of air, A ds, of $\rho A \, ds \, (K_1/r_1^2) \cos \theta_1$ in the +V direction, and the other a force of $\rho A \, ds \, (K_2/r_2^2) \cos \theta_2$. The air is accelerated to the right and represents an inertia force to the left (negative). Its magnitude is the product of mass per second, $\rho \, VA$, and the change in speed, dV, giving the term $- \rho \, VA \cdot dV$. Summing the forces,

$$A \, dp = \rho A \left[(K_1/r_1^2) \cos\theta_1 ds + (K_2/r_2^2) \cos\theta_2 ds \right] - \rho VA \cdot dV \qquad \text{A4-6}$$

Noting in the sketch that $\cos\theta_1 ds = dr_1$ and $\cos\theta_2 ds = dr_2$ and dividing by A gives

$$\frac{dp}{\rho} = \frac{K_1}{r_1^2} dr_1 + \frac{K_2}{r_2^2} dr_2 - V \, dV \qquad \text{A4-7}$$

Substituting the value of ρ from equation (A4-2), the first term in (A4-7) becomes $\dfrac{P_o}{P_o} \dfrac{dp}{p^{\frac{1}{\gamma}}}$

and the integration of all terms in (A4-7) gives

$$\frac{P_o^{\frac{1}{\gamma}}}{P_o} \frac{P_o^{1-\frac{1}{\gamma}}}{1-\frac{1}{\gamma}} = -\frac{K_1}{r_1} - \frac{K_2}{r_2} - \frac{V^2}{2} + C \qquad \text{A4-8}$$

where

$$C = \frac{P_o^{\frac{1}{\gamma}}}{P_o} \frac{P_o^{1-\frac{1}{\gamma}}}{1-\frac{1}{\gamma}} + \frac{V_o^2}{2} \qquad \text{A4-8a}$$

and the subscript o refers to the undisturbed stream. Dividing equation (A4-8) by the first term in (A4-8a) as before, noting that $\gamma P_o / \rho_o$ equals the square of sound speed, c_o^2, and raising both sides to the $\dfrac{\gamma}{\gamma-1}$ power gives the answer:

$$\frac{p}{P_o} = \left[1 + \frac{\gamma-1}{c_o^2} \left(\frac{V_o^2}{2} - \frac{V^2}{2} - \sum_1^n \frac{K}{r} \right) \right]^{\frac{\gamma}{\gamma-1}} \qquad \text{A4-9}$$

For $\gamma = 1.4$, which it is for planet Earth, equation (A4-9) becomes

$$\frac{p}{P_o} = \left[1 + \frac{0.4}{c_o^2}\left(\frac{V_o^2}{2} - \frac{V^2}{2} - \sum_1^n \frac{K}{r}\right)\right]^{3.5}$$ A4-10

The force field potential term $\varphi = \sum_1^n \frac{K}{r}$ in (A4-9)

and (A4-10) is put in summation form because the equations obviously hold for an unlimited number and distribution of force centers, but if there is only one the term reduces to K/r. When all the velocities are zero, (A4-10) reduces to the static equation (A4-5), as it should. Also, when $\sum K/r = 0$, (A4-10) reduces to a conventional compressible flow energy equation.

THERMAL CONSIDERATIONS

Isentropic, acceleration-controlled compressible flow is here analyzed to determine the temperature anywhere in the flow field as a function of velocity. The perfect gas law is

$$p = g \rho RT$$ A4-11a

where the new symbols are R, the gas constant, and T, the absolute temperature. Dividing (A4-11a) by an identical expression with subscript o to denote free stream conditions yields

$$\frac{p}{P_o} = \frac{\rho}{\rho_o} \frac{T}{T_o}$$ A4-11b

Evaluating ρ/ρ_o by the adiabatic relation (A4-2) gives

$$T/T_o = (p/p_o)^{\frac{\gamma-1}{\gamma}}$$

$$p/p_o = (T/T_o)^{\frac{\gamma}{\gamma-1}}$$

These relations are general except in the boundary layer where the concept of recovery factor is necessary to account for the energy of turbulence. If the pressure ratio is computed by equation (A4-10), the temperature ratio can be computed by (A4-11c). An inspection of equation (A4-10) and comparison with (A4-11d) shows that the quantity in brackets is the temperature ratio,

$$T/T_o = 1 + \frac{0.4}{c_o^2}\left(\frac{V_o^2}{2} - \frac{V^2}{2} - \varphi\right) \qquad \text{A4-11e}$$

Without the force potential $\varphi = 0$ and at the stagnation point where $V = 0$, equation (A4-11e) reduces to the well-known conventional stagnation-temperature equation in Mach number form.

This is the equation which worries aeronautical engi-

$$T_s/T_o = 1 + 0.2\, M_o^2 \qquad \text{A4-11f}$$

neers about the heating of the nose and leading edges of conventional vehicles and makes them wonder why UFOs don't overheat. However, with a field energy potential φ_s at the stagnation point the temperature ratio is

$$T_s/T_o = 1 + \frac{0.4}{c_o^2}\left(\frac{V_o^2}{2} - \varphi_s\right) \qquad \text{A4-11g}$$

With the value of $\varphi_s = K/r_s = V_o^2/2$ suggested by equation (13-3) to prevent shockwaves, $T_s/T_o = 1$. There is no temperature rise.

At this point we should bring out a natural thermal limitation of the flow theories herein presented. A reduction in air flow temperatures below the liquefaction point oxygen at -183 degrees F (277 degrees R) can result in the liquefaction of oxygen in minute droplets. This in turn violates the gas laws, continuity equations, etc., and wind tunnel experience shows that when this happens local shockwaves occur. This is most apt to happen at high flight speeds, together with high values of force potential alongside, to stagnation point air that has had all its original kinetic energy removed and then flows around the side. A good guide is to be cautious of local Mach numbers above about M = 2.14, although the boundary layer plays a counteracting role for stagnation point air.

To avoid overcooling the air, students of airflow can lower the value of K, move the force center closer to the stagnation point, or consider a redistribution of force centers, if required for specific cases.

C. Equations of Airflow for Bodies of Revolution

In this section, the equations of motion for axially symmetric, irrotational, steady-state, compressible flow around bodies of revolution are developed. The body is stationary, pointing left, while the undisturbed air flows from left to right parallel to the x-axis at supersonic speed. (Actually, the equations are general as to speed.) Cylindrical coordinates are used, with the x-axis lying along the cylinder centerline, and y is the radius of any concentric circular cylinder. Because of symmetry, only two coordinates are needed. At the stagnation point, x and y are zero, the flow comes in along the -x axis, while the +x axis is within the body. A repulsive force field center is located within the body at $x = a$, $y = 0$, while others may be located at $x = b$, etc. as desired.

Symbols used:

V	velocity
u	component of V in the +x direction
v	component of V in the +y direction
c	local speed of sound
x	axial distance, positive to the right
y	radial distance, positive outward
a	force field center x-coordinate
r	distance from field center to any point P
p	pressure
ρ	mass of air per unit volume
T	absolute temperature
U	"body-force" potential per unit mass of air (Kaufmann)
γ	ratio of specific heats

φ   velocity potential

Subscripts:

o   refers to free stream, far from body

x   partial derivative with respect to x, of whatever quantity

y   partial derivative with respect to y

xx   second partial with respect to x

yy   second partial with respect to y

xy   second partial with respect to x and to y

The equation of continuity is independent of the existence of force potentials and fields and can be obtained for this case from any good reference on compressible-flow aerodynamics. For example, *The Theory of Transonic Flow* presents the following equation (Guderley 8):

$$(y \rho v)_y + y(\rho u)_x = 0 \qquad \text{A4-12}$$

Taking the indicated partial derivatives of products

$$\rho v + yv\, \rho_y + y\, \rho v_y + yu\, \rho_x + \rho\, yu_x = 0$$

We now introduce the gas laws by noting that the square of the speed of sound equals the rate of change of pressure with density. This may be written in the following form (Ferri 19):

$$\rho_y = P_y / c^2 \qquad\qquad \rho_x = P_x / c^2 \qquad \text{A4-13}$$

Substituting these expressions into equation (A4-12a) and dividing by ρy yields the following equation of continuity with gas law

$$\frac{v}{y} + v_y + u_x + \frac{v}{\rho c^2} P_y + \frac{u}{\rho c^2} P_x = 0 \qquad \text{A4-12b}$$

We now develop Euler's equations taking into account the field forces and the potentials from which they are derived. Following *Fluid Mechanics* (p. 374), where Dr. Kaufmann writes Euler's equations including a "body force" on unit mass of air which is derived from a potential he calls U. The force in the x direction is $X = -U_x$, and in the y direction is $Y = -U_y$, where the subscripts mean that partial derivatives are to be taken with respect to x and to y. He leaves U otherwise undefined. We define it as the potential for an inverse square repulsive force field, $U = K/r$, where r is

$$r = \sqrt{(x-a)^2 + y^2} \qquad \text{A4-14a}$$

We also note that $\qquad r_x = (x-a)/r \qquad\qquad$ A4-14b

and $\qquad\qquad\qquad r_y = y/r \qquad\qquad\qquad$ A4-14c

whereas $\qquad -U_x = (K/r^2)r_x = K(x-a)/r^3 \qquad$ A4-14d

and $\qquad\qquad -U_y = (K/r^2)r_y = Ky/r^3 \qquad$ A4-14e

Physically, K/r^2 is the force on unit mass of air at distance r and in the direction of r, and when multiplied by the direction cosines r_x and r_y give the components of force in the +x and +y directions.

Kaufmann writes (in effect) that the acceleration of air in the +x direction equals the sum of the forces on unit mass of air in that direction, including the field potential force.

$$u\,u_x + v\,u_y = -U_x - p_x/\rho$$

This is Kaufmann's equation 225 on page 374 of his book, simplified to 2-D from his 3-D case. Substituting the value of $-U_x$ from (A4-14d) into 225 and rearranging gives

$$p_x/\rho = -u\,u_x - v\,u_y + K(x-a)/r^3 \qquad \text{A4-15a}$$

and a similar treatment for the y direction yields

$$p_y/\rho = -v\,v_y - u\,v_x + Ky/r^3 \qquad \text{A4-15b}$$

Note that since x is negative ahead of the body the unconventional force term in equation (A4-15a) reduces the pressure gradient as it should, and forces the term u_x to take on negative values, which is its reason for existence.

Substitute p_x/ρ and p_y/ρ from (A4-15) into (A4-12b), combining continuity, the gas law, and the force-acceleration relations into a single equation. After performing the indicated multiplications and pairing similar terms, we note that one pair combines as $-(uv/c^2)(v_x+u_y)$. Irrotational (non-spinning) flow has been assumed because in the main body of the flow the air viscosity effects are negligible, and the flow is free from shockwaves. As may be verified by any aerodynamic text, irrotational flow means that $v_x = u_y$, and the above term pair becomes $-2(uv/c^2)u_y$. The final result is

$$\left(1 - \frac{u^2}{c^2}\right)u_x - 2\frac{uv}{c^2}u_y + \left(1 - \frac{v^2}{c^2}\right)v_y + \frac{v}{y} + \frac{K(x-a)u}{c^2 r^3} + \frac{Kyv}{c^2 r^3} = 0$$

A4-16

With $K = 0$ equation (A4-16) is a well-known conventional equation for axially symmetric compressible flow. With K a positive constant it is a new or unconventional equation applying to unconventional flying objects controlling the airflow with an acceleration field. If there is a distribution of acceleration field centers the coefficients of u and v in the last two terms will be summations.

Some natural boundary conditions are:

$u = u_o$ at $x = -\infty$	(a)		$u = u_o$ at $y = \infty$	(d)
$v = 0$ at $x = -\infty$	(b)		$v = 0$ at $y = \infty$	(e)
$u = 0$ at $x,y = 0,0$	(c)		$v = 0$ at $y = 0$	(f)

A4-17

At body surfaces $v/u = (dy/dx)_{surface}$ except at $x,y = 0,0$. (g)

In equation (A4-16), c^2 is the square of the local speed of sound which varies with local temperature in the following manner:

$$c^2 / c_o^2 = T / T_o$$

Combining this proportion with equation (A4-11e) gives

$$c^2 = c_o^2 + 0.2\,(V_o^2 - V^2 - 2\varphi) \qquad \text{A4-18}$$

where $\varphi = K/r$ for a single field center and $V^2 = u^2 + v^2$. Equation (A4-18) is also a conventional equation with $\varphi = 0$ (Kaufmann 379, equat. 602, for example).

According to the general theory of fluid mechanics, if a flow is energy-conservative (irrotational and without heat transfer) all fluid properties are point functions of space coordinates and a velocity potential φ exists for which $u = \varphi_x$ and $v = \varphi_y$. Then $u_x = \varphi_{xx}$, $v_y = \varphi_{yy}$, and $u_y = \varphi_{xy}$. Equation (A4-16) then becomes

$$\left(1 - \frac{\varphi_x^2}{c^2}\right)\varphi_{xx} - 2\frac{\varphi_x\varphi_y}{c^2}\,\varphi{xy} + \left(1 - \frac{\varphi_y^2}{c^2}\right)\varphi_{yy} = -\frac{\varphi_y}{y} - \frac{K(x-a)}{c^2 r^3}\,\varphi_x - \frac{Ky}{c^2 r^3}\,\varphi_y$$

$$\text{A4-19}$$

Again c^2 is to be replaced by its equivalent expression (A4-18) and is therefore a function of φ_x, φ_y, x, and y. With or without the acceleration field terms, the mathematical description of equation (A4-19) is the same. It is a nonlinear, non-homogeneous, second order partial differential equation in the dependent variable φ. While the equation is linear in the second order derivatives, their coefficients are highly nonlinear. The non-homogeneous first order terms on the right have coefficients which are functions of x and y only. In fact, φ and all its partial derivatives are functions of the space coordinates x and y. Since the solution of this equation in analytical form is highly unlikely, its solution—or what is the same thing, the solution of equation (A4-16)—may be considered to be the task of establishing the ordinates of a φ-surface above an x versus y base by numerical means. When established, the φ-surface will everywhere have a slope in the $+x$ direction equal to u and a slope in the $+y$ direction equal to v, as well as conform to the boundary conditions (A4-17).

This complex airflow analysis is necessary only if the air-control fields allow air pressures and air densities to vary much from atmospheric values. If the UFO uses both repulsive and attractive fields to maintain constant pressure and density in the airstream, the simple analyses of Appendix 3 are applicable, and the flow over any streamline body follows a subsonic flow pattern, no matter what the UFO speed.

Appendix 5
Interstellar Travel Theory

A. The Earth Reference Frame

APPLICABLE THEORY

If large changes in gravity fields are not encountered, which is generally true in interstellar space, and if the observer is essentially unaccelerated (on a time average basis), as is the case for a planetary observer, the special theory is adequate as a basis for making the relativistic velocity and time calculations for space travel. This is because for gravity free space and for an unaccelerated observer the general theory of relativity reduces to the special theory in differential form (see Bohm, ch. 30).

FUNDAMENTAL RELATIONS

The relativistic differential equations needed are given in text books, such as Bohm's *The Special Theory of Relativity*, and in papers, such as Sanger's *Flight Mechanics of Photon Rockets*. The three basic differential equations needed are summarized below. They are the relations between the on board differential values of velocity dv', time dt', and mass dm', and the corresponding observed values dv, dt, and dm as functions of the ratio of observed velocity to light velocity v/c.

$$dv/dv' = 1 - (v/c)^2 \qquad \text{A5-1a}$$

$$dt'/dt = \sqrt{1 - (v/c)^2} \qquad \text{A5-1b}$$

$$dm/dm' = \frac{1}{\sqrt{1 - (v/c)^2}} \qquad \text{A5-1c}$$

Multiplying (1a) by (1b) yields a necessary acceleration relation

$$dv/dt = (dv'/dt') \left[1 - (v/c)^2\right]^{3/2} \qquad \text{A5-1a}$$

A helpful way to visualize these relations is to observe that as v/c approaches 1, $1 - (v/c)^2$ approaches zero. Consequently, observed velocity increments and observed accelerations, (A5-1a) and (A5-1d), approach zero as do the on board time increments, (A5-1b). On the other hand, the increments of observed mass tend toward infinity.

OBSERVED ACCELERATING TIME

The observed accelerating time t_a is obtained by substituting a' for dv'/dt' in equation (A5-1d) and transposing

$$a'dt = dv/ \left[1 - (v/c)^2\right]^{3/2} \qquad \text{A5-1d}$$

With a' constant, integration (Pierce-Foster 23, No. 142) yields

$$\frac{a't}{c} = \frac{v/c}{\sqrt{1 - (v/c)^2}} \qquad \text{A5-2}$$

The quantity $a't/c$ is the observed time parameter and a' is the vehicle on board acceleration. The value of a' agrees with observed acceleration at departure.

OBSERVED VELOCITY AND DISTANCE

Equation (A5-2) can be rearranged to explicitly express observed velocity in terms of the observed time parameter.

$$\frac{v}{c} = \frac{a't/c}{\sqrt{1 + (a't/c)^2}} \qquad \text{A5-2a}$$

Note the observed approach of v/c to unity at large values of the time parameter. The observed distance traveled during the acceleration period s_a is obtained by substituting equation (A5-2a) into the observer relation

$$s_a = \int_0^t v \, dt$$

giving

$$s_a = \int_0^t \frac{a't \, dt}{\sqrt{1 + (a't/c)^2}}$$

From *A Short Table of Integrals* (Pierce-Foster 22, No. 135):

$$s_a = (c^2/a')\left[\sqrt{1 + (a't/c)^2} - 1\right] \quad \text{consistent units} \qquad \text{A5-3}$$

To change units to light years, divide by c and the number of seconds in a year, giving

$$S_a = \frac{c/a'}{31.5576 \times 10^6}\left[\sqrt{1 + (a't/c)^2} - 1\right] \quad \text{light years} \qquad \text{A5-3a}$$

ON BOARD TIME

The next step gets to the heart of the problem. The on board elapsed time t' must be computed in terms of the observed time t. First consider the elapsed time during the accelerating period t'_a. For this purpose, equation (A5-1b) is integrated (Bohm 164). Then, in terms of the observed parameters, the on board accelerating time is

$$t'_a = \int_0^t \sqrt{1 - (v/c)^2} \, dt \qquad \text{A5-4}$$

where the variation of v/c must be prescribed. Substituting equation (A5-2a) into (A5-4) gives

$$t'_a = \int_0^t \frac{dt}{\sqrt{1 + (a't/c)^2}} \qquad \text{A5-4}$$

From *A Short Table of Integrals* (Pierce-Foster 22, No. 128):

$$a't'/c = \sinh^{-1}(a't/c) \qquad \text{A5-5}$$

Equation (A5-5) gives the on board time parameter as a function of the observed time parameter. The equivalent expression for on board accelerating time in years is

$$T'_a = \left(\frac{c/a'}{31.5576 \times 10^6}\right)\left(\frac{a't'}{c}\right) \quad \text{years} \qquad \text{A5-5a}$$

As explained in Section XVIII, the mission profile consists of a period of on board constant acceleration, a coasting period at maximum speed, and a deceleration time equal to the acceleration time. Using S for interstellar distance in light years and S_a for the accelerating distance (A5-3a), the observed coasting distance in light years is

$$S_c = S - 2S_a \qquad \text{A5-6}$$

Dividing (A5-6) by the observed constant velocity gives observed coast time:

$$T_c = \frac{S - 2S_a}{v/c} \quad \text{years} \qquad \text{A5-7}$$

Since coasting conditions are constant, the on board coasting time T'_c is obtained by multiplying equation (A5-7) by the time ratio (A5-1):

$$t'/t = \sqrt{1 - (v/c)^2} \qquad or$$

$$\text{A5-8}$$

$$T'_c = \left(\frac{S - 2S_a}{v/c}\right)\sqrt{1 - (v/c)^2}$$

The total on board time is

$$T' = T'_c + 2T'_a \qquad \text{A5-9}$$

where T'_a is obtained from equation (A5-5a). The on board time problem is thus complete.

OBSERVED TIME

The observed time in years is

$$T = T_c + 2T_a \qquad \text{years} \qquad \text{A5-10}$$

T_c is given by equation (A5-7) and the observed accelerating time can be obtained from the observed time parameter as follows:

$$T_a = \frac{c/a'}{31.5576 \times 10^6} \cdot \frac{a't}{c} \qquad \text{years} \qquad \text{A5-11}$$

where $a't/c$ is given by equation (A5-2).

B. The On Board Reference Frame

Those who have studied relativity know that in a planetary reference frame no vehicle exceeds the velocity of light. This fact is demonstrated by equation (A5-2), which shows that for a vehicle with acceleration a', observed velocity v/c approaches 1 as time goes to large values. But what does it mean physically when an on board integrating accelerometer says that light speed is being exceeded? The vehicle passengers can sense that the vehicle accelerometers are reading correctly and therefore should be believed.

If the acceleration continues long enough, for example for 3.54 days at 100 g acceleration, the passengers believe they have reached and are beginning to exceed the velocity of light. For them it is true. They sense no increase in mass and decrease in acceleration as witnessed by the Earth observer. The most basic principle of relativity, and Einstein's inspiration for the creation of the theory, is that *all* physical laws properly formulated hold good in *all* reference frames. We may not discriminate against the on board reference frame. If the on board accelerometers and integrating accelerometers (speedometers) are in working order, they may be believed by the passengers. Even if the reader does not accept this as true, he will soon see that the concept is in every way consistent with relativity from the Earth observer's viewpoint, and that its use greatly simplifies space-travel computation.

By my ideas herein explained and proven, the effective speed of a space vehicle (to those on the vehicle) accelerating at an acceleration a' is

$$v_e' = a't \qquad \text{A5-12}$$

where t is a non-relativistic Earth-clock time and a' is constant. Dividing equation (A5-12) through by light speed gives the effective speed in units of light speed

$$v_e'/c = (a'/c)\,t \qquad 0 < v_e'/c < \infty \qquad \text{A5-12a}$$

Of course, no one disagrees with equation (A5-12a) at a v_e'/c much less than 1. However, it may be considered valid at all speeds from the viewpoint of the on board passenger's reference frame. By the use of this concept, space travel computations are greatly simplified relative to the corresponding relativistic computations pertaining to the Earth reference frame.

If the acceleration a' is variable

$$v_e'/c = \frac{1}{c}\int_0^t a'\,dt \qquad \text{A5-12b}$$

The computation of effective vehicle speed in the on board reference frame is non-relativistic for all values of v_e'/c and all manners of acceleration.

The use of equations (A5-12) through (A5-12b) as the basis of on board relativity as set forth in the following analysis is, I believe, an original contribution to the subject of space-travel relativity.

CONSTANT SPEED

We now come to the second simplification. The distance traveled at constant speed (as in coasting) equals the product of effective speed and on board time, another non-relativistic computation.

$$s = v_e' \, t' \qquad \text{consistent units} \qquad \text{A5-13}$$

Dividing by c

$$s/c = (v_e'/c) \, t' \qquad \text{light seconds} \qquad \text{A5-13a}$$

If we now divide by the number of seconds in a year, the on board time is in years T′ and the distance in light years S

$$S = (v_e'/c)T' \qquad \text{A5-13b}$$

Derivation: To simplify the arguments, assume that the constant speed travel was arrived at by a previous period of constant acceleration. That this restriction is not necessary will become clear when nonconstant acceleration is discussed later. The vehicle starts the constant speed run at a speed of $v_e'/c = a't/c$ by our definition (A5-12a).

We first write the accepted and more or less obvious Earth-observer relation for the distance traveled in light years in terms of the constant relativistic velocity v/c (Einstein number) and the elapsed Earth time in years, T.

$$s = (v/c)T \qquad \text{A5-7a}$$

We now use the time-ration factor to convert Earth time to on board time:

$$T = T' / \sqrt{1 - (v/c)^2}$$

Substituting this expression for T into equation (A5-7a) gives:

$$S = \frac{v/c}{\sqrt{1 - (v/c)^2}} \, T' \qquad \text{A5-7b}$$

But by equation (A5-2) the fractional function of v/c in (A5-7b) is equal to and may be replaced by $a't/c$ which is in turn our effective speed v_e'/c. Making this substitution, (A5-7b) becomes

$$S = (v_e' / c)\, T' \qquad\qquad \text{A5-13b}$$

and the result is established. This particular cornerstone of my effective-speed method of computing interstellar vehicle performance was noticed while inspecting the pertinent equations as I sought meanings and simplifications that might result from using the on board reference frame. Solving equation (A5-13b) for T' gives the time the interstellar passengers must wait to travel a fixed distance in light years:

$$T' = S / (v_e' / c) \qquad\qquad \text{A5-13c}$$

Equations (A5-13) through (A5-13c) are valid for all values of v_e'/c from zero to infinity. Whether or not the vehicle "really" goes faster than light is academic; performance-wise, it behaves as though it does. The time it takes to go to the various stars can be mainly computed by simple arithmetic. That is the real point.

The effective on board velocity method is illustrated by Table A5-1, where it is compared with the usual Earth reference frame method. Table A5-1 gives the computation of the on board time it takes to go 1 light year distance at the various values of constant effective speed listed in column 1. Column 2 is simply a reminder that the distance in each case is 1 light year. Column 3, which is column 2 divided by column 1, gives the on board time in years T' to travel a light year by the new method. (Try computing column 3 mentally.) The remainder of the table, columns 4 through 7, show how to make the same computation by Earth-observer relativity. Both the correctness and the extreme relative simplicity of the new method, equation (A5-13c), are obvious.

Table A5-1   On Board Time Computations
Vehicle velocity constant

1	2	3	4	5	6	7
Const speed	Dist.	On-board time	Einstein number	Earth time, T	Time ratio	On-board time
v_e'/c	S Lt-yr	T' years	v/c Eq. A5-2a	$\dfrac{S}{(v/c)}$ years	$\dfrac{T'}{T} = \sqrt{1-(v/c)^2}$	$T' = T\left(\dfrac{T'}{T}\right)$ years
0.5	1.0	2.0	0.44721359	2.2360680	0.89442719	2.0
1.0	1.0	1.0	$1/\sqrt{2}$	$\sqrt{2}$	$1/\sqrt{2}$	1.0
2.0	1.0	0.5	0.89442719	1.1180340	0.44721359	0.5
10.1	1.0	0.1	0.99503719	1.0049876	0.9950372	0.1

Explanations of columns 4, 5, 6, and 7 follow:

Column 4 v/c is computed by equation A5-2a with

$$a_e't /c = v_e' /c.$$

Column 5 is column 2 divided by column 4.
Column 6 is the ratio of on board time to Earth time.
Column 7 is Earth time times the time ratio. Of course, this
   column agrees with column 3.

Comment: Column 1 was here assumed, to give exact numbers. Normally, column 1 is computed by v_e'/c = a't / c. This is also the first step for the Earth-observer relativity. In the latter case, the computations are just begun, while with the Newtonian-like super-light-speed concept the computations are nearly finished. Surprising, isn't it?

This "any speed goes" theory passes two criteria for "correct" theory.

1. Prediction with precision.

2. Usefulness. Its simplicity (to this point) would save time even for a mathematician making spacecraft performance computations. Also, its simple concepts can place space travel computations at senior high school and college freshman levels.

ACCELERATION IN TERMS OF EFFECTIVE SPEED

Equation (A5-3) giving distance traveled at constant on board acceleration was derived on the basis of Earth-observer relativity. However, the only independent variable is a't / c which is effective speed v'/c. Making this substitution gives

$$S_a = \frac{c/a'}{31.5576\times10^6}\left(\sqrt{1 + \left(v'_e / c\right)^2} - 1\right) \quad \text{light years} \qquad \text{A5-3b}$$

Similarly, equation (A5-5) giving the elapsed on board time during constant acceleration or deceleration becomes in the effective speed concept

$$a't'/c = \sinh^{-1} (v'_e /c) \qquad \text{A5-5a}$$

Therefore, including coasting travel along with travel at constant acceleration and deceleration, all the mathematics we have used is consistent with the effective (unlimited) speed concept.

I am pleased to note that because equation (A5-2) was integrated with variables separated it is a general equation valid for any acceleration history as is also true of equation (A5-2a). In the effective-speed concept, (A5-2a) becomes

$$\frac{v}{c} = \frac{\left(\dfrac{v'_e}{c}\right)}{\sqrt{1 + (v'/c)^2}} \qquad \text{A5-2c}$$

This conversion from effective speed to Einstein number is a perfectly general relation that can be used in any manner. See effective speed definition (A5-12b) for example. This is why the derivation of equation (A5-13a) is not limited to the use of speed definition (A5-12a).

For a better understanding of effective speed procedures some finite-increment, step-by-step computations will be made of the accelerated flight of an interstellar vehicle. An Earth observer watches a vehicle leave Earth at a constant acceleration of 100 g in the on board reference frame. He computes the effective speed, daily progress, and on board time on a daily basis and records the results in Table A5-1 for a period of 10 Earth days. Because we have equations (A5-3b) and (A5-5a) available, step-by-step procedures are not necessary, but merely educational, and the results will be checked by these two equations. First we take time out to derive needed equations in finite-increment form.

By substituting equations (A5-2c) into (A5-1b), it is easy to show that the ratio of on board to Earth time in incremental form is

$$\frac{\Delta T'}{\Delta T} = \frac{1}{\sqrt{1 + (v'_e/c)^2_m}} \qquad \text{A5-14}$$

where the subscript m is used to indicate the mean value of v'/c or the value at the middle of the Earth-time increment. We also put equation (A5-13b) in the obvious incremental form

$$\Delta S = (v'_e / c)_m \, \Delta T' \qquad \text{A5-13d}$$

Eliminating T' from equation (A5-13b) by relation (A5-14) gives

$$\Delta S = \Delta T \, \frac{(v'_e / c)_m}{\sqrt{1 + (v'_e / c)^2_m}} \qquad \text{A5-15}$$

and, finally,

$$\Delta T' = \Delta S / (v'_e/c)_m \qquad \text{A5-13e}$$

Table A5-2
Vehicle Progress for 10 Earth Days
(6.238 On Board Days)
On board acceleration constant at 100 g.

(1) Earth days out	(2) Vehicle speed	(3) Mean speed	(4) Distance	(5) O.B. Time Incr	(6) O.B. Time
	v'_e / c	$\left(v'_e / c\right)_m$	ΔS Lt-days Eq. (A5-15)	$\Delta T'$, days = $\dfrac{\Delta S}{\boxed{v'_e / c}}$	T', days Sum of (5)
0	0				0.00000
		0.14112	0.139735	0.990189	
1	0.28224				0.99018
		0.42336	0.389861	0.920874	
2	0.56448				1.9110
		0.70560	0.576529	0.817077	
3	0.84672				2.7281
		0.98784	0.702768	0.711419	
4	1.12896				3.4395
		1.27008	0.785693	0.618617	
5	1.41120				4.0581
		1.55232	0.840666	0.541554	
6	1.69344				4.5997
		1.83456	0.878030	0.478605	
7	1.97568				5.0783
		2.11680	0.904183	0.427146	
8	2.25792				5.5054
		2.39904	0.923022	0.384747	
9	2.54016				5.8902
		2.68128	0.936957	0.349440	
10	2.82240				6.2396
			sum, 7.07744 Lt. days		

Explanation of Table A5-2:

Column (1) is Earth days from departure.

Column (2) gives effective vehicle speed v'_e / c at the end of each day from equation (A5-12a) using a' = (100)(9.8) = 980 m/sec sq., c = 3×10^8, and t = 86,400 sec at the end of the first day, etc. This gives an effective speed of 2.8224 times light speed at 10 days.

Column (3) is the effective speed at the mid-point of each E-day.

Column (4) is the incremental distance S obtained by using the values of $(v'_e / c)_m$ from column (3) and $\Delta T=1$ in equation A5-15.

Column (5) is obtained by dividing column (4) by column (3) giving the on board time as a decimal fraction of an Earth day.

Column (6) is a running sum of column (5).

Notes for Table A5-2:

1. The sum of column (4) is 7.077441 light days or 0.01938 light years. This corresponds to a value of 0.01935 obtained from equation (A5-3b) which is accurate. The slight difference is due to the large time steps.

2. The elapsed on board time of 6.2396 days from column (6) corresponds to the more accurate answer of 6.2384 from using $v'_e / c = 2.82240$ in the equation (A5-5a). The lack of perfect agreement is entirely due to the coarse daily time steps used.

3. One should note that column (4) is the distance traveled (Lt-days) in unit time (1 Earth day). The distance traveled in unit time is the definition of speed. Here the unit of time, the Earth day, is the unit the space travel antagonists have always used to tell us that space travel is impractical, improbable, and—until recently—impossible. As acceleration time increases, column (4) values approach but never reach 1. That is why we are bombarded with the dogma that nothing goes faster than light.

In the on board reference frame, the travelers are constrained to use the on board time for the on board speed definition: on board speed equals distance traveled per unit of on board time. Divide the incremental distances of column (4) by the corresponding incremental times of column (5) and the speed is $(v'_e / c)_m$ of column (3), which can have any value. Obviously the speed depends on whose definition is used!

4. The simplicity of the method is evident. The speed columns are just the speed at the end of the first day 0.28224 times the days from launch. In column (3) the days from launch always include a half day. Column (4) is equal to the Einstein number, and column (5), the time increment, is obtained by the same simple idea used in Table A5-1 to obtain T' of column 3 of that table.

5. The essential check of the tabular method as pointed out in notes 1 and 2 demonstrates the theoretical

integrity and overall consistency of the super-light-speed concept.

6. Because all speed computations are linear, it is a simple matter to include any arbitrary history of on board acceleration in the tabular form of this theory. Just add a new column giving the arbitrary acceleration values a', and a second column giving the corresponding increments of $\Delta v_e'/c = a'\Delta t/c$. Then the running sum of $\Delta v_e'/c$ gives the v_e'/c correct for column (2) of Table A5-2. The remaining procedures remain unchanged.

NATURAL PHILOSOPHY

In modern physics the mathematical approach has been adopted to the point where it is often easy to lose sight of physical meanings. How fast a spaceship can go in the passenger's reference frame will be discussed (as it must be) in terms of the definition of speed. Speed is the distance traveled per unit of time. When speed is constant, the equivalent definition is distance divided by time. To avoid getting sidetracked in semantic disagreements, one must very carefully specify: what distance and what time? These two questions become decisive.

At this point we deviate to note what we do *not* do. We properly ignore statements which are true only in the stationary observer or Earth reference frame. For example, we often hear, "As light speed is approached by any object its mass tends toward infinity. Therefore no material object can reach the speed of light." This is a truism in the Earth observer reference frame and is probably why an Earth observer has never witnessed an object going faster than light speed in a vacuum. The increase in mass referred to is the mass of the object's kinetic energy in the Earth reference frame. In a vehicle reference frame the kinetic energy of the vehicle is zero and the vehicle mass is its rest mass. The argument simply doesn't apply. Incidentally, subatomic particles often travel through water faster than light travels through water, so "nothing travels faster than light" without further qualification is a loose statement. To reiterate, we adhere strictly to (1) relativity, and (2) speed definitions.

In the definition of on board speed as distance divided by time, the value of time is the one quantity about which there can be little doubt. All relativists will agree that in the on board reference frame the time is the on board time read by the passenger's on board clocks, expressed by the symbol T', years. The distance, which we might ordinarily think of as non-controversial, is the quantity that is a problem. According to the theory of relativity, in the on board reference frame the distance traveled is foreshortened by a factor given by the Lorentz contraction ratio, $\sqrt{1 - (v/c)^2}$, where v/c is the Einstein number. This ratio has the same value as the time factor, T' /T.

The relativist says,

"The distance traveled depends on the speed and the speed is v/c = S '/T ', where S ' is the foreshortened distance

$$S' = S\sqrt{1 - (v/c)^2}$$

and S the distance as viewed from Earth at zero speed. Crediting the vehicle with the foreshortened distance always results in a speed S ' /T ' less than 1."

The practical navigator says he knows that the interstellar distances S look like they are reduced to S' while he is underway, but when he arrives at destination and looks back, the distance he has traversed is again S, the same value it had before he started. The navigator says,

"There is nothing permanent about S ', but there is about S. When I arrive, the distance I have accomplished is S. I strongly object to measuring distances with a rubber meter stick. On the other hand, the on board time is always less than Earth time and it is permanent. On board elapsed time doesn't slip back to Earth time when you stop. My estimate of speed is S / T' = v'_e / c which reaches values much greater than 1 on most trips. For simplicity I bookkeep all distances as Earth reference distances. Of course, that's why I get effective speeds greater than 1. It just depends on whether you credit the ship with the distance S or S ' in the definition of speed."

There one has both views. The reader has his choice.

Appendix 6
Propulsion Equations

In this appendix are developed the ordinary equation for rocket speed, the relativistic equation for rocket speed, and an equation for the ultimate speed of a vehicle carrying its own energy supply, each in terms of the ratio of initial to final mass (mass ratio). Also developed is the theory for switching from the complete energy conversion mode to relativistic rocketry at an intermediate speed. Introductory material gives the relationship between propellent mass fraction and mass ratio.

A. The Dependence of Mass Ratio on Propellent Fraction

For a one-stage vehicle, the propellent mass fraction is defined as the ratio of initial propellent mass to gross vehicle mass at takeoff. The inert mass fraction is the ratio of structural plus payload mass to gross mass. By these definitions the propellent mass fraction plus the inert mass fraction equals 1. The vehicle mass ratio is defined as the ratio of initial or gross mass to the final or inert mass when the propellent is used up.

Letting m be the final mass, m_i the initial gross mass, and m_p the initial propellent mass, we note that m equals m_i minus m_p. Then the mass ratio is

$$\frac{m_i}{m} = \frac{m_i}{m_i - m_p}$$

Dividing the numerator and denominator by m_i gives the relation between propellant factor and mass ratio:

$$\frac{m_i}{m} = \frac{1}{1 - m_p/m_i} \qquad \text{A6-1}$$

Conversely,

$$\frac{m_p}{m_i} = \frac{m_i/m - 1}{m_i/m}$$

A6-1a

B. The Rocket Equations

Relativistic rocket theory does not differ much from Newtonian rocket theory which will also be derived in the process. Equating the product of mass and acceleration to the rate of change of momentum, and using m for instantaneous mass, v' for on board velocity, t' for on board time, v_j for jet velocity, and d for the differential sign,

$$m \, dv' / dt' = -v_j \, dm / dt'$$

where the negative sign indicates that the rate of change of mass is negative. Canceling dt' and separating variables

$$dv' / v_j = - dm / m$$

A6-2

Integrating,

$$v' = v_j \log_e (m_i/m)$$

A6-3

Equation (A6-3) is the standard non-relativistic rocket equation for vehicle velocity in terms of jet velocity and mass ratio.

It can be seen from equation (A6-2) that the relativistic effects on mass cancel out. To incorporate relativistic effects in (A6-2) we introduce equation (A5-1a) of Appendix 5 to convert v' to the observed velocity v.

$$dv' = dv / \left(1 - v^2/c^2\right)$$

A5-1a

Substituting the value of dv' in (A6-2) and letting $v_j = c$,

$$-c \, \frac{dm}{m} = dv / \left(1 - v^2/c^2\right)$$

A6-4

Integrating, using Pierce-Foster's table (p. 9, No. 49),

$$\log \frac{m_i}{m} = \frac{1}{2} \log \frac{c+v}{c-v}$$

Taking the antilogs

$$\frac{m_i}{m} = \sqrt{\frac{c+v}{c-v}} \qquad \text{A6-5}$$

Equation (A6-5) is the recognized photon rocket equation for full conversion of mass to jet kinetic energy, but applies equally for all zero-rest-mass particles, such as gravitons.

C. Mass-Energy Conversion

If a vehicle converts part of its own mass to energy, and that energy is converted to vehicle kinetic energy without losses, no vehicle carrying its own energy supply can do better. This gives a true speed limit for self-energizing vehicles. Again we let:

v = vehicle velocity
c = light speed
m_i = initial rest mass
m = vehicle rest mass when vehicle has velocity v
m_r = vehicle relativistic mass at velocity v
m/m_i = reciprocal mass ratio

The initial energy equivalent of the entire vehicle is, by Einstein's mass-energy relation,

$$E_i = m_i c^2 \qquad \text{A6-6}$$

The vehicle relativistic mass is given by the Lorentz transformation:

$$m_r = \frac{m}{\sqrt{1 - (v/c)^2}} \qquad \text{A6-7}$$

Multiply (A6-7) by c^2 to get the final energy, E_f:

$$E_f = \frac{mc^2}{\sqrt{1-(v/c)^2}}$$ A6-7a

Since energy is conserved,

$$E_f = E_i$$

Substituting from (A6-7a) and (A6-6) gives

$$\frac{mc^2}{\sqrt{1-(v/c)^2}} = m_i c^2$$

Canceling c^2 and rearranging gives the reciprocal mass ratio:

$$m/m_i = \sqrt{1-(v/c)^2}$$ A6-8

This is the highest possible reciprocal mass ratio when all the energy is carried along.

To demonstrate that equation (A6-8) reduces to the proper low-speed result, expand

$$\frac{mc^2}{\sqrt{1-(v/c)^2}}$$

with the binomial theorem to obtain

$$\frac{mc^2}{\sqrt{1-(v/c)^2}} \approx mc^2 + \frac{1}{2} m v^2 + \ldots$$

and note that except for terms inconsequential at low velocity the total final energy equals the final rest mass energy plus kinetic energy. Equating final to initial rest energy

$$mc^2 + \frac{1}{2} mv^2 = m_i c^2$$

the obvious low-speed result is obtained.

$$\frac{1}{2} mv^2 = (m_1 - m) c^2$$ A6-9

It is an interesting philosophical point to observe that if m from equation (A6-8) is substituted in equation (A6-7) there results $m_r = m_i$. This means that the stationary observer sees no change in vehicle mass. To him the loss of mass to energy conversion exactly equals the gain in vehicle kinetic mass due to approaching light speed. This is quite a departure from the approach to infinite mass of an object propelled toward light velocity by an external power source.

D. Propulsion Mode Switch-Over

A switch-over from static field propulsion to zero-rest-mass rocketry at the observed switch-over speed, v_2/c, all with full energy conversion, can be computed by utilizing equation (A6-8) in conjunction with (A6-4). We retain the subscript i for initial conditions, 2 for switch-over, and 3 for final conditions. Integrate equation (A6-4) between m_2 and m_3, and v_2 and v_3 (Pierce-Foster 33, No. 49). This gives

$$- \log m \bigg]_2^3 = \frac{1}{2} \log \frac{c+v}{c-v} \bigg]_2^3$$

Substituting limits,

$$\log \frac{m_2}{m_3} = \log \sqrt{\frac{c+v_3}{c-v_3}} - \log \sqrt{\frac{c+v_2}{c-v_2}}$$

Since the difference in logarithms is the log of the ratio

$$\frac{m_2}{m_3} = \sqrt{\frac{c+v_3}{c-v_3} \cdot \frac{c-v_2}{c+v_2}} \qquad \text{A6-10}$$

In equation (A6-8) apply the subscript 2 to m and v and divide equation (A6-10) by (A6-8). After factoring and canceling the ratio of m_i to m_3 is obtained.

$$\frac{m_i}{m_3} = \frac{1}{1 + v_2/c} \sqrt{\frac{1 + v_3/c}{1 - v_3/c}} \qquad \text{A6-11}$$

This equation gives the lowest possible overall mass ratio at the speed v_3 for a vehicle carrying its own energy supply which started out in a mode with vehicle mass being completely converted to vehicle kinetic energy and switched at speed v_2 to a rocket mode with jet velocity c.

E. Proton Fission into 3 Antiquarks

In section C, the limiting (reciprocal) mass ratio for a given speed was derived based on the assumption that mass is converted to energy according to $E = mc^2$. In this section is derived the effect on the mass ratio-speed relationship by the energy released in the fission of protons and neutrons into 3 antiquarks as explained in Section XIX-F. The super energy release

$$E_b = 2m_p c^2$$

is assumed all converted to vehicle kinetic energy as a limiting case. Here m_p is the proton mass, but may also stand for propellant mass. Let m be the initial inert mass. Using the same symbols as previously, with subscripts f meaning final and i initial, the mass-energy conservation equation is

$$E_f = E_i$$

Detailing

$$\frac{mc^2}{\sqrt{1 - (v/c)^2}} = mc^2 + 2m_p c^2 \qquad \text{A6-12}$$

or

$$m\left(\frac{1}{\sqrt{1 - (v/c)^2}} - 1\right) = 2\,m_p$$

and

$$m_p/m = \frac{1}{2}\left(\frac{1}{\sqrt{1-(v/c)^2}} - 1\right) \qquad \text{A6-12a}$$

The rest-mass definitions give

$$m_i = m + m_p \qquad \text{A6-13}$$

or

$$m_i/m = 1 + m_p/m \qquad \text{A6-13a}$$

Substituting (A6-12a) into (A6-13a) gives the final mass ratio

$$m_i/m = 1 + \frac{1}{2}\left(\frac{1}{\sqrt{1-(v/c)^2}} - 1\right) \qquad \text{A6-14}$$

In this form of equation (A6-14) the number 2 may be thought of as an energy performance coefficient comparable to 1 for the energy release due to the complete annihilation of matter. This equation gives high-speed mass ratios approaching half (reciprocal mass ratios twice) as great as equation (A6-8).

If the starship both accelerates and decelerates on an energy supply carried along (not launched by a home-based beam or expendable booster) it is appropriate to square the mass ratio given by (A6-14). Squaring twice to allow for a homeward trip (as most physicists do) seems unnecessary in this case as there will be a supply of protons and neutrons available at most any destination visited.

Since this analysis presupposes the validity of the quark theory of matter, it is reasonable to also assume the structural mass of the vehicle is zero or negative, as Dr. Winterberg has suggested. The only positive mass at the final destination is then the passengers and their equipment, which we call the payload.

Appendix 7
Analyses of UFO Fields

A. Field Intensity

The spherically symmetric fields of nature all obey the same rules connecting field intensity (strength) and the field geometry, which is simply the geometry of a sphere. Early analytical investigators of fields, such as Faraday, used a successful concept called lines of force to represent field strength. He let total number of lines of force represent total field strength and defined intensity as the lines of force passing through unit area normal to the lines. Where the lines of force are close together, the field strength is high; and where they are far apart, the field strength is low. In the case of a spherically symmetric field, the lines of force are radially oriented and uniformly distributed, a fixed number emanating from the central source of the field and crossing imaginary spherical surfaces, distant r from the center. The concentration of lines at each imaginary sphere is the total number of lines N divided by the surface area, giving an intensity

$$I = N/4\pi r^2 \qquad \text{A7-1}$$

From this we see that the intensity, or field strength, varies inversely as the square of the distance from the field center for a geometrical reason.

It is simpler mathematically to lump $N/4\pi$ into a field-strength constant K giving for spherical fields

$$I = K/r^2 \qquad \text{A7-1a}$$

For an acceleration field the intensity is the force on unit mass. When the force is positive as in (A7-1a) the force is in the direction of +r. It is a repulsive force. If the sign of the intensity is negative

$$I = -K/r^2 \qquad \text{A7-1b}$$

the force on unit mass is directed opposite to r, or toward the center of the field as in gravity. Both repulsive and attractive spherical fields may be used in the airflow control theories developed in Appendix 4 and discussed in Section XIII.

In all of physics, whenever an old theory is applied to a new domain a principle called *analytic continuation* applies. It means that the new or extended theory be sufficiently consistent with the old that when the new theory is applied to the old domain the original known result is obtained. To make the UFO propulsive-field theory consistent with spherical field properties, the line-of-force idea is adapted to the field beam, which gives a field intensity that varies inversely with the beam cross-sectional area for purely geometrical reasons.

To write this variation in mathematical form, consider a hovering UFO at height h above ground level, emitting a diverging propulsive field beam as in Figure A7-1. Let x be the distance from the UFO to any point in the beam. We may project the beam back to a virtual focal point distant x_o above the UFO.

If A_o be the cross-sectional area of the beam at the UFO, where x equals zero, the area at any other station x is

$$A = A_o \left(\frac{x_o + x}{x_o} \right)^2 \qquad \text{A7-2}$$

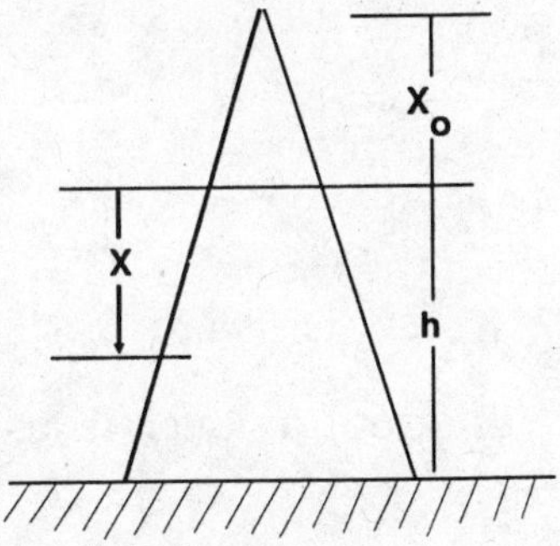

Figure A7-1.

If I_o be the intensity of the field beam at the UFO the intensity ratio at station x is

$$I/I_o = A_o/A = x_o^2 / (x_o + x)^2 \qquad \text{A7-3}$$

representing the field intensity at the UFO by $I_o x_o^2 = K$, equation (A7-3) becomes $\quad I = K / (x_o + x)^2 \qquad$ A7-3a

B. Field Energy Variation

For spherical acceleration fields, the field potential energy is defined as the work necessary to bring a unit mass from far away to any point distant r from the field center. For a repulsive field, the work done is bringing unit mass from "infinity" to radius r is equal to the integral of the applied force over the distance:

$$E = \int_{\infty}^{r} -\frac{K}{r^2} dr = \frac{K}{r} \Big]_{\infty}^{r} \qquad \text{A7-4}$$

$$E = K/r \qquad \text{A7-5}$$

This is a standard result for a repulsive field.

The potential energy to bring unit test mass from far away to any point in the field beam is now computed. Again the field force on unit mass is positive (downward), but the opposing force to move unit mass against the field force is negative. The energy to move unit mass from ∞ to x is

$$\left[E = K \int_{\infty}^{x} -\frac{dx}{(x_o + x)^2} = K \frac{1}{x_o + x} \right]_{\infty}^{x} \qquad \text{A7-6}$$

$$E = \frac{K}{x_o + x}$$

If ground level is used as the potential energy datum

$$E_{gl} = \frac{K}{x_o + x} - \frac{K}{x_o + h} \qquad \text{A7-6a}$$

The derivative or gradient of (A7-6) with respect to x is

$$\frac{d}{dx} \frac{K}{x_o + x} = \frac{K}{(x_o + x)^2}$$

and since the intensity is equal to minus the gradient

$$I = \frac{K}{(x_o + x)^2}$$ is the same as equation A7-3a.

If any confusion arises with respect to the direction of the field forces, and energy sketch gives a reliable criterion. A unit test mass, or any mass, always wants to go down the energy hill. If we plot energy against distance below saucer from equation (A7-6) and assume a linear variation of energy in the field generators we have the energy distribution shown in Figure A7-2.

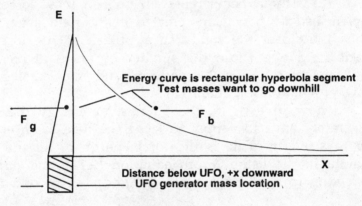

Figure A7-2.

From Figure A7-2 we see that the energy slopes are proper to give a thrust or lift force on the generators, and masses in the beam receive a download.

As discussed in Section XIX, for the force field to have static-field properties it must consist of field-exchange quanta that have a reflection property in massive substances like earth and water. The direction turnaround is 180 degrees. According to this hypothesis, it is relatively unimportant at modest altitudes whether the beam is tightly or widely focused, for each exchange quanta reflects back toward the UFO in either case.

Each exchange-quanta is massless and uncharged and travels at light speed carrying positive momentum. Consider such a Uon quanta which has reflected at the ground and has returned to re-reflect at the UFO. During its re-reflection at the UFO, at the instant in time separating its absorption and re-emission downward, it has delivered twice its momentum to the ground and twice its momentum to the UFO. One may multiply this momentum 2p by the number N reflecting per second to obtain the UFO thrust and ground reaction which are about equal:

$$T = 2pN$$ A7-7

Not all of the exchange quanta make it back to the UFO. Of those that do get back, some may penetrate the UFO without being reflected. Both of these losses are replenished by new Uons created in the field generators. Thus the closer the field can approach a true loss-free static field operation, the smaller the amount of work the generators have to perform and the smaller the power demands on them.

We now investigate the amount of energy the field generators have to supply to bring the field-beam energy up to strength. This is the total energy of all the Uon quanta in the beam. From equation (A7-7) the number reflecting from a given mass (ground) per second is

$$N = T/2p = T/2\left(\frac{ke}{c}\right) = Tc/2(ke)$$

where (ke) is the kinetic energy quanta. But the round trip frequency is c/2h where h is the hover height, so the number of quanta n in the beam is

$$n = \frac{N}{c/2h} = \frac{Tc}{(c/2h)\,2\,(ke)}$$

Multiply the first and last members by (ke) to get the total kinetic energy in the beam, E_k

$$E_k = hT$$ A7-8

The distance h is actually the hover height plus the mean ground penetration distance. This interesting equation indicates that the dynamic energy in the beam of a hovering UFO is a little greater than the work it would take to raise the UFO from ground level to hover height. Equation (A7-8) is a very favorable result because according to this basically static field theory the minimum energy the UFO has to supply to form the beam is *small*. Also, according to equation (A7-8) the UFO could raise itself from ground level to height h with its beam with the same amount of energy it would take to do the same job with hydraulic jacks, cranes, or a powerful elevator!

C. Equations for UFO Field if Generated by Positron-Electron Annihilation

As outlined in Section XIX-E, use is made of physicist D.D. Ivanenko's statement that it is possible for a positron-electron reaction to result in a gravitational output. An ideal cycle is visualized in which electrons are accelerated downward (in a hovering UFO) in vacuum to strike quiescent positrons, giving a downward momentum to the reaction products. Let p_{grav} be the resulting momentum of gravitons, antigravitons, and directed component of x-ray photons from the reaction. It is assumed that the reaction also gives off randomly directed photon pairs without net momentum. In this idea cycle, the total energy of the random photon pairs is fed back to an electric field to accelerate the electrons onto the positron target. Let

v	=	electron speed
m_e	=	electron rest mass
m_p	=	positron rest mass
c	=	light speed
p	=	momentum
E	=	relativistic energy

For momentum conservation, equate the momentum output p_{grav} to the relativistic beam momentum input:

$$P_{grav} = vm_e / \sqrt{1 - (v/c)^2} \qquad \text{A7-9}$$

and the corresponding output beam energy E_{grav} equals cp_{grav}:

$$E_{grav} = cvm_e / \sqrt{1 - (v/c)^2} \qquad \text{A7-9a}$$

The energy of the photon pair is equal to the beam kinetic energy which it supplies

$$E_{photon\ pair} = m_e c^2 / \sqrt{1 - (v/c)^2} - m_e c^2 \qquad \text{A7-10}$$

We now equate the positron plus electron energy before reaction to the energy of the reaction products:

$$m_p c^2 + m_e c^2 / \sqrt{1 - (v/c)^2} = E_{grav} + E_{photon\ pair} \qquad \text{A7-11}$$

Substitute (A7-9a) and (A7-10) into (A7-11):

$$m_p c^2 + m_e c^2 / \sqrt{1 - (v/c)^2} = cvm_e / \sqrt{1 - (v/c)^2} + m_e c^2 / \sqrt{1 - (v/c)^2} - m_e c^2$$

$$\text{A7-11a}$$

Simplifying and noting that $m_p = m_e$

$$2 m_e c^2 = cvm_e / \sqrt{1 - (v/c)^2} \qquad \text{A7-11b}$$

which means the annihilation mass supplies the energy of the directed reaction products. Cancel, square, and solve for v/c:

$$v/c = \sqrt{4/5} = 0.8944 \qquad \text{A7-12}$$

This beam speed puts all the gravitons, antigravitons, and residual photons in alignment with the UFO axis for parallel focusing. Because the beam momentum to energy ratio varies as v/c, at lower electron speeds there is excess energy to give lateral dispersion. Lowering electron speeds therefore results in progressive defocusing.

The gravitational output of this reaction is without experimental confirmation. See text for other reservations. Perhaps high beam energy and high collision kinetic energy would promote the probability of occurrence.

Author's Technical Biography and Credentials

Paul R. Hill (1909-1990) spent a lifetime in the field of aeronautics, on the cutting edge of research and development. He received his B.S. in Mechanical Engineering with Aeronautics Option (Specialty) from the University of California, Berkeley, in 1936. He also participated in graduate courses at the University of Virginia Extension during his employment with NACA, but he considered himself primarily self-educated in mathematics and analysis.

The following is his impressive technical resume, including illuminating anecdotes, which unquestionably establishes his credibility in his field and makes his a voice to be reckoned with in the arena of UFO research.

Professor of Aeronautics, Polytechnic College of Engineering, Oakland, California, September 1936 to June 1939.

Employee of the Langley Research Center (LRC), Hampton, Virginia, under the National Advisory Committee for Aeronautics (NACA) and the National Aeronautics and Space Administration (NASA), July 1939 to July 1970, in the following three divisions:
Physical Research Division (PRD)
Pilotless Aircraft Research Division (PARD)
Applied Materials and Physics Division (AMPD)

A. Official positions held at Langley Research Center *(all but first are line-management positions in the research department):*

Aeronautical Research Scientist
Head, Rocket (Model Propulsion) Section, PARD

Head, Preflight Jet Section, PARD
Head, Performance Section, PARD
Head, Performance Aerodynamics Branch, PARD
Assistant Chief, PARD
Assistant Chief, AMPD
Associate Chief, AMPD, with technical supervision
 in my areas of competence over 7 branches:

Aerospace Mechanics Branch. Included orbital and other analytical mechanics, space navigation, horizon physics measurements for spacecraft orientation, re-entry problems.

Aerothermochemistry Branch. Included ultra-high-speed fluid mechanics, thermodynamics, material combustion and erosion, atmospheric contamination.

Chemistry and Physics Branch. Spacecraft materials with emphasis on plastics for spacecraft application, Radiation Physics Lab.

Flight Projects Branch. Operated all of LRC's rocket-vehicle flights out of Wallops Island, Cape Kennedy, and Vandenberg, including Scout-launched satellites until the Scout Project Office was established for that phase.

Propulsion Branch. Handled all of NASA's extensive in-house research on solid fuel rocket motors. The Lewis Laboratory handled liquid fuel rocket research.

Space Environment Branch. Operated satellites to measure meteoroid impact rates and penetration rates as a function of material thickness. Research on meteoroid shielding techniques with ground-based meteoroid simulation guns. Operated large vacuum facilities at liquid helium temperatures to simulate the vacuum of outer space. Spacecraft materials and mechanisms tested under combined vacuum and solar radiation.

Spacecraft Systems Branch. Emphasis on manned systems for space stations, space laboratories, and interplanetary missions. Included research on space-erectable and inflatable structures, underwater astronaut space simulations, regenerative life support systems with a closed environmental test chamber, and a control laboratory for research on gyroscopic control of spacecraft.

B. Special Assignments by NACA and NASA, sometimes to other Agencies:

Member, NACA Special Subcommittee on Rocket Engines. Coordination of NACA's rocket research with that of industry. Research planning.

Member, AEC ad hoc Committee for Nuclear Propulsion, Technical Advisory Board (served as aerodynamicist requested by AEC, supplied by NACA). Spent one summer at Oak Ridge doing the aerodynamic design of a supersonic nuclear-powered airplane. Wrote part of TAB's final report. Given complete personal tour of laboratories by Director.

Member, Army ad hoc Committee for Ballistic Missiles (served as aerodynamicist and rocket expert requested by Army). Committee recommended a design for the Mid-Range Ballistic Missile which became the Army's very successful MRBM.

Member, LRC Planetary Missions Technology Steering Committee. This committee's jurisdiction included Viking Project planning.

Member and chairman, LRC Space Science and Technology Steering Committee, Planetary Entry Deceleration Panel. Research planning.

Chairman (6 years), LRC Manned Orbital Research Laboratory Steering Committee. Coordinated and planned LRC's interdivisional research applicable to manned space missions.

Consultant, NASA Office of Advanced Research and Technology. Requested by OART, supplied by LRC, for expertise in the area of space laboratories and their supply. The Shuttle concept arose from these NASA planning sessions in response to the clear need for better supply (reusable vehicles).

Member, NASA Office of Advanced Research and Technology, Space Station Review Group, with responsibility in the area of Design Integration. Purpose was to supervise the NASA-Industry Space Station Studies.

Consultant, AEC. In a light vein, the following anecdote regarding a consulting assignment illustrates my point, made in the text's Introduction, that, in the absence of hard data, qualitative data sometimes suffices. In the late 1940s, Dr. Brodsky of the AEC's Sandia Laboratory made an urgent call to Dr. Floyd Thompson, LRC's Chief of Research, for help with the second generation bombs. The bomb prototypes were fishtailing! Thompson took Dr. R.R. Gilruth and me and hastened to Sandia to examine the problem. The first day, we looked askance at the bomb aerodynamics and examined the transverse flight accelerometer data. Everyone suspected the aerodynamics. On the second day, I requested to see the bomb again, sitting in its cradle. With both hands, I grabbed the bomb by the tail and shook it with all my might. I mentally noted amplitude and frequency response. With this "data" I pinpointed the problem as aeroelastic and prescribed a stiffer structure. The Sandia scientists wouldn't believe it, least of all Dr. Brodsky, and a small wager was made. Two months later, Dr. Brodsky paid me a visit, along with the one dollar he now owed. The bomb was cured.

C. Sample Research/Personal Involvement

P47 Fighter. Early in World War II, I did the aerodynamic prototype design and 0.4 scale model tests in the 19-Foot Pressure Tunnel for the Republic P47 Thunderbolt fighter and long-range bomber escort plane. The prototype consisted of a new fuselage design and concept in which all the internal air was taken in the nose inlet (there were no air scoops) and a wing and tail design that Republic had used for an older fighter, which I adapted to the new fuselage. Partly due to its heavy armament of 8 50-caliber machine guns mounted in the wing leading edges and to its heavy armor, it achieved a 10-to-1 margin of kills to losses, and the two top aces of World War II did it with the "Jug." However, its clean aerodynamics cannot be overlooked. The P47 must have been aerodynamically clean (the model tests proved that it was), for it was reported to have a top speed in level flight of 430 mph—outstanding for a 2000 hp propeller-driven fighter weighing 16,000 pounds. No enemy plane could outrun it in level flight, nor could any get away from it by diving. In those days, things were so secret that scarcely anyone knew that the P47 had a NACA aerodynamic design and much less that it was laid out by a junior employee.

I wrote the first report on supersonic ram-jet engine theory to be published by the NACA (*Parameters Deter-*

mining Performance of Supersonic Pilotless Airplanes Powered by Ram-Compression Power Plants). A ram-jet engine is a ram-compression engine without moving parts. It is like a turbojet without the turbocompressor, because at supersonic speeds the high pressure due to speed is sufficient. Dr. Gilruth, who was then setting up the Wallops Island flight base, was assigned as chairman of the editorial committee; this was heretofore unheard of. At the last meeting of the editorial committee, Dr. Gilruth invited me to set up a ram-jet flight program at Wallops Island.

In the late 1940s, I initiated and supervised the NACA's ram-jet flight research program at Wallops Island. All ram-jet vehicles were rocket boosted to Mach number 1.8 when the ram-jet engines were ignited. The vehicles then accelerated under ram-jet power on nearly vertical trajectories to speeds between Mach 3.2 and 3.7, depending on the design and type of fuel used. Typical accelerations were 2 to 3 g's. In a certain time period, ram-jet missiles—the Bomark missile, for example—were used for anti-aircraft defense by the Navy.

I had design responsibility for two unique wind tunnels:

(1) Design responsibility for the test section, test procedures, tunnel cooling, instrumentation, and calibration of the NACA's Flutter Research Tunnel. This was the first tunnel to be operated with other than air; it circulated freon gas because of its high density. It was also the first tunnel in which the heat equivalent of the thousands of driving horsepower had to be removed by refrigeration. (This is reminiscent of the UFO problem of handling high powers without overheating!)

(2) Complete design responsibility for the first supersonic tunnel in the United States to operate with full supersonic temperatures, 500 degrees F. or 960 degrees R. for Mach 2. Called the Preflight Jet, this "blow-down" open-jet tunnel was used for ram-jet research and high-temperature aeroelastic studies under my supervision, in my position as Head, Preflight Jet Section. The two tunnels required giant heat exchangers of opposite types, one for cooling, the other for heating.

Initiation and direction of supersonic heat transfer and skin friction in-flight measurements at Wallops Island on the RM-10 research model which was designed by W.J. O'Sullivan and me. The slip-flow tests described in Section XIV-D of the text were done in this program.

Carried out the first kinesthetically-controlled "flying platform" research program, 1950-53. This program, discussed in Section XI-G of the text, was both my work and my hobby.

Initiation of LRC's research on spherical solid fuel motors. These achieved propellant mass fractions of about 0.94 (6% structure).

Initiation of space station technology research in the 1960s.

> Inflatable and other self-erecting space structures.
> Regenerative life-support systems.
> Closed environmental chambers for life-support systems tests.
> Laboratory for study of direct gyro control. Credit for this item must go to Dr. Peter Kurzhals, and credit for all four items is shared with Robert Osborne, Head of the Spacecraft Systems Branch, which I set up.

Invention, with David Thomas, of lunar low-gravity simulation applicable to lunar transport-flyer research. With David Thomas and invited professional test pilots, I personally engaged in and directed the program.

D. Awards

Tau Beta Pi for scholarship, University of California.

NASA Exceptional Service Medal for "Outstanding Scientific Leadership" in initiating, coordinating, and conducting research on space station technology. NASA Headquarters, 1969.

Citation, with $1,000, for outstanding scientific leadership in directing research applicable to space laboratories and other spacecraft. Langley Research Center, 1970.

E. Authorship

Author of about 30 diversified technical papers; most published by NACA and NASA, others in technical journals.

Retired from NASA July 10, 1970.

I began a more concentrated study of unconventional flying objects about January 1974, resulting in the drafting of this book.

It is my hope that some of the "outstanding scientific leadership" for which I have been credited in my research on spacecraft for human operation has rubbed off on my research on alien-operated spacecraft, as I prefer to think of them. Thus I think of my current work as a shift from one type of spacecraft to another. Of course, these craft penetrate the atmosphere, but here too I have a suitable background of aerodynamic experience to have some insights. I explain what I can with today's science and marvel at the aliens' advanced science for that residue of technology currently unexplainable. At least I don't discuss "other planes of existence" and like concepts, which have an ample background in the thinking of the Middle Ages, but none whatsoever in science.

The world of UFO students has literally and openly been crying for scientific assistance and explanations. This book is my answer.

Works Cited

Anon. "The New Particle Mystery: Solid Clues Lead to Charm." *Science*, 189 (August 1975), 443-44.

APRO Bulletins.

Baker, Robert H. *Astronomy, Eighth Edition.* Princeton, NJ: D. van Nostrand Co., Inc., 1964.

Blum, Ralph, with Judy Blum. *Beyond Earth: Man's Contact With UFOs.* New York: Bantam, 1974.

Bohm, David. *The Special Theory of Relativity.* W.A. Benjamin, Inc.

Burt, Eugene H. *UFOs and Diamagnetism.* New York: Exposition Press, 1970.

Churchill, Ruel. V. *Operational Mathematics.* New York: McGraw Hill, 1968.

Coffin, Joseph. G. *Vector Analysis.* New York: John Wiley & Sons, 1938.

Committee on Science and Astronautics, U.S. House of Representatives. Symposium on Unidentified Flying Objects, July 29, 1968.

Condon, Dr. Edward U. *Scientific Study of Unidentified Flying Object.* New York: Bantam, 1969.

Edwards, Frank. *Flying Saucers—Here and Now.* New York: Bantam, 1967.

Edwards, Frank. *Flying Saucers: Serious Business.* New York: Bantam, 1966.

Ferri, Antonio. *Elements of Aerodynamics of Supersonic Flows.* New York: The Macmillan Co., 1949.

Ford, Kenneth W. *Basic Physics.* Waltham, MA: Blaisdale Publishing Co., 1968.

Guderley, K.G. *The Theory of Transonic Flow.* Pergamon Press, 1962.

Hall, Richard, ed. *The UFO Evidence.* Washington, D.C.: NICAP, 1964.

Halliday, David, and Robert Resnick. *Physics, Part II.* New York: John Wiley & Sons, 1962.

Hill, Paul R. *Parameters Determining Performance of Supersonic Pilotless Airplanes Powered by Ram-Compression Power Plants.* NACA ACR L6D17, 1946.

Hill, Paul R., David Adamson, Douglas Foland, and Walter Bressette. *High-Temperature Oxidation and Ignition of Metals.* NACA RM L55L23b, 1956.

Hynek, Dr. J. Allen. *The UFO Experience.* Chicago: Henry Regnery Co., 1972.

Ivanenko, D.D., and Yu S. Vladimirov. "Matter and Physical Fields," Part One of *The Earth in the Universe.* Translated 1968. Available from U.S. Dept of Commerce Clearinghouse, Springfield, VA.

Kaufmann, Dr. Walter. *Fluid Mechanics.* New York: McGraw Hill, 1963.

Keyhoe, Maj. Donald E. *Flying Saucers From Outer Space.* New York: Henry Holt and Co., 1953.

Kuhn, Thomas S. *The Structure of Scientific Revolutions.* Chicago: University of Chicago Press, 1962.

Lorenzen, Coral. *Flying Saucers, The Startling Evidence of the Invasion From Outer Space.* New York: Signet Books.

Lorenzen, Coral, and Jim Lorenzen. *Encounters with UFO Occupants*. New York: Berkeley Publishing Corp., 1976.

Lorenzen, Coral, and Jim Lorenzen. *UFO: The Whole Story*. New York: Signet Books, 1969.

Lorenzen, Coral, and Jim Lorenzen. *UFOs Over the Americas*. New York: Signet Books, 1968.

Markowitz, William. "The Physics and Metaphysics of Unidentified Flying Objects." *Science*, September 15, 1967.

McCampbell. *UFOlogy: New Insights From Science and Common Sense*. Belmont, CA: Jaymac Co.

Michel, Aime. *The Truth About Flying Saucers*. New York: Pyramid Books, 1967.

Miller, Joseph S. "The Structure of Emission Nebulas." *Scientific American*, October 1974, p. 39.

Pierce-Foster. *A Story Table of Integrals, Fourth Edition*. New York: Blaisdell Publishing Co.

Ribera, Antonio, and Rafael Farriols. *Platos Volantes Sobre España [Flying Saucers Over Spain]*.

Robinson, Arthur L. "Particle Psysics: Evidence for Magnetic Monopole Obtained." *Science*, 189: 778, 815-16.

Ruppelt, Maj. Edward J. *The Report on Unidentified Flying Objects*. Garden City, NJ: Doubleday and Co., 1956.

Sanger, Eugene. *Flight Mechanics of Photon Rockets*, as translated by ATIC, Wright-Patterson A.F. Base, Ohio. Stuttgart: 1956.

Saunders, David R., and Roger Harkins. *UFOs? Yes! Where the Condon Committee Went Wrong*. New York: Signet Books, 1968.

Stair, A.T., Jr., and H.P. Gauvin. *Research on Optical Infrared Characteristics of Aurora and Airglow.* Bedford, MA: Optical Physics Lab, A.F. Cambridge Research Laboratories.

Steiger, Brad, and Jean Whitenour. *Flying Saucers Are Hostile.* New York: Universal Publishing & Distributing Corp.

Tietjens. *Fundamentals of Hydro and Aeromechanics.*

Vallee, Jacques. *Anatomy of a Phenomenon: Unidentified Objects in Space.* New York: Ballantine, 1965.

Vallee, Jacques, and Janine Vallee. *Challenge to Science: The UFO Enigma.* New York: Ballantine, 1977.

Weber, Prof. Joseph. *General Relativity and Gravitational Waves.* New York: Interscience Publishers, Inc., 1961.

Weidner, Richard T., and Robert L. Sells. *Elementary Modern Physics.* Boston: Allyn and Bacon, Inc., 1968.

Winterberg, F. *Quarks Possibly Are Negative Mass Monopoles.* Reno, NV: Desert Research Institute, Atomkernenergie (ATKE) Bd. 26 (1975) Lfg. 1.

INDEX OF NAMES

INDEX OF PLACES

GENERAL INDEX

Acceleration diagrams, 148, 153, 157

Acceleration fields, 95-97; direct evidence of, 98-108

Acceleration loading on occupants, 219-24, 320; field superposition (cancellation), 220; neutralization in dirigibles, 220-21; neutralization in scout vehicles, 222-24

Acceleration of UFOs: linear acceleration, 48; turning acceleration, 47; optical effects of, 50

Aerodynamic cooling, 214-16

Aerodynamic heating, 208-18, 326; effect of slip-flow, 216-18; control at stagnation point, 212; control on side walls, 214; normal stagnation temperature, 209

Airflow control. See supersonic airflow control.

Aliens, 245-61, 335

Artifacts, 225-44, 332; angel hair, 237-44; magnesium isotopes, 233-34; suacer fragment, 235-36; Ubatuba magnesium, 226-34

Astronomical facts summary, 333

Beast-like dwarf, 246-47, 335

Blades in annular ring, 131-32

Bow shockwave, 181, 194-95, Fig. XIII-3

Collectors, 249-50

Color-energy chart, 61

Computerized study, 11

Configurations, 12

Conical UFO (misnomer), 13, 59, 65, 143-44, 145

Conical-hat UFO, 12, 57

Cosmic exploration, 254-58, 335

Cosmic scientist, 255, 335

Cyclic field, 123-30, 321

Data sources, 27

Definition of UFO, saucer, 27

Dirigible UFO, 12, 174-77, 220-22

Disciplines, 24

Ellipsoidal UFO, 12, 34, 198-06, 71-71

Energy supply, 288-94, 328

Excited molecules, 60, 65-66

Extraterrestrial, 245-61, 335

Field as exchange quanta, 294, 295, 312, 330

Field-engine properties, 312; energy relations, Appendix 7; field focusing, 131, 135-36, 143-44, 312; replacement for heat engines, 311. See also positron-electron annihliation.

Field-suspension of UFOs, 281-83, Appendix 7

Flying shoes, 258-61

Force diagrams, 146

Force fields (or acceleration fields), 95-97; cyclic nature, 122-25; evidential data, 98-108; signaling system, 182; speed-of-light fields, 97; suspension of UFOs, 281-83, Appendix 7; type evaluation, 109-18

Geigercounter data, 70-71, 74, 75

Gravitons and antigravitons, 297-98

Gravity shielding, 35

Gravity as energy source, 294-95, 328

Hardness, 37, 235-36

Hoppers and flyers, 247-49, 258-61

Hum, whine, buzz, etc., 119-23, 125-30, Appendix 1

Humaniod occupants, 245-61, 335; classification, 251

Identification of UFOs, 40

Internal heating, 284-85

Ionization of atmosphere: brightness, 64-65; color-energy chart, 61; color spectrum of nitrogen gas, Fig. III-2; color spectrum of air, Fig. III-3; excited molecules, 60; inonized molecules, 60; illumination from ionized air, 54; indistinct outline by

HAMPTON ROADS
PUBLISHING COMPANY, INC.

Thank you for reading *Unconventional Flying Objects*. Hampton Roads is proud to publish an extensive array of books on the topics discussed in this book—topics such as UFOs, the government's cover-up, and more. Please take a look at the following selection or visit us anytime on the web: www.hrpub.com.

UFOs and the National Security State

Chronology of a Cover-Up: 1941–1973

Richard M. Dolan
Foreword by Jacques F. Vallee, Ph.D.

Uncovering what the government knew about UFOs and when they knew it, Dolan unearths countless violations of U.S. air space by UFOs and attempts by air force jets to intercept them, the official policy of government secrecy, and civilian efforts to reveal the truth.

Paperback • 510 pages • ISBN 1-57174-317-0 • $16.95

The Phoenix Lights

Lynne D. Kitei, M.D.
Foreword by Paul Perry
Introduction by Gary E. Schwartz, Ph.D.

On the night of March 13, 1997 Lynne Kitei, a well-respected Phoenix physician, suddenly found herself a key insider in a complex mystery that has baffled humanity for centuries. Kitei used her video camera to record a massive triangular array of lights moving silently but in unison above the city. *The Phoenix Lights* is a well-researched, photograph-filled account of the story behind the lights; of the theories, cover-ups, facts, and denials that surrounded this event.

Paperback • 248 pages • ISBN 1-57174-377-4 • $16.95

www.hrpub.com · 1-800-766-8009

Hampton Roads Publishing Company

. . . for the evolving human spirit

HAMPTON ROADS PUBLISHING COMPANY publishes books on a variety of subjects, including metaphysics, spirituality, health, visionary fiction, and other related topics.

For a copy of our latest trade catalog, call toll-free, 800-766-8009, or send your name and address to:

HAMPTON ROADS PUBLISHING COMPANY, INC.
1125 STONEY RIDGE ROAD • CHARLOTTESVILLE, VA 22902
e-mail: hrpc@hrpub.com • www.hrpub.com